KNOWLEDGE AND THE ENDS OF EMPIRE

KNOWLEDGE AND THE ENDS OF EMPIRE

Kazak Intermediaries and Russian
Rule on the Steppe, 1731–1917

Ian W. Campbell

CORNELL UNIVERSITY PRESS   ITHACA AND LONDON

Publication of this book was made possible, in part, by a grant from the First
Book Subvention Program of the Association for Slavic, East European, and
Eurasian Studies.

First published 2017 by Cornell University Press
Printed in the United States of America

Library of Congress Cataloging-in-Publication Data

Names: Campbell, Ian W., 1984– author.
Title: Knowledge and the ends of empire : Kazak intermediaries and Russian rule
    on the steppe, 1731/1917 / Ian W. Campbell.
Description: Ithaca : Cornell University Press, 2017. | Includes bibliographical
    references and index.
Identifiers: LCCN 2016037425 (print) | LCCN 2016038404 (ebook) |
    ISBN 9781501700798 (cloth : alk. paper) | ISBN 9781501707896 (epub/mobi) |
    ISBN 9781501707902 (pdf)
Subjects: LCSH: Kazakhstan—History. | Kazakhstan—Relations—Russia. |
    Russia—Relations—Kazakhstan. | Russia—History—1689–1801. | Russia—
    History—1801–1917.
Classification: LCC DK908.85 .C36 2017 (print) | LCC DK908.85 (ebook) |
    DDC 958.45/07—dc23
LC record available at https://lccn.loc.gov/2016037425

For Lindsey and Simon

No words can ever suffice.
I wrote you 100,000 of them anyway.

Contents

Acknowledgments

Listing all the debts I have incurred in a decade of work on this book would require a separate appendix. I will do my best to enumerate the most significant ones here. If I have omitted your name, please know that it was both intentional and personal.

Time and again, different organizations have paid for me to sit around and read with the promise that I would eventually write something. At the University of Michigan a full funding package from the History Department included multiple Foreign Language and Area Studies fellowships. A Fulbright-Hays DDRA grant supported my research in Russia and Kazakhstan in 2008–2009. A postdoctoral fellowship at Harvard's Davis Center for Russian and Eurasian Studies let me be part of new conversations and gave me access to the treasure trove that is the Widener Library. The administration of UC-Davis permitted me to take that postdoc, while granting a generous startup package that funded two more summers of archival work in Russia. I am both grateful to have been given these opportunities and sad that the current generation of graduate students does not enjoy the same access to them.

I am especially grateful for the thorough training I received in Russian and Eurasian history at the University of Michigan. Valerie Kivelson was my first teacher of Russian history, in 2002, when I wandered into her medieval Russian history course certain only that I didn't want to be a chemistry major anymore. I doubt either of us would have guessed that the conversation would still be going 15 years later. Douglas Northrop arrived at Michigan exactly when I was looking for someplace to do a PhD. In the intervening decade he has modeled the kind of scholar I hope to be: knowledgeable both broadly and deeply, scrupulously rigorous, kind, and fair. I'm grateful to him for taking a chance on me. Bill Rosenberg and Peter Holquist have also been cherished mentors and teachers during my graduate training and beyond.

Cornell University Press has been a dream to work with throughout this process. I thank Roger Haydon for finding this project worthwhile, for his restrained good sense in editing, and for his forthrightness about the entire enterprise. Susan Specter's guidance through the production process has been invaluable. Carolyn Pouncy's attentive copyediting saved me from several embarrassing errors. Bill Nelson did terrific work on the maps. The two outside readers of the original manuscript gave very helpful comments, with one going so far as to make marginal notes on the whole thing. This is a rare display of collegiality that I hope to pay forward.

An early version of part of chapter 5 appeared as "Settlement Promoted, Settlement Contested: The Shcherbina Expedition of 1896–1903," *Central Asian Survey* 30, nos. 3–4 (2011): 423–436; fragments of the book appear in another essay, "The Scourge of Stock-Raising: *Zhŭt* and the Transformation of the Kazak Steppe," in *Eurasian Environments: Nature and Ecology in Eurasian History* (Pittsburgh), edited by Nicholas Breyfogle.

I've been fortunate to count many colleagues in this field as friends, and still more fortunate to impose on those friends for help with this book. Many of them have read parts of the manuscript at different stages and made suggestions that improved it tremendously: Maria Blackwood, Sarah Cameron, Michael Hancock-Parmer, Anna Graber, Maya Peterson, Kimberly Ann Powers, Rebekah Ramsay, and Charles David Shaw. Julia Fein's generous commentary on Dissertation Reviews was invaluable. Yuri Slezkine and Victoria Frede kindly gave me the opportunity to present some ideas from the book at UC-Berkeley's History *kruzhok*, and I had the chance to workshop two chapters at Harvard thanks to Laura Adams and Terry Martin. Special thanks to Pey-Yi Chu and Cathy Frierson for making our office at Harvard a congenial, simpatico space in which we still managed to get some work done. Thanks also to Alexander Morrison for his unfailing generosity in sharing notes and references (and, not least, for absorbing the wrath of the reading room attendants in Almaty sometimes). Zaure Batayeva and Jonathan Washington double-checked some tricky Kazak translations.

I would not have accomplished half of what I did in Almaty without the support and guidance of Aigul′ Aubakirova. She, Yuri Shneidemiuller, and their families welcomed me kindly and looked out for me; it would have been a lonely and boring time without them. In St. Petersburg, I have come to think of my room in Liudmila Pirogova's apartment as a second home. I am grateful to her for hours of conversation and more than a few good meals.

At UC-Davis I entered a wonderfully collegial and supportive department that gave me everything I could have asked to succeed. Many of my colleagues and graduate students were subjected to drafts of parts of the manuscript: David Biale, Diana Davis, Edward Dickinson, Omnia El Shakry, Katie Harris, Elliott Harwell, Quinn Javers, Sally McKee, Matthew Vernon, Charles Walker, and Louis Warren. Their comments and willingness to share their experience were invaluable to me. Further, two quasi-official institutions kept me entertained and reminded me of the world outside the printed word. I am happy to acknowledge the value of the weekly assistant professors' beer(s) meet-up with Quinn Javers, Marian Schlotterbeck, Matthew Vernon, and Adam Zientek. Equally important, not least for keeping the beer belly away, were frequent bike rides through rolling

California farmland with the peloton of Ari Kelman, Pablo Ortiz, Simon Sadler, and Charles Walker.

My parents, Gregory and Ann Campbell, have supported me unfailingly. Growing up in rural northern Michigan, they stretched to put resources and opportunities to think, learn, and create at my disposal. Since then, they have been constant supporters of a research program and a career that keep me from visiting nearly as often as they have a right to expect. My brother, Baird Campbell, is a brilliant and critical reader who suffers no fools, making him an ideal interlocutor when I am stuck in my thinking and writing.

The most important people to acknowledge are those to whom this book is dedicated. Lindsey Malta entered my life in 2007, when this project was just beginning, and has never been spared a day without it. In the intervening years she has endured a series of crummy apartments, patchy Skype chats, and the February wind off the Moika as I saw it to completion. Despite these various trials, she stuck it out. Hence the second half of the dedication, to our son Simon Charles, who arrived when the manuscript was out for review and made the revision process happier than I could have imagined. I love you both more than words can say.

A Note to the Reader

Script, transliteration, and toponymy come with a welter of unpleasant political questions in contemporary Eurasia. The choices I have made in this book represent one effort to find a compromise between orthographic fidelity and comprehensibility for a broader audience. Thus, for well-known place names and individuals I give the most common English form (St. Petersburg, Abai Kunanbaev instead of Qŭnanbaiŭli). For less familiar locations I use the place name employed in the Russian Empire at the relevant time (e.g., Vernyi, not Almaty). I transliterate Russian according to the Library of Congress system. For Kazak I use the Allworth (1971) system, with the exception that the "short i" character is rendered as i. My very choice of "Kazak" (as opposed to, e.g., "Kazakh" or "Qazaq") is one more such compromise. When quoting from other authors I employ their transliterations as given.

All prerevolutionary dates are given according to the Julian calendar.

Introduction

Early in 1870, faced with a seemingly routine question about the salary and provisioning of Cossack troops on the Siberian steppe's long border with China, the War Ministry of the Russian Empire sent out a confused request for data: "In order to decide the question raised in the War Ministry about allowances [*dovol'stvie*] for Cossack forces serving on the Chinese border, it is necessary to have information about whether or not the Ukek picket and the former picket Chandygapui, located in Biisk district of Tomsk province, are actually located on the Chinese border."[1] If information is the lifeblood of the state, the Russian Empire always tottered on the edge of anemia. This was the case for isolated corners of the countryside of "European" Russia, the fate of which after the emancipation of the serfs was materially influenced by a lack of statistical data about its inhabitants.[2] But it was even more true in parts of the empire that were far from major metropolitan centers and populated by people of different lifeways, customs, and languages than obtained in the Slavic core. This book is, at its core, the story of the Russian Empire's attempts to remediate this fundamental problem in one strategically important but difficult-to-govern region. The story of conquest and rule on the Kazak steppe is inseparable from the production of knowledge about it by Russians and Kazaks alike.[3]

On one hand, in its borderlands, the Russian Empire continued to lack some of the basic desiderata of other European empires down to 1917 (Alexander Morrison, for example, notes the absence of a cadaster for Turkestan).[4] On the other, the knowledge of which it could dispose—what the historian C. A. Bayly would call its "archival depth"—grew exponentially between the initial incorporation of the Kazak steppe in the early 1730s and the empire's collapse two centuries later.[5] Superficially, the achievements of the tsarist state on the steppe during this interval would seem to signify a familiar and straightforward correlation between knowledge and state power. Increased tactical and topographical knowledge, circulated in specialist journals, facilitated a rapid military movement south to the oases of Turkestan. By the end of the 1800s, specialized agronomic and statistical surveys proliferated in support of a rapidly growing movement of Slavic agriculturalists to the steppe. As "civilizing" voices within the empire promoted the Russian language and tsarist institutions as conduits for the skills and habits that raw, wild nomads needed in order to modernize themselves, a small but vocal group of local intermediaries accepted their arguments. By many of the indices according to which an empire can be judged, Russian imperialism in Central Asia and the Kazak steppe was a success, and the knowledge that Russian scholars and bureaucrats amassed about these regions, with the significant assistance of Kazak intermediaries, played an important role in it. Yet even as this empire succeeded, according to the terms it had set itself, its policies prepared the ground for a major revolt on the eve of the revolutions of 1917, while further isolating an autonomist movement whose participants had previously shown themselves willing to participate in its institutions. This seeming contradiction is best explained by exploring the knowledge that Russians and Kazaks produced about the steppe in its social and administrative context.

This is not meant to be another in a long line of deconstructionist studies of the representations and categories of imperial rule, or a simple statement of the power of discourse to oppress.[6] Rather, I am inspired by the work of historians and philosophers of science who are interested not in the construction, per se, of categories and concepts but in the manner in which people form and revise beliefs on the basis of the information at their disposal.[7] Ian Hacking, discussing the natural sciences, has identified three aspects of social-constructivist arguments and proposed that constructivists and their opponents exist on a continuum with respect to each: contingency (that is, ideas might have emerged differently than they did); nominalism (the world is structured through human representations); and explanations of stability (whether because of objectively existing reality or social consensus).[8] By Hacking's definition, much of this book's own epistemological foundation is social-constructivist. But by no means does this exhaust the list of questions that can usefully be asked about the co-construction of the steppe and its population by the Russian Empire and its intermediaries on the Kazak steppe.

Tsarist bureaucrats were desperate to produce the sort of knowledge that would help them to formulate and apply policy on the steppe. At the same time, once the Russian Empire created the sparse institutions (newspapers and schools) that made its *mission civilisatrice* in the region anything more than rhetorical, it represented itself, and in particular the Russian language, as conduits to a world of useful knowledge outside the wild, benighted steppe. In both respects, tsarist attitudes about knowledge created discursive and institutional space for Kazak actors to represent themselves and advance their own interests. The Russian Empire's encounter with the steppe, though certainly characterized by unequal power relations, was thus an exchange of knowledge, whereby Kazak and tsarist actors represented themselves and one another *to* one another. Many of these representations had long-lasting social and political repercussions. Tracing both is the fundamental task of the present work.

Power, Knowledge, and Russian Expansion

Such a program cannot avoid engaging with the enormous body of criticism and meta-criticism of the relationship between power and knowledge in imperial settings. Scholars of Russian imperialism have been debating this question for almost two decades now, mostly through the prism of the ur-text on this problem, Edward Said's *Orientalism*.[9] The consensus of specialist studies of individual scholars and institutions is that Russian orientalism was subtler and less monolithic than Said's model would lead one to expect, that it was diverse and fundamentally apolitical.[10] But there remain lingering doubts about whether this work tells us anything unique about Russian orientalism; scholars of other colonial empires have shown just as clearly that orientalism is not a monolith, and that the connection between scholarship and policy can never be simply assumed.[11] We are left with a familiar scholarly dynamic: after years of focused empirical research, a broad theoretical text is shown to be imperfectly applicable to all times and climes.

This approach to the power-knowledge relationship can be criticized, even on its own grounds, in two ways. First, while the empirical study of intellectual biography is useful as a means of restoring historicity to scholars subordinated to a totalizing orientalist paradigm, the history of texts and ideas does not end at the effects their authors wished them to have. This is an idea which literary critics have developed since the 1940s, and it was forcefully stated by Bruno Latour with respect to the hard sciences in the 1980s.[12] In this book, we will frequently have occasion to see administrators take scholars' ideas in drastically different directions from those they had intended. Accordingly, to understand the relationship between scholarship and imperialism, knowledge and power, particularly in an autocratic state, it is necessary to trace the circulation and genealogy of ideas from scholarly writing to imperial administration as thought, practiced, and lived. Second, among Russianists, a focus on the philologically oriented classic disciplines of orientology has blinded scholars to disciplines—geography and statistics in particular—where the relationship between knowledge and state authority was much clearer. Following too closely in

Said's footsteps has left us with a consensus view of the relationship between power and knowledge that is at variance with the historical record on the Kazak steppe.

Meanwhile, the historiography of other European empires provides us with sharper tools of analysis for this same problem. In this sense the work of Bernard Cohn and C. A. Bayly is particularly notable. Cohn's studies of knowledge production and British rule in India see classification and categorization as closely connected with governing; the imperatives of rule shaped what he calls "investigative modalities" by which appropriate knowledge was gathered and worked up into usable forms.[13] In this project orientalism *stricto sensu*, understood as the knowledge of languages, was a prerequisite for, or a silent partner in, the production of the really useful knowledge surveys and censuses could offer.[14] State building depended on specific processes of documentation and classification, some purely administrative, others developing into scholarly disciplines; the burden of Cohn's scholarship is to trace the connections between these processes and the instrumentalization of knowledge in specific historical contexts.

Bayly's critique of Said that "orientalism . . . was only one among a variety of localized engagements between power and knowledge" stems from a similar historicizing impulse but goes farther in stressing the weakness of the British colonial state and the importance of local intermediaries and forms of knowledge.[15] What Bayly terms the colonial information order was "erected on the foundation of its Indian precursors," leaving the British little choice but to adapt themselves to older networks and forms of knowledge.[16] Though this adaptation saw the gradual rise of colonial "experts" and a gradually heightened understanding of local conditions, it neither destroyed the old information order nor totally undermined the authority of indigenous ways of knowing. At key moments, most notably during the mutiny of 1857, British administrators revealed their fundamental ignorance of the country and inability to come to grips with the information order that had preceded them. Producing knowledge in colonial contexts, Bayly shows, must always depend in some measure on indigenous actors, networks, and understandings; the outcomes of this cooperation, though, are rarely predictable or straightforward.

Taken together, Bayly and Cohn invite us to carefully investigate the conditions of knowledge production as an administrative tool and as a social process. On the Kazak steppe, a weak imperial state was conscious of what it did not know and fumbled, gradually, toward ways of thinking and learning that would remediate its problems. Kazak intermediaries, engaging with the tsarist state, were only too happy to present themselves as the bearers of useful knowledge. They were a vital part of the historical linkage between knowledge and power, though the lines between their knowledge—indeed between any expert knowledge—and the articulation of policy were rarely straight.

Historicizing Kazak Intermediaries

When we follow these methodological cues, situating both Kazak intermediaries and the knowledge they produced in their social and intellectual context, a new story emerges. The Russian Empire's incorporation of the steppe occurred without any very clear idea of what to do with it, only a general sense that it needed to change and develop. Nor were the investigations that scholars and administrators undertook to clarify this problem characterized, at first, by any great unanimity. Studies of pastoral nomadism, of religion, of customary law, and of flora and fauna were often meant to answer urgent questions of policy formation. Some Kazaks, by leveraging and emphasizing their insider knowledge of these issues, were able for a time to give their own answers to these questions; their success in selling these answers, in turn, depended largely on the particular administrative and social milieu in which they functioned. Historians of African colonialism have noted "a significant difference in the lives of intermediaries" as the colonial state matured.[17] Over the course of nearly two centuries, so too did the role and authority of Kazak intermediaries evolve.

From the first moments of the steppe's incorporation (conventionally dated to 1731), until well into the 19th century, tsarist officials disposed of shockingly little useful data about its internal politics and environment. They ruled mostly from a chain of fortifications in the north with both broad acceptance that there were fields in which they could not intervene and a heavy dose of savoir faire, rather than systematized knowledge.[18] What emerged close to the line was a sort of frontier society, with significant cultural intercourse, trade, and creolization.[19] Deeper in the steppe lay a world whose politics, customs, and environment tsarist administrators knew and understood little; local guides, purveyors of information rather than knowledge, were indispensable to carrying out even basic tasks.

Both strategic considerations and new conceptions of governance changed this finely balanced situation. Tsarist officials perceived their artificial frontier in the northern steppe as vulnerable (as frequent raids proved it to be). Drawn away from the line on punitive and strategic expeditions, imperial Russian troops gradually engulfed much of the steppe. This movement, in turn, brought more Kazaks than before under the direct control of the tsarist state, though the models of rule to which they were subjected varied. This was a move that, if it was not accomplished in a fit of "absence of mind," occurred largely owing to strategic considerations—with little clear thought about what might be done with the steppe once it was part of the empire.[20] So too, at the same time, did the models of rule to which some Kazaks were subjected change; from 1822 on, Kazaks in the Siberian (eastern) steppe were ruled directly through *okrug prikazy* (district administrative centers with police and court functions, with both Russian and Kazak representatives).[21]

As more land and people on the steppe became answerable to tsarist administrators, and the latter's intentions for them evolved beyond mere stability or pacification, the nature of the tsarist state's dependence on non-Russian intermediaries changed. This was especially the case after the promulgation of the Provisional Statute of 1868, which massively expanded the still modest budgets and staffs of the colonial administration. Trained at first in a small handful of Russian-language schools in provincial centers, these intermediaries were principally the humble clerks, scribes, and translators who were the lifeblood of the imperial state.[22] Some Russophone Kazaks, however, would go still farther, actively studying their kinsmen and native environment and publishing their findings. These latter, in the historian Alida Metcalf's scheme, were "representational" intermediaries producing knowledge about the steppe and its inhabitants for tsarist administrators.[23] Starved for knowledge as they were even late in the nineteenth century, local and central administrators tended to welcome these contributions, although strategic and political priorities (themselves not uniform) constrained the range of acceptable findings.

The uncertain situation in the steppe was a microcosm of the Russian Empire's attitudes toward imperial diversity in the second half of the nineteenth century. In a study of conversion and apostasy in the Volga-Kama region, Paul Werth argues that, beginning in the late 1820s, the imperial model favored by the old regime began to shift from one emphasizing dynastic loyalty (and thus permitting substantial diversity) to an assimilative, nation-state model.[24] Crucially, for Werth, this transition always remained incomplete, making the Russian Empire "something *between*" and hindering its ability to create a consistent confessional policy for the Muslims and animists of the region.[25] Robert Geraci, in his Kazan'-centered investigation of identity politics, comes to broadly similar conclusions: there were competing models of assimilation for non-Russian subjects of the empire (and, indeed, fundamental doubts about its desirability), reflecting mutually incompatible notions of Russian nationality.[26] On one hand, tensions like this were pernicious for the maintenance of imperial rule; on the other, there was no monolithic imperial policy for non-Russian subjects to submit to or reject but a panoply of options among which they could navigate.

Geraci notes that, in the last years of the Romanov dynasty, the Russian Empire lurched sharply toward the political Right, rejecting assimilative models in favor of maintaining difference.[27] Similarly, it was around the turn of the twentieth century, despite the apparent promise of the new representative institutions gained after the Revolution of 1905, that maneuvering space for Kazak intermediaries closed with shocking alacrity. Central administrators developed a new set of priorities linked to the economic modernization of the empire that manifested themselves, on the steppe, principally in a policy of mass resettlement of peasants from the European part of the empire. A developing body of statistical and agronomic data, itself the logical continuation of earlier knowledge production both on the borderlands (geography and travel narratives) and in the core (statistical studies of peasant households), supported and enabled this policy. Indeed, the Main Administration of Land Management and Agriculture (GUZiZ), responsible for peasant resettlement, was probably the Russian Empire's most epistemologically confident organization after 1900.[28] Local assistants continued to play a vital role in the functioning of the frequent land and economic surveys that GUZiZ carried out. But Kazaks who sought to go farther, to productively engage with the new conception of their environment GUZiZ was peddling and thus oppose mass resettlement, in both the Russian and nascent Kazak-language press, found their arguments coldly received by all decision makers influential enough to do something about it. Nicholas Dirks describes, for the Indian case, the marginalization, appropriation, and silencing of local voices as the imperial epistemic regime consolidated itself.[29] Kazaks employing arguments suited to an earlier moment found themselves on the end of a comparable process.

Gallingly for these proud and educated intermediaries, after Petr Arkad'evich Stolypin's parliamentary coup of June 3, 1907, these decisions were being taken without even token representation from the Kazak steppe in the State Duma.[30] This exclusion, on the grounds of the political immaturity of the region's population, had chiefly political valences. It was meant to create a more conservative, Russo-centric, and (hopefully) compliant representative body. But it also was rooted in particular understandings of social evolutionism, nomadism, and Islam that were current in the early twentieth-century Russian Empire.[31] As the fruit of the Russian Empire's civilizing mission, and living proof that politics was not completely beyond Kazaks' ability to comprehend, Kazak autonomists questioned this as well, with little success, seeking rights within an empire whose priorities now ran contrary to what they understood the interests of their people to be.[32] Their attempt to negotiate their rights on the basis of their status as cultural insiders and local expertise ran aground when the other side ceased to negotiate.

The vast majority of the Kazaks who were most materially affected by resettlement did not read or publish in the journals where these arguments took place. Still, they had ways of making their feelings known, most conspicuously in the Central Asian revolt of 1916. This revolt was, in equal measure, the product of a botched requisition of the labor of Kazaks and other Central Asians (not ordinarily subjected to the military draft) and of the changing lifeways and declining economic conditions among the nomads that resettlement caused. The former was, on several levels, a failure of the tsarist state to engage with Kazak intermediaries; the latter was a failure of the statistical data on which resettlement so confidently rested. As the post-Mutiny British state in India simultaneously strengthened itself while ignoring some networks of which it had previously been part, so too did tsarist policymakers on the steppe distance themselves from useful and important ways of knowing the steppe, with disastrous consequences.[33]

The Central Asian revolt was pacified quickly enough wherever it flared up, with serious punitive campaigns against the nomads in its aftermath. It is difficult to say what might have followed had the February Revolution not occurred soon after in Petrograd, although the hints we can find suggest that a gallingly brutal vengeance was being prepared. But the revolution did happen, and the joyful recounting of February's events and call for support of the new government that appeared in a March issue of the Kazak-language newspaper *Qazaq* spoke for many intellectuals.[34] With hindsight, it is clear the regime that would emerge after the Russian Civil War in what became the Kazakh SSR would hardly prove more fortunate for intellectuals or ordinary Kazaks than the one that preceded it.[35] As in so many other locales in the empire, though, by February 1917 on the Kazak steppe the tsarist regime had so alienated potential allies that many were no longer willing to stand up for it.

Intermediaries, Agency, and Power

A signal part of the imperial turn in Russian history has been an interest in the ways in which minority groups shaped, participated in, and responded to imperial ideologies and practices of rule, fueled by the opening of local and republic-level archives and opportunities to study non-Russian Eurasian languages. The most important methodological contribution of these works is to, as Virginia Martin put it, view the subjects of their study (Kazaks, for Martin) as "historical agents, rather than . . . recipients of historical change."[36] Other scholars, such as Robert Crews and Austin Jersild, have, in different contexts, demonstrated that tsarist institutions served as sites of contestation of the meanings of identity and imperial rule, even as local elites shared the civilizing assumptions of their tsarist interlocutors.[37] The present work broadly confirms these findings.

Insisting on the agency of Kazak intermediaries as historical actors, even though they shared many of the basic improving and "civilizing" assumption of their interlocutors, means they cannot be seen as engaged in mimicry, or as simply inevitably adopting the views of an all-powerful imperial state.[38] This, in turn, flies in the face of a historiographical tradition that imputes tremendous power to the structures and discourses of colonial rule. David Scott, for one, positioning Toussaint L'Ouverture as a "conscript of modernity," his decisions constrained by the inexorable change modernity implied, leaves his subject precious little freedom of thought or action.[39] Similarly, Partha Chatterjee has highlighted the contradictions in Indian nationalism, "because it reasons within a framework of knowledge whose representational structure corresponds to the very structure of power nationalist thought seeks to repudiate."[40] A later attempt to "claim for us, the once-colonized, our freedom of imagination" posited that anticolonial nationalism operated by bifurcating the world into material and spiritual domains, acknowledging Western superiority in the former while insisting on the distinctiveness of the latter.[41]

This does not seem to have been the case on the steppe, though. A timeless and ill-defined construct like "modernity" does not suffice to explain the range of choices (and their disappearance) available to Kazak intermediaries. Both the land and people of the steppe were unknowable, or at least imperfectly knowable, to the tsarist state. In that context, Kazak intermediaries could collaborate in a way that was in the main fruitful for the empire, and fully accept its modernizing materialist imperatives, while maintaining a degree of intellectual autonomy and agency.[42] If tsarist observers, practically to a man, saw the steppe as backwards with respect to the Russian metropole, they neither did so in the same way nor agreed on how that backwardness was to be remediated. Civilization, after all, might take many forms, and many roads might lead to it. Mobilizing local expertise gave Kazak actors, for a time, a limited voice in such debates. These intermediaries sought influence, and through it subjecthood, through the currency of knowledge. Even in presenting it within a modern, or European, framework, they had opportunities to shape the practice of imperialism on the steppe. It was resettlement that changed this situation, and there was nothing inevitable about that policy developing when and as it did.

It might, perhaps, be argued that choosing the sort of imperialism to which one is subject is hardly a choice. Given the apparently irreversible fact of conquest, though, it was a choice that Kazak intermediaries were often prepared to make. Even putatively "European" ways of knowing, in the context of a weak state and an alien environment, provided sufficient space for this to be less than a complete surrender to the ideologies and practices of Russian imperialism.[43]

Sources

A topic as broad as the circulation and use of knowledge in an enormous region over the course of more than a century is, without some sort of heuristic for selecting sources, unmanageably broad. Since the genesis of this project was in the study of Kazak intermediaries, my strategy has been to read outward from sources that they produced, pursuing issues in which they were interested in both archives and the scholarly press. To access the views of these Kazak intermediaries, I have used both the collected works of more celebrated figures (such as Chokan Valikhanov and Älikhan Bökeikhanov) and, to shed light on more obscure figures, periodicals both in full runs (*Kirgizskaia stepnaia gazeta* [The Kazak steppe newspaper, Kaz. Dala ualaiatïnïng gazetï]) and collections (*Ai-qap* and *Qazaq*). For archival work, the mixed administrative status of the region that came to be known as the Kazak steppe has meant archival research in gubernatorial and ministerial collections in St. Petersburg, Moscow, and Almaty. Colonial archives have their limits and their silences, but as Ann Stoler has suggested, they can be productively read "along the grain"—here meaning as reflective of what the tsarist state cared to know, and what crucial actors made of that knowledge.[44] For scholarly periodicals, the logical starting point was works that Kazaks themselves cited as important or influential. This is not a perfect science, and I have erred on the side of reading broadly in hopes of finding unexpected connections. But it means, for instance, that seeing the importance of peasant resettlement in the Kazak-language periodical press after 1900 led me to devote a significant proportion of my archive time in St. Petersburg to the collections of the Resettlement Administration. If this, and other choices I have made, inevitably reflects my own interests and preoccupations, I would contend that it has also been a fair reflection of the preoccupations of the subjects of my study.

A Note on Comparisons

Although the present work is not explicitly a work of comparative history, it cannot avoid engaging with scholarship on other colonial empires. This is especially the case for South Asian history, a field in which, as Tony Ballantyne has noted, "the knowledge/power relationship has become a central preoccupation."[45] Making such comparisons, however, flies in the face of a *Sonderweg*-ish preoccupation with the unique nature of Russian imperialism and runs the risk of effacing the real historical differences between the Russian Empire and its contemporaries.[46] Some meditation on the nature of the comparison thus seems warranted.

Many of the more commonly employed arguments in favor of and explanations for the Russian Empire's purported "uniqueness" fall apart on closer inspection. There is, first, a regrettable trend of simply repeating the rhetoric of tsarist colonizers as though it were historical fact; these claims for the uniquely benevolent nature of tsarist imperialism may be dismissed out of hand.[47] More serious is Alexander Etkind's recent argument that the Russian Empire's urban elites had a quasi-imperial relationship with the Orthodox peasantry of rural Russia, but this argument leaves important questions unanswered when looking at the Kazak steppe (or, for that matter, at Turkestan), where ethnic Russians came to enjoy significant legal preferences over indigenous people.[48] The Russian Empire was continental, not a thalassocracy, but it is unclear why the journey from, say, Moscow to Omsk (1,500 slow miles over bad roads) should have been easier, or less productive of a sense of otherness, than the short steam route from Marseilles to Tunis. Russia had a long and complex historical relationship with the lands it ultimately conquered and colonized, but readers of, for example,

Benjamin Disraeli's *Tancred* will understand that this was also the case for the imperial powers of western Europe. The elite of the tsarist empire was multi-ethnic in a limited way, but the Scots who rose to high positions in British India would dispute that there was anything new or unique in that.

Ultimately, the Kazak steppe existed in a legally discriminatory regime, as an object to be conquered, pacified, and civilized. By 1917, more than a million Slavic settlers took advantage of this legal discrimination to expropriate land from Kazak nomads. All the while, there were practical (if not always explicit and legal) barriers to the advancement of "Asiatics" in local administration. Tsarist administrators wrote of a *metropoliia* and *koloniia* and were clear that the steppe provinces fell into the latter category. Of course, the steppe had its particularities, and in this it differed not a whit from any colony that has ever existed. But it is clear that, if the colonial empires of the late nineteenth and early twentieth centuries were a genus, the Russian Empire was one more species of them.[49]

The differences that existed between Russian imperialism, in the form that it took on the Kazak steppe, and the imperialism of other European powers only add some local particularities to this study, rather than invalidating engagement with other historiographies. The weakness of the tsarist state, relative to some of its counterparts, made it if anything particularly dependent on non-Russian intermediaries. The diversity of legal arrangements to which the metropolitan core of the empire came with different ethnic groups and territories; the weak and late development of mass Russian nationalism; and the persistence of a dynastic, rather than nation-state, model of imperialism all lent unusual strength to local actors' demands that their knowledge, experience, and visions of the future be taken seriously. At the same time, in a highly illiberal state like the Russian Empire, local knowledge did not have to count for anything. Policy could be, and was sometimes, formulated arbitrarily. Thus the position of intermediaries and the expertise they claimed to provide was always precarious, and ultimately subject to the whims of district chiefs, governors, and ministers. In this precarious position lie the reasons for the closing of the space Kazak intermediaries had made for themselves after the turn of the twentieth century.

Chapter Outline

This book develops its argument in six chapters. Chapter 1 familiarizes readers with the geography and environment of the steppe and the basics of nomadic society. If this is a common approach to academic histories of Central Asia, though, this chapter forces readers to see the steppe as tsarist administrators would have before 1845; it familiarizes them with the administrators' assumptions as well as the significant gaps in their knowledge of the region.[50] The efforts to close these gaps by two institutions, the General Staff and the Imperial Russian Geographical Society (IRGO), are the subject of the following chapter, which treats the writing of the Provisional Statute of 1868 as a case study concerning the effectiveness of those efforts.

The Provisional Statute was, by design, open to modification, an experimental document produced in the context of acknowledged ignorance of local conditions. This, in turn, created especially propitious conditions for local actors to influence the way that they were ruled. Thus chapter 3 is a case study of a different sort—a biographical study of the ethnographer and educator Ibrai Altynsarin (1841–1888). It introduces the concept of "repertoires of governance" to explain both the options and the limitations that Altynsarin's engagement with tsarist knowledge production and administration entailed.[51] Chapter 4 further treats Kazaks' engagement with the civilizing mission of the Russian Empire, specifically its claim to represent a more scientifically and technologically advanced civilization, through the work of the *aqïn* (bard) Abai Kunanbaev and the pages of *Kirgizskaia stepnaia gazeta* (KSG). It demonstrates that, even as some Kazak intermediaries accepted these civilizing claims, local experiences and experimentation were vital to their articulation in practice.

The question of peasant colonization, from the 1870s on, shaped the decision space that Altynsarin and other intermediaries could operate in. Once the tsarist state committed to such a policy (after 1896), there was no more room for debate. The final two chapters of the book explore this dynamic from two different angles. The first focuses on a series of statistical research expeditions to the region and the use (and misuse) of their data. Ultimately, such statistical data provided what seemed to be a scientific basis for peasant colonization, without harming the interests of Kazaks who remained nomadic.[52] From the perspective of expropriated Kazaks, however, this was an illusion. The last chapter, thus, explores the ideas behind Kazaks' (and other Central Asians') economic and political estrangement from the Russian Empire and their attempts to claim a role for themselves, and defend their interests, within the space of discussion and debate in which they had previously operated.

The failure of imperialism that the Central Asian revolt of 1916 represented had two layers: of the way the tsarist state had chosen to know the steppe, on one hand, and of relations with the intermediaries it had cultivated for decades, on the other. This book shows both why this failure came to be and why Russian and Kazak observers alike might not have expected it to occur.

SEEING LIKE A HALF-BLIND STATE

Getting to Know the Central Eurasian
Steppe, 1731–1840s

Frequently, English-language academic books about Central Asia begin with an introductory sketch, a set piece that introduces readers to the particularities of local geography, history, and lifeways.[1] This is an entirely reasonable approach. The unfamiliarity of the region even to well-educated English readers suggests the necessity of reviewing its particularities from the outset. An introductory sketch helps fine-grained monographs about the social and cultural history of Central Asia to reach a broader audience.

However, for the present work, which aims to historicize and contextualize the very sources such a sketch might be based on, such an approach is awkward at best and impermissible at worst, for two reasons. First, synthesizing the views of outside observers over a wide range of years, from drastically different genres (travelogues, ethnographic narratives, administrative reports), makes it difficult to understand how these views changed over time. Second, adopting such an omniscient perspective makes it difficult to enter into the subject position of tsarist administrators assigned to the steppe. Over bad roads, raids or disorders might take months to report; such basic data as the location of major landforms were disputed and subject to revision.[2] Tsarist administrators, well into the nineteenth century, were situated in islands of certainty in the midst of a sea they barely knew.

Working through the sources an educated Russian might have been able to consult during the first century of tsarist rule on the steppe can help us to better understand the difficulties that administrators at the local level, or in the chanceries of St. Petersburg, might have faced in understanding the region. A comprehensive survey of the ephemera produced by various early expeditions is not my goal here. Rather, I have triangulated among three bibliographical sources to produce a synthetic view of the steppe on the basis of the knowledge contemporary observers actually had at hand. Two of these bibliographies give a sense of administrative perspectives, the views that were accessible to the civilian and military officialdom of tsarist Russia. The first of these is attached to a fundamentally military text, compiled by the General Staff officer Lev Feofanovich Kostenko, *Sredniaia Aziia i vodvorenie v nei russkoi grazhdanstvennosti* (Central Asia and the establishment in it of Russian civil order).[3] The second is the *Turkestanskii sbornik* (Turkestan collection), a collection in 594 volumes of published works concerning Central Asia begun at the order of K. P. von Kaufman, governor-general of Turkestan from 1867 to 1882. For academic views I have referred to an index to work on the Kazaks compiled by the ethnographer Aleksei Nikolaevich Kharuzin, published in 1891.[4] Combined, these references provide a guide to the sort of knowledge a curious, well-educated, and well-resourced administrator, scholar, or amateur could have obtained during the eighteenth and the first half of the nineteenth centuries. The increased volume of works cited after roughly 1840 represents a new era in the tsarist state's regime of knowledge production and will be treated in its place. Works not appearing in either of these bibliographies were, effectively, dead to Russian readers. Uncited, out of print, sometimes never even in print, the information and perspectives they contained were of questionable relevance to the practice of rule.[5]

Taken together, the writings of scholars and travelers to the steppe reveal a striking blend of similarities and inconsistencies. A consistent and self-justifying narrative of the history of the steppe's entry to the Russian Empire clashed with shifting perceptions of the quality of its land and character of its inhabitants. That shift, in turn, was conditioned by the gradual acculturation of outside observers to steppe environments and lifeways, on one hand, and evolving perspectives on the state's role in this remote borderland on the other.[6] By the 1840s, the dominant view was that nomadism was primitive, and that Kazak nomads were difficult for the tsarist state to deal with. Yet it was unclear whether the steppe environment permitted any other lifeway, and thus whether changing the Kazaks was feasible or desirable. This complex of enduring and contradictory ideas, it seemed, could be remedied only by further study.

Agents, Sources, Networks: How to Know a Borderland

The beginning of the Kazak steppe's incorporation into the Russian Empire can be dated to the early 1730s. It was in the fall of 1730 that the ruler of the Small Horde of the Kazaks, Abulkhair-khan, gave a petition asking to accept him, with his people, as subjects of the Russian Empire, and in February of the following year that Empress Anna Ioannovna gave the conditions under which she would accept them, which she finally did in 1734.[7] The Middle Horde would follow a few years later, bringing most Kazaks of the northern steppe under nominal tsarist control. Although these lands had not been completely unknown to tsarist administrators before their incorporation, the establishment of regular relations (and thus an increased stake in knowledge production) eventually produced a significant increase in the quality and variety of data available.

Long before the establishment of Russian suzerainty over the steppe, the texts of early modern travelers to Central and South Asia like the Russian-born Afanasii Nikitin and English-born Anthony Jenkinson offered incidental, frequently inaccurate information about the lands and seas they had crossed to get there.[8] By the early seventeenth century, through a range of channels, enough was known about the steppe to include it in the *Kniga bol'shomu chertezhu* (Book of the great sketch map), "a lengthy list of geographical information compiled on the basis of [a map commissioned by Tsar Boris Godunov] and supplemented with additional information by cadastral books."[9] Similarly, the famed "ethnographic map" of the Siberian cartographer Semen Ul'ianovich Remezov displays, with borders of unlikely precision, "lands of the Kazak horde," the "Bukharan kingdom," and the "Khivan state [*derzhavstvo*]."[10] Maintaining relations with the new imperial subjects, constructing fortifications, and establishing trade both laid bare the deficiencies of this fly-by-night approach and provided opportunities to take a new course.

Initially ordered in 1734, the brainchild of the statesman and autodidact Ivan Kirillovich Kirillov (1695–1737), the Orenburg Expedition was meant to construct a line of forts along the Russian Empire's frontier with the Bashkirs, another Turkic-speaking, nomadic people. It would thus also provide a base from which to rule the Kazaks to the south of the line and for further enterprises in Central Asia.[11] This political mission was also equipped with engineers, geodesists, and other scholars, for good reason, as the lower basin of the Volga River, in which the Orenburg Expedition was based, was "a region little-known to Kirillov and his colleagues."[12] In an ironic turn, probably the greatest contribution to tsarist understandings of the history and environment of the steppe came from a Vologda merchant's son with no formal education, originally a bookkeeper to the expedition, Petr Ivanovich Rychkov.[13] Rychkov's *Istoriia Orenburgskaia* (History of Orenburg) and *Topografiia Orenburgskoi gubernii* (Topography of Orenburg province) would serve as key works for understanding the region, alongside the service reports of other bureaucrats in the region, for decades after their publication.[14]

By far the most significant attempt to gather scholarly information about the lands of the Empire during the eighteenth century (including lands that Kazaks inhabited) was a set of group expeditions that took place under the auspices of the Imperial Academy of Sciences between 1768 and 1774.[15] These travels, commissioned by Catherine II in a gesture befitting an enlightened despot, and under the direction of the German zoologist Peter Simon Pallas, left, by any standard, a tremendous amount of raw data.[16] This data, however, was highly empirical, weakly systematized, and often available in limited print runs or not translated into Russian, hence limiting its utility and interest in Russia beyond a small circle of specialists.[17] An indispensable reference point of later research, and a key part of tsarist understandings of the population and environment of the steppe, the voluminous works of the Academic Expeditions needed a devoted reader, and serious work, to be of more than academic interest.

The majority of the remaining public sources of information about Central Asia and the steppe, prior to the 1840s, came from officers and bureaucrats serving at the line or commanded beyond it for specific purposes. These authors, increasingly, were able to access and respond to the writings of previous researchers, correcting what they perceived as errors of interpretation and fact while adding their own useful data. The first half of the nineteenth century saw a series of geological expeditions to the steppe, including those of Ivan Petrovich Shangin (1816) and K. A. Meier (1826), while the celebrated Alexander von Humboldt favored the Russian Empire with a visit in 1829.[18] Military men of several ranks, following the will of their monarchs, took the opportunity of being assigned to missions to the khanates of Central Asia to, as one of them put it, "obtain precise information about insufficiently known countries" as they traveled, though these works, too, sometimes remained obscure.[19] The standard reference, for years after it was published, was the three-volume *Opisanie Kirgiz-Kazach'ikh, ili Kirgiz-Kaisatskikh, ord i stepei* (Description of the Kazak hordes and steppes) by Aleksei Iraklievich Levshin (1798–1879), a son of the steppes of southern Russia who, on assignment to Orenburg from the Ministry of Foreign Affairs, carried out ethnographic observations of the Kazaks and extensive research in the archive of the Frontier Commission there.[20] Based, moreover, on two years of archival and library research in St. Petersburg, Levshin's work was unquestionably the state of the art when published in 1832.

The Kazak steppe, then, was subjected over the first century of its incorporation into the Russian Empire to a familiar process of production and reproduction of knowledge. The balance of this chapter seeks to introduce readers to the gaps and contradictions in this body of its knowledge even as it introduces them to pastoral nomadism and the particularities of the steppe environment.

For local and central administrators, such lacunae were every bit as important as the knowledge that they did possess.

The Past

The toponym that I consistently translate as "Kazak steppe" (usually *kirgizskaia step'* or *kirgiz-kaisatskaia step'*, with a range of spelling variations, in Russian sources) was, at its base, a political term. Eliding multiple environmental assemblages, it simply designated the place beyond tsarist fortifications and redoubts chiefly inhabited by people who called themselves Kazaks, but whom outside observers called *kirgiz*, to avoid confusion with the tsarist irregular troops, Cossacks, who populated those fortifications.[21] Thus travelers were able to use the Russian border as a reference point dividing not only environments but safety from danger, civilization from its absence.[22] How these people had come to inhabit the places they now occupied, however, and how they had come to organize themselves as they did, was a matter of some debate, an aspect of the steppe's past that, with few written sources available, tsarist observers had difficulty grasping.

Virtually the only point on which tsarist observers could agree was that the people with whom they now had contact was divided into three major groups, or hordes, the Great, Middle, and Small. Despite some weak hypotheses about the origins of this nomenclature, the consensus was that there was no good evidence as to how this division had taken place (a question that bedevils even twenty-first-century historians).[23] Conflict existed, however, on the question of where these people had come from, a confusion that emerged from the misapplication of the term "kirgiz" to multiple groups of people. Thus, in a synthetic work, the academician Johann Georgi confused the present-day Kazaks with the ancient Yenisei Kirgiz, forebears of today's Khakass and, in some versions, Kyrgyz peoples.[24] This was hardly his idea alone. Most likely, Georgi drew or misread it from the earlier work of G. F. Müller, part of the "academic party" of the Second Kamchatka Expedition and, as the historian Han Vermuelen has argued, a progenitor of the discipline of ethnography.[25] Later commentators, with the advantage of hindsight, took him to task for it. The more likely version, Levshin argued, on the basis of multiple sources including what he termed Kazak "legends" (*predaniia*), was that the people who called themselves "Kazaks" were actually a confederation of multiple tribes who had arrived to the Central Asian grasslands from different places and at different times.[26] People under this name, he noted—quite incorrectly—had been known to Asian historians long enough to be one of Chingghis Khan's numerous conquests, and, after the collapse of the Golden Horde, emerged as independent, regularly warring both with other nomadic peoples and the sedentary polities to the south of them.[27] The territory they occupied grew and shrank in correspondence to their fortunes in war; Levshin noted that they had expanded piecemeal during the seventeenth and eighteenth centuries.[28] The steppe Kazaks were a tribal confederation that had become something more than that and had played the game of early modern Eurasian politics more successfully than its neighbors.

None of these were matters of purely antiquarian interest. The question of the origins of the different ethnic groups that composed the Russian Empire raised questions as to whether or not the "Kirgiz" Kazaks were related to the "true Kirgiz," or how fully the Kazaks were connected to the various "Tatar" populations around them. In the long run, although tsarist observers were of many minds as to their precise origins, Kazaks did seem more distinct than not from the ethnic groups that surrounded them, and this would prove vital to the tsarist state's approach to governance. The idea of Kazaks as a loose confederation, one which still relatively recently "occupied only the middle part of their present-day lands," tended to weaken their territorial claims to the steppe.[29]

Characteristically, the story grew much more consistent when tsarist writers reflected on their own actions on the steppe. A reliable and politically useful master narrative of the region's political incorporation into the Russian Empire quickly emerged; over time, it was referenced and reified.[30] The Russian Empire, when Abulkhair-khan first proposed that he and the Small Horde become subjects, was but one among several influential outsiders in the political arena of the steppe, and perhaps not even the most useful available ally (a list that included the Qing Empire and the small khanates of Central Asia). Scattered over a large area, the various Kazak hordes also faced diverse enemies. Kazaks' khans and sultans treated their oaths of fealty as flexible, seeking out the alliances that would offer maximum advantages as their circumstances changed. (Ablai-khan, of the Middle Horde, was a particularly skillful practitioner of this art.)[31] For Ablai, who considered himself a subject of neither the Russian nor the Qing Empires but sought good relations with both, such behavior was self-explanatory.[32] To bureaucrats with their own epistemic biases about international politics, though, such actions took on a drastically different meaning: betrayal.

In his history of the incorporation of the Small and Middle Hordes, Levshin, listing the numerous instances of Abulkhair-khan's *derzost'* (impudence), thundered:

> However little sincerity there was in statements of obedience to Russia by the Kazaks' masters [*vladel'tsy*]; however vain were their promises to give captives, protect caravans, and so forth, at least from the time

they were taken as subjects until 1743, neither they themselves nor those under their power made bold to make overt raids on our borders and fortresses. In this year they carried out unusual feats of impudence; and who was mainly guilty of them? That same Abul-khair, who did not cease to assure the Russian government of his faithfulness and of his fulfillment of all the obligations of a diligent subject.[33]

A careful observer of the Middle Horde, Ivan Grigor'evich Andreev (1744–1824), levied similar charges against Ablai and his successors for their continued dalliances with the Qing Empire, undoubtedly consequences of their "frivolity, and [devotion] to deep-rooted, ancient, fickle oriental customs."[34] Despite unceasing gestures of generosity on the part of the tsarist court, providing salaries to loyal rulers, and even building fortifications at their request, rulers remained untrustworthy, and the borders of the empire only conditionally safe.[35] Targeted administrative reforms, similarly, had not made the region or its inhabitants much more tranquil or politically stable.[36] Only in the Middle Horde, one traveler was convinced, had good government created any progress.[37] The other two hordes, even in the 1820s, remained "devoted to plunder [grabezh]."[38]

Understanding the recent past as they did, as a result both of their unfamiliarity with steppe politics and the uncertainty and danger many undoubtedly experienced when commanded there, tsarist administrators arrived at a consistent and promising solution for managing such a seemingly capricious people.[39] This, simply, was demonstrative violence instrumentalized as a tool of fear to keep the region pacified. Petr Rychkov, writing in the wake of the tumultuous early 1770s, which had seen the attempted flight of the Kalmyks to Zungharia, the Pugachev rebellion, and increased Kazak raiding amid the chaos, argued for the necessity of strengthening frontier garrisons.[40] The language he used to make his case was suggestive: "And so that these frivolous and inconstant people would have threats from the Russian border and line, and would not dare to approach fortresses so impudently and spread their raids beyond them, as it was last year, 1774 (a better year than others, although they did not join the famous scoundrel Pugachev), for this it is urgently necessary to establish and maintain in these fortresses such a militia, as would be in correspondence to their light and fast raids."[41] Levshin, on reflection, also situated the history of Russian rule as a dialectic of reward and punishment. When gifts and administrative reform inevitably failed to do the job, "necessity compelled [the tsarist government] to run to arms in order to punish predators who could not be convinced by any means and continued to attack the Orenburg border."[42] Levshin's convictions, in this respect, ran deep. "Centuries of experience and observation," he proclaimed, had proven that Russia could only achieve its goals on the steppe through an (unlikely) change of

Kazaks' national character or by forcibly restraining them.[43] Anything else was a half-measure, a needless expense on ungrateful and frankly dangerous subjects. Such views, established in a key text, militated against taking a more active approach to governance on the steppe; reformers or "civilizers" would have to make a strong case.

Despite the wasted resources and frequent false starts, most argued, the Russian Empire had not erred in accepting the "voluntary submission" of the Kazaks of the Small and Middle Hordes. Perhaps unsurprisingly, men who made their careers on the frontier argued passionately that they were not involved in a massive boondoggle. Given Kazaks' unedifying history of raiding both Russian settlements and the property of other peoples subject to the Russian Empire, but now within the fortified lines, Petr Rychkov argued, having them as subjects, however nominal, at least did not worsen the situation. Rather, once they brought influential Kazaks to heel, tsarist administrators could persuade them to release captives and make efforts to direct their raiding elsewhere.[44] Some years later, Levshin concurred, directly addressing an audience perhaps dubious of the need for control of the steppe, and showing surprisingly little concern for security issues: "However frequent are the attacks, disturbances, and raids, carried out by the Kazaks within their neighboring dominions, trade makes up for all these losses and makes their proximity very profitable, especially for China and still more for Russia."[45] Kazaks were essentially primary producers of animal products, carrying out exchange trade at Russian forts for grain and finished goods, a trade that offered substantial profits to merchants (especially unscrupulous ones) and the imperial fisc.[46] Both the steppe and the more lucrative Central Asian khanates to which merchants traveled were full of dangers, which Kazak guides could help to surmount or survive, if sufficient force kept them in line.[47] Moreover, were the steppe to be pacified, it would be possible for caravans to travel through it to Central Asia in still greater numbers.[48] To synthesize this line of thought: though the tsarist state gave much to the Kazak steppe and its leaders in the century that followed its submission, only to be repaid by bad faith, its efforts were compensated in other ways. The relationship was worth continuing.

Such an emphasis on security and trade suited the modest ambitions of a frontier state well enough, though these ambitions would later grow. Through the first half of the nineteenth century, the way that prominent authors understood the steppe's past under tsarist rule tracked well with the way that many administrators understood its future. It also corresponded to the land and people tsarist observers saw before them, a dry and harsh landscape populated almost exclusively by pastoral nomads. In the long run, though, a more thoroughgoing incorporation of the region would require new undertakings, including agricultural settlement. Perceptions of the potential of the steppe environment were vital to discussions of the possibilities, and limitations, of such enterprises. Even in a period of limited interest in settlement, by collecting data about the natural world, scholars, travelers, and administrators weighed in on the question of its place within the empire.

The Present: Land

Beyond its status as a political term, "Kazak steppe" had both geographic and ethnographic connotations. "Steppe" in the sense of a landscape was familiar enough, in the abstract, even to tsarist observers more accustomed to city life or more heavily forested environments. After all, before Abulkhair had even considered becoming a subject of the tsar, the Russian Empire had held flat, treeless, semi-arid grasslands—the lower basins of the Don and Volga Rivers, as well as the Black Sea littoral of contemporary Ukraine.[49] Some of the lands that entered into the "Kazak steppe" were comparable to them, a point which the physician Khristofor Bardanes, attached to Johann Peter Falck's academic expedition, noted explicitly.[50] Others, however, were far outside the ken of any unprepared observer. For the Kazak steppe was also something protean, a space defined by human behavior. As Bardanes put it, its *real* boundaries were "those limits . . . beyond which they do not nomadize, or cannot do so."[51] These vast lands encompassed desert wastes, grasslands, and oases seemingly propitious for sedentary life. It fell to tsarist observers to try to make sense of this diverse array of landscapes.

On the Russian side of the Kazak steppe, at least, it was fairly easy to define where it ended and Russian possessions began. These boundaries, beyond fortresses, were a pair of major waterways, the Ural/Yaik River (in the west, flowing south to the Caspian Sea) and the Irtysh River (in the east, flowing north to the Ob' River, and thence to the Arctic Ocean).[52] It was also clear enough, in the tsarist geographical imaginary, that the Kazak steppe, lying largely east of the Ural Mountains, was a part of Asia rather than of Europe.[53] What tsarist observers perceived as the indefiniteness of borders between "Asiatic" peoples, and the simple fact of distance from Russian possessions, made it trickier to establish a similar boundary to the south, where the Kazak hordes ran up against the khanates of Turkestan. Petr Rychkov proposed the Sary-Su ("yellow water"), a river originating in what is today central Kazakhstan, as a southern border of Orenburg province, while Levshin noted that Kazaks did not migrate south of the 42nd parallel.[54] The Caspian Sea served as an approximate western limit, while a line of Qing fortifications in present-day Xinjiang province stretching north to Russian borders offered a firmer one in the east.[55] Even Levshin, with the most complete data available at the time, refused to estimate what a huge surface area fell within these bounds.[56] To provide an idea of the distances and scale involved, though, in 1841 the scholar and diplomat Nikolai Khanykov calculated the area occupied by the Small and Bukei Hordes alone at 900,000 square versts, significantly larger than the state of Texas.[57] Coming up with some sort of scheme to make sense of a region so vast and diverse was a heuristic necessity, for both busy administrators and scholars who were beginning to think more systematically.

Efforts to do so resulted in the development of very elaborate schemes of classification. The diplomat Iakov Petrovich Gaverdovskii (approx. 1770–1812), in the only part of his extensive work published during the nineteenth century, identified four different zones (*polosy*) within the steppe, on the basis of their soil, elevation, vegetation, and climate.[58] Not to be outdone, Levshin delineated no less than seven climactic zones.[59] As a practical matter, though, most observers recognized two major divisions of the steppe (the oases of Semirech'e being outside of imperial control, and thus of the sight of the state, at this time). These were simple axial divisions, north-south and east-west. In terms of soil, vegetation, and hydrology, these lines divided regions familiar and comfortable to forest-dwelling agriculturalists from the world of the nomads.

A line that Levshin defined around the 51st parallel divided what he considered to be the most fertile, least sandy part of the Kazak steppe from the less promising regions to its south, with a second region of limited fertility stretching to roughly the 48th parallel.[60] The vast majority of tsarist observers drew this distinction between a lush, productive northern zone and the "infertile" south, although with less precision.[61] The soil above this line was the prized *chernozem*, black earth, the high humus content of which promised fertility and years of good harvests.[62] Further to the south, the soil grew poorer, with rich humus replaced by sandy, rocky, or salty and alkaline soils (*solonchak*).[63] These soil conditions had an obvious influence on the flora characteristic of the two regions. In the north, tsarist observers luxuriated in the possibility of introducing forms of agriculture similar to those of European Russia.[64] The south, on the other hand, seemed a bunch of reeds and grasses at best, perhaps useful to Kazaks, but monotonous and scanty to outsiders.[65] Less explicable was the seeming difference between the west and east, regions ultimately subordinated to the governor-generalships of Orenburg and Western Siberia, respectively, and which I will refer to throughout as the "Orenburg" and "Siberian" Kazak steppes. The eastern Kazak steppe, in areas where the soil had sufficient fertility, could boast a reasonable amount of forest cover, until it grew stony and naked on its far eastern edge.[66] Farther to the west, in contrast, the available forests were "very insufficient."[67] I have found no attempts to explain this difference, but the lack of trees even on the best parts of the Orenburg steppe seemed a problem to be solved and a serious limiting factor on its present and future prospects.

Another general limiting factor was the lack and uneven distribution of sources of fresh water. Here, too, the north came out far ahead. River valleys were the most promising areas for grain cultivation, providing moisture for crops and potable water for humans and dray animals. Unfortunately, as Levshin put it, beyond a few first-rank rivers (the Ural and Irtysh) and their major tributaries (the Ilek, flowing into the Ural; and the Tobol and Ishim, reaching the Irtysh), the vast majority "flow[ed] only in spring and at the start of summer" before drying up.[68] Both the Orenburg and Siberian steppes thus could boast only one major river and several minor ones boosting the fertility of the land, ribbons of life in an otherwise dead landscape.[69] Toward the south, the dryness of the climate reduced the flow of even fairly significant rivers, making valleys "uncomfortable" (neudobno) even for nomads during the summer.[70] The largest bodies of standing water (the Aral and Caspian Seas in the west, Lake Balkhash in the southeast) stood in the middle of particularly inhospitable deserts; smaller ones were undrinkable and ephemeral, useful only as sources of salt.[71] While some of these, especially the Syr-Darya River, Aral Sea, and Caspian Sea, offered hope for commercial navigation, the overwhelming message of scholarship and travel literature was that the southern Kazak steppe was a difficult place to survive as Russians were accustomed, much less thrive.[72]

The one thing that all of these subdivisions of the steppe had in common, in the eyes of tsarist observers, was their climate. In this the consensus was fundamentally correct: despite some small regional variations, this was one of the most continental climates on earth, with sharp transitions between hot and cold, little atmospheric precipitation, unbearable heat in the summer, and cold in the winter that could literally be deadly.[73] Fearing diseases of the eyes and respiratory system that they believed were caused by moist, cold air in enclosed spaces, tsarist observers were unanimous in lauding the salutary influence this bracing climate had on the indigenous inhabitants of the steppe.[74] All the same, the limits that it placed on human economic activity, without significant ameliorative work (irrigation, chiefly, where it was possible), appeared to be clear.[75] Yet some basic points remained disputed. While Gaverdovskii considered changes in elevation the defining factor in the Kazak steppe's climate, creating microclimates of varying suitability for habitation,[76] Khanykov marshaled an impressive mass of quantitative data to argue that it was the openness of the region from the north (and hence to polar winds) that produced its basic continentality.[77] Moreover, he asserted, glittering generalities about the climate were insufficient, though earlier researchers, for lack of equipment and time, were not to be faulted for relying on them; on the basis of new data for the 1820s and 1830s, he set it as his task to "establish plausible limits for the general expressions 'very cold' and 'very hot.'"[78] More precise quantitative data would enable both predictions for locations where measurements had not been taken and the establishment of isotherms, connecting locations within the Kazak steppe with locations elsewhere on the globe with comparable mean annual temperatures.[79] Although Khanykov never completed the essay where he began these calculations, similar methods would be used, in later years, to support arguments about the possibility of cultivating various crops in Central Asia.[80] For the time, though, all that could definitively be said about the climate of the region as it related to human activity was based on subjective experiences of the heat and cold, actual attempts at cultivating certain crops, and rank speculation.[81]

The image of the Kazak steppe environment that emerged in the work of early tsarist scholars and travelers was thus a blend of certainty and ambivalence. The rough natural divisions of this huge and diverse landscape seemed evident, but their sources and significance were altogether less clear. To the extent that much of it seemed unpromising for the lifeways tsarist observers were accustomed to, though, the steppe also seemed well suited to a different set of social and economic practices: pastoral nomadism. This, in turn, stood out as the key fact of Kazak life, the fundamental difference between them and the state to which they had sworn fealty, and a potentially serious obstacle to tsarist ambitions on the steppe.

The Present: People

Kazaks were by no means alone as nomadic subjects of the Russian Empire. Still, their curious habits provoked much commentary and speculation from observers unaccustomed to their seasonal movements and the social structures that supported them. Under imperial eyes, even at this early stage, nomadism was an idea with many valences: an environmental adaptation, a civilizational marker, a means of social organization, and a fact to be dealt with in matters of diplomacy and governance. It was held to be the determining factor in Kazak institutions and behavior, and the disputed question of whether their environment or character would permit them to live any other way thus bore strongly on perceptions of their future within the empire.

Nomads are notoriously tricky for modern states to deal with, to the point of cliché, slipping through the boundaries they draw and the institutions of surveillance they hope to establish.[82] Of course, comprehensive censuses were not common anywhere in the world before the nineteenth century, but tsarist observers saw the production of knowledge as particularly difficult among "a half-wild people ... ceaselessly mov[ing] from place to place with their homes, and whom the single word 'census' may bring to agitation."[83] Mobility, and not

the overall weakness of the tsarist frontier state, was thus to blame for the pau-
city of data available about Kazaks' numbers and wealth. Population estimates
focused, as a practical matter, on the number of men of fighting age each horde
could place on a battlefield, and even these varied widely: between 30,000 and
70,000 in the Middle Horde; roughly 30,000 in the Small, though only 20,000 had
been observed; in the unlikely event that the two hordes fully unified, the total
figure might make 100,000, or might make less.[84] Still less reliable was information about nomads' wealth, which outside observers could only estimate down
to orders of magnitude, and in broad strokes. Kazaks seemed to be rather less
wealthy than they claimed they had been in the past,[85] but the upper strata of the
population still held an enormous number of animals—1,000–3,000 sheep and
"often" 1,000–2,000 horses.[86] The vague picture that emerged from these statistics was of a thin population leading an extensive lifestyle—some tremendously
wealthy, others so poor in livestock that they had lost the ability to nomadize.[87]

Because of seasonal changes and the rate at which livestock ate grass, Kazaks
made several major migrations per year, a process that Khanykov summarized
in purple prose:

> When the sun with its spring rays frees the northern steppes from their
> snowy shroud and calls lush grasses forth from the renewed earth for
> a short life, the Kazaks and their herds hurry to build their strength, so
> as to bear the painful feelings of the other times of the year. But their
> ease does not continue for long. At the start of May, the most expansive
> [privol'nye] parts of the steppe's surface almost always offer a yellow
> plain of sad appearance, covered with grass burnt by the sun; then the
> Kazaks every week must move their light dwellings from place to place
> and, wandering along the banks of streams and springs, only by con-
> stant motion save their herds and themselves from a hungry death.[88]

The fall was also a dry time, filled with preparations for winter, which was
a time of limited mobility and the most difficult, dangerous time of year. The
holdings of even the wealthiest nomads were not reliable, in this view—they were
dependent on their unrestricted movement and acts of God.

Although it would have been easy, from a sedentary perspective, to dismiss
seasonal migration as disordered wandering, some tsarist commentators had a
fairly strong understanding of the ordering principles beneath the system. On
one hand, they created stronger links between individual hordes and specific
territories than had historically been the case: the Small Horde occupied the
Orenburg steppe and lands bordering the Caspian Sea; the Middle the Siberian
steppe; and the Great had its pastures in Semirech'e and what is today called Xinjiang.[89] On the other, they believed that the clan (rod), a subdivision of the horde,

provided the fundamental structuring principle of Kazak life, including during pastoral migration, and had a clear idea of these clans' preferred summer and winter pastures (Kaz. *zhailau* and *qïstau*, respectively).[90] If tsarist administrators had little success in keeping nomads within state boundaries, they at least knew where to expect them to appear. They believed, further, that this was a stable situation and, more critically, that these divisions of pasture were analogous to territorial subdivisions with which they were more familiar:

> In each clan rules among them he who is richest and is considered among them the wisest [*razumneishim*], but as the titles of these clans derive from their very antiquity, and as they are very populous, and occupy good-sized areas [*na nemalykh okruzhnostiakh*], one can compare them with our districts or cantons [*uezd, volost'*], having their own special administrators, which they call elders. They unite toward a single goal only in such cases when there is an inevitable need for it or the good of the whole clan demands it. . . . Every Kazak knows to which clan he belongs, and from clan to clan they do not move.[91]

Such regularity did not prevent conflicts among clans, despite, Levshin argued, their best intentions.[92] Rather, they clashed frequently over territory and resources, acting in the service of much narrower political and economic interests.[93] But there was, at least, a form and a logic to both seasonal movement and conflict, ratified by generations of tradition: clans and subclans moved seasonally along established routes, stopping at locations (*urochishcha*) to which they had defined rights of use.[94]

In fact, pastoral nomadism defined how Kazaks organized and governed themselves in several respects. Tsarist commentators, though, drew largely negative conclusions about the institutions that mobility conditioned. Lacking written laws because of their illiteracy and purported ignorance, they settled disputes through folk judges, in some versions according to "natural laws," in others according to "established customs and the provisions [*zakonopolozheniia*] of the Koran."[95] Over time, through the publications of Levshin and Grigorii Spasskii, there emerged a rough understanding of the existence of a body of customary law created under Tauke-khan (1650–1715), the *Zhetï zharghï*, establishing compensation for various crimes (including payment of a *kun*, blood money, for murder).[96] In the future, this emergent understanding would send tsarist administrators on a chimerical quest to ascertain and codify customary law.[97] Early on, though, commentators were more inclined to note practical problems: weak enforcement of rulings based in customary law forced dissatisfied litigants and their relations to run to the strategy of *baranta* (Kaz. *barïmta*), the theft of livestock in order to obtain satisfaction again in court or to compensate one's losses, a practice most common during the summer and fall migrations, and which inevitably favored the strong.[98] Indeed, mobility generally lent itself to weak leadership and to frequent situations where the right of the strong prevailed; people dissatisfied with their leaders would simply abandon them for others who better suited their "wild" inclinations, a privilege that sedentary peoples lacked.[99]

Such a rough-and-ready system of justice and administration might, in the right context, have found some measure of approval, in a Rousseau-inspired way, praising the simple and pure morals of people living in a state of nature according to natural laws.[100] But early tsarist observers do not seem to have thought about Kazaks and the steppe in this way. The farthest they traveled down the path of cultural relativism was to note that weak leaders potentially offered administrators a divide-and-rule strategy and to pay lip service to understanding the role that baranta played in Kazak life—that it was a ritualized, regulated phenomenon, rather than an unending cycle of theft and murder.[101] Tsarist observers discerned the existence of a ruling "white bone" elite that had the hereditary right to ruling positions (as khans or sultans), and sought to ally with them to stabilize a leadership situation that Levshin described as "anarchy."[102]

In short, by the time Levshin wrote in the early nineteenth century, these were not noble savages. They were simply savages, and, Levshin acidly noted, if Rousseau had gained any experience of what life was like among them, he might not have wasted so many words on the subject.[103] They caused themselves to suffer, impoverished themselves, and held their own development back.[104] Pastoral nomadism was, at best, something the Russian Empire could succeed in spite of.

This negative view of pastoral nomadism became even more strongly established as scholars and administrators fell under the influence of an Enlightenment-inspired social evolutionist telos, according to which pastoral nomadism was only a slight step beyond hunting and gathering, and still far behind sedentary lifestyles supported by agriculture or commerce.[105] Nomadism's sins against order and civil development, it seemed, were numerous, and did not stop at supporting an atrophied justice system dominated by a few influential grandees. The medical doctor Al'fons Iagmin laid the case out clearly in a short book dedicated to the sometime governor of the Orenburg region, Vasilii Perovskii:

> The history of the sciences and arts, and accordingly of medicine, among each people, begins with the history of its civil order. This is why, where civil order has not yet emerged, we would in vain seek out sciences and art, taking these words in their real meaning. The Kazaks support this truth in the most obvious way by their example. Until now they, constituting a separate people from educated nations, stood aloof from these latter, and,

evading any collision with them, remained in a rough and almost wild condition. The reasons for this consisted: first, in the nomadic character of the Kazaks, the general attributes of Muslim peoples, to which they belong according to their faith; second, in the geographical position of their country, because the Syr, or Seikhun River, divided this tribe from sedentary tribes, and the lands that lay to the north and northeast of the land of the Kazaks, were always inhabited by nomadic peoples.[106]

Mobility thus militated against the very prerequisites of intellectual or cultural advancements.[107] What remained were a variety of absurd superstitions and rituals that were at best accidentally useful and at worst dangerous.[108] Nor did it permit the full development of a religious hierarchy that might have softened morals and sharpened minds, a quintessentially Catherinian idea that retained adherents into the first half of the nineteenth century.[109] Rather, they were at best ignorant Muslims, at worst not truly Muslims at all—recent pagans who lacked their own mullahs and mosques.[110] The essence of their religion was not civil order but a few easily mimicked rituals (washing, circumcision, avoidance of pork) and deeply held, inconvenient prejudices against Russians and other "unbelievers."[111] For administrators who believed that force was the only possible way to deal with "Asiatics," here was more evidence in favor of their views.

The vast majority of generalizations about Kazaks' character were similarly grounded in their nomadic lifestyle and similarly pessimistic. Nikolai Rychkov accused Kazaks of ignorance (strongly associated with nomadism), slyness, and unbridled self-interest.[112] Shangin found them capable of inhuman cruelty and to possess a character "as inconstant as their way of life."[113] Both Bardanes and Pallas wrote that they displayed an unseemly suspicion of their Russian interlocutors.[114] Levshin thought them simply cowardly and greedy.[115] Such views, by definition ethnocentric, were in no small part the result of imperial Russian observers seeing the usual practices of steppe politics and warfare through a sedentary European lens. Positive evaluations, where they existed, tended to focus on their traditions of hospitality and the good qualities of Kazak women, apparently kind and hard-working people tyrannized by their husbands.[116] No particular efforts were made to reconcile these sometimes contradictory reports—for one high-ranking observer, S. B. Bronevskii, contradiction was the very essence of the Kazaks' being—nor to problematize the idea that a group of people could be said to have a "character."[117] Heedless of the small contradictions in these ethnographic reports, the fundamental difference between observer and subject—steppe and sown, sedentary and nomadic— seemed to affirm that these new subjects of the empire had a wide range of qualities that made them difficult and dangerous.

An evolutionary perspective on human societies implied that Kazaks might at some indefinite future time become other than what they were. After all, many of the worst traits of their "patriarchal" society were similar to laws and practices that had characterized now-advanced European societies during late antiquity and the Middle Ages.[118] All that was needed to make such an argument was to prove that nomadism represented a choice, and that sufficient parts of the Kazak steppe were suitable for sedentary agriculture to make advancement possible. Many tsarist observers were prepared to do exactly that. Bronevskii, for example, argued that pastoral nomadism was rooted in Kazaks' preference to remain wild and free: "[they] not only do not have sedentarism but, considering it as bondage to remain in a single place, hold fixed [*postoiannuiu*] life in contempt."[119] Moreover, both past and present offered numerous examples testifying that agriculture was possible on the Kazak steppe. Nikolai Rychkov, for example, noticed evidence at the Kara-Turgai River, within the Orenburg steppe, that the people who had inhabited it before the Kazaks had cultivated grain there.[120] Other observers exulted that hard-working Kazaks, in both the Siberian and Orenburg steppes, had been able to extract good harvests from soil that did not seem to have much potential.[121] A good enough environment made sedentary life possible, and that, by the logic of the time, meant that good government could make cultural advancement possible.[122] In sum, multiple viewpoints existed on this question, and taken to their logical conclusions, these viewpoints would lead to contradictory policy implications.

If these assertions could be shown to be untrue, though, then there was no alternative but to see Kazaks as permanently troublesome subjects, unlikely to be civilized, and best turned to the Russian Empire's advantage by force and coercion. Levshin, with a dominant position in scholarly and administrative discourse, laid out the logic of this viewpoint clearly: "It is impossible to presume that all Kazaks could be turned from shepherds into farmers, for, not speaking already of their aversion toward this way of life, they have too few places suitable for grain cultivation."[123] This, however, was nothing to mourn over. Since the Kazak steppe was "created as if on purpose for nomadic life," its inhabitants could serve the empire far better as wealthy herders than as poor farmers.[124] This was unlikely to leave Kazaks any more civilized, cultured, or inherently tractable than they currently were, but it would render them manageable through established methods, and had the virtue of corresponding to what Levshin viewed as environmental realities. At the time when Levshin wrote, maintaining, rather than effacing, difference still seemed to have its advantages.

In the century or so that followed Abulkhair-khan's original "submission" to Russian rule, tsarist administrators and scholars developed a firm set of understandings of nomadism and the problems it presented, although some aspects of this consensus seem unlikely or simply wrong in hindsight. Nomadism's status in Kazak life, though—as immutable or potentially changeable—was already open to dispute. Soon, geopolitical change and a reordering of internal priorities would lend particular importance to the question.

From one perspective, during the first century of its suzerainty over the Kazak steppe, however nominal, the Russian Empire produced a limited but useful sort of knowledge about Kazaks and the land they inhabited. The history of Kazak subjecthood, written as it was happening, amply justified Russia's presence in the region. Information about terrain, however rough and incomplete, sufficed as a guide to the most important travel routes and the locations where the most influential clans and leaders might be found.[125] A complex web of facts and stereotypes about nomadic life was flexible enough to justify any approach to imperial rule that might have seemed desirable—civilizing, if one apprehended the Kazaks through the prism of evolutionism, or a forceful, borderlands strategy, if environmental determinism came to the fore. The tsarist state saw the Kazak steppe clearly enough to maintain nominal control over it, control that, despite occasional rebellions, seemed to be growing stronger.

At the same time, some serious gaps stand out. Population figures were never better than a guess, and data about the environment was poorly systematized. Trying to take as a single whole a massive land area comprising several distinctive environmental regions, and whose residents were subject to divergent influences from without, produced a mass of contradictions. By the 1840s there remained fundamental disagreements about which lifeways the steppe could support, as well as about the civilizational aptitudes of its residents. Such uncertainty was productive, or at least not fatal, at the early stages of imperial rule. But it would present serious problems when, in the 1860s, the conquest of Turkestan completed the encirclement of the steppe, making it an internal province of the empire.

The Russian Empire conquered the Kazak steppe without well-defined intentions for it; more than that, though, it conquered the steppe without knowing a great deal about what it actually was. The 1850s and 1860s were a time of feverish scholarly and legislative activity in the empire, with new institutions appearing to support the research that, it was hoped, could resolve its increasingly apparent difficulties.[126] The administrative reforms that took place on the steppe in the 1860s were a test case for this new era of knowledge production: could scholars and administrators move beyond generalities and contradictions to develop positive and useful facts about the region?

2

INFORMATION REVOLUTION
AND ADMINISTRATIVE REFORM,
CA. 1845–1868

In his three-volume statistical manual concerning the Russian Empire's Oblast of the Siberian Kazaks (abolished, and parceled out into new borders, the same year the manual was published), a relatively obscure officer of the tsarist General Staff, Nikolai Ivanovich Krasovskii, paused to reflect on the position of his study in comparison to those that preceded it:

> Until now, we have not had any kind of data, of any sort of precision, on the basis of which it would have been possible to make definitive judgments about the climate of the steppe, rather than speaking in general phrases. . . . Atmospheric observations, by which it would have been possible to make judgments about the particularities of one area or another, were not carried out in any of the steppe settlements, nor are any being carried out right now. . . . Because of a lack of zoological and botanical research, it has barely been possible to say anything about the influence of the steppe climate on the development of organisms in different parts of this region, which is very interesting in both respects. Finally, with the information we have, it is also difficult to indicate to what extent climactic conditions here support human life.[1]

Krasovskii had little personal or professional interest in the ephemera of scholarly geography and orientology. The Russian Empire had, by the time his work was published in 1868, moved its military lines south to the oases of Turkestan, enclosing a region that, while it went under the general name of the "Kazak steppe," was ecologically diverse and populated by nomads of strange habit and questionable loyalty. Neither he nor the higher officials who gave him the assignment had any clear idea of what could be done with this new internal province—if it could be made productive, how it might be defended, or what institutions best suited it. Krasovskii offered up his three volumes as a first batch of reliable, practical data that might answer these and other questions of governance.

Krasovskii's writings stood in contrast both to the older scholarship described in chapter 1 and to the recent self-assessments of administrative organs on the steppe. One of these, the Orenburg Frontier Commission, even in the 1850s groused that it had no "precise and direct information" about the quantity of people and livestock under their authority.[2] Uncertainty about the environment, the atmosphere, and the population was not simply a matter of administrative bean counting. A failure of knowledge about the climate or environment militated against making judgments about the region's suitability for human habitation, or for agriculture. Population figures were the only available basis on which to estimate and project the tax revenues coming from the region. Projected revenues, in turn, were vital to any plan of administrative reform or assessment of current administrative performance.[3] In a very real way, then, approximate and unreliable population statistics left the future of the steppe provinces hazy.

In the 1860s, when the Kazak steppe became an internal province of the Russian Empire as a result of the conquest of Turkestan, a challenge and an opportunity emerged. It was axiomatic that this area required a new governing statute, but producing one would require a huge amount of study and fieldwork in a short amount of time. The task of the military and state administrators appointed to deal with this project, a group that came to be known as the Steppe Commission, was to collect as much information about the region as possible, complement its reading with fieldwork and interviews with influential locals, and ultimately recommend a statute on the basis of what its members had learned. Reading scholarship and delving into decades of bureaucratic correspondence—treated as an archive of administrative precedent and recent steppe history—members of the commission were expected to know the steppe as thoroughly as any man in the Russian Empire could before coming to their decisions. In a sense, this was a test case of Krasovskii's bold statements about the merits of new research in comparison to what had come the century before, and an opportunity to address the Frontier Commission's laments: was the existing state of knowledge about the steppe actually sufficient to lead determined administrators to a coherent and effective policy?

This question, implicit in the Steppe Commission's assignment, can be answered by reconstructing the intellectual world in which it operated and comparing the state of tsarist knowledge by the mid-1860s with administrative reform as actually practiced on the Kazak steppe. Russophone Kazak intermediaries were a small but significant part of this intellectual world, so reconstructing it also entails allotting to local knowledge and expertise a proportional role in the narrative—as part of a conversation rather than something decisive.

Neither the relationship of knowledge to power nor the relationship of Kazak intermediaries to knowledge production was straightforward. Bureaucrats studied the steppe in great detail and duly, in 1868, produced a Provisional Statute to rule it. Yet the Provisional Statute, meant to act for only a two-year period, represented a choice not to decide permanently in the absence of sufficient factual information. It was a best guess, and the men responsible for it would not commit to a guess for the long term. The knowledge of Kazaks had a fate similar to that of other would-be experts in the making of the statute. It was actively solicited, and occasionally valorized as being particularly important, yet also subject to being misread or discarded when the commission's understandings, or the priorities of its superiors, were at odds with it. The Provisional Statute, ultimately, was a case of orientalism *manqué*. The institutional culture of the era demanded that administrative decision makers study the objects of their decisions to the best of their abilities, and demanded that decisions and principled viewpoints be justified by established facts. But when the facts were not sufficient or incomplete, decisions were temporary and cautious. In its aftermath, the very epistemological uncertainty at the foundation of the Provisional Statute set the stage for a new era of debate and uncertainty about the steppe's future.[4]

New Institutions and New Attitudes

The decades before the Steppe Commission began its work witnessed an ongoing change in the Russian Empire's apparatus of knowledge production, a change that encompassed both its purpose and the training of its key actors. This change primarily took place under the auspices of two institutions. One, the Imperial Russian Geographical Society (IRGO), founded in 1845 and enjoying the direct patronage of Grand Duke Konstantin Nikolaevich, was an institution that transcended specific political affiliations.[5] It was, like the geographical societies of London and Paris that inspired it, an imperial "information exchange" at which curious people of diverse political and professional backgrounds presented new findings.[6] It was not, however, devoid of patriotic goals. From its very inception, the society was inspired by "the necessity of having geographical and statistical information of Russia . . . acknowledged by both the government and private individuals."[7] This, in turn, was a characteristic gesture of the prehistory of the Great Reforms—an attempt to gather useful, practical information to further the well-being of the empire's population and the good running of the state.[8] While IRGO, early on, patronized above all ethnographic studies of Russian people, its ambit quickly extended to promoting research of imperial borderlands and translations into Russian of major European scholarly works, such as Carl Ritter's massive *Erdkunde* (Geography).[9] Many of its most visible early participants—for example, the brothers Dmitrii and Nikolai Alekseevich Miliutin—were also regular participants in the salon culture of St. Petersburg in the late 1840s, where they discussed the work of such chic and radical thinkers as Saint-Simon, Proudhon, and Fourier. Although these service-oriented men tended to pass over the political content of the work of such utopian socialists, they drew from it an ironclad faith in the progressive, ultimately perfectible nature of human knowledge—a proposition as applicable to the remote borderlands of the empire as to peasant hovels deep in the countryside.[10]

Among the most active participants in IRGO, both organizationally and as members of its Asian expeditions, were members of a professionally distinct intellectual elite, alumni of the General Staff Academy—the other institution responsible for the change in knowledge production that took place on the borderlands in the 1840s and 1850s. The key discipline in this change was military statistics; its chief exponent was Dmitrii Miliutin, first a professor at the General Staff Academy under Nicholas I, later Alexander II's long-serving, reformist minister of war. Miliutin's military statistics had three branches (study of the territory, population, and state structure), each held to be potentially relevant to the conduct of war: the human and material resources that could be mobilized, the administrative mechanisms through which they could be accessed, and the political considerations that influenced the probability of war's outbreak in one region or another.[11] The General Staff had long gathered statistical information for its own private use. But beginning in 1857, at Miliutin's urging, its officers began work on a new series, *Materialy dlia statistiki i geografii Rossii* (Materials for the geography and statistics of Russia), which produced for all interested readers and institutions comprehensive sketches, with all the disciplinary rigor of military statistics, first of the 36 provinces of "European" Russia, then of the balance of the empire.[12] With such a broad conception of the details necessary for a comprehensive military survey, these volumes offered useful material for more than strictly military tasks. For the steppe, they were the absolute *summa* of what it was possible and desirable to know. Moreover, within the institutional culture Miliutin fostered at the General Staff and, later, at the Ministry of War, good scholarship was among the keys to professional advancement. Any graduate of the academy worth his salt, on campaign in the steppe or Turkestan, produced an article or two, sometimes for the military trade publications *Voennyi sbornik* and *Morskoi sbornik*, other times for presentation at the learned societies of Moscow and St. Petersburg.[13] With the Ministry of War still closely involved in governance on the steppe, there was no dividing line between the authors of these geographical and statistical works and the men responsible for the region's day-to-day rule. They were either closely acquainted with one another or, at times, one and the same person.

Under these conditions, it is unsurprising that the question of administrative reform on the Kazak steppe was decided by a study commission. The 1860s were a moment of confident positivism in Russia's public life, particularly within the institutions that were entrusted with governing Central Asia and the steppe. Serving orientalists and statisticians, no doubt seeking in part to buttress their own role and authority, publicly argued in favor of the importance of expert knowledge in administration even as they warned of dire consequences in its absence.[14] If the past had been an era of uncertainty, the chance now existed to do better and, by bringing the right knowledge to bear, govern the steppe wisely.

Forming the Steppe Commission

The unification of the Russian Empire's Orenburg and Siberian defensive lines in 1864 necessitated the reexamination of the separate administrative systems under which the Orenburg and Siberian steppes had previously been

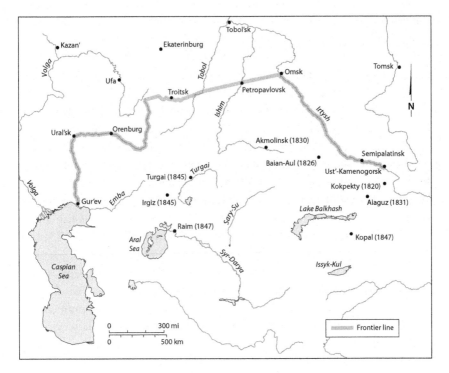

MAP 1. Tsarist frontier line and settlements within the steppe to ca. 1850

ruled. The movement of tsarist troops to the south and east had made the former Governor-Generalship of Orenburg and Samara unmanageably big. Nor
was it clear what cities as distant from one another as Samara and Shymkent
could possibly have in common. Samara province was thus lopped off from
the former governor-generalship on February 2, 1865. With the lines united,
all regions with a majority-Kazak population were, to one degree or another,
internal components of the empire, and the distance between them and the
frontier would only grow during the Turkestan campaigns of 1865–1868.
Moreover, the first domino of administrative reorganization had fallen. The
opportunity to study and standardize, impulses so characteristic of the era of
the Great Reforms, was now present on the steppe as well.[15] Thus Alexander
II ordered the ministers of internal affairs and war, Petr Valuev and Dmitrii
Miliutin, to research which principles ought to constitute the basis of a fundamental administrative restructuring of the steppe.[16] For Miliutin in particular,
the pioneer of military statistics and an active patron of young, talented, well-
informed officers, this was an opportunity to bring governance into line with
the state of the epistemological art concerning the Central Asian borderlands.
He proposed the organization of a study commission, to which Valuev readily
agreed.

So as not to lose the opportunity that spring travel conditions presented,
the two ministers moved quickly. The study commission, known as the Steppe
Commission (1865–1868), was to consist of one representative apiece from the
War Ministry, Ministry of Internal Affairs, Orenburg Governor-Generalship,
and Western Siberian Governor-Generalship, thus ensuring that the interests
of all the most relevant administrative instances were represented in its discussions.[17] These roles were quickly filled by a blend of ambitious and experienced officials. The War Ministry appointed Aleksandr Konstantinovich Geins
(1833–1893), a colonel of the General Staff and, until recently, a student at its
prestigious academy.[18] Another General Staff officer, Capt. Aleksandr Petrovich
Protsenko, was the choice of the Western Siberian authorities, while the new
governor-general of Orenburg, Nikolai Andreevich Kryzhanovskii, appointed
Gen. Karl Kazimirovich Gutkovskii (1815–1867), an officer of Polish ancestry known for his expertise in steppe ethnography and geography.[19] Valuev
entrusted his ministry's role to Fedor Karlovich Girs (1824–1891), part of a
long-serving and influential family of Swedish Lutheran administrators, a well-
traveled troubleshooter within the ministry and a member of its council.[20] It
was Girs who would serve as the chairman of this multiethnic, multiconfes-
sional group, bound together by a patriotic commitment to state service and
intellectual devotion to the collection of practical, useful knowledge. A month
later, all deputies available in St. Petersburg had developed a detailed program

of no less than 17 questions concerning basic administrative principles, the effectiveness of Kazak and Russian courts, tax structures, land use, public health, education, and religious affairs.[21] Even at the time, probably, it beggared belief that four men, at least two of whom knew no local languages, could travel more than 6,000 versts (about 4,000 miles) through difficult country and provide satisfactory answers to so many questions within a year—no matter how sincere their efforts and deep their expertise. Yet the tsarist state was making a serious wager that they could do exactly that, budgeting more than 17,000 rubles for the first year of the commission's work alone.[22] Despite the magnitude of the task, Girs and Geins set off from St. Petersburg late in June, arriving in Omsk, center of the Oblast of the Siberian Kazaks and the Western Siberian Governor-Generalship, on July 16.[23]

Tours like this were a quintessential tool, in the Russian Empire of the nineteenth century, for bringing about rapid administrative change, particularly in regions which were remote, lesser known, or distinct from the common structure of the European provinces.[24] On one hand, they enabled rapid data gathering by picked men of the tsar or his relevant ministers, with some participation by local actors. On the other hand, they permitted the ministries of St. Petersburg to bypass years of correspondence with local governors and their own assorted departments and quickly introduce proposals to executive organs. To effect change in this highly bureaucratic empire was an Augean task—statutes contradicted one another, paperwork got lost, powerful local governors died or were replaced by men with radically different views and an equal amount of power. Study commissions, with the right patronage and equipped with sufficient authority, could get around this mass of paperwork and personalities. Indeed, in the case of the Steppe Commission, all correspondence on matters pertaining to Kazak administration, no matter how far discussions had advanced, was simply halted, and the relevant files were presented to Girs for consideration in the commission.[25] Valuev and Miliutin happily took the opportunity an extraordinary institution presented to achieve a greater level of coordination than was usually possible. In short, this was a blunt administrative instrument intended to resolve problems that had been quite literally piling up for decades in the chanceries of Orenburg, Omsk, and St. Petersburg.

Once in the field, the commission's occupations were varied. They spent some time going native, living in Kazak *auls* (villages) chosen expressly for their "less spoiled" character, and conversing with influential members of the native administration.[26] In the Siberian steppes, their circuit (*ob"ezd*) took approximately five months; with the approach of the bitter Siberian winter, they returned to Omsk to pull files from the provincial archive, interview members of the Russian administration, and write up, according to a division of labor agreed in advance, their observations.[27] Some then returned to St. Petersburg for the winter. The following May, they departed for Orenburg, the steppes adjacent, and Turkestan.[28] By the spring of 1867, when the legwork was complete, much had changed. The massively unsatisfactory nature of the temporary administration of "Turkestan province," the administrative unit created to manage the newly conquered territories south of the Syr-Darya River, moved the problem of its reform to the front of the line.[29] Moreover, the very personnel had changed. Gutkovskii passed away early in 1867, depriving the Orenburg steppe of its representative; Geins, having done the lion's share of the work in compiling a governing statute for Turkestan, accepted a prestigious appointment as an aide to that region's new governor-general, Konstantin von Kaufman, which would give him the opportunity to put his recommendations into practice. But their replacements came from the same small pool of General Staff experts and experienced frontier administrators as before. Orenburg's new deputy was Major-General Viktor Dandevil', an experienced Central Asian hand as former commander of the Syr-Darya line of fortifications.[30] The War Ministry, meanwhile, would now be represented by an acknowledged authority on steppe affairs, Col. Lev Lavrent'evich Meier, who had literally written the book on the Orenburg Kazaks.[31] At the insistence of the governor-general of Orenburg, Nikolai Andreevich Kryzhanovskii, they were joined by another military man, Major-General of His Majesty's Suite Lev Fedorovich Balliuzek, a provincial governor in the Orenburg region who had, independently of the commission, undertaken his own study tour of his province.[32] It was this slightly changed group of officers that was responsible for pulling together a draft statute, explaining unclear points to local administrators, and, crucially, justifying the legislation they proposed in a special note. On New Year's Day of 1868, Girs presented the fruits of two and a half years of tiring travel and intellectual labor to Miliutin.[33] But before following the commission's proposed statute through the work of legislation, it is first necessary to analyze in detail the assumptions and information on which it based its conclusions. The Steppe Commission was, explicitly, a study commission—so what did it study? And what was the relationship between the knowledge it had at its disposal and the legislation it proposed? Sizable scholarly and administrative traditions had developed, by 1865, concerning all the questions most pertinent to administrators: Kazak lifeways; the applicability of reformed metropolitan institutions; and religious affairs. In all cases, members of the Steppe Commission had to navigate between what seemed true to them and administrative expediency. The knowledge of Kazak intermediaries, whether published in Russian or obtained through conversation on the spot, was more grist for this mill, an important but not decisive factor in settling debates.

Land and People: Sedentarizing and Civilizing the Steppe

The question of administrative reform on the steppe turned foremost on the question of its suitability to be ruled, now or in the future, along lines similar to the rest of the empire—whether it should permanently remain a borderland apart or could ultimately progress to *grazhdanstvennost'* (loosely translatable as "civil order").[34] However, this question itself turned on a series of others: could Kazaks become civilized while remaining nomads? If they could not, did their environment permit them to settle on the land? And if they were to become sedentary, who or what would effect such a transition, and in what time frame? By the time the Steppe Commission entered the field, the scholarship it could draw on indicated that the steppe was a coherent unit, more broadly suited than not for sedentary life and the civic development that came with it. But the more finely grained questions continued to lack clear answers, and demanded the commission's intervention.

Of the lands the Steppe Commission was to study, the most notoriously wild and uncivilized was the steppe of the Small Horde, governed from Orenburg and stretching to the banks of the Caspian Sea. This was the wild, anarchic steppe that Aleksei Levshin described in his widely read account. Levshin's argument about the inherent wildness of the Orenburg steppe was not terribly complicated. It showed early flashes of the geographical determinism that came into vogue in radical intelligentsia circles much later, in the 1860s. Nomads presented a set of inherent problems for any state that wanted to govern them—an assumption that, by the 1860s, was widely shared.[35] The sun-scorched sands and scrubby brush of the Orenburg region seemed unpromising for any lifeway but pastoral nomadism. Consequently, the Orenburg Kazaks were likely to remain at their present stage of development, and it only remained to the tsarist government to manage and pacify them as best it could. Later, the military statistician Ivan Fedorovich Blaramberg (1800–1878) expressed somewhat more optimism than Levshin about the influence of tsarist administration on nearby Kazaks. Still, his general conclusion was nearly the same:

> The nomadic way of life is a necessary consequence of the main industry of the Kazaks, animal husbandry, and the character traits common to all Asiatics—laziness and carelessness. They cannot in any way get the

hang of [*srodnit'sia*] the idea of settling for two very important reasons. First, condensed into a small space, by what would they satisfy their uncountable herds, which give them clothing, food, and everything needed for life? Second, this would deprive them of the mobility with which they are now able to evade their enemies and satisfy their deep-rooted passion for baranta [livestock theft].[36]

Both environment and a vaguely understood national or racial character militated against making the Orenburg Kazaks anything other than what they were.

For years, this image of the Orenburg steppe and its inhabitants fit comfortably with the priorities of the man who ruled both. The long-serving governor-general of Orenburg, Vasilii Alekseevich Perovskii (1794–1857), had been a frontier administrator of the old school. Improvement and "civilizing" did not enter into the list of Perovskii's tasks. Defense of the frontier from raids did, and in this, he felt, it was possible to deal with nomads. Indeed, his concern with security led him to oppose, on principle, permitting Kazaks to take up agriculture even in regions where environmental conditions permitted it. Rather, he hoped to transform the Orenburg Kazaks into consumers of Russian grain and manufactures, "softening" their wild morals as raiding the Russian border ceased to be in their economic interests.[37] Such priorities dovetailed nicely with a system of indirect rule that placed significant power in the hands of Kazak administrators and foresaw little direct intervention in Kazak lives by the tsarist administration. Into the 1850s, the way scholars viewed the Orenburg steppe and the limited aspirations that administrators had for it were utterly complementary.

The Siberian steppe (populated by the Middle Horde) and Semirech'e (populated by the Great Horde) were generally viewed as much more promising areas for nomads to settle on the land, with all the attendant civilizational benefits. Despite an uninhabitable hole in the center of the region, the notorious "Hungry Steppe," this was the area that seemed to offer the most promise for integration with and utility for the rest of the empire. Some of this was the result of a more direct system of rule introduced by Mikhail Speranskii in the 1820s, governing territory through okrug prikazy (district administrative centers that included Russian officials) instead of delegating matters to Kazak sultans. Whatever this system's deficiencies—and reform-minded observers, by the 1860s, were convinced that they were numerous—it had proven preferable to simply abdicating the responsibility to govern.[38] But environmental factors also played a role here. Unlike the harsh Orenburg steppe, the majority of this region seemed to offer resources sufficient for Kazaks to sedentarize, and Russians to take root, without significant effort. Krasovskii identified a variety of locations highly favorable for agriculture in the northern steppe, principally in the hills west of the Ishim River. Attempting to erase any doubts as to his objectivity, he noted, with unlikely precision, that "in these areas, chernozemic soil [i.e., black earth, with high humus content] occupies, out of each 100 desiatinas, about half (40.8%)."[39] Semirech'e stood out still further, as the Russian presence there grew, its left flank tremendously fertile and offering the possibility "to develop grain cultivation there and firmly establish [*uprochit'*] the Kazaks' sedentarism," which they would surely be able to do with the appropriate governmental encouragement.[40] The two halves of the steppe seemed like separate worlds—one ruled directly, developing gradually, and offering still further possibilities, the other seemingly condemned to remain an eternal backwater.

Already before the Steppe Commission went to work, there was significant criticism of this state of affairs in Orenburg. Perovskii's successor in Orenburg—the handsome, charming, but sickly Aleksandr Andreevich Katenin—quickly attempted to undo much of the work his predecessor had done when he came to power in 1857.[41] He was particularly galled by Perovskii's principled opposition to agriculture and sedentarization of the Kazaks and, in a memorandum of early 1859, attempted to systematically destroy all of his arguments. The subtle dependency and submission, based on commerce with Russian grain merchants at the Orenburg Line, that Perovskii envisioned seemed to Katenin a pale facsimile of the guarantees of stability that sedentarized Kazaks would offer: "The dependence and obedience of a sedentary people are incomparably more strengthened by the fact of their attachment to their dwellings and crops, that they will not dare to abandon them and go off God knows where, like nomads, and by the fact that these dwellings and crops, as punishment for insubordination, can be wiped out [*razoreny i istrebleny*]."[42] But this principled viewpoint would have been for naught if the Orenburg steppe was as unpromising a landscape for agriculture as Levshin and his ilk argued. Thus, although it is not clear which sources he used, Katenin also argued that Perovskii's assessment of the steppe environment was needlessly pessimistic. He embraced a different sort of environmental determinism than Blaramberg had. If there were sufficiently large areas with promising conditions for sedentary life after all, there was no reason the Orenburg Kazaks could not ultimately progress to agriculture, commerce, and grazhdanstvennost' as all societies should. Katenin noted that the small amount of land suitable for agriculture was only small relative to the vast total surface area of the Orenburg region. However, huge swaths of the Tobol', Turgai, and Ural/Yaik river valleys, in particular, were completely suitable for cultivation with minimal effort.[43] Consequently, to fix the Kazaks in one place—in this instance, without any particular mention of further Russian colonization—was both desirable and, in many areas, feasible.

But this was a long-term goal, and in the immediate term, Katenin was clear that nomads and farmers alike could be improved. Later in 1859, he would make an even bolder proposal: moving the affairs of the Orenburg Kazaks from the management of the Ministry of Foreign Affairs to that of the Ministry of Internal Affairs, like any other province of the empire. His reasoning stemmed equally from recent strategic shifts in Central Asia and a sanguine understanding of the influence of Russian rule on the Orenburg steppe: "The Trans-Ural Kazaks have turned from a half-wild people into real subjects, and Russia's border with Central Asia already goes not along the Ural, but along the Syr-Darya River and Ust-Urt [plateau]. . . . In terms of the degree of their dependence on the State, of their inner administrative structure, and of external security, the Trans-Ural steppe is now exactly the same province of the empire, as the steppe of the Kazaks of the Siberian department."[44] This was a slightly optimistic view of things at a time when the Russian Empire's front military lines, in the Orenburg and Siberian steppes, were not yet united. There were still significant security threats from the south. But Katenin's perspective stands out as important. It offered a new and drastically different conception of the environmental possibilities of the Orenburg steppe. At the same time, it established intellectual and administrative precedents for treating the Orenburg and Siberian steppes identically—and for treating them both as internal provinces of the empire—*even before the steppe had been fully engulfed by Russia's march to the south.*

It only remained for the established facts about the Orenburg steppe to catch up to Katenin's views (carried on by his successor, Aleksandr Pavlovich Bezak). The future member of the Steppe Commission Meier provided the goods. In his military-statistical manual on the Orenburg steppe, Meier, son of a family of evangelical St. Petersburg merchants and an officer of the General Staff, summarized the arguments in favor of sedentarism, agriculture, and the *mission civilisatrice* there.[45] Near the Orenburg line, there was much land suitable for grain cultivation, and sufficient precipitation to do without expensive irrigation canals.[46] Moreover, grain could be grown farther south, at the Syr-Darya, and he was much less pessimistic than other commentators about Russians' ability to adapt to the new agricultural methods needed to thrive there.[47] All this would in no way interfere with Kazaks' pastoral nomadism on unsuitable lands, for only through such mobility "[was] it possible to extract some use from many parts of [this] vast territory."[48] But still further, he argued, even superficially unpromising lands gave hope for future development, or at least utility, under the proper stewardship. He drew particular attention to the productive fruit and vegetable gardens at Fort Alexandrovsk, established by an enterprising officer of its garrison, "on the high plateau Ust-Urt, known for its infertility, and surrounded on all sides by naked, stony steppe and cliffs," and noted that nearby Kazak gardens were still more numerous and productive.[49] This was, effectively, the most logical conclusion to the shift of thinking about the Orenburg steppe among tsarist officials that had begun years earlier. In general, Meier presented evidence that human action could triumph not only over wild morals, regardless of the environment, but over the environment itself. Specifically, his data showed that the Russian Empire need not restrict itself to fortifications outside the steppe and resign itself to minimal control within it. Meier had already shown himself to favor the desirability of this idea; now he also vouched for its practicability.[50] A public opponent of the indirect "frontier" system of government that had characterized the Orenburg steppe, Meier also envisioned its environment as propitious for sedentarism in a way that would allow all the civilizational benefits of direct rule to flower there.[51]

Meier presented a raft of quantitative and qualitative data to justify his positions. His military statistics of the Orenburg steppe, when released in 1865, undoubtedly represented the state of the art in terms of information about the region. In effect, on the backs of several previous administrators and scholars, he had created a new fact—the Orenburg steppe as a civilizable, habitable place, basically compatible with its Siberian neighbor.

Even as the developmental possibilities of Orenburg caught up to the Siberian steppe in the tsarist official mind, local officials in Western Siberia were expressing new ambitions and preparing for a new phase in the life of the region. Since there were obviously, it seemed, lands suitable for agriculture that Kazaks were not making use of, the governor-general of Western Siberia, Aleksandr Osipovich Duhamel (1801–1880), proposed that peasant colonization of the region entrusted to him "could bring great benefits both with respect to civilizing the Kazaks, as well as for the development among them of agriculture and other trades characteristic to sedentary people."[52] Duhamel and his council favored caution; the precise quantity of land in the governor-generalship was unknown, as was its quality, but permitting settlers to rent from Kazaks would allow some to set themselves up in the region while protecting the nomads from any potential harm.[53]

When the Steppe Commission entered the field, then, scholarly and bureaucratic views of the steppe were in a state of dynamic tension. On one hand, by the mid-1860s, it was well established that, from the Caspian Sea to Lake Balkhash, from the Tobol' River to the Syr-Darya, the steppe was more civilizable and usable than not. This basic uniformity, in turn, permitted the entire region to be understood not as a set of distinct biomes, with their own histories, demanding unique treatment, but as something essentially coherent—the *Kazak* steppe. On the other hand, new ideas were emerging about the agents by whom, and the time scale according to which, the steppe might be sedentarized and, hence, civilized, questions that the commission would have to decide.

Local Institutions and Metropolitan Goals

Tsarist administrators, facing the steppe, confronted an administrative system sharply distinct from the one in the European parts of the empire, particularly with respect to the judiciary. Law, among the Kazaks, centered around the figure of the *biy*, a judge-cum-orator appointed by popular acclamation who gave his rulings publicly, in accordance with customary law (*adat*). Particularly complicated disputes, or those involving appeals, could instead be subject to the decision of an assembly of biys. Such an independent judiciary, ruling according to principles basically unknown to tsarist administrators, seemed intolerable for reasons of imperial prestige and control alike. Thus Virginia Martin has argued, from 1822 (the year of Speranskii's Rules [*Ustav*] on the Siberian Kazaks, i.e., those of the Middle Horde) on, tsarist administrators attempted to "[use] law to 'civilize' the Kazaks gradually in a colonial mission that mixed the material goal of settlement of the nomads with the cultural goal of 'softening' the morals and changing the customs that did not coincide with Russian legal sensibilities and cultural norms."[54] The continued existence of the biy court and the customary laws that supported it were only possible to the extent that they supported imperial prerogatives—independence from the expanding tsarist bureaucracy was no longer on the table. While Martin's argument is difficult to dispute over the long run, the question of if or how to incorporate the biy court into tsarist administrative structures was a challenging one for the scholars and bureaucrats of the Russian Empire. The mid-nineteenth century, rather, was a time of contingency and ambivalence on this issue, the resolution of which had as much to do with the particularities of tsarist administration as what bureaucrats actually knew about customary law on the steppe.

Although the tsarist state pursued different administrative strategies in the Orenburg and Siberian steppes before the 1860s, its strategies with respect to the biy court were broadly similar in both. The Statute on Orenburg Kazaks of 1844 permitted biys to adjudicate only in criminal matters involving minor losses of property (less than 20 silver rubles in value) and civil suits worth less than 50 silver rubles. All other matters were subject to courts-martial (*voennyi sud*) or the final judgment of the Orenburg Frontier Commission.[55] Russian courts also functioned as an appellate instance above the biy court, to which dissatisfied Kazaks were permitted to turn.[56] Although Speranskii's rules of 1822 presented biys the right to judge in all civil matters among Kazaks [216], it also set the tsarist oblast administration above the biy court as an appellate body [218] and subjected biys to punishment for abuses of power [220].[57] The overall gesture, as Martin puts it, was "to control and redefine the practice of adat to suit imperial purposes."[58] Tsarist administrators attempted to bring the biy court under the supervision of imperial institutions as much as was feasible and practical.

By the 1850s, both of these arrangements appeared to be running into significant problems, prompting reform proposals from the Orenburg governor Katenin. Katenin reported that the relatively limited competency of the biy court according to the 1844 statute suited neither tsarist nor local Kazak administrators well. The former had difficulty conducting investigations, since the nomads of the Orenburg steppe could easily hide or flee, whereas the latter were most often illiterate, unaware of imperial laws and ignorant of what their superiors were asking of them.[59] Moreover, investigations of criminal affairs lasted for years, taxing the Frontier Commission's limited resources and burying it in so much paperwork that it had little hope of catching up.[60] The solution seemed to lie in a wholesale expansion of the traditional biy court. Matters taking place exclusively among the Kazaks, it seemed to Katenin, even cases of baranta, murder, and quite large civil suits, could be left to the discretion of the independent court of biys. Only when Kazak misbehavior left the bounds of the steppe or involved Russians was it necessary to involve Russian law and tsarist institutions.[61] Such a change would eliminate needless paperwork, free the Frontier Commission to pursue more pressing matters, be more comfortable for Kazaks, and put the force of law behind the de facto state of affairs that already existed on the Orenburg steppe.

Katenin reasoned primarily as a practically minded administrator, and objections to his proposal had more to do with rough stereotypes of nomadic behavior or concerns with imperial prestige than any deep knowledge of the workings of the biy court. Justice Minister Viktor Panin and Dmitrii Bludov, head of the Second Section of His Majesty's Own Cabinet, fretted about the position of Russians with respect to the Kazak court and the way this court would judge serious and violent crimes, respectively.[62] When the matter reached Valuev in 1863 (after Katenin's death), he agreed to the principles behind the reform but, beyond Panin and Bludov's objections, disagreed that Kazaks could be trusted to come to independent judgments about murder and horse theft. If some expansion of the biy court was necessary "at this stage of [the Kazaks'] civil development," placing the tsar's imprimatur on the payment of the kun (blood money, Kaz. qŭn) for murder was completely out of the question.[63] Valuev rather endorsed, and submitted to the Council of State, a modified version of Katenin's proposal, according to which the activity of the biy court would be both less extensive and further bureaucratized.[64] Before the matter could advance further, though, thanks to a request for further consideration from Katenin's successor, Bezak, it came to a standstill. It still remained unresolved in 1865, when the Steppe Commission was created.[65]

Discussion of such local initiatives took place, necessarily, in parallel with initiatives emerging from St. Petersburg in the era of the Great Reforms. In the discussions that led up to the implementation of Russia's judicial reforms of 1864, providing for simplified, public, adversarial jurisprudence, it was necessary to determine the applicability of the principles underlying the new courts to regions outside of "European Russia" proper. To this end, in 1863, the Main Administration of Western Siberia commanded its bureaucrat of special orders, I. E. Iatsenko, in the company of the Russophone Kazak nobleman Chokan Chingisovich Valikhanov (1835–1865), to make a survey of public opinion among "honored people"—sultans, biys, and other influential Kazaks.[66] The majority of Kazak elites in the Siberian steppe gave their assent to various forms of regulation of the biy court by the tsarist state, a view that Iatsenko reported in good faith.[67]

The next year, however, Valikhanov composed a scathing note (not published until 1904) on what he had observed during this study tour. Though the note was unpublished during the 1860s, in light of Valikhanov's connections in St. Petersburg and Omsk, and its parallels with the views of other elite Kazaks that the Steppe Commission recorded, it is worth considering carefully.[68] Valikhanov clearly believed that the combined weight of his life experiences allowed him to understand much better than Iatsenko what had taken place. Valikhanov could boast inside knowledge of Kazak culture, particularly the practices of its elites. At the same time, his years of experience of tsarist education in the school for military cadets (*kadetskii korpus*) in Omsk and his subsequent service (mostly scholarly) to the tsarist state lent him a familiarity with the core principles and goals of tsarist institutions. Thus Iatsenko, he charged, had naively believed that "Kazak opinion" was uniform and unproblematic. But in Valikhanov's understanding, the wealthy and powerful sought to maintain, even increase their influence, and formalization of the traditional court of biys was simply another means for them to do so.[69] The biy court, which Valikhanov evaluated positively as a speedy, informal, and impartial institution, could only have a positive role in Kazak life if it remained independent of a state which elites would doubtless try to co-opt. In Valikhanov's view, then, the bureaucratization and regulation of the biy court promised no sort of civilizing mission, but continued and expanded abuses by the worst pretenders to the position—and the situation would remain so until Kazaks had developed further mentally and civilizationally.[70] Thus an organ that was intended to slowly introduce a spirit of grazhdanstvennost' to the steppe would, because of the tsarist state's failure to carefully consider local conditions, do exactly the opposite.[71]

Still, despite disagreements about the precise implementation, both local and central reform proposals now concerned themselves with *which variant* of the biy court would best suit metropolitan priorities. All of these discussions took place in the context of a strikingly positive appraisal of the biy court by tsarist administrators. True, some commentators considered Kazaks' purported national weakness for bribery a strong case against the complete independence of the biy court.[72] Yet others argued that, in areas with less governmental interference, "inviolable self-administration and the court of biys" were to be thanked for the Kazaks' rapid development.[73] Thus Valikhanov's historicist insistence on the necessity of preserving the independence of the biy courts at the Kazaks' present developmental stage was not simply the voice of a lone indigene crying out, unheard, for the preservation of national customs. Rather, there were real and widely shared concerns about the desirability of imposing Russian bureaucratic forms on Kazak customary law. Moreover, biys frequently appeared in Russian travelogues of the era as examples of the sort of local elites Russians could work with, as useful sources of information and confederates in a range of official and private missions.[74] In short, if individual biys were fallible, and the precise status of this customary institution with respect to tsarist administrative organs remained open to question, there was genuine feeling in favor of its preservation in some form.

The archive of administrative debates which the Steppe Commission could draw on, and the opinions of its local informants, thus pointed strongly towards making the biy court, in one form or another, part of the steppe's future. But this was largely a principled decision, based on a thousand-foot view of what the biy court was. Positive appraisals of the biy court took place with very little awareness of what Kazak customary law actually consisted of, beyond a few fragments. According to Martin, administrators in the Siberian steppe attempted to codify customary law no less than five times between 1838 and 1854, with none of the resulting collections passing muster administratively.[75] Farther south, in Turkestan, the customary law of the Great Horde Kazaks had not even been codified by the mid-1870s, nearly a decade after it had been accepted as the basis of administration of the region's nomads.[76] What was known with certainty, though, was that the old compromise between customary law and imperial administration had obvious problems. Instead, bringing the biy court, with its supposed quickness and openness, into the orbit of the state aligned well with the priorities of tsarist jurisprudence during the era of the Great Reforms.

When the Steppe Commission was sent into the field in the summer of 1865, all discussion of judicial reforms among the Russian Empire's Kazaks formally ceased, so that the commission could take it up anew. Years of documentation were forwarded to Girs, and members of the commission read these reams of ministerial and gubernatorial correspondence as a primary source concerning the recent history of the steppe.[77] Their task would be framed by the research and debate that had come before them—only aware of the content of Kazak customary law in broad strokes, but generally enthusiastic about it, if only in a transitional role. But the duration of this transition, the degree of bureaucratization to which customary law should be subject, and the reach of the biy courts, all remained open to further study.

"True Islam" and Confessional Politics

If, among the questions the Steppe Commission was asked to deal with, the court of biys was far from the experience of its members, matters of religion were much less so. The early modern tsardom of Muscovy had been, in its trade and diplomatic relations, as much a part of the Islamic world as of Christendom, and the Russian Empire had governed Muslim subjects since the conquest of the khanate of Kazan' in 1552. Since that time, it had conquered and incorporated several other rump khanates of the Golden Horde, engaged in a century-long struggle for control of the Caucasus that had, in the person of Imam Shamil, strongly religious overtones, and fought a series of wars against the Ottoman Empire. When Russian scholars and administrators faced the Kazak steppe in the mid-nineteenth century, they were equipped with historical understandings of policy successes and failures with respect to Islamic institutions. Moreover, on the basis of centuries of experience of interaction with Muslim polities and peoples, they had a strong idea of what Islam looked like—and equally of what constituted heterodox or deviant practice.

This idea was based strongly in institutions, texts, and practices, very similarly to the way that educated urban observers delineated "correct" Russian Orthodoxy from deviant behaviors in rural areas.[78] Orthodox Muslims prayed five times a day, abstained from eating pork and drinking alcohol, followed sharia, and had their own mosques, prayer houses, and schools. If such institutions and rituals made Muslims legible as such to the Russian Empire, they also, for a long time, provided this dynastic, pragmatic, and utterly undergoverned polity with a surrogate means of establishing order in newly incorporated or remote regions.[79] Through the mid-nineteenth century, in the tsarist official mind, good religious order and good administrative order looked identical. Alternatively, in a more pessimistic view, an established and well-regulated religion was simply too dangerous to interfere with.

To such observers, whatever was happening among the Kazaks, it was not Islam. Contemporary scholars have a robust understanding of the roots Islam had established in the multiethnic steppe by the nineteenth century, furthered by commercial and intellectual exchanges among Kazan', Ufa, Orenburg, Petropavlovsk, and other urban centers.[80] Moreover, as Devin Deweese has convincingly demonstrated, Islamic conversion was central to the identity of Central Asian nomads from the fourteenth century on.[81] However, this perspective, valuable as it is, is irrelevant to the views of a tsarist administrator. Responsible for maintaining external security and internal tranquility, often over vast areas and with little assistance, deluged with wide-ranging petitions relevant to the religious lives of those they governed, such men had to make snap decisions on the basis of whatever combination of scholarly information and personal prejudice was characteristic to them. Through the 1860s, all available sources continued to hold that Kazaks, irrespective of location and administrative system, were only barely Muslims. Meier neatly summarized this view and the panoply of factors held to have brought it about:

> The Kazaks, as is known, are Muslims and are usually considered Sunnis, however this is based on exactly nothing, because generally speaking, this people at present is very undeveloped in regard to religion and itself does not know definitively which religious sect it keeps to. The majority of the Kazaks have only a very muddled [*smutnoe*] understanding about the existence of two sects of Islam—Sunni and Shia. Further the very essence of their religion is completely unknown to them. The reason for this, likely, is partially their nomadic way of life, and partially the fact that they lived, and continue to live, surrounded by people of different confessions: Christian, Muslim and pagan, who are all hostile to one another.[82]

Even in the more settled Siberian steppes, Krasovskii argued, "the Kazak should be considered a Muslim in appearance only, and only temporarily."[83] (More pruriently, the traveler and orientalist P. I. Pashino suspected that Kazak men converted to Islam not out of any deep religious conviction, but because the lawfulness of polygyny helped to satisfy their libidos.)[84] Kazaks did not know what tsarist observers expected them to know. Nor did they do, in rituals or in daily life, what tsarist observers expected them to do. As travelogues and more serious ethnographies repeated these ideas, their authors both framing one another's expectations and citing one another, the superficiality and transitional character of Kazak religious beliefs became something close to an established fact.[85]

The questions of whether or not Kazaks were truly Muslim, how they had become whatever they were, in what directions their beliefs were trending, and under what influences, were deeply connected to basic questions of governance. What role, for example, was religious education to play in government-sponsored schools? Were Orthodox missionaries to be presented the steppe as a field for conversion, as among the animist populations of the empire, or had Islam taken root deeply enough that doing so would be unproductive, or even dangerous? Most of the Muslims of the Volga-Ural river basin were subordinated to the authority of the Orenburg Muslim Spiritual Assembly (OMDS): were Kazaks to join them? All of these issues generated substantial bureaucratic correspondence in the years leading up to the comprehensive reforms of the Steppe Commission. Moreover, in administrative discussions of all of these issues, the idea that Kazaks were recently converted and deeply heterodox Muslims at best had the effect of removing Islam from Kazak identity. Any construction of mosques, hiring of imams, or support of *medresse*s and *mekteb*s (Islamic higher and primary schools) became, by definition, a sign of insalubrious influences from without— since Kazaks, as they had been understood, did not behave like that.

It was, in fact, just such views of Kazaks' religious history that inspired proposals for a radical departure from the earlier tsarist norm—control and management of non-Christian confessions through institution building—in the mid-1860s. Their most vocal proponent was Kryzhanovskii, after his appointment as the new governor-general of the Orenburg region in 1865. Kryzhanovskii was an unapologetic propagandist of Orthodoxy who made little effort to veil his disdain for Islam and those who confessed it. In an initial report to Alexander II, summarizing his first year of activity in the region, he professed his horror, among other things, that the Orthodox faith had suffered so there as Islam grew stronger. This general trend was also notable among the region's dominant population, the Kazaks, and the growing convergence (*sblizhenie*) of a people "who were for a long time indifferent to any faith with the Bashkir and Tatar clergy is very harmful, especially if one considers that in the newly obtained Turkestan province religious fanaticism is essentially developed in the people even more than among the Bashkirs and Tatars."[86] Acting to stem this rising tide, he took a series of measures which boiled down to asserting greater state control over Muslim institutions in the region, rather than assuming that these institutions, left to police themselves, would produce sufficient control of their subject populations.[87] Emboldened by Alexander II's approval of his actions, early in 1867, Kryzhanovskii submitted to Valuev a still more developed anti-Islamic program.[88] Alongside an 18-point proposal to weaken "fanaticism" among the sedentary Muslims of the region, he advocated an unprecedented level of state intervention in Kazaks' religious life: permitting Orthodox clergymen to teach in schools with Russian and Kazak boys, and to teach from the Gospel to both at once; a zealously enforced ban on the residence of Tatar and Central Asian "immigrants" in the steppe; substantially reduced content in those Muslim religion classes that were to remain for Kazaks.[89] All these measures taken together, he argued, would in time win the still waffling, not truly Muslim Kazaks back from "fanaticism" and permit grazh-danstvennost' to flourish among them.[90]

In light of the support he had received from the tsar, and the increasingly frosty attitudes toward Islam in administrative circles in the 1860s, Kryzhanovskii would probably have been surprised at the negative reception these proposals received from two successive ministers of internal affairs.[91] Neither Valuev nor his successor, A. E. Timashev, had much to say against Kryzhanovskii's premise, nor against the goal he sought to pursue. Rather, their concerns centered more on the extreme character of some of his measures, what seemed to be his sketchy under-standing of Islam in Turkestan and the steppe, and consequently the resistance that such measures were likely to engender.[92] Thus Kryzhanovskii's views repre-sented, in their way, one logical conclusion to the idea that Kazaks were Muslims in name only. They were also an important precedent, for in the 1860s, his power in Orenburg was only beginning to wax. But the outcome of this matter points to both the circulation of knowledge and administrative practices among multiple regions of the empire and to hints of a different, more aggressive way of thinking about the place of Islam in Kazak life and identity.[93]

Perhaps coincidentally, at mid-century it was two of the Russian Empire's Kazak intermediaries—from elite families, and having received a first-class edu-cation in the imperial cadet colleges in Omsk and Orenburg—who expended the greatest effort in trying to convince their superiors that they had erred on the question of Kazaks and Islam. Valikhanov we have already met. His analogue, in the Inner Horde, was Khodzha Mukhammad-Salikh Babadzhanov (1832–1871). Both were mid-level functionaries of the tsarist state—Valikhanov in the Main Administration of Western Siberia, Babadzhanov sporadically in several lower-level administrative positions—and active participants in the learned societies of the metropole.[94] As with Valikhanov's self-representation in discussion of the court reform, in both scholarship and administration, a large part of their value lay in status as sources of "insider" information, difficult or impossible for Rus-sians to access, and their ability to present that information in a form and style to which administrative and scholarly audiences were accustomed.

In the case of Islam, as we will see, the value that some administrators placed on these Kazak interlocutors did not guarantee the adoption of their ideas. This was still more the case because Valikhanov's views of the matter, at least, were extraordinarily complicated. In one of his major works on steppe religion, he stated flatly that "Islam has not yet gotten all the way into [v"elos'] our [Kazaks'] flesh and blood."[95] As an ethnographer, moreover, he devoted substantial atten-tion to what he believed were traces of older pagan belief and ritual in contempo-rary Kazaks' religious praxis.[96] Yet privately, he disdained claims that Kazaks were not true or incomplete Muslims. His personal notes on Levshin's description of the Kazaks are, in this respect, as instructive as they are venomous. Dismissing the earlier scholar as "too captivated by the ignorance of the people he describes," he continued:

> The two Kirgiz-Kaisaks, whom A. I. Levshin asked what faith they belonged to [*kakoi oni very?*]—it is likely that they did not fully understand something in the sense of the question and, puzzled by its novelty, did not find a response beyond the easiest in such situations: 'I don't know.' Any Kazak knows that he is a follower of Muhammad and that he is a Muslim; maybe he does not understand the meaning of the word, but all the same this constitutes his pride in front of non-believers. From childhood he hears constantly, that he is a Muslim, and that all others, apart from Muslims, are kafirs, judged by God for eternal punishment in the other world. After this is it possible to state, that a Kazak does not know his faith?[97]

Valikhanov was personally irreligious, and certainly did not see Islam as part of the desired long-term future of the steppe under imperial rule.[98] But his private thoughts on Levshin appear to have influenced his policy recommendations. Caution was necessary, and missionary work, along with other "energetic measures" toward the introduction of Christianity, was undesirable.[99] Loyal to the empire he served and desirous of advancement in its hierarchy, Valikhanov argued that actively promoting Christianity, rather than simply interfering with the further spread of Islam (for some of his anti-Islam recommendations were similar to Kryzhanovskii's), could only harm the state and its subjects alike.

Babadzhanov, himself a member of a *khoja* lineage (a "sacred" clan claiming descent from Muslim saints), expressed much less hesitancy on the matter. Rather, in a set of "notes of a Kazak on the Kazaks" (1861), he positioned Islam as something important to Kazaks, and claimed that their ignorance of basic doctrine, and local variations on the same, were simply the product of a lack of formal education.[100] He faulted the Tatar mullahs responsible for teaching religious law to Kazak boys, where they existed, not for imposing an alien religion from without, but for their extraordinary strictness, and because, he claimed, "together with the laws of Islam, they give the Kazakhs their folk superstitions."[101] In this version, then, Kazaks were both Muslim and being corrupted by the heterodox popular religious practices of another ethnic group—not the other way around. Indeed, Babadzhanov linked the "progress" that the Inner Horde had made during the nineteenth century precisely to the establishment, under Khan Dzhanger Bukeev (1803–1845), of schools in which the formal study of Islamic law and Russian literacy were combined.[102] Islam was thus a part of Kazakness and potentially highly compatible with both cultural progress and imperial rule.

With respect to Islam, then, as in the cases of judicial institutions and the steppe environment, potential reformers had a diverse and often internally contradictory body of knowledge at their disposal, consisting of published scholarly accounts and bureaucratic archives. Kazaks were only superficially and insincerely Muslim—unless one chose to listen to the Kazaks who had weighed in on the matter, and argued that Kazaks were no less Muslim for not conforming to doctrinaire expectations. This superficial religiosity (unless it wasn't) permitted, even demanded, that the tsarist state take all possible measures to bring Kazaks to Orthodoxy—unless some of these measures were too dangerous. The track record of what previous administrators had attempted to bring about on the steppe, and how they and their successors evaluated the results, was available in the archive for any potential reformer to recover as the history of the steppe. When preparing their statute for an often tortuous review process, members of the Steppe Commission navigated among imperial archives, scholarship, and their perceptions of administrative priorities and preferences. After nearly three years of work on the questions developed here, and others, it was time to see if they had developed a solution to problems of governance on the steppe that their superiors would find palatable.

The Provisional Statute of 1868: An End or a Beginning?

Girs and his colleagues presented their draft statute for review on New Year's Day of 1868. It represented their decision on a range of questions—about land use, intellectual and civil development, the court of biys, religious practices, steppe geography, and the very unity or lack thereof of the steppe—that had plagued scholars and administrators for decades. True, not all of its provisions shone by their originality; some regulations were easily borrowed from, or directly inspired by, what was already on the books elsewhere in the empire.[103] But in others, thanks to memoir sources and the explanatory note the commission attached to its draft, the interactions between fieldwork and the preconceptions of its members become clear. At the same time, analysis of the review process, which took most of 1868 in different administrative instances, reveals contradictions between the commission's decisions and earlier, but still viable, ways of knowing the steppe.

Asked whether its original premise, that the Kazaks should all be ruled according to a single system, was valid, the commission was unanimous: "Study in detail of local conditions and the life of the people convinced the commission that the Kazaks comprise one people [*odin narod*] according to their ancestry, understandings about religion, language, and way of life, and that therefore identical administration is necessary for them."[104] To subordinate all the empire's Kazaks to a single statute was one problem, but to draw borders that satisfied strategic considerations and administrators' prerogatives was another. What the commission established as an ethnographic fact—that Kazakness was the fundamental factor unifying the steppe, to the exclusion of Tatars, Bashkirs, or Sarts— did not come with a readymade administrative outcome.

All potential borders presented advantages and disadvantages. For Geins and Gutkovskii, the apparent new fact that Kazaks were one people fit well with their desire for unity of military command over a long and insecure border and control over the uniform implementation of reforms in the formerly divided steppe. Thus, in 1866, they submitted a separate opinion, advocating that the entirety of the Orenburg and Siberian steppes, and large parts of the newly conquered parts of Turkestan, be united in a single Governor-Generalship of the Steppe, centered on Fort Vernoe (present-day Almaty).[105] This was a minority opinion, though, within a commission that inclined more toward finding convenient ways to administratively parcel out the Kazaks. The motivations for doing so varied. Kryzhanovskii offered a range of justifications for keeping the new Turkestan territories subordinate to Orenburg while letting the Siberian steppe go its own way. Though he cited Orenburg's importance as an established point of the Russian civilizing mission, and the connections between Kazaks living in the proposed Orenburg and Turkestan Governor-Generalships, the most likely impulse for his proposal was to maintain his own authority as "the tsar's viceroy" over a vast swath of territory.[106] Officials in the Ministry of Internal Affairs, much more committed than Kryzhanovskii to the development of grazhdanstvennost', feared that any sort of administrative merger of Kazak hordes formerly governed separately would inspire them to unite politically, with potentially dangerous consequences for Russian rule.[107] Such arguments, which ultimately won out, were not the exclusive product of a "divide and rule" strategy, but also based on practical considerations.[108] These included, for example, the impossibility of monitoring Turkestani affairs from Orenburg, more than a thousand miles away. Moreover, actually drawing the borders required awareness of Kazaks' established trade and migration patterns.[109] When dividing the steppe, ethnographic data was only one consideration, to be placed alongside other questions of governance less susceptible to scholarly argument.

Neither did simple answers present themselves with respect to the possible sedentarization of the Kazaks, and the closely connected questions of land and property laws. On one hand, a special commission based in Omsk—the capital of the Siberian steppe—argued that private property, at least in winter camps, already existed among the region's Kazaks, and that creating legal institutions in support of it would only further Kazaks' rapprochement with Russians and the civil order they represented.[110] This support would, moreover, permit individual Kazaks to rent their land to Russian settlers. In the context of earlier discussions of colonization and rental it is clear that the civil order private property was meant to inculcate was that of sedentary life.[111] In sum, both the environmental and economic conditions of the Siberian steppe were propitious for a transition away from nomadism.

In response to this proposal, the Steppe Commission provided its own body of facts. Certainly, Girs and his colleagues shared the long-term goals of sedentarization and Russianization with their Siberian interlocutors. But they disagreed that the time was currently right for it, as according to their observations, few Kazaks had any understanding of property beyond communal rights. The few who did know of private property, as a local informant named Ali-Mukhamet Seidalin informed Geins, had used that understanding to accrue vast holdings and exploit their neighbors.[112] Until such time as this changed, to prevent abuses and the undue suffering of pastoral nomads, the commission agreed with Bezak's older opinion that "for now the only possible form of land use among the Kazaks, because of their nomadic way of life, is communal [*obshchestvennaia*]."[113] As a transitional measure, it agreed to permit Kazaks to construct buildings on their own sections at winter camps, which having been improved could then be inherited and alienated.[114] But the large-scale expansion of private property in land, and the natural constraint of pastoral migration that came with it, would still be a long time in coming.

Perceptions of the steppe environment also informed the commission's view of the *agents* of the Kazaks' eventual sedentarization. Insofar as they only saw signs that Kazaks had settled down in regions where mobility was not needed for survival, they concluded that it would be a mistake to expect mass, planned colonization to be a success, for in this respect, the open expanses of the map were deceptive.[115] Much of the steppe, especially around Orenburg, could never be used for agriculture. What was instead needed, they argued, was voluntary and free colonization, which would cost the government little and resolve by itself the issue of the steppe's suitability as a settler colony—those settlers who chose unpromising areas would simply change occupations or leave.[116] This cautious approach, they argued, would also protect Kazak stock raising, with benefits for the nomads themselves and for the economy of the entire Russian Empire.[117] Land could come from the state or could be yielded by whole Kazak societies, by communal vote, hopefully obviating the concerns of the commission's interlocutors that individual property would lead to land sales that benefited a few individuals, rather than the community as a whole.[118] The small settler colony that would organically result from all this would be an archipelago of Russian trade and agricultural settlements, mixing with sedentary Kazaks in regions suitable for settlement, and floating on a sea of pastoral nomads gradually civilized by the proximity of towns.

If, so the commission argued, the current state of its knowledge supported such an approach, this position was also essentially an abdication of the responsibility to make a final decision on colonization and sedentarization until better data came in. The author of the commission's explanatory note suggested that to make any substantive conclusion about the possibility of large-scale colonization "without an economic survey, by means of which alone it is possible to positively define the quantity of suitable lands, would be premature."[119] Meanwhile, the few surveyors at the disposal of the Ministry of State Properties were already overburdened with their existing work, and could not hope to take on the gargantuan new task of surveying the steppe.[120] Caution and propriety thus demanded a gradual, hands-off approach. But the positivist assumptions beneath this formulation set the stage for a radical change in policy within three decades. When the tsarist state determined that it had the capacity to survey the steppes, caution would go out the window, and a measure meant to protect nomads and their way of life would lead toward their destruction.

The commission maintained a similarly cautious, transitional approach with respect to the court of biys, hewing closest to what might be called the "Katenin line" of expanding its competency. Certainly, its members had been won over by the positive evaluations its local interlocutors shared. These Kazaks shared Chokan Valikhanov's views. The biy court, a good and useful thing, had been ruined by its mixing with the administration and the arbitrary behavior of Kazak bureaucrats, in particular, interfering with its decisions; a more independent biy court would better serve its purpose.[121] After a conversation with Seidalin, Aleksandr Geins expressed a principled view of the matter in his diary: "I will try to restore [the biy court] by all possible means."[122] Moreover, in the understanding of the steppe's recent history that the commission developed, moments when Kazaks were judged exclusively according to the general laws of the Russian Empire "served not toward the joining [*soedinenie*] of [Russians and Kazaks] but, the opposite, toward their separation [*raz"edinenie*]."[123] Their interviews and experiences had demonstrated that certain crimes which seemed threatening to order on the steppe, most notably baranta, were so closely linked to the existing socioeconomic life of the Kazaks that they should remain under the traditional court.[124] However, they could not agree to a fully independent court system, as their local informants had suggested. Rather, they proposed a system of multiple, overlapping courts, through which the tsarist state would gradually increase its control of the steppe legal system (by means of the election and support of official biys and the right of Kazaks to turn to the tsarist legal system).[125] But the first and fundamental principle of this reformed court system, as Katenin and others had suggested, was, as Girs put it, "the restoration of the [Kazak] 'people's court' [narodnyi sud]."[126] Ethnographic knowledge and good administrative sense both seemed to point in this direction.

These proposals of the Steppe Commission, more than any others, panicked the ministries to which they were sent for review. Vladimir Butkov, chairman of the now-defunct Siberian Committee and a key figure in the development and implementation of the 1864 court reform, took a law-and-order position on the question of baranta: "Baranta, as is known, consists in armed attacks of one mass of Kazaks on another and is accompanied by the forcible driving off of livestock, seizure of others' property, and often even murder. It is obvious after this that baranta combines in itself elements of the most destructive character and therefore belongs directly to the category of actions that violate social order and tranquility."[127] Leaving it outside the activity of tsarist administration was thus folly. Representatives of Gorchakov's Ministry of Foreign Affairs went even further than Butkov in raising principled objections. If the commission truly believed that concessions were a transitional measure, they asked, gradually introducing civic-mindedness to half-wild nomads, then how did accepting those nomads' false understandings of obviously violent and dangerous crimes work toward that goal?[128] Not only would the commission's proposals fail by the very standards it had set itself, they would also harm the prestige and authority of the imperial government in the eyes of the Kazaks, perhaps irrevocably.[129] In the face of such organized and widespread opposition, the commission was forced to back down. The final text of the Provisional Statute kept baranta and murder under the jurisdiction of Russian courts, according to the general laws of the Russian Empire.[130] On the court issue, within a relatively small decision space, panic won out over ethnographic expertise, even as the administrative priorities of commission members had triumphed over the views of local actors.

With respect to confessional issues, members of the commission unanimously kept to the Russian scholarly consensus.[131] When Kazaks had become subjects of the Russian Empire in the 1730s, Girs wrote in the explanatory note, they had been only nominally Muslims: "they did not have, on the whole enormous area of their steppes, a single mosque; they did not have their own clergy."[132] Catherinian policies in support of Islamic institutions had been a serious mistake, allowing an alien religion to gain a foothold on the steppe.[133] All, however, was not lost, as the vast majority of Kazaks had still "yielded [poddalsia] but little to the Muslim spirit."[134] The religious future of the steppe, rather, stood at a decisive impasse—either the tsarist administration could take active measures against the further spread of Islam, or it could permit the trend the commission observed to continue unchecked. In the latter case, both the security of the region and the prospects of the Russian Empire's civilizing mission, embodied by other articles of the proposed statute, would be deeply threatened. Unsurprisingly, given this understanding of the stakes, the commission chose an active defense, proposing, in a secret note, severe restrictions on the construction of mosques and the presence of non-Kazak clergy, as well as the complete separation of the Kazak steppe from the OMDS.[135] They went further, too, advising that conversion of wavering Kazaks to Orthodoxy had a high likelihood of success and recommending the establishment of a missionary society for the region.[136]

This conclusion was not surprising. After all, the commission had been asked, in its initial program, to assess Orthodoxy's prospects in the steppe, a leading question that suggested that higher-ups in St. Petersburg were interested in receiving exactly the answer the commission provided. More surprising is the evidentiary support the commission chose to marshal in favor of its position, in which Valikhanov's writings on Islam played the leading role.[137] Gutkovskii, a former teacher in the Omsk cadet school and a man with whom Valikhanov corresponded, is the most likely connection between the late Kazak scholar and the commission. But Valikhanov would not have recognized the use his words were put to in the commission's explanatory note. Valikhanov counseled caution, explicitly arguing against missionary activity, but the commission argued that fears about conversion only had a place in the sedentary oases of Turkestan, where Islam was more established. Adding its own judgments to insider knowledge, the commission used Valikhanov's words to argue in favor of a policy he did not support. If Islam was generally a problem to be solved for tsarist administrators by the 1860s, here the facts provided by a local informant, adapted to signals from higher ministerial spheres, were made to speak in favor of a particularly activist approach.

Asked for their opinions on the draft statute in the spring of 1868, the local governors-general, Kryzhanovskii and A. P. Khrushchov (of Western Siberia), had few substantive further comments on it.[138] But outside of administrative spheres, during the spring, two of the Russian Empire's most respected figures in Central Asian affairs, Levshin and Nikolai Khanykov, began to make their feelings known. Their disagreement was not particularly, contrary to the indications of the memoir literature, based on a power struggle between long-serving experts and inexperienced young bucks from St. Petersburg.[139] The late Gutkovskii, after all, had put in almost two decades of dedicated service in the Siberian steppe, and Meier was a well-established and widely published expert. It was, instead, a conflict of different ideas about the steppe and its inhabitants, in which claims of experience and deep knowledge were sooner constructions to establish one's authority than facts to be taken at face value.

Levshin was approaching 70 years of age when the Council of State solicited his opinion on the Steppe Commission's draft early in 1868. He had made himself, by any standard, a glittering career after his journey to Orenburg. A leading figure in IRGO's early days, he had risen in the civil service to the high rank of actual privy counselor, and served as assistant minister of internal affairs during the 1850s. Now enjoying an honorable sort of semi-retirement, he leapt into action when called, convinced that the commission had erred in its fundamental assumptions, even that the very task it had been asked to complete was wrong. He laid a series of points before the Council of State, but most could be reduced to a single fundamental issue: the Kazaks, especially those of the Orenburg steppe whom he knew best, were not so peaceful and ready to be governed as the commission believed. Hence the incomprehensibility of permitting any sort of land use other than communal for nomads who did not know the meaning of individual use.[140] Hence the danger of replacing traditional clan leaders with elected officials.[141] Hence the eternal need to be on guard against Kazaks' raids and brazen disrespect towards all representatives of law, order, and civilization.[142] Perhaps the Siberian steppe was different, and the new statute applicable there— he could not, he modestly concluded, say for sure. But all the study, travel, and consultation that the members of the Steppe Commission had undertaken could not convince Aleksei Iraklievich Levshin that they knew the Orenburg steppe better than he. He urged the Council of State to reject the statute they proposed.[143]

Khanykov, writing from his own semi-retirement in Paris, where he had finally been presented with the opportunity to develop the extensive materials collected during his earlier travels, expressed a similarly dim view, but for different reasons. Even more explicitly than Levshin, he called into question the expertise of the commission's participants. It should have been expected, he wrote, that Girs would make the major errors Khanykov found in the draft, as the man was "completely unfamiliar with the orient [s vostokom]."[144] Chief among the errors he identified were an unseemly faith in and fascination with the court of biys, which he argued would remain powerless; entrusting the nomads with election of their own local administrators; and an overly complicated bureaucratic system that would never satisfy the Kazaks it was meant to serve.[145] The only good point of the project was the aspect Levshin despised most—beginning to establish the foundations of private land property.[146]

But Khanykov, in particular, had rooked himself. The sort of expertise he offered enabled him to tear a proposal down, but not to build anything new back up. He was critical both of traditional Kazak institutions and the new, more actively interventionist bureaucratic system. Meanwhile, the Steppe Commission had been at work for three years, Tsar Alexander had expressed his personal wish to see a unified administration of the Kazaks, and getting the interested ministries and local governors to agree even as much as they had was a rare occurrence.[147] In that context, members of the commission and their superiors had to deliver *something*. By failing to give the facts he provided a practical orientation, Khanykov excluded himself from any further influence on the matter.

Levshin's work suffered a fate that was perhaps crueler for a scholar, or at least more ironic. Members of the commission charged that, based as it was on experiences in the 1820s, some of Levshin's information was simply out of date. The Orenburg steppe was no longer wild and dangerous, but pacified.[148] Not content to stop there, though, they added a further indignity—citing Levshin's own work, still a widely cited reference work, against him (rather than directly referring to Meier's much more recent account):

> Analyzing the position of the Kazak steppes [earlier in the century], so well known in Aleksei Iraklievich Levshin's splendid work, published in 1833, one can surmise that, if the organization of the Orenburg Kirgiz had been in Speranskii's hands, their administration would have been organized just as in the Siberian steppe. Later, the systems drifted still further apart: in the Siberian steppe, alongside the gradual extension of the Speranskii statute to all Kazaks, our colonization also developed. Along with this, the most important of the occupied points, having become the seats of district [*okrug*] administrations, became centers of trade. By the combined actions of administration and colonization, our ways engulfed, more and more, the life of the nomadic people. The whole matter went so successfully that the tranquility and good order [*blagoustroistvo*] of even recently occupied parts of the steppe, like the former Kopal and Alatau districts, exceeded . . . parts of the Kazak steppe that had long been annexed.[149]

It was, at the last stage, the triumph of the nurture-over-nature argument, a case that the steppe ought to be civilized—in the various meanings administrators would come to ascribe to the word—and that this could be brought about quickly and painlessly. The Committee of Ministers, in agreement with the Council of State, when it heard Miliutin and Timashev's final presentation in October 1868, introduced no further substantial changes to the redaction of individual statutes. But its decision had a sting in its tail. Perhaps Khanykov and Levshin's notes had troubled them, or perhaps it was a decision taken in accordance with the commission's own frequent acknowledgment that its work would need to be adjusted further in the future, according to the indications of experience.[150] At any rate, because the proposed statute reflected such a substantial change from existing legal codes for the steppe, the ministers decided it would be "most prudent" to approve the statute for an initial, two-year, experimental term, presenting to the local governors-general the right to change or omit parts of it as needed.[151]

This decision was a logical outcome of the positivist attitudes that suffused tsarist institutions during the 1860s. The Provisional Statute was flexible to a fault, devolving significant power to local administrators as their understanding of the steppe and its population grew clearer. But it also wordlessly anticipated a moment of epistemological certainty, when that flexibility would be legislated out of the system, and claims to command new or improved data could not be leveraged into influence.

The Provisional Statute created a framework for the gradual advancement of imperial governance into Kazaks' lives to a much greater extent than had hitherto been considered possible or desirable. It established legal mechanisms for the establishment of Russian urban settlements within the steppe; enmeshed local Kazak administrators in a web of bureaucratic formulae and procedures; grouped clans and tribes into cantons and villages (*volost', aul*) according to administrative convenience rather than existing kinship connections; and significantly strengthened the resources of province- and district-level chanceries. All of these changes had to do with the persistent metropolitan goal of making Kazaks more governable, both morally and practically. However, in most cases, they also aligned with understandings, in tsarist scholarship and among administrators, of local conditions and tradition, and were justified in such terms. Over the following two decades, moreover, their articulation would depend on the ability of bureaucrats and subjects alike to amass and present knowledge of the local population and environment.

Ultimately, and despite the sweeping changes they introduced, the most important fact of the Provisional Statute was its very provisionality—a sense that it was a placeholder awaiting further development. This, in turn, was a direct product of the consciousness of members of the Steppe Commission, as well as of higher government instances, that they disposed of incomplete and imperfect knowledge at a fundamental level. Constructing a framework for imperial governance, they left the details to time, experience, and attentive further study. This compromise solution satisfied the concerns of all interested parties. It quashed the possibility that any single bureaucrat could be held responsible for the reform's failure while satisfying the basic assumption of the commission's members: that good governance and good knowledge were connected, and that as the state of knowledge improved, the laws it supported would have to change as well. In the long run, though, further change was no simple matter of accruing complete or precise knowledge of the steppe. When large-scale administrative reform *did* ensue more than two decades on, in 1891, it occurred not only in the context of increased knowledge of the steppe and its inhabitants but the rise of new and distinct conceptions of what both might mean to the Russian Empire.

In the interim, the reform that the steppe wound up with was highly characteristic of the 1860s—decentralized, but far from autonomous. The emphasis on fact finding and future revision, if anything, increased further the power of local bureaucrats reporting directly to the ministries placed over them. In particular, many of the men who were entrusted with diagnosing the problems the Provisional Statute had not foreseen had been deeply involved in the Steppe Commission. Balliuzek returned to the Orenburg region, where he served as military governor of Turgai province almost until his death. Kryzhanovskii, his authority slightly reduced from what he had dreamt of, but still considerable, was governor-general of Orenburg until he was removed from power in disgrace in 1881. Protsenko was governor of Semipalatinsk province in the late 1870s and Turgai province in the mid-1880s. Geins became one of the empire's foremost troubleshooters in Asian affairs. First called to serve as the right-hand man of Konstantin Petrovich von Kaufman (the governor-general of Turkestan and a major patron of scientific and scholarly research) in the late 1860s, he would return to the steppe to temporarily fill Balliuzek's position in Turgai province in 1878. In short, governance on the steppe during the 1870s and 1880s was in many ways a continuation of the work of the original Steppe Commission—an extended fact-finding mission.

But these governors were not omniscient, and were self-aware enough to be conscious of the limitations of their knowledge. Because of this, in the context of the Provisional Statute's experimental character, anyone who could claim authoritative local knowledge had a strong chance of influencing the implementation and revision of the statute. Kazaks and Russians alike, working independently or under the auspices of learned societies, hurried during these two decades to make their conclusions known. The correctness of the information they provided, though, would be decided as much by the views of those in power as by actually existing material conditions.

AN IMPERIAL BIOGRAPHY

Ibrai Altynsarin as Ethnographer
and Educator, 1841–1889

After it was first promulgated in October 1868, the Provisional Statute remained
as much a wish as a living, functional document. On the open, unsettled frontier
near the shores of the Caspian Sea, the proverbially wild Kazaks of the Adai clan
met the proclamation of the statute and new elections with armed resistance that
took months to fully suppress.[1] Some of its projected districts and district centers
did not exist, and construction was at times impossible at the Steppe Commission's designated locations.[2] Most of all, the new administrative structure the
statute envisioned, with expanded state involvement in canton- and village-level
elections and judicial affairs, rendered the tsarist state dependent in new ways on
the good will and expertise of Kazak intermediaries.

A proposed change to the instructions provided to canton and village administrators illustrates the scale of this dependence:

> With a view to the best possible eradication of theft, robbery, and
> baranta among the Kazaks, the canton administrator is obligated to join
> to villages Kazaks notable for their bad behavior who nomadize mostly
> separately from villages, and establish over them appropriate observa-
> tion by trustworthy Kazaks. The canton administrator and village elder
> are also obligated to know all the backwaters [*glukhie mesta*] in the can-
> ton and in the village, in which, predominantly, malefactors hide out,
> and to inspect them as often as possible.[3]

Whether hunting down criminals, translating documents, or teaching in schools, low-ranking Kazaks were the ball bearings that kept the ramshackle machine of tsarist rule on the steppe running. Local, insider knowledge was their stock in trade; it provided them with both limited routes to professional advancement and the means to advance their own political agendas.

The career of one such Kazak intermediary in the steppe remade by the Provisional Statute, Ibrai Altynsarin, is the subject of this chapter.[4] Over the course of a prolific career, Altynsarin, a well-born but poor Kazak of the Middle Horde's Qïpshaq clan, rose to a position of some influence in local educational affairs. He wrote ethnographies of his fellow Kazaks, compiled pedagogical materials, and maintained correspondence with some of the most prominent orientalists of his day. Although the extent of his rise and the strength of his connections with tsarist administrators were exceptional at the time, he was a model for future generations of Kazaks in their interactions with the tsarist state. His administrative service and intellectual endeavors brought him into close contact with a diverse body of ideas and practices for governing the vast Turgai province (part of the Orenburg Governor-Generalship through 1881) and its increasingly ethnically diverse population. His biography is a chronicle of the thought and practice of Russian imperialism in the Kazak steppe during the mid-to-late 1800s.[5]

The indefinite nature of the Provisional Statute and the continuing weakness of the tsarist state on the steppe created space for the knowledge of an intermediary figure like Altynsarin to influence policy under certain conditions. It can be difficult, however, to tease out Altynsarin's own historicity, relationship to imperial power, and agency in light of the sheer number of historical narratives his career has been made to serve. In various contexts, Altynsarin has been described as a class enemy advocating Russian missionary activity and colonialism; a great "democratic enlightener" of the Kazak steppe, bringing the benefits of Russian culture to a benighted region; and a proto-nationalist, "working for the development of national literature and culture in the area of forming a Kazak literary language."[6] Indeed, it is precisely the protean nature of Altynsarin's life and work, moving within varied structures of power, and mediating between tsarist institutions and Kazak life, that has enabled historians to squeeze him into the Procrustean beds of Soviet "friendship of peoples" historiography, or of contemporary nationalism.[7]

As an author and as an administrator, Altynsarin confronted a tsarist state that could be frightfully arbitrary and was rarely unified in its visions of the steppe's future, or its purpose within the Russian Empire. His professional milieu included both Orthodox missionaries and local administrators who were deeply opposed to preaching Orthodoxy to imperial subjects of other religions. It included old hands who had been on the steppe for years before the Provisional Statute and new men who made their careers precisely in the expanded administration after 1868. In short, he encountered what I would describe, playing on Jane Burbank and Frederick Cooper's framework for comparative imperial history, as repertoires of imperial governance.[8] Within the loose framework the Provisional Statute provided, a set of interrelated problems confronted tsarist administrators: should Kazaks become sedentary, and if so, how? To what extent could their Muslim faith be accommodated, and for how long? Should the Turkic dialects they spoke be promoted or replaced by the ruling language of the empire, Russian? Such questions had a limited number of solutions, but the answer to one did not determine the answer to another. Rather, provincial governors and district chiefs combined them as seemed best according to their understanding of the land and people entrusted to them.

Altynsarin's was one more voice in this polyphony. Like any other thinking subject of the empire, he navigated and combined a range of potential futures for the steppe and a range of measures to achieve them. Unlike many administrators, though, Altynsarin was able to insist on his own status as a Kazak—his deep familiarity with the land and people of Turgai province—to advance his views. At the same time, the reception of those views depended deeply on the particularities of Turgai province's ever-changing administrative structure, a side effect of the way that the Provisional Statute granted Altynsarin's superiors broad freedom of thought and action in their measures. Following his career through varied institutions and superiors provides an opportunity to "do history historically" in response to well-worn debates about the place and influence of metropolitan ideas and practices among colonial elites.[9]

Over the course of his career, Altynsarin compiled his own repertoire of ideas about the present and future of the steppe. The idea of "Kazak" as a separate category of identity had orientalist valences and distinctly imperialist ends. But in Altynsarin's hands it served other purposes. The sense of Kazak groupness he articulated, in language and religion, was compatible with some ideas of Russian rule on the steppe but much opposed to other visions.[10] His understanding and representation of the local environment enabled him to promote a program of Kazak economic modernization without moving to sedentary agriculture and without peasant colonization, even as the latter in particular began to appear on administrative agendas. Later in his life, as a school administrator, he had the opportunity to put these ideas into practice, proposing institutions and textbooks that promoted his understanding of Kazak culture while developing the forms of knowledge and vocational skills most appropriate to local conditions. Yet state power mattered tremendously to the success of all of Altynsarin's enterprises. Even in a supervisory role, converting intellectual agency to practice depended not only on Altynsarin's ability to project expertise, but also on the shifting priorities of tsarist administrative personnel.

Formative Years: Language and Ethnic Particularism

Born in the northwestern Kazak steppe in 1841, near what would later become the city of Kustanai, Altynsarin was orphaned at a young age and adopted by his grandfather, a biy named Balgozha.[11] He was biographically similar to other Kazaks engaging with the undermanned local imperial institutions of his era: born into a family that enjoyed high social status and was interested in maintaining it. Accordingly, in 1846, his grandfather presented a five-year-old Altynsarin as a candidate to enter a proposed school under the auspices of the Frontier Commission in Orenburg, intended to train Kazak boys as clerks, translators, and scribes for a range of administrative offices.[12] After much debate between officers of the Frontier Commission and central authorities in the Ministry of Foreign Affairs, the school finally opened in 1850, and Altynsarin and ten other Kazak boys composed its first class.[13] Here, in a small stone building on Orenburg's Bol'shaia Nikolaevskaia Street, across a courtyard from the buildings of the Frontier Commission, they studied a curriculum that included several

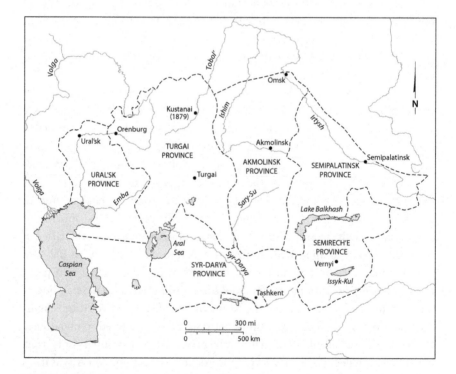

MAP 2. Territorial divisions of the Kazak steppe after the Turkestan and Provisional Statutes

languages (most prominently Russian and Tatar), formal study of the Koran, and arithmetic.[14]

The nine-year-old Altynsarin's adjustment to this new environment was not easy. He begged school authorities to let the older Kazak man who had accompanied him and his classmates on their journey to school remain with them, a request the authorities granted.[15] His talents, however, soon showed themselves. When this first group of Kazak boys finished their course of study with a public examination in 1857, Altynsarin was ranked fourth out of 22 boys, with excellent marks in all subjects and a reputation as a voracious reader.[16] Now qualified for state employment, he began his working life at the age of 16 at the bottom rung of the ladder, serving as a scribe for his grandfather, who by this time was the administrator of a group of Kazaks of the Qïpshaq clan.[17] He climbed quickly and was soon appointed a junior translator in the Frontier Commission at Orenburg, working directly under its head, the celebrated orientalist Vasilii Vasil'evich Grigor'ev (1816–1881).[18]

Altynsarin's time at the Frontier Commission proved formative intellectually and interpersonally. Spending his workdays in Grigor'ev's reception room, he spent much of his time reading books from Grigor'ev's personal collection. Grigor'ev also provided his young subordinate with translations of unfamiliar Russian words. According to one account, the notoriously prickly Grigor'ev's fatigue with this arrangement drove the young Kazak into the tutelage and friendship of another young scholar, Nikolai Ivanovich Il'minskii (1822–1891), a devoutly Orthodox alumnus of the Kazan' Ecclesiastical Academy recently commanded to Orenburg.[19] As with Grigor'ev, Altynsarin's relationship with Il'minskii first focused above all on language acquisition, with Il'minskii later recalling: "Altynsarin appeared at my place every evening from seven to twelve. Our conversations mainly consisted in explanation of words."[20] From this small seed, a warm relationship grew. Il'minskii remarked that Altynsarin was "always a welcome guest" in his household, and their correspondence continued, with interruptions, until Altynsarin's death in 1889.[21] Soon, however, a new professional opportunity, facilitated both by the young Kazak's excellent track record and his personal acquaintance with Grigor'ev, separated the two friends. In 1860, four schools for Kazaks were opened under Russian fortifications in the steppe; Altynsarin accepted the invitation to teach in the one at the Orenburg fortress, a location that later developed into the city and provincial center of Turgai.[22]

These four schools were a cherished project of Grigor'ev's, and he fought hard with his superiors, especially the martinet Aleksandr Pavlovich Bezak (1800–1869), who began his service as governor-general of Orenburg in late 1860, to build them in the form he had envisioned. Critics of the existing school for Kazak boys in Orenburg had described it as overly influenced by Tatars, expensive, and not corresponding to the needs of steppe life as they understood it. What was needed for the next stage in educating the Kazaks was not a well-appointed, centrally located building with an extensive curriculum, they argued, but a set of schools lasting no more than four years, built with any materials locally available, deeper in the steppe, with teaching in Kazak rather than Russian. "The simpler the schools are," Grigor'ev wrote in 1859, "the closer they are in appearance to the Asiatics', the better."[23] The new schools were to inexpensively and unobtrusively satisfy a demand for literacy training in the new ruling language, providing an alternative to the dreaded Tatar mektebs.[24] Altynsarin and his fellow alumni of the Orenburg school, proficient in Russian and Kazak, were the heralds of Grigor'ev's wish to adapt imperial schools to local tastes.

Altynsarin endured great personal difficulty after accepting this new appointment. Bureaucratic wrangling meant that the school was not opened until four years after he accepted the position, and in the intervening years he was forced to teach children informally, as they came to him.[25] Moreover, the post took him far away from family members to whom he had economic responsibilities, and Altynsarin's petitions to Grigor'ev for a transfer closer to home were variously denied or left unrealized owing to a lack of suitable replacements.[26] The situation began to improve only in 1863, when Altynsarin took the step of moving his entire household to the Turgai River.[27] The school under his supervision was finally opened the following year.

For the next five years Altynsarin taught Kazak and Russian students alike. Among other materials, he used his friend Il'minskii's *Samouchitel' russkoi gramoty dlia kirgizov* (an 1861 textbook of the Russian language), compiled with the help of another local intermediary, Bakhtiarov, and printed in the Arabic script.[28] Il'minskii's choice of the Arabic script was controversial. Grigor'ev, who commissioned this "textbook of Russian language for Kazak schools, in Russian and Kazak," favored the Cyrillic script for writing Kazak.[29] This choice, he argued, was not only better suited to the complicated, vowel-rich sound system of the Kazak language; it would also gradually reduce the influence of Tatar language and culture (strongly associated with the Arabic script) among the Kazaks.[30] Nor was Il'minskii himself yet firmly decided on the issue. His first attempt at a dictionary of Kazak, with an attached grammar, was printed in a modified Cyrillic script so elaborate that Grigor'ev took him to task for it.[31] Vernacular-language education, in the steppe provinces, came with a range of administrative choices and no single clear answer.

Nor was vernacular-language education itself remotely uncontroversial. Still in its relative infancy in the early 1860s, it had multiple meanings for its proponents and detractors alike. Il'minskii is most widely associated with this approach, which was originally applied in schools for the Baptized Tatars (*kriasheny*) of the

Volga River basin. In this context, delivering the content of religious texts to the recently converted in a language they understood was intended to prevent their backsliding into apostasy.[32] Such a perspective implied a moral and spiritual perspective on the Russianization (*obrusenie*) of nondominant nationality groups, according to which Orthodoxy, rather than the Russian language, bore the most important components of Russian identity.[33] In this view, to educate the small nationalities of the empire in their own language was to facilitate their moral rapprochement with the numerically and politically dominant population of the empire.

The historian Tomohiko Uyama has described Russia as a "particularist empire," in which the ways that bureaucrats perceived different ethnicities resulted in divergent policy outcomes.[34] And indeed, outside of the Volga basin, the specifics of this spiritual Russianization were rather different. In the Turkestan Governor-Generalship, the local population was considered so staunchly Muslim that any attempt to convert it would engender serious resistance. Thus the highly influential first governor-general of the region, Konstantin Petrovich von Kaufman (1818–1882), pursued a policy of *ignorirovanie* (ignoring), permitting a high degree of local autonomy in religious affairs and vernacular-language schools free of any missionary valence.[35] Bilingual schools were meant to achieve cultural transformation, but still "incorporated Muslim religious instruction for non-Christian pupils."[36] Here the value of vernacular education, as the historian Daniel Brower notes, was strictly pragmatic. Russian-language instruction, and the secular cultural transformation that was to accompany it, could not occur in a largely illiterate society without teaching native-language literacy first.

In both the Volga basin and in Turkestan, further, there were those tsarist administrators who doubted the utility of vernacular education. Its opponents believed that the benefits of linguistic Russianization could not be sacrificed for the sake of a moral project of vague character and uncertain timeline. For the Volga, an 1867 article in the official *Zhurnal Ministerstva narodnogo prosveshcheniia* (Journal of the Ministry of Education) acknowledged the deficiencies of religious education conducted exclusively in Russian, while simultaneously articulating high-level fears relating to vernacular religious education.[37] Critics expressed fears that the local vernacular could not accurately render the content of missionary teaching.[38] Moreover, the creation of official languages from "scanty" dialects (*narechiia*) would necessarily involve borrowing from Tatar, and "such an artificial strengthening of the Tatar element on the eastern borderland of Russia and the merging [*sliianie*] of *different* foreign groups into *one* foreign mass, even under the condition of their serious Christian enlightenment, cannot in any way be desirable."[39] Others expressed a diametrically opposite fear—since "a language is a people" (*iazyk—eto narod*), providing "small peoples" with their own language would inspire feelings of national particularity and separateness from the ruling Russian nationality.[40]

Conversely, in Turkestan, the criticism was less of vernacular education per se than of the goal toward which it strove. In the work of the notoriously hysterical missionary Mikhail Miropiev, use of Russian alongside the vernacular was hopefully a waystation toward the outcome he desired most—education of Turkestan's Muslims on the basis of the principles of Orthodoxy.[41] Ignorirovanie was not a satisfying compromise, for Miropiev. If Russian-language education gradually softened native culture, perhaps, in the long run, administrators' caution would no longer be needed, and the policy could be abandoned.

The ethnographic and orientological consensus was that religion on the steppe was closer to the situation among the converted peoples of the Volga basin than to Turkestan. Certainly the authors of the Provisional Statute, citing Levshin and Valikhanov, had believed Kazaks to be nominal Muslims at best, with significant traces of shamanist belief still present. The passage of time did not dispel this impression. Even in 1880, in a strikingly Islamophobic essay on Central Asian religion, the orientalist and pedagogue Nikolai Ostroumov had described Kazaks as "neophytes" in Islam.[42] Il'minskii's views on vernacular education among the Kazaks were very much of a piece with this consensus. Using the Kazak language in schools, for Il'minskii, would gradually win Kazaks away from Islam, exposing them "to the advantages of Russian civilization over Islamic culture and draw[ing] them into cultural alignment with Russians."[43]

Grigor'ev's views were less obviously missionary than Il'minskii's, but he was also a notorious Tatarophobe and endorsed the use of vernacular Kazak as a means of reducing Tatar influence in administrative, commercial, and religious affairs.[44] Early administrators had chosen to conduct correspondence in the language they called "Tatar" (actually the old Tatar or "Turki" language) for a number of reasons. It had the considerable advantages of an agreed-upon script and a written literary tradition, and was already known to literate intermediaries. Orenburg and its environs boasted a substantial Tatar minority.[45] But Grigor'ev, Il'minskii, and others were prepared to argue that Tatar no longer suited the needs of Russian governance there. Many administrators associated Tatars particularly strongly with Kazaks' "conversion" to Islam. Therefore, in the wake of the secret and seriously Islamophobic attachment to the Provisional Statute on Islam in the steppe, there was good reason to believe that Petersburg shared their views.[46]

From the first attempts to educate *inorodtsy* (aliens) until the last days of the empire, script and language alike had a politics in the steppe, and an inherent part of that conversation was the production and use of educational materials.[47] However, it does not follow from this that Russian-educated Kazaks associated the same politics with these issues as their interlocutors. While Altynsarin's later career as an educator would take place at the center of this controversy, he had begun to form his own impressions of the problems inherent in steppe education and their solutions at a young age. He was relatively pleased with the results provided by Il'minskii and Bakhtiarov's textbook, and developed a preference for the use of the Arabic script for Kazak that was not always practicable as his career advanced. Writing to Il'minskii in 1871, he argued that while Cyrillic script rendered Kazak phonology with greater fidelity than Arabic, and that the introduction of the former would create less dissatisfaction than some believed, books printed in Cyrillic would not "be grafted [*priv'iutsia*] to the Kazaks as easily and quickly as could be supposed."[48] Script was less important than ensuring the widest possible dissemination of correct content. Thus the same logic that led Il'minskii to argue for vernacular education justified a defense of one specific variant of it, using the Arabic script, for Altynsarin.

At the same time, as we will see, both the content and the intent of Altynsarin's vernacular education would move in directions that Il'minskii would hardly have predicted. Even as he was satisfied with Il'minskii's textbook, Altynsarin's correspondence displays his frustration with other issues arising at the fortification's school. Students, he complained, robotically learned the phrases they required to serve in the colonial administration, without gaining any useful moral or intellectual knowledge.[49] Moreover, they were too mobile. Their parents could, and did, recall them from school at any time, whether or not they had learned anything, for any reason (including Altynsarin's attempts to exert some sort of discipline and moral education on them). At this early stage of his career, the young teacher could think of no solution to the issues facing him beyond stricter discipline (a solution he claimed to abhor). Questions of moral education, of the *content* rather than simple fact of language pedagogy, and of student mobility (and its reasons) would concern him for the rest of his life. It was after pondering these questions that an older Altynsarin, more experienced in administrative and educational affairs, developed a vernacular curriculum that both grew out of his understanding of local conditions and gave Islam a different, more central place in Kazaks' imperial subjecthood than many administrators wanted.

Ethnography: Envisioning Kazakness

As the curious young Altynsarin turned from reader to author, he encountered his superiors' ongoing concern with delineating Kazaks as a discrete ethnic group. Among the underlying assumptions of the Provisional Statute was that Kazaks were both a distinct and united ethnicity, demanding uniform administration. For Altynsarin, this delineation of Kazakness was vital to advancing his own agenda; that he himself was a Kazak was meant to lend legitimacy to his ideas of how Kazaks should fit into the Russian Empire. A set of ethnographic sketches of Kazaks of the Orenburg region , composed while he was working at the Turgai in 1867, established this conceptual baseline for his later work.

Altynsarin's sketches featured prominently in the first issue of the *Zapiski* (Notes) of the Orenburg division of IRGO, published in 1870. At the founding of the Orenburg division, Governor-General of Orenburg Nikolai Andreevich Kryzhanovskii stated that, among other tasks, its members could "render the government and Russia an invaluable service by attentive study of the character, history, qualities, deficiencies of religion, and prejudices of all the various tribes populating the Orenburg region," since "without this information it is hard to act or, more accurately, one can only act at random [*na-obum*]."[50] It was an entirely fitting speech for a former associate of the Steppe Commission to give. Kryzhanovskii's vision of ethnography and other scholarly domains was primarily oriented towards the production of useful facts, whose utility would be determined by the extent to which they brought benefit to what he called "our common Fatherland."[51] But whether or not the superficially prosaic details of an ethnographic sketch had utility in imperial governance, Kryzhanovskii's statement also represented an invitation to intermediate figures like Altynsarin to represent themselves and their ethnographic visions to scholarly and bureaucratic publics. The Provisional Statute was representative of a broad trend, in the 1860s and 1870s, whereby tsarist administrators framed their approach to governance through ethnicity. When replying and using this frame, Altynsarin and other intermediaries had the opportunity to deploy their local expertise in the service of drastically different interpretations of ethnic difference.

In his sketches, devoted to the ceremonial practices surrounding weddings and funerals, Altynsarin presented the Kazaks as distinct from surrounding ethnicities, as well as their Muslim co-religionists outside of Eurasia. This may not have been surprising, given his interactions with Il'minskii and Grigor'ev, both of whom were at pains to argue that Kazaks were different from (and threatened by) "Tatar" outsiders. Altynsarin went beyond this, associating positive values with Kazaks' distinctiveness and valorizing rituals seen as primitive or irrational by some metropolitan observers. Though Altynsarin never explicitly advanced the argument that "the Kazaks" (*kirgizy*) were distinct, his work presupposed an ethnic difference. Kazak practices were timeless and primordial; any observed deviation was due to the influence of non-Kazaks living on the steppe. In the undated past, "when the only rulers of social relations among the Kazaks were customs and legends," it had been common practice for close friends to promise their children to one another even before the child's birth. This custom began going out of fashion by the late 1860s, a development Altynsarin argued was "related to some . . . influence of the neighboring peoples."[52] The distinctiveness of Kazak practices was further underlined by the distinction Altynsarin drew between his subjects and the global community of Muslims. He noted that, while Kazaks had a strong taboo against marriage within seven degrees of kinship, such arrangements with close relatives "[were] observed among all Muslims besides the Kazaks."[53] Such arguments were consonant with a larger effort by Altynsarin and other observers to disassociate Kazak from "Tatar" culture; the former, in this view, had both a distinct lexicon and distinct set of behaviors.

Scholars and administrators alike described the absence of rationality as critical to the distinction between Kazaks and "Tatars." If the latter were, in Grigor'ev and Il'minskii's eyes, fanatical Muslims hostile to everything Russian, Kazaks were not as far down the path, talented and possible to civilize gradually. Altynsarin made a similar case for the marital and funereal rites of the Kazaks he described in general terms. Practices that might have been described as wasteful and exotic were, in his account, explicable and comprehensible within the logic of those who embraced them.[54] Polygyny, in this telling, was a reasonable response to infertility or the absence of romantic love, rather than a remnant of barbaric patriarchy. Similarly, marriage taboos and betrothing children to one another before their majority created alliances that served to prevent internecine strife.[55] Explaining the logic behind local practices did not, however, constitute an endorsement. Altynsarin skewered practices he considered to be harmful or outdated, such as those restricting the behavior of newly arrived daughters-in-law (kelīn) toward their husbands' male relations.[56] But he set himself up in these sketches as a thinking intermediary (rather than a passive observer), representing both the internal logic and the deficiencies of his subjects. Altynsarin's version of Kazakness was unique and rational, but also open to improvement from without, an idea he would carry forward as an educator within the tsarist administration. Emphasizing Kazaks' rationality at once asserted their difference from the much-feared Tatars (as well as Turkestani Muslims) and validated a civilizing mission on the steppe. Such views also had the potential to support specific claims on the financial and institutional support of the colonial administration. Small wonder that some intervention-minded administrators embraced them.

Altynsarin's authority to represent Kazaks as a coherent group was contested and constrained in this volume not by another Kazak but by an ethnic Russian commentator and former acquaintance of Altynsarin's from the

Frontier Commission, V. N. Plotnikov. Although he claimed to esteem the article, Plotnikov found much to criticize in Altynsarin's work. Focusing on minor details and emphasizing the diversity of Kazak practices, he framed his critique in terms that brought to the fore divergent views of the purpose and proper framing of ethnographic data: "[Errors] happened, probably because . . . Mr. Altynsarin wrote his article as a general sketch of the Kazak wedding, *not having a scientific goal in mind*."[57] In Plotnikov's view, a "scientific" sketch would have gone into finer detail; the issue was with Altynsarin's decision to subjectively choose certain practices as representative rather than passively reporting what he saw. In this way, Plotnikov denied the claim that Altynsarin, as a cultural insider, was best placed to represent the steppe to a scholarly audience. Giving disciplinary ideals of objectivity pride of place, Plotnikov argued that Altynsarin's account required the interpretation and gloss of a more educated Russian administrator before it could be considered "scientific."

In a sense, this episode signifies a major trend in Altynsarin's administrative career. His linguistic and ethnographic endeavors went beyond defining what was unique about Kazak culture—Altynsarin first had to convince his audience that a discrete entity called "Kazak culture," characterized by identifiable words and practices, existed. But he was never the only actor engaged in these projects, and if he was able to find agreement that such particularism, expressed within the framework of the empire, was desirable, others could contest his views through different readings of script, religion, language, and economic change. The ethnic and administrative hierarchies of Russian imperialism on the steppe created a problem of reception for Altynsarin the author *and* Altynsarin the administrator. Activities and ideas within the broad repertoire current in scholarly and administrative circles had a good chance of being heard, and created opportunities for choice among the colonized. This was a flexible but inherently limited arrangement.

Education: Kazakness for the Empire

As the new "civilizing" institutions and administrative organs associated with the Provisional Statute gradually fell into place, non-Russian intermediaries like Altynsarin had new opportunities to advance their professional and political agendas. At first, he requested and received a transfer away from the Orenburg fortress school to become a clerk in the administration of Turgai district.[58] Over the following decade, he proved useful as an investigator of natural disasters and suspicious deaths among the Kazak population of the district, while also briefly serving as a judge.[59] Thus by the mid-1870s he was well established as an intelligent and trustworthy agent of the imperial administration. But the most famous role Altynsarin found, from the early 1870s on, was in developing educational programs for the new Russo-Kazak schools of Turgai province. Here, gradually rising to a supervisory position, Altynsarin further delineated what did, and did not, make a Kazak, while embedding all of his work within a model of imperial citizenship.

By allotting a subsidy of 8,000 rubles to each of the steppe provinces for education, the Provisional Statute facilitated greater intervention in Kazaks' cultural life than had hitherto been possible.[60] This represented a commitment, on paper, to a *mission civilisatrice* whose feasibility and desirability had been subject to doubt within recent memory, most notably by the former Orenburg governor Vasilii Perovskii. Cooperation from local administrators was absolutely necessary to putting such a civilizing mission into practice, as the relatively slow growth of Kazak schools in the neighboring Semipalatinsk and Akmolinsk provinces indicates. With Perovskii out of the picture, Turgai province boasted both the will and the means to educate. Even in this relatively propitious environment, though, multiple administrative instances contested the establishment of schools, and the process of setting them up dragged on for an unusually long time. Kryzhanovskii acted quickly to solicit recommendations from a committee headed by Turgai province's new military governor, another former Steppe Commission man, Lieut.-Gen. Lev Fedorovich Balliuzek (1822–1879). Balliuzek argued for a gradual and adaptive approach, focused on centralized teacher training and mobile schools closer to the lifeways of the target Kazak population.[61] This may have been an ideal approach, but Kryzhanovskii feared to lose the state subsidy and demanded that new, permanent school buildings be constructed, even before any judgments about their staffing or curriculum took place.[62] In this fear he was correct; the initial allocation of 8,000 rubles for the province was reduced to 3,465 in 1872, forcing Kryzhanovskii to appeal to the Finance Ministry (with little success) and establish an additional tent tax on the Kazak population of the province.[63] The civilizing project thus shambled forward, deeply desired by some but inconvenient in the eyes of others. Turgai province's few state schools, years after the promulgation of the Provisional Statute, were shoddy and suffered from low attendance.[64] In the absence of funding, teachers, and adaptation to local conditions, the goals that advocates of educating inorodtsy set themselves were unlikely to be met.

Using the Kazak language in the classroom became a key strategy to salvage these goals after 1870, when a new law on educating inorodtsy established a preference for vernacular education.[65] Then-Minister of Education D. A. Tolstoi

strongly supported this measure, as did Il'minskii, who, when asked for his opinion on the new Kazak schools in 1870, "insisted" on the Kazak language for Kazak
schools and argued that the language and exposition of the subject matter there
should be "understandable for the old and young and for any illiterate Kazak."[66]
But not all administrators agreed that Tatar needed to be rapidly replaced as the
lingua franca of the steppe. Balliuzek, so ready to adapt to the difficulties pastoralist lifeways presented for education, believed that Tatar's greater distribution
made it a valuable means of disseminating useful knowledge among the population.[67] Though his opinion was in the minority, his conclusion and the logic by
which he arrived at it are useful reminders of the multitude of meanings and
methods associated with the Russianization of the steppe. Multiple languages,
structures, and goals were part of Russia's repertoire of imperial governance.[68]
Combining them in accordance with their personal convictions and understanding of the population they served (and environment in which they worked), officials of the tsarist state exerted an agency that was constrained more by rank and
status than ethnicity.

Starting in the early 1870s, Altynsarin's involvement in these issues reached
a new stage. To adapt the schools to the steppe so fully as to staff them with
Kazak teachers would have meant limited choices even relative to the chroni-
cally understaffed world of rural pedagogy. Meanwhile, Kazak-language
teaching materials beyond Il'minskii's 1861 textbook were practically absent.
Il'minskii thought, however, that he knew a solution to both problems in the
products of the now-defunct Orenburg school for Kazaks, and his mind fell
especially to Altynsarin. Not knowing with certainty "if Altynsarin is still alive,"
he recommended his old friend as curious, talented, and strongly interested
in Russian letters. If the young Kazak had not lost these qualities, he wrote
to the Ministry of Education, it might be useful to invite him to Kazan', provide him with special training as a teacher, work with him on compiling textbooks for the proposed schools, and release him to teach in one of the new
institutions.[69] Il'minskii correctly guessed Altynsarin's attitudes. The young
Kazak expressed a willingness to collaborate on such a project the following
year.[70] However, when Kryzhanovskii and Tolstoi actually called a conference
to discuss the Cyrillicization of Kazak and production of textbooks in the local
language, Altynsarin, who had been specially invited by Kryzhanovskii, was
unable to attend.[71] In his absence, the new texts were produced by the guard-
ian (*popechitel'*) of the Orenburg school district, Petr Alekseevich Lavrovskii,
who, like Il'minskii before him (but much in the face of current administrative
opinion), wrote them in Arabic script. Since these would not do, Lavrovskii,
on Il'minskii's advice, asked Altynsarin to take up the task; the latter succeeded
in compiling a language textbook and reader in Kazak, Cyrillicized against his

own convictions, but in accordance with MNP policy, in time for publication in 1879. On September 1 of the same year, with the enthusiastic recommendations of Il'minskii and his former superior, the district chief of Turgai district, Col. Ia. P. Iakovlev, he was named director of Kazak schools for Turgai province, a position he held until his death.[72]

Altynsarin's textbooks quickly became staples in classrooms throughout the steppe. His *Kirgizskaia khrestomatiia* (Kazak reader) was widely enough used to gain a second edition years after its initial appearance in 1879.[73] It combined, in conception and practice, a range of purposes dear to the heart of Altynsarin and, in different ways, to his closest interlocutors as well. Moral education (*vospitanie*, rather than the transfer of scholarly knowledge, *obrazovanie*), had long been at the core of Il'minskii's educational programs for inorodtsy. Moreover, in the early 1880s, the vice-governor of Turgai province, Vladimir Fedorovich Il'in, blamed Kazaks' "moral underdevelopment" (*nravstvennoe nedorazvitie*) for many of the practical failings of the Provisional Statute.[74] Altynsarin, for his part, had hoped to morally improve his pupils from his first days teaching at the Orenburg fortification. The didactic tools he used toward this end were varied, and such variation, in turn, reveals the complex relationship in his mind between Kazakness and metropolitan culture. Altynsarin wrote some morally instructive stories for the volume himself, while adapting others from the fabulist I. F. Krylov and, especially, I. I. Paul'son, an innovative pedagogue who developed a reader for Russian primary schools in 1871.[75] The lessons of these short stories were simple. "*Tïshqannïng ösiety*" (A Mouse's Advice), for example, promoted respect for one's elders, while "*Dadandïq*" (Ignorance) lampooned charlatans in the religious and medical professions, and "*Ädep*" (Politeness) highlighted the importance of a respectful demeanor and good etiquette regardless of social station.[76] Fundamentally, these were arguments for basic morality, rather than providing worldly or practical knowledge. Similarly, Altynsarin exhorted his readers to strive for education as a matter of both personal interest and the common good: "The literate person knows life in all its beauty/The literate person can achieve his dreams," whereas his generation "grew old in blind ignorance/[and] brought little good for our people."[77] While morality was thus an ambiguous category in Altynsarin's work, he constructed it in such a way as to urge pupils to further study and service, which included—but was not limited to—teaching in lower-level steppe schools.[78] Such service to the people would occur within a framework of expanding imperial governance, providing the steppe with trained and honest servitors and enabling Kazaks to make the best of their political integration to the empire.

At the same time, Altynsarin maintained his interest in cultivating a sense of Kazak distinctiveness. His reader had a strongly folkloristic component.

Its final three sections consisted of Kazak-language songs, proverbs, and riddles, many collected by Altynsarin himself.[79] This process of selecting and transcribing oral literature, under the premise that such literature was in the Kazaks' own language, created the appearance of greater lexical and grammatical regularity than had previously existed.[80] Thus both word choices (*dadandïq* for ignorance, instead of *nadandïq* or *sauatsïzdïq*) and pronunciation (*patsa* and *keshkentai* for "tsar" and "small," rather than *patsha* and *kïshkentai*) favored the part of the steppe where Altynsarin had spent most of his life.[81] Moreover, while Altynsarin's attitudes toward Tatar culture were far less negative than those of Grigor'ev or Il'minskii,[82] he employed it as a foil against which to juxtapose Kazakness in the introduction to the *Kazak Reader*. Unlike the Tatars, he argued, "the Kazak people is uncorrupted, and its strivings are not restricted to a narrow framework [i.e., not restricted to religious questions alone]; it thinks freely."[83] Tatar became, in this formulation, the language of dry religious formalism, unsuited to the tasks Altynsarin hoped lay in his pupils' future. Instead, he selected texts with the chief consideration that "the tales in the book were predominantly in the spirit of the Kazaks," thus conflating useful knowledge and Kazakness even as he advanced the assumption that such an identity was extant and coherent.[84] He further called other Kazaks to compile vernacular textbooks for a people he depicted as ignorant but unspoiled, and receptive to useful innovations properly presented.[85] In a seeming paradox, for Altynsarin, it took educational materials written with the distinctiveness of Kazak language and culture in mind to shape his pupils into people equipped to bear the same privileges and duties as other groups within the empire. His sense of Kazakness was not at odds with a concept of imperial subjecthood based on moral and civil, rather than ethnic, criteria.

Accordingly, although Altynsarin devoted significant energy to vernacular-language education and to creating a Kazak language from the cloth of local dialects, he also felt strongly that educated Kazaks should have some ability in Russian. Just as his duties as school inspector were beginning, he fretted, in an unpublished manuscript, that Kazaks' lack of facility in the language of the metropole left them vulnerable to abuse: "All tribes under the White Tsar's authority can at least report to the authorities about their needs via their own confederates [*edinomyshlenniki*] either in oral or written form; while we [Kazaks], when need appears, seek out at first some man knowing Kazak and Russian, with whom we go to the authorities, not knowing whether or not this guide [*vozhak*] is suited to truthfully and effectively translate our words."[86] Studying the Russian language would eliminate the role such corrupt middlemen had on the steppe while simultaneously fostering subjecthood on equal terms with all other ethnic groups of the Russian Empire, alike in their subordination to the ruling dynasty. Moreover, such a course of study would both facilitate Kazakhs' *sblizhenie* (coming together) with Russians and provide access to the technical and scientific information they currently required to develop themselves.[87] Therefore, as necessary as it was to reach Kazaks in their local language, he continued to write to Il'minskii that the main goal in Kazak schools was "teaching Kazak children Russian language and orthography [*pravopisanie*]."[88] In this view, a bilingual system of education neatly blended local and imperial prerogatives.

Moreover, while Il'minskii and his ilk focused on vernacular education as a means of spiritual (read: Orthodox) rapprochement, Altynsarin's moral-educational project was to be centered around Islam.[89] His goals in this sphere were underlined by the compilation and publication, in 1884, of a Kazak-language Islamic catechism, *Müsïlmanshïlïqtïng tütqasï* (also published under the title *Shariat ul-Islam*).[90] This slender volume consisted of four sections, in which were explained the confession of faith (*shahada*), the five actions obligatory for all Muslims, and other moral prohibitions and recommendations; it also included translations into Kazak and explanations of Arabic prayers for a variety of special occasions.[91] Although many tsarist administrators were at best hesitant about Islam's future within the empire, Altynsarin's catechism was an important component of his attempt to arrive at a form of Kazakness that was compatible with imperial subjecthood. Altynsarin, explaining the need for his book in 1882, complained that although Kazaks had long been interested in learning the tenets of their religion, obstacles to this from the imperial administration had driven them into the waiting arms of Tatar and "Bukharan" mullahs, engendering ignorance and chauvinist attitudes toward non-Muslim ideas.[92] This was not only contrary to the interests of the empire but anti-Islamic, since Muslim law "nowhere refuses the need to teach secular sciences, whichever people they emerged from."[93] This concern for rationality, propriety, and adaptability in religion also pervaded descriptions of *gushur* and *zaket* (two forms of obligatory almsgiving) composed in the early 1880s; the former in particular had, after the Russian advance through the steppe to Turkestan, outlived the purpose it had been ascribed in local practice.[94] Islam was not primordial, in this presentation; it had previously adapted and evolved in light of changing conditions, and Russian rule was but one more change requiring adaptation, while potentially offering benefits to believers.

There were also, however, valences to Altynsarin's catechism that were potentially less friendly to state aims.[95] Altynsarin signaled his intent for the book to be used as broadly as possible by begging Il'minskii to permit its publication in Arabic script, broadening the base of literate users and not marking the text as dangerously alien.[96] Yet the language of the text had to be Kazak, rather than Arabic, which had hitherto played a large role in steppe religious praxis. The implications of using Arabic were pernicious, since it was impossible for "simple people" [qara khalïq] to learn Arabic, and "there is no book written in our Kazak language that is comprehensible for everyone to read, or understandable for simple people if one reads it aloud to others."[97] Hence the necessity of a book written in language that ordinary people could understand; ignorance of one's own religion, he claimed in his introduction, threatened apostasy (küpïrlïk).[98] But the specificity of the local language, paradoxically, also connected his readers to a global religious community, one to which many imperial Russian observers considered Kazaks to belong only weakly. Similar transnational gestures by other confessions within the empire, even other Muslims, bore the suspicious taint of irredentism.[99] Portions of the Russian Empire's Muslim community were also organizing vernacular-language Islamic education at roughly the same time, although there does not seem to have been any direct connection between them and Altynsarin.[100] Il'minskii and others saw an opportunity in what they perceived as weak Islamicization on the steppe, but Altynsarin sought to reform their beliefs beginning from the axiom that Islam was a vital part of Kazakness. To be a Kazak, for Altynsarin, was to be a good Muslim; to be a good Muslim was to focus on the content, rather than form, of prayers and rituals, and to remain open to secular knowledge as mediated through the educational institutions and common language of the metropole.[101]

Such secular knowledge became increasingly important, in Altynsarin's mind, as acts of God and a steady increase in the presence of Slavic peasants in Turgai province put pressure on the pastoral nomadic lifeways that most of its Kazaks practiced. Pastoralism was, if anything, a more likely candidate to serve as the unifying basis of Kazak culture than Islam or language. But could it endure under such conditions? Altynsarin's schools, and his other writings during the 1880s, represented one attempt to resolve this issue.

Education, Environment, and Lifeways

Altynsarin shared his Russian interlocutors' assumptions that sedentary life was superior to pastoral nomadism. The clearest evidence of this is in his plans for a set of showpiece two-class central district schools, the focal point of his educational agenda and the first things he and his superiors wished to see built. On the surface, these new institutions had the potential not only to prepare students for higher study but to train a new generation of useful, bilingual administrators

from the Kazak population proper, combining moral education, language training, and rudimentary knowledge of a few scholastic subjects.[102] The lessons they
would learn there, however, would go beyond the moral and informational; the
two-class schools were also to introduce selected youths to the material norms
of sedentary life, Russian-style. In these model institutions, Altynsarin wrote
to Il'minskii, students should "get accustomed to sedentarism, tidiness, and a
healthy view of things."[103] This core idea, also reflected in later requests for funding, found its expression in several ways.[104] The two-class school building was a
permanent structure, usually built of wood or stone, and furnished according to
the Russian taste.[105] Kazak boarders, rather than sitting on the floor, on carpets or
on trunks, would be seated in rows of desks, in large rooms with fixed walls and
heated with iron stoves. If pupils were given food adapted to the "Asiatic taste,"
they were expected to eat it with metal knives, forks, and spoons.[106] Students also
slept alone and wore uniform clothes provided by the school administration.[107]
All of this represented a radical change in the material world of the new schools'
pupils, who were asked now to see the benefits of a culture that was not only sedentary but specifically European. (Although other sedentary ethnic groups, notably the Tatars and Bashkirs, also populated Turgai province, official reports on
the state of Kazak schools, to which Altynsarin undoubtedly contributed, evinced
concern that the student body of the two-class schools not be dominated by an
"Asiatic element.")[108] The new order, also reflected in the curriculum of trade
schools opened later, represented both a post-Enlightenment belief in the progressive nature of sedentary life and, seemingly, an acceptance of the superiority
of the colonizer's culture.

Yet even as Altynsarin agreed with other administrators on the benefits of
sedentarism, he rejected their views of how Kazaks were to be made to settle
on the land, and how they were to live once they settled. The 1870s were an era,
in some quarters, of growing interest in experimental peasant colonization of
the steppe, and in encouraging Kazaks to take up agriculture. The impetus, as
during the compilation of the Provisional Statute, came from Western Siberia. Administrators here discussed colonization in 1874, hoping by expanded
settlement within the steppe, rather than under district administrative centers,
on one hand to develop agriculture, industry, and trade, and on the other to
provide Kazaks "the best example . . . [of] sedentary life and diligent work [*tru-
doliubivaia deiatel'nost'*]."[109] Subsequently, a new governor-general of Western
Siberia, N. G. Kaznakov, developed an argument that, among other things, limited colonization would help Kazak nomads during difficult years, especially
when livestock died in large numbers owing to pasturage failure (*zhŭt*) during
severe winters. Kazaks would learn how to sow grain from colonists and dis-
cover that settling on the land could save them from a cold and hungry death.[110]

Colonization, sedentarization, and moving to grain cultivation were now not just matters of profit and stability for the Russian Empire, but matters of the welfare of a huge nomadic population.

Altynsarin contested these assumptions at a critical juncture, in the aftermath of the severe winter of 1879–1880, when a zhŭt placed him, along with the rest of Turgai province, in a tense struggle for survival. This was a moment when the beliefs of the Western Siberian administration (which, Altynsarin acidly noted, "are not alien to our administration, either") seemed to have proven justified.[111] As Altynsarin put it, these administrators proposed to "replace the unstable method of the people's welfare, animal husbandry, with a more stable one, agriculture, and in accordance with this to turn the nomadic way of life of the people as quickly as possible to sedentary, even if by forcible measures."[112] But, as a "steppe man" (*stepniak*) who had grown up in the region and was intimately familiar with its environment, Altynsarin thought differently.[113] His overall impression was that most of it was unfavorable for agriculture, and that stock raising represented a useful adaptation to its arid, barren landscape. Knowledge of the steppe environment, the economic practices of Kazaks, and the particular needs of the local population permitted Altynsarin to argue that the steppe's future was not, and could not, be fully agricultural.

Although he was quick to acknowledge the suffering that the winter of 1879–1880 had caused, Altynsarin argued strongly against the idea that this necessitated a shift to agriculture for the Kazaks. It was not only the mobile pastoralist economy, he noted, that could be ruined by an act of God, as evidenced by the fact that "our city of Turgai bears adversity just the same as do the Kazaks."[114] Indeed, Kazaks were in the habit of making stores of food and hay for themselves and their livestock in case of emergency, but had, like the residents of the city of Turgai, simply been overwhelmed by the immensity of the disaster that faced them.[115] Further, it was unclear that a shift to agriculture was even possible. Since his first days as a clerk of the Turgai district administration, Altynsarin had noted that much of the region was, because of its soil, climate, and vegetation, unsuited to grain cultivation, and that even artificial irrigation of fields was of limited utility owing to the remoteness of reliable sources of fresh water.[116] True, Kazaks had successfully tilled some, more propitious areas for years, as Altynsarin was well aware from his earlier administrative work.[117] But in other dry and sandy regions, "the only possible occupation . . . [was] animal husbandry."[118] To the extent that agriculture was possible on the steppe, Kazaks had already begun experiments in the field on their own initiative; compulsion was unnecessary.[119] And colonization by Russian *muzhiks*—"in terms of their mental development, no better than Kazaks"—was a particularly undesirable form of compulsion.[120]

It was possible, Altynsarin thought, to make use of imperial institutions and resources to develop the steppe in a way that made the best use of local conditions, but without colonization. Rather than a forced and unpromising transition to agriculture, encouraged by colonists of dubious merit, it would benefit both individual Kazaks and the empire as a whole if the steppe were made not a second breadbasket [*zhitnitsa*] for the empire, but rather its "stockyard" [*skotnyi dvor*]. Such an approach would make the best use of both local environmental conditions and knowledge already well established in the population.[121] Under this regime, Kazaks would become partially sedentary, orient their production toward commercial markets rather than subsistence, and adapt their earlier practices in light of advances in agriculture and stock breeding made elsewhere. The school system of Turgai province, under Altynsarin's supervision, developed to support just such an order of things.

Rather than transitioning to agriculture, Altynsarin believed, educated Kazaks would do best to leverage the expertise, the environment, and the products with which they were already familiar. Toward this end, vocational schools were a crucial part of the educational network he envisioned. (In practice, though, their expense rendered them a secondary priority, below language pedagogy.) This was, at first, in line with the Ministry of Education's instructions of 1878 concerning the development of vocational education throughout the empire. Within the framework of these instructions, Altynsarin was also able to exert influence, based on his perception of Kazaks' needs as part of the empire, on its practical articulation. Many local administrators in the steppe were fully in favor of such innovations as a means of facilitating its economic transformation.[122] Altynsarin, for his part, argued in 1882 to V. N. Dal', Lavrovskii's replacement, that such institutions would be beneficial in light of the Kazakhs' ongoing transition to sedentarism, but also took pains to provide for students' training in Russian literacy.[123] First planned in the city of Turgai, the vocational school was a special supplement to the two-class school, not a replacement, and had to recapitulate what Altynsarin considered the most important part of the latter's curriculum. Later, discussing the introduction of vocational training to central schools, Altynsarin argued against the idea that there was anything unique about Kazaks' developmental needs. Rather, "it goes without saying that if general professional education is acknowledged as beneficial among all the long already sedentary and more or less cultured peoples of the Russian empire, in the Kazak people, still in a transitional state from the nomadic way of life to sedentarism, it is still more necessary for the direction of this young people, just only beginning cultured life, toward proper [*pravil'noe*] economic and moral development."[124]

At the same time, these vocational plans were firmly grounded in the specific conditions of the steppe environment (considered a constant) and market (changing rapidly in the context of Russian expansion). The Kazaks, he wrote, "are natural shepherds, their life and sympathies are closely joined with animal husbandry. But it is also known that they use this natural wealth only in its raw form, and as much as is required for their nomadic life."[125] Thus the program of the proposed vocational schools was focused principally on the small-scale manufacture of items that could be made from readily available materials: leather and felt from animal skin and hair, boots and clothing from that leather and felt, and soap from animal fat.[126] Carpenters and mechanics (*slesary*) would also be necessary, to manufacture the finished goods that Kazaks would demand as they became more sedentary; eventually, women and girls were to be admitted to introductory classes in sewing, knitting, and weaving.[127] Altynsarin's vision of a steppe populated by artisans rested on an unstated assumption about the problems of the mobile pastoralist domestic economy. The idea that household skills that already existed among the Kazaks needed to be taught as academic subjects indicates that Altynsarin was chiefly interested in correcting the perceived irregularity of cottage industries. If imperial Russian ethnographic accounts from the late nineteenth century can be trusted, it would have been difficult to find a Kazak woman unfamiliar with sewing or felt making.[128] The idea that household tasks needed to be studied as academic subjects marked mobile pastoralist practices as needing improvement from external sources, while simultaneously valorizing the teachings of the new trade school as rational, efficient, and scientifically approved.[129] Altynsarin's rejection of one common plan for the steppe's economic development, then, still took place in a context that rejected mobile pastoralism as a viable plan for the future. The steppe would become sedentary, just not agricultural.

But in the immediate term, Altynsarin believed, it was much more important to reach Kazaks literally where they lived. This meant adapting the only schools most Kazaks would ever see, at the cantonal level. Ostensibly, these lower-level schools, offering a simple curriculum focused on Russian literacy and Muslim catechistics, were to prepare students for the two-class school, from which they could then advance to gymnasia or *Realschulen*. The system that Altynsarin put forward when Il'in, temporarily serving as the provincial governor, solicited his opinion in 1883 went even further down the path of adaptation by reaching into a grab bag of plans suggested by earlier administrators:

> In my opinion, the arrangement [*ustroistvo*] of [cantonal] schools, being exclusively among the Kazaks, should be adapted to the life conditions of this people, in view of which they should winter with the Kazaks, when they winter, and migrate, when they migrate. Thus,

for example, having chosen a central place in the canton, generally convenient in economic respects, it is necessary in my opinion to build of local materials (light brick and etc.) as solid and warm a building as possible, with a class room, sleeping hall . . . and a kitchen with a vestibule and storeroom. Here the Kazak children may be taught for seven and a half months, that is, from September 15 to May 1, when the Kazaks usually migrate off for the summer. From the first of May the school should move, like the remaining Kazaks, to a tent and migrate together with one of the influential officials [*dolzhnostnoe litso*].[130]

The necessity of running schools for inorodtsy on a shoestring budget had plagued administrators since Grigor'ev, in whose more humbly built schools Altynsarin had occupied his first teaching post. The problem of student mobility, which militated against completion of the course of study, had vexed Altynsarin since his early days at the Turgai. A few months before his proposal to Il'in, Altynsarin was so concerned that the ignorance of truant students would reflect poorly on the schools that he proposed attendance simply be made compulsory.[131] Balliuzek, in contrast, in his earlier consultations with Kryzhanovskii, had proposed that schools would be most successful when they moved together with the Kazaks. It is unclear if Altynsarin came to a similar conclusion on his own or was drawing on Balliuzek's earlier proposal. What is important, though, is what this episode tells us about the position of sedentarism and mobility among the serving officials of Turgai province. Many students would not continue their education beyond the canton school. Although a sedentary lifestyle had its benefits in terms of hygiene, morality, order, and governability, mobile pastoralism did not create a primordial wildness, impossible to overcome, in pupils. Altynsarin certainly envisioned sedentarism as part of the eventual future of the steppe. But his emphasis on moral and linguistic education meant that the initial change—the only change, for many—could be accomplished without abandoning the pastoral mobility that made Kazaks economically and culturally distinct. Kazaks would be the agents of their own economic change and accomplish it, with the help of metropolitan resources, on their own timeline.

A summation of Altynsarin's thought and its implementation within the school system of Turgai province reveals a range of surprising intermediate positions. Kazaks were Muslims, not missionary fodder, but needed to become better Muslims so they could better absorb secular lessons from elsewhere in the Russian Empire. They needed their own language, delivered to them in a script they were comfortable with, but so that they could be imperial subjects on an equal basis with others, not so they would form an independent nation. They ought to become sedentary but not farm, intensifying the stock raising they already knew well, and with a minimum of peasant colonization. In short, Altynsarin's career shows how an intermediary figure bought into many of the civilizing assumptions of the imperial Russian state, but leveraged his expert knowledge of local languages and environments to transform the methods by which they were to be put into practice. Collaboration and autonomy went hand in hand as, citing expertise his interlocutors lacked, Altynsarin found his own space within the Russian Empire's repertoires of governance.

The Dilemmas of Leadership

For all the originality of his thought, though, and his projection of local expertise as a means of advancing his viewpoints, Altynsarin remained a mid-level functionary of an autocratic empire subject to frequent changes of leadership. The success or failure of his ideas—indeed his very effectiveness as an intermediary—depended on cultivating allies within and outside of Turgai province. One prolonged illness or leave of absence on the part of a sympathetic governor could delay or scuttle years of work. The presence of arbitrary state power in Altynsarin's life represents a final layer of uncertainty in his position; local knowledge did not count for anything if Altynsarin's superiors thought they knew better or wished to pursue a different policy.

In 1882 and 1883, during one of the Ministry of Internal Affairs' endless attempts to revise the Provisional Statute in light of experience, the authorities of Turgai province sought to use Altynsarin's ethnographic expertise to their advantage. The provincial governor, Aleksandr Petrovich Konstantinovich, along with Vice-Governor Il'in, complained that neither the subdivision of the province into administrative cantons and villages nor the election of indigenous leaders for these units corresponded to Kazak lifeways. Rather, these artificial units drew together Kazaks with incompatible economic interests; under such circumstances, local elections were a life-or-death struggle.[132] It was necessary, rather, to change both the way territory was divided and the order of local elections within sub-units. As evidence, Il'in presented a long poem circulating among the Kazaks of the province that Altynsarin had transcribed and translated, a lament characteristic of the *zar zaman* (troubled times) school of Kazak poetry.[133] Its anonymous author juxtaposed a pre-tsarist pastoral utopia against the miseries, especially the bloody internecine strife that accompanied elections, brought on by the Provisional Statute.[134] Il'in forwarded it to the ministry, arguing that it represented "the view of the people on the deficiencies of local administrative institutions," a view he happened to share.[135] All the pieces for a revision of a law meant to be revised ad hoc seemed to be in place.

Yet nothing came of it. When his opinion was solicited, Aleksandr Petrovich Protsenko, then military governor of neighboring Semipalatinsk province (located in a separate governor-generalship), flatly denied that any change in election procedures was necessary.[136] Worse was to come from the governor of another steppe province, Ural'sk, Prince Grigorii Sergeevich Golitsyn. Golitsyn's frame of reference was diametrically opposed to that of the poem's author. To his mind, it was the vigorous implementation of the Provisional Statute that was responsible for progress on the steppe; the pre-tsarist era was a time where only the strong ruled, holding ordinary people "almost in slavery."[137] Nothing more came of the matter, and when the new Steppe Statute finally came down in 1891, it bore little resemblance to the changes that Il'in and Konstantinovich, with Altynsarin's backing, proposed.[138]

Even in the field of education, where Altynsarin's authority would seem likely to have been strongest, provincial politics delayed and transformed his proposals, which had only mixed and conditional success. His most successful intervention had to do with the introduction of Islamic education. If the administrative context in which Altynsarin worked tended to be hostile to Islam, this hostility was not uniform or unchanging. Tolstoi, during his time (1866–1880) as minister of education, was simultaneously ober-procurator of the Holy Synod, responsible for the civil administration of the Orthodox Church, and made his reputation in part by agitating against the multiplication of Muslim clergy and writing a near-slanderous account of the role of the Catholic Church in Russian history.[139] At the same time, he seems neither to have been very religious himself nor to have taken his duties at the Synod very seriously. Il'minskii, in contrast, toward the end of his life composed screeds against the dangers allegedly represented by Jadidism, a Muslim educational movement based on new methods of teaching literacy, open to secular knowledge, and interested in modernizing the Russian Empire's Muslim subjects.[140] (He was evidently unaware that Altynsarin's catechism, to which he had assented, however grudgingly, had broad similarities with this project.)[141] The few Orthodox missionaries working on the steppe encountered harsh working conditions, a frequently hostile administration, and won few converts.[142] And indeed, although there were dissenting voices (for example, Lavrovskii), Islamic education was introduced to Russo-Kazak schools early on, with the permission of the highest authority in the province, Governor Konstantinovich.[143] The factors motivating Konstantinovich and his advisors differed somewhat from the explanations Altynsarin later provided in his catechism. Konstantinovich wanted both to bring the "fanaticism" preached in Islamic schools under state control and avoid alienating the Kazaks by giving the appearance of a missionary agenda.[144]

Islamophobia, preached with particular ferocity by Il'minskii's colleagues in Kazan', and present to some degree in most parts of the imperial administration, was not connected directly to any strategy of governance.[145] Instead, the range of potential responses such attitudes might generate was capable of incorporating the efforts of actors with much more positive views of Islam. Space for negotiation and compromise did not always form between intermediate figures from the inorodtsy and their governors. The publication and use of Altynsarin's catechism, though, shows that it could.

On the other hand, the cantonal schools, so important to Altynsarin's synthesis of mobility, civilization, and imperial loyalty, were a long time in coming. Administrative and material concerns both played a role in the delay. At first, there were not enough Kazak teachers to staff cantonal schools, but with a teachers' seminar functioning, that was no longer a concern by 1886. At that point, with personnel and funds prepared, responsibility fell on Protsenko, who had moved over from Semipalatinsk at the end of 1883 to assume gubernatorial duties in Turgai province. For reasons Altynsarin professed not to know, Protsenko significantly reduced the annual tax collection and diverted the funds that remained, previously intended for the first canton schools, to the building of a new central school.[146] This represented, Altynsarin claimed, an unnecessary and illegal action, since Kazaks who had donated money for canton schools expected them in their own cantons.[147] He argued his case passionately, noting that locally based schools would provide a more tangible moral and economic benefit to the population, and protect it from unscrupulous go-betweens (imagined, unsurprisingly, to be Tatar).[148] But only during Protsenko's last year in office, 1887, did cantonal schools receive the funding Altynsarin felt was their due, after a campaign that brought Il'minskii and, through him, Minister of Education I. D. Delianov onto their side.[149] By the start of 1888 he had succeeded in opening six of them, and planned to establish five more by the end of the year.[150] These canton schools, it appears, were not actually built set up along the lines Altynsarin had proposed in 1883; the 1887 budget for canton schools in Turgai province makes no mention of the tents, dray animals, or moving equipment that would have been necessary for such an undertaking.[151] But the change in leadership from Protsenko to the progressive Iakov Fedorovich Barabash augured well for Altynsarin's program. The network of low-level schools he envisioned multiplied quickly, and the village schools that began to appear after 1889 were mobile.[152]

Altynsarin, however, did not live to see most of this. The exhausting regimen of travel (up to 500 miles each way from his home) and work to which he had devoted himself overwhelmed him, as it did so many tsarist bureaucrats at the edges of the empire. He died of a respiratory ailment on July 17, 1889, having inspired and trained a new generation of Russophone Kazaks, just a few years before the role of such figures would be newly and balefully circumscribed.

The repertoires of rhetoric and governance Ibrai Altynsarin encountered over the course of his career presented him, like any other administrator, with options. Altynsarin worked within these options and applied his own understanding of the present state and future direction of a population and environment he was familiar with to articulate and defend original views of the possible future of the steppe. If Altynsarin's mind was not colonized, though, Turgai province certainly was, and this basic fact constrained both the range of choices available to him and the likelihood that his ideas would come to fruition. In the hierarchical administrative world of the Russian Empire, a project could succeed with the support of a patron like Barabash or Il'minskii, or founder on the opposition or indifference of a powerful figure like Protsenko. Any career-minded bureaucrat had to deal with this reality. Altynsarin, though, was not only consciously different by ethnicity and confession from most of his professional interlocutors, he was often selected because of his difference, granting his superiors access to local knowledges that they variously used or disregarded. The product of an early "civilizing" project on the steppe, he exerted, within bounds, a substantial influence on what that project ultimately became. The Ojibwe/Dakota author Scott Lyons has provocatively employed the "X-mark"—the signature placed on agreements with the US government by American Indians—as a symbol of both the coercive pressures exerted by imperial institutions and the agency of natives in casting their lot with them.[153] Altynsarin's life and career in service to the tsarist administration of the Kazak steppe represented just such a compromise.

That same administration, though always multiple and contested, was changing during Altynsarin's lifetime and after his passing. The direction in which it was moving would gradually become less favorable to local knowledge of the sort Altynsarin deployed in his defense. On one hand, under A. E. Alektorov and A. V. Vasil'ev, educational institutions were built in Turgai province along the lines Altynsarin had proposed, with the addition of simple, cheap, and mobile village schools adapted to local lifeways. In the first years of the twentieth century, Turgai province would remain well ahead of the other steppe provinces with respect to the quality and sheer number of its schools. In these schools, Altynsarin's textbooks found broad application. His promotion of an Islam both more doctrinally correct and compatible with Russian governance became less acceptable, although still within the realm of what many administrators would countenance. But Altynsarin's opposition to peasant colonization of the steppe could not have survived long into the twentieth century, as a new set of laws and a new set of facts developed in support of it.

As tsarist policy became both more Islamophobic and more focused on peasant colonization in the 1890s, the next generation of Kazak intermediaries would be harder put than Altynsarin to argue for a different religious, economic, and cultural future for the steppe within the Russian Empire. While tsarist policies remained hesitant and multivalent, Kazaks and Russians with profoundly varied relations to the imperial center continued, at times, to find common ground. The mutual intransigence they would find in one another by the turn of the twentieth century, though, would ultimately prove decisive—and divisive.

4

THE KEY TO THE WORLD'S TREASURES

"Russian Science," Local Knowledge, and the Civilizing Mission on the Siberian Steppe

Sometime in 1894, Abai Kunanbaev (1845–1904), a Middle Horde Kazak of distinguished ancestry educated in both an Islamic medresse and Russian schools, penned the following words of admonition to his fellow Kazaks: "Russian knowledge and culture are the keys to the world's treasures. Whoever has these keys will gain everything else without particular effort."[1] Abai was not alone among the Kazaks of the Siberian steppe (Akmolinsk and Semipalatinsk provinces) in propagandizing the value of Russian education. In the context of the Russian Empire's recent, seemingly irreversible conquest of the steppe, this seemed a sensible adaptation to changing realities. With the benefit of hindsight, it also appears, on the surface, to reflect absolute surrender to the modernizing impulses of an encroaching empire, acceptance of its material superiority, and the abdication of the value of nonmetropolitan knowledge practices. A closer look at the intellectual life of the Siberian steppe at the fin-de-siècle, however, presents a more complicated picture, one in which Kazak intellectuals accepted the civilizing assumptions of some of their tsarist interlocutors while using their knowledge of local conditions to craft arguments about how these visions ought to be implemented. As the nineteenth century drew to a close, though, their space to craft such arguments, and their hope of seeing them come to fruition, was on the wane.

More than four decades after Ronald Robinson's influential thesis, it has become a truism to suggest that the success or failure of empires depends to a significant degree on their ability to create incentives for local cooperation, outside of the dominant nationality group.[2] These incentives go beyond the materiality of salary, status, and rank. They extend to the creation of intellectual and ideological common ground—a sense that imperial officials and their colonial subjects, rulers and ruled, participate in the same project for similar reasons. On the Siberian steppe, science and knowledge as mediated through metropolitan institutions and language functioned, briefly, as such a common ground. It appeared in a smattering of colonial schools, local learned societies (statistical committees and subdivisions of IRGO—institutions involved with what would later be called regional study or *kraevedenie*), and an official bilingual newspaper, the *Kirgizskaia stepnaia gazeta* (hereafter *KSG*).[3] In all of these arenas, a "civilizing" message expressed in scientistic language, emphasizing the rationality of European science and its potential to improve the world, both constructed Kazak backwardness and offered Kazaks an instrument by which—on those terms—to improve themselves.[4]

The administrative, social, and economic context in which this common ground formed was changing rapidly. Experiments with peasant colonization continued throughout the 1880s; by the mid-1890s, with the formation of a Resettlement Administration and the appearance of thousands of irregular colonists (*samovol'tsy*) fleeing the famine of 1891–1892, it had decidedly hit a new phase, if well short of its peak. More than two decades after its initial two-year term, the Provisional Statute was finally replaced in 1891 by a Steppe Statute (not implemented until 1893). This statute, while drawing Kazaks more closely into the bureaucratic structure of the Russian Empire, also enabled colonization by declaring that surpluses of Kazak land, as state property, were subject to seizure for other purposes.

Before Kazak observers' very eyes, the steppe was changing. Yet the ways in which it might change remained contingent and contested, with Kazak intermediaries and tsarist administrators alike expressing a range of views. Common ground formed on the basis of a shared premise among Kazak intermediaries and "civilizing" tsarist administrators that a civilizing mission was desirable and feasible, that the steppe and its population both required improvement and could be improved through the action of imperial institutions. This very premise excluded numerous voices, both Kazak and Russian. Among the civilizers, it seemed likely that the steppe's future would involve Kazaks settling on the land. The appearance of colonization on the political agenda, the actual appearance of colonists on the steppe, and the continuing association of pastoralism and backwardness all pointed in this direction. Yet even as many official observers wrote in favor of sedentarism and a move from pastoralism to agriculture, and many Kazaks agreed with them, significant doubts rooted in perceptions of the steppe environment also appeared about the feasibility of such a transformation.

In this context, local knowledge, some of it collected and developed by Russian scholars (amateurs, in the vast majority of cases), appeared both as a means of seeking the adaptations that would permit a move to agriculture and as a defense of pastoralism. If Russian knowledge was the key to the world's treasures, knowledge of the local environment was vital to debates about what lay inside the chest.

Failures to Converge

Among both Kazaks and imperial Russians, there were many who either did not see the tsarist conquest of the steppe as positive or were skeptical of the possibilities of a civilizing mission there. Attention to these alternative views of conquest and rule highlights the intellectual agency of both Kazaks who saw something useful in metropolitan epistemologies and of imperial Russians who viewed the steppe and its population as worthy objects of development. The action of the present chapter—the mixing of local knowledge and new scholarly findings, applied to debates about the future of the steppe—occurred to the exclusion of these other systems of thought and knowledge.

The most prominent critical perspective, for Kazaks, lay in the work of the so-called *zar zaman* (troubled times) poets, most famously Shortanbai Qanaiŭlï (1818–1881), Mŭrat Möngkeŭlï (1843–1906), and Dulat Babataiŭlï (1802–1871). These bards (*aqïn*) have not enjoyed a good press over the past century. When mentioned at all in histories of Russian imperialism on the steppe or of Kazak literature, they have been caricatured as "ideologues of the powerful people of the feudal order [*feodal'noi verkhushki*]," owing to which they "related negatively to everything new in the economy, politics, and culture of Kazakh society of the era."[5] This is a mistaken approach. Rather, these poets' production, orally distributed widely around the steppe, represent an alternative view of the relationship between Kazakhs and the Russian Empire, one which, judging by its "broad popularity," was likely shared by many.[6] If many Russophone Kazak intermediaries viewed the conquest of the steppe as both a misfortune and an opportunity, the *zar zaman* bards saw it exclusively as a misfortune. The pre-conquest steppe, in their telling, was a fantastically wealthy pastoral idyll, where "herds were like clouds on the foothills/and hooves rang out like rain/you couldn't count the herds of horses."[7] A moral and spiritual decline, though, had left Kazaks as easy prey for the Russians (literally, for Shortanbai: "The Russians . . . are the eagle [*berkït*], we the fox"), spoiling this idyll, with little hope for recovery.[8] Shortanbai would go so far as to develop eschatological associations with the conquest and its aftereffects, invoking the approach of the end times (*aqïrzaman*).[9] In short, the conquest was a misfortune of historical proportions for Kazaks, and lamenting it remained the only option.

Reading against the grain of official documents celebrating tsarist civilizational and educational achievements makes it clear that such views were not exclusive to bardic lamentation. The intentions of regular exhortations against Kazak ignorance from Kazaks and Russians alike are obvious enough, but the fact of their repetition suggests that their targets were rarely receptive to the message.[10] When the editors of the *KSG* groused, for example, that the Kazaks of Omsk, seat of the Steppe Governor-Generalship, opened a Muslim primary school without any plans to offer instruction in the Russian language, they positioned it as an unfortunate half-measure.[11] It might, however, just as easily be interpreted as embodying an alternative view of the forms of education and knowledge that the founders of this school found valuable. In broad terms, the sheer numerical preponderance of Islamic schools in comparison with Russo-Kazak schools supports such a reading.[12] This was neither active resistance nor the hopeless lamentation of the zar zaman, but clearly, many Kazaks remained unconvinced that the Russian Empire and its institutions offered them something useful.

For that matter, a significant group of tsarist administrators did not see the steppe and other borderlands as worth the effort of civilization and development, as it was unlikely to reward the effort and funds invested. For the Turkestan Governor-Generalship, Daniel Brower has described the tension between reformist, civilizing officials and others who saw in the region only perpetual danger, best managed by strict military rule.[13] In the steppe, too, different provincial governors assigned drastically different priorities to "civilizing" projects. Ibrai Altynsarin's Turgai province, for example, had an educational system that by all accounts was far ahead of Akmolinsk and Semipalatinsk (the provinces of the Siberian steppe), where in the 1890s schooling remained in the same condition "that it was in in the 1860s."[14]

Partha Chatterjee has presented these strategies of rule as two sides of a single imperial coin, the "pedagogy of violence" and "pedagogy of culture," both latent within the protean, durable practice of imperial power.[15] At a fundamental level, this view is difficult to argue against, but it also tends to obfuscate the motivations of colonial administrators and their subjects in cooperating with one another. The big tent called "empire," on the Kazak steppe (and in most other imperial settings), held a range of potential lived experiences and outcomes. To appreciate the role of local knowledge in debating the future of the steppe, it is necessary to disentangle civilizing and noncivilizing perspectives on imperialism from one another.

Viewing the steppe as a locus of danger, to be kept in check, rather than a venue for a civilizing mission, a way of thinking with a long history among Russian administrators, found new support in some academic quarters, particularly the growing discipline of physical anthropology.[16] Two separate anthropological observers, V. D. Tronov (a doctor in Zaisan district of Semipalatinsk province) and N. Zeland (observing the Great Horde Kazaks of Semirech'e) came to strikingly similar conclusions about their subjects.[17] Both expressed grudging admiration for the Kazaks they observed in a noble-savage sort of way, noting their keen powers of observation and, it was claimed, tremendous tolerance for physical hardship.[18] But these animalistic traits were themselves no more than the scant positive manifestations of the squalor surrounding their Kazak subjects. Kazaks, according to Tronov, lived a "lower animal life" devoid of intellectual pursuits, organized industry, or any concerns beyond remaining satiated at all times while expending as little work as possible.[19] The inevitable results of this primitive lifestyle were ignorance and shocking immorality, manifested above all in widespread rates of syphilis infection. Zeland, similarly, grouped Kazaks among the world's primitive (*pervobytnye*) peoples, blamed the problems the Great Horde faced on laziness and ignorance, and took a particularly dim view of their squalid and disordered domestic life.[20] For both, the cultural level of the nomads they observed was leagues behind the rest of the civilized world.

So far, there is nothing unexpected about this—as we will see, the views of both Kazak and Russian "civilizers" also depended on the construction of Kazak backwardness. Zeland's conclusion, however, was as striking as it was inimical to any sort of civilizing project: since Kazaks "must take a place behind cultured peoples not only in their amount of factual knowledge, but in terms of suitability for its acquisition and cultivation," all previous attempts to educate them had "not brought forth any significant fruit."[21] Unlike Japan, the classic fin-de-siècle case in favor of the developmental possibilities of "Asiatics," the Kazak steppe was miserable and always had been. It was impossible to revive, according to this line of thinking, what had never been lively before. No kind of regulation or policy could change the fundamental backwardness of the steppe. It could only be managed.

Thus there was no inherent reason for the interests of Kazak intermediaries and tsarist administrators to converge on the Siberian steppe. For many, clearly, mutual intransigence and the maintenance of difference were closer to the norm. Choosing a different course of action required both institutional space and intellectual labor.

Spaces of Convergence

In the hierarchical world of the Steppe Governor-Generalship (the successor, from 1882, to the Governor-Generalship of Western Siberia), it is hardly surprising that the institutions which brought Russian and Kazak civilizers together were based on statist calculations. Both the *KSG* and various regional-studies publications had their origins in what local governors and governors-general understood as the greater good of Russian imperialism on the steppe. However, various governors had drastically different goals in view, and attracting Kazak participation was not a given. The spaces of convergence that administrators, scholars, and a smattering of local Kazaks created on the steppe were thus fragile and dependent on mutual good will, specific configurations of authority, and intellectual common ground.

The *KSG* was the creation of Gerasim Alekseevich Kolpakovskii (1819–1896), first governor-general of the steppe, but it particularly flourished under the supervision of his successor, Baron Maksim Antonovich Taube (1826–1910). Originally a supplement to the *oblastnye vedomosti* (official provincial gazette) of Akmolinsk province, it was eventually attached to the official newspapers of Semipalatinsk and Semirech'e provinces as well. Published in dual texts (Russian and Arabic-script Kazak), and containing both an "official" section (new regulations and orders) and an "unofficial" one (social commentary and articles), it was available for the modest annual subscription of two or three rubles.[22] In the first issue, released on New Year's Day, 1888, the editors described its broad ambit:

> The special 'addition' to *Akmolinskie oblastnye vedomosti* is published, by order of the Steppe governor-general, so that the native Kazak population may get acquainted with the measures and instructions concerning the Kazak steppe and Kazak public administration of local and higher authorities, and to spread useful information among the Kazaks about the nature of the country and the daily life [*byt*] of its inhabitants—economic (stock raising, development of grain cultivation, exchange trade, etc.) and spiritual (customs, legends, tales, development of literacy, etc.).[23]

The same opening issue appealed for Kazaks themselves to act as contributors, to "talk about their real needs" via the newspaper.[24] It was thus, from its inception, both a didactic and a dialogic institution. Kolpakovskii, Taube, and the editors working beneath them would set the tone and the terms of what cooperation looked like, and Kazaks who found the paper's message compelling would further its mission by contributing their own writings. During the decade-plus it was published (1888–1902—microfilms for 1889 are missing), it occasionally drew the ire of central administrators and, more often, struggled for non-Russian contributors.[25] Still, it succeeded in publishing a surprising range of materials ranging from local folklore to European history, summaries of recent scientific research to humble, homegrown methods of dealing with common problems.[26]

Publications also evolved around local statistical committees, especially the one based in Semipalatinsk province and subordinated to the Ministry of Internal Affairs. These were institutions common to all provinces of the Russian Empire, and responsible for gathering such diverse data as population statistics, harvest data, and information about the state of various business enterprises, and reporting it to provincial authorities and the Central Statistical Committee in St. Petersburg.[27] This was the so-called "obligatory work" of Semipalatinsk's statistical committee, and its desired relationship to a strong state at all levels is clear enough.

From 1898 on, though, the statistical committee also took upon itself the publication of the annual *Pamiatnaia knizhka Semipalatinskoi oblasti* (PKSO). Between 1898 and 1902, the *PKSO* combined the usual functions of such *pamiatnye knizhki* (directory-style information about local administrators and businessmen, as well as a calendar of important events) with lengthy articles about Kazak culture, the history of the Kazak and settler populations of the province, and its flora, fauna, agriculture, and animal husbandry, among other subjects.[28] In 1901, moreover, Semipalatinsk also witnessed the opening of a subdivision (*pod"otdel*) of the Omsk-based Western Siberian division of IRGO. Many of the authors who published in this subdivision's *Zapiski* were the same ones who had written in the *PKSO*, and an uptick in its publications coincides with a sharp fall in long-form contributions to the *PKSO*. Thus it seems likely that the subdivision effectively replaced the *PKSO* as a forum for publishing regional studies.

The study of flora, fauna, and populations at the local level came with multiple political valences.[29] In Semipalatinsk, this was particularly the case, given its place within the political geography of the Russian Empire. This modest city on the Irtysh River, a center of colonial rule, was also a place of exile. Fyodor Dostoevsky, who met Chokan Valikhanov during a stay in Semipalatinsk following his release from the "house of the dead" in Omsk, is the most famous of these exiles, but there were dozens more throughout the second half of the nineteenth century, living in Semipalatinsk under the observation, secret or otherwise, of the tsarist gendarmerie. Among them were both followers of the famed radical Nikolai Chernyshevskii and participants in the failed Polish revolution of 1863. In a context where state organs lacked sufficiently educated bureaucrats, these educated but politically "unreliable" people often carried out state-sponsored research concerning Semipalatinsk oblast. Steeped in the rationalism and materialism of radical culture of the 1860s, and conscious of the small-deeds liberalism of the reform era, many were equally eager to carry out research independently.[30] Kazakhstani historians have devoted highly empirical monographs to the scholarly activity of these exiles, including Nikolai Iakovlevich Konshin (the most frequent contributor to the *PKSO*), E. P. Mikhaelis, and I. I. Dolgopolov.[31] It cannot be assumed a priori that the oppositional politics of such figures was manifested as opposition to imperial rule on the steppe. Liberalism, a highly fraught concept for the Russian Empire under the best of circumstances, has never consistently functioned as a barrier to imperial expansion.[32] But regional study did mean that when political exiles or other oppositionally minded figures wished to criticize colonial rule as practiced around them, they had the opportunity to gloss strong criticism as factual scholarship, and useful to the state that had sponsored it.

In their way, then, all of the *KSG*, *PKSO*, and *Zapiski* of Semipalatinsk's branch of IRGO were marginal publications. The *KSG* assumed an interventionist perspective on governance and Kazak civilizational aptitudes, neither of which were universally shared, and both of which could vanish for no other reason than a change of governor-general. The regional-studies publications were not entirely produced by exiles, of course, but had their share of participants who had already attracted the ire of the state. The publications themselves would also turn out to be, at times, the objects of administrative displeasure.[33] Yet they remained an important part of the practice of imperial rule in the Siberian steppe for more than a decade—one configuration of the relationship between colonizers and colonized, metropolitan and local knowledge, among several.

The *KSG* actively solicited Kazak participation in its endeavors, but the regional-studies organizations also were sites of interethnic exchange. Abai, for example, was a member of the Semipalatinsk Statistical Committee from 1886.[34] A younger Kazak, an alumnus of the Omsk Technical School and Imperial Forestry Institute, Älikhan Bökeikhanov, contributed material to the *PKSO*.[35] Involving Kazaks in such projects, in light of the few Russian-language schools in the governor-generalship and dim physical-anthropological views of their intellect, took some intellectual gymnastics. Here, social-evolutionist views and a *longue durée* view of history proved useful. Toward the end of the *KSG*'s print run, one V. Ivanov made a case for relativism and the tutelage that it implied: "European peoples, who now bear all the marks of higher culture, were not always so. They, during their improvement [*sovershenstvovanie*], passed through a certain series of steps, one of which is the very one at which the Kazaks stand at present, the nomadic way of life."[36] Kazaks could thus be improved within a relatively short timeframe, given the appropriate models and incentives. If this flew in the face of received anthropological wisdom about nomads, the jurist and ethnographer Ivan Ivanovich Kraft, serving in neighboring Turgai province, offered a justification for efforts to reform and uplift the Kazaks that fit well within the paradigm of fin-de-siècle racial thinking. In a report to the Imperial Archaeological Commission reprinted in the *KSG*, Kraft not only hypothesized that Kazaks' former slaves (Russians and sedentary Central Asians) had assimilated with the nomads in centuries past, but that this had had measurable positive effects:

> Should we not see, in this mixing of blood of a higher race with the blood of the natives, one of the reasons that the Kazak nationality is not undergoing the fate of many foreign tribes, some of which live in even better conditions—that is, extinction, but displays vitality [*zhivuchest'*], viability, and striving toward higher culture? Does not one of the reasons that the Kazaks are freely and skillfully moving to agricultural life, reaching the same level as, and sometimes outstripping, the original farmers, Russian colonizers, stem from this freshening of the blood [*osvezhenie krovi*]?[37]

In this view, Kazaks were neither ordinary nomads nor comparable to the various "small peoples" of Siberia who tottered on the edge of extinction under tsarist rule.[38] They were intelligent and adaptable and, as we will see below, their adaptability promised advantages greater than a hands-off policy could offer.

Kazak cooperation, the other side of the equation, stemmed from several factors, some easier to evidence than others. If not all Russian-educated Kazaks came from elite-born families, it is clear enough that collaboration with tsarist institutions and values offered a new and potentially viable source of authority, one which could be deployed against what they viewed as the pernicious influence of native authority figures.[39] The bare fact of the conquest of the steppe, and the apparent wealth and strength of the Russian Empire, suggested unflattering comparisons and the necessity of accepting whatever tuition tsarist officials might offer. Abai, overstating the case for dramatic effect, wrote that this material gap was so wide that "there can be no words about the Russians. We cannot even be compared with their servants."[40] These incentives dovetailed well. If existing authority figures stood in the way of material progress, new leadership and new alliances were needed.

Harder to document, but undoubtedly important, is the affective side of the matter. In the context of Soviet "friendship of peoples" historiography, desperate to identify "good" Russians within reactionary tsarist imperialism, such relationships between Kazaks and Russians as existed were widely celebrated.[41] Abai's relationship with Mikhaelis (and S. S. Gross), in particular, has been made to bear tremendous explanatory weight for his behavior later in life. The historian Äbish Zhirenchin, for example, notes that Abai and Mikhaelis's friendship began when

Abai requested a novel by L. N. Tolstoy from the Semipalatinsk city library that Mikhaelis was reading at the time.[42] Regardless of the provenance of these stories, the "friendship" narrative emerged so quickly after Abai's death—Bökeikhanov, in a 1907 obituary, attributed to Mikhaelis and Gross "a huge influence on Abai's education and enlightenment"—that there is doubtless some fact beneath the layers of myth.[43] In a context where few prominent Kazaks would not have felt the heavy consequences of arbitrary administrative rule, it does not seem far-fetched to think that social intercourse, even friendship, with people who approached them as potentially talented and interesting seemed preferable to approaching administrators who saw them as comically backward "children of nature," or to simply failing to engage wholesale.[44]

Thus Kazaks and Russians alike had significant incentives to participate in a set of institutions that were vital to envisioning (and, under some conditions, enacting) imperial rule on the steppe, despite their precarious position relative to the administration and motley band of contributors. The space for discussion within these institutions, though, was more restricted than it had been during the era of the Provisional Statute, owing to policy changes both locally and in St. Petersburg.

Resettlement and Colonization: A New Phase

By the 1890s, the heyday of both the *KSG* and *PKSO*, peasant colonization loomed far larger on the administrative agenda than it had in the 1880s, when Ibrai Altynsarin proposed that Kazaks could settle on the land and intensify their stock raising without the tutelage or encouragement of peasant colonists. The resettlement of Slavic peasants to the Kazak steppe was not yet at its zenith, but migration law and the actual movement of peasants changed the situation such that colonization could not be dismissed, or left unaddressed, in discussions of what Kazaks' future might hold.

A new phase in the tsarist state's thinking on peasant migration, from a stance that was initially hesitant and distrustful of such mobility, can be dated to 1881, when Alexander III granted his support to a provisional, restrictive law permitting peasants to migrate in order to ameliorate the landlessness felt by some in the empire's inner provinces.[45] The year 1889 witnessed a less restrictive and better-publicized law on general migration, which offered limited state aid, contingent on the availability of free state land, for peasants whose reasons to migrate "merited attention."[46] The 1890s were, in several respects, a period of intensification of this policy. The Steppe Statute of 1891 developed land law on the steppe in a manner that made it possible to free up state lands for peasant migrants. The Provisional Statute of 1868 had declared all pastures used by Kazak pastoralists to be state property, granted to them on rights of long-term rental; according to article 120 of the Steppe Statute, any of these state lands that turned out to be surplus to Kazaks' use (*izlishki*) could be seized and placed at the state's disposal.[47] Peasants also arrived outside the prescribed order of migration, fleeing the terrible famine of 1891–1892; by 1896, the new Trans-Siberian Railway had been built as far east as the Ob' River, making travel to the new lands easier and faster. The same year, in the wake of a series of measures "designed to encourage migration," a special Resettlement Administration formed to supervise settler movement, and an expedition under the leadership of the zemstvo statistician F. A. Shcherbina began work on clarifying the amount of surplus land available for settlers.[48] In short, this was a period of ever-growing institutional and financial commitment to peasant resettlement to the steppe. In light of earlier administrative fantasies positioning the peasant as a *Kulturträger*, able to help Kazaks to settle on the land and teach them agriculture, such commitments implied both the means and the agents by which Kazaks might be "civilized."

The expanding presence of settlers on the steppe, and the development of a legal and institutional apparatus that facilitated their movement, was the single most important issue motivating discussions of the future of the region. As we will see, tsarist administrators and Kazak intermediaries alike offered a range of arguments about the feasibility and desirability of colonization, sedentarization, and agriculture on the steppe. But these discussions could only take place given the existence of intellectual common ground, which in the *KSG* and regional-studies publications consisted of two important points: first, that Kazaks were uncivilized, and required improvement; second, that scientific knowledge verified by experience was the most likely means of bringing about such improvement.

The Mutual Construction of Backwardness

Ensconcing the steppe in a narrative of civilizational progress required, in contrast to the zar zaman bards, a more negative view of the distant (i.e., pre-conquest) past of the steppe than of its present condition. At the same time, the view of the present could not be so uniformly positive as to obviate the possibility of further progress under imperial tutelage. In the *KSG* and regional-studies publications, Kazak intermediaries and tsarist administrators co-constructed a steppe that was midway between primordial wildness and European civilization. Its further progress depended on targeted state interventions.

In the narrative the *KSG* presented, the pre-conquest steppe had been a remarkably dismal and dangerous place. Here, a single passage from an early issue of the *KSG* may stand in for many specific complaints that developed later on:

> To the number of such [vast] borderlands belong Russia's Central Asian possessions, extending from the coast of the Caspian Sea to Kul'ja, and from Orenburg to the Pamirs. Populated by the remainders of khanates that were, at one time, mighty by their physical strength, the territory of Central Asia served as an arena for mutual hostility, attacks, and pillaging of peoples of various races [*raznoplemennykh narodov*], while they were not subordinated to Russian power by the force of necessity, a power which was called, in order to protect its borders, to impose order and tranquility in the heart of the Central Asian steppes.[49]

Things remained relatively grim, when the paper's editors were in a mood to admonish, during the 1890s. Kazak correspondents and governors alike complained of the continuing problems that horse theft caused for farmers and nomads, and the apparent corruptibility of native administrators remained an ongoing concern for both groups as well.[50] That this situation had improved at all over the course of the nineteenth century was entirely attributed to tsarist institutions. In this sense, a late piece on the achievements of Tsar Alexander II was a metonym for the entire experience of Russian rule on the steppe: the tsar-liberator had conferred (*darovat'*) a wide range of careful administrative reforms on the steppe, setting the historical stage for their further progress.[51] Thus, the "scenario of power" that the *KSG* and the civilizing governors who patronized it represented was one according to which Kazaks and the steppe had come as far as they had only by their halting acceptance of imperial tutelage; they would go further only by acquiescing in it more deeply.[52]

One particular manifestation of this administrative beneficence would be in overcoming the ignorant superstition that Kazaks were believed to exhibit in their daily lives. The pages of the *KSG* were filled with descriptions, by turns mocking and pitying, of ordinary Kazaks' beliefs, from Russian and Kazak authors alike. An anonymous author, in 1895, laid the blame for low population growth and high mortality directly at Kazaks' feet. Though the bracing steppe air promoted good health, he claimed, a witches' brew of unhealthy practices, including keeping unsanitary winter dwellings, early marriage, and the dubious treatment offered by folk witch doctors (*znakhari, baksy*), had consigned Kazaks to a miserable existence and possible extinction.[53] Not content with a general condemnation of folk medicine, the paper at times offered lurid descriptions of the particular fates suffered by Kazaks who had turned to folk healers instead of district doctors and medical assistants (fel'dshery).[54] Still higher on the list of horrors, a Kazak correspondent contributed an anecdote from the late Ibrai Altynsarin, who had, during his time as a district judge in the 1870s, tried vainly to save a woman buried alive because of the superstition and blind adherence to ritual of her fellow villagers.[55] In short, evidence was mounting from the KSG's correspondents, regardless of ethnicity, that Kazaks' ignorance had reached the point of becoming fatal. In 15 years of newspapers, not a single defender of folk healers emerges. If this undoubtedly reflects the editorial priorities of the newspaper, it also demonstrates that its editors had some success in recruiting Kazaks who found that editorial line reflective of their own experiences and needs.

There are strong similarities between these descriptions of Kazak squalor and ignorance and ethnographic descriptions of the Russian peasantry and urban lower classes at the same time.[56] In the village, in the slum, and on the steppe, such rhetoric was deployed in the service of a range of transformative agendas. The specificity of the imperial situation in the Kazak steppe lay in the institutions, practices, and sources put forth as the sources of that transformation.

Finally, the pastoral nomadism that continued to be Kazaks' predominant lifeway, as practiced toward the end of the nineteenth century, appeared to have serious deficiencies. Undoubtedly, the most prominent of these was Kazaks' "carelessness" (bespechnost') in taking care of their livestock. This carelessness, it seemed, was reflected above all in a failure to think about anything beyond their most immediate needs and pleasures:

> The Kazaks completely forget that winter will return again: they do not trouble about preparation of fodder for livestock, even though they would completely have been able to do so in most cases, and pass the whole summer in idleness, delighting their sinful bellies [uslazhdaia svoiu greshnuiu utrobu] with koumiss [fermented mare's milk] and mutton and spreading steppe news from village to village instead of doing business. But outside their expectations, once more winter arrives with storms, blizzards, and frosts; it, the villain, catches the Kazaks unawares, and completely unprepared to face it.[57]

In a regular year, perhaps, this would not constitute a death sentence, as hooved animals would still be able to dig sufficient food from beneath the snow. But when the fodder was inaccessible, whether because snow drifted too deeply on the open steppe or because, after a thaw, it was covered in a thick crust of ice, a frightful moment arrived. This was the dreaded *zhŭt*, most severe every 10–12 years, and paired with the appositive "the scourge of stock raising" (*etot bich skotovodstva*) in the *KSG*. Discussions of zhŭt had several dimensions. In Konshin's hands, for example, a historic zhŭt of the 1840s provided an occasion to meditate on the failings of earlier tsarist administrations, less competent and less concerned with their population's welfare.[58] But it was, by and large, a rhetorical device used to criticize nomads perceived as lazy, backward, and unproductive.

Zhŭt, like the "superstitious" medical treatments offered by charlatans, had an underlying and miserable objective reality to it.[59] Outside observers estimated that severe events could carry off anything from 10 to 70% of Kazakhs' livestock.[60] Pastoral nomads' opportunities to adapt were always limited— under the best of circumstances, they could only hope to combine the backbreaking labor of physically removing deep snow and shattering ice, slaughtering as many animals as possible, and ultimately fleeing to warmer, drier areas.[61] But it was also a phenomenon that had, apparently, recurred for centuries on the grasslands, and while suffering was undoubtedly great in the short term, the natural reproduction of livestock covered the losses quickly.[62] Thus envisioning zhŭt itself as a disaster necessitating humanitarian intervention needed intellectual labor, a concept of the necessity of intervening in subjects' lives that goes under the broad heading of governmentality.[63] On the steppe, as elsewhere in the Russian empire, this developed gradually over the course of the nineteenth century, with state sponsorship of smallpox inoculations and the piecemeal introduction of microcredit institutions (*ssudnye kassy*) for the neediest nomads.[64] It is in this sense that we can understand zhŭt as a constructed phenomenon, although the remedies proposed for it varied widely. Editorials in the *KSG* and correspondence sent in from steppe Kazaks drew the consequences of zhŭt in the most serious terms, preparing the ground for arguments in favor of sweeping economic change. One correspondent from Turgai province lamented that "the famous rich man D. B., who had more than 3,000 horses, now has only 80. Ch., who formerly had more than 5,000 horses, now has about 100. Many rich Kazaks, who owned small herds, do not now have a single horse. By the spring, merciless hunger raged. . . . With the dying of livestock disappeared the main means the Kazaks had for survival, since during the spring and summer the population consumes milk and dairy products."[65] The winter the *KSG*'s anonymous correspondent described, 1891–1892, was legendarily difficult around the Russian Empire, and played a role in the notorious famine at that time in the Volga River basin.[66] Exceptional circumstances like these, though, seemed to require fundamental change, for the nomads' own good. If they could not think to take precautionary measures on their own, they would need to learn new approaches from tsarist institutions and the more "enlightened" of their kinsmen.

Kazaks' seeming carelessness was also expressed in their unwillingness to intervene in their animals' reproduction, prizing quantity over quality in livestock and simply releasing the best animals into their herds and flocks with no attention to potential improvements in the breed. As a result, as one commentator put it, "stock raising in general and horse keeping in particular among the Kazaks are in decline."[67] Wolves were another source of losses due to insufficient watchfulness. If the problem here seemed less intimately connected with human survival than was zhŭt, there was nevertheless both a strong incentive for change and a set of solutions that, to outside commentators, seemed obvious.[68] Cultural change and the appropriate support from state institutions (most notably state-run stables) could ensure not only survival but prosperity for willing nomads.[69]

Like many humanitarian interventions, remediating such concerns about pastoral nomadism promised a hefty payoff for the intervening Russian Empire. Animals bred for specific qualities had clear purposes within European Russia. In an internal report, Kolpakovskii argued that no finer light cavalry horse existed in Europe than the tough, nimble Kazak breed, which could be used in large numbers if Kazaks could be prevented from spoiling it.[70] The building of the Siberian railroad promised a good market for the meat and fat of Kazak sheep—fat for manufacturing the tallow candles commonly used by most strata of the population, meat to feed workers at the factories of the Urals region.[71] To secure these benefits to the empire (and, the editors of the KSG argued, to themselves), though, Kazaks would need to accept what Bruce Grant has described as the "gift of empire," permitting themselves to be civilized on Russian terms: "So as to satisfy the European market, the nomadic population must meditate upon its economy—shake off apathy and laziness from itself and take up stock raising on more firm foundations. They should replace their careless relationship toward existence of their livestock with more attentive care [ukhod] and keeping of animals, selection of stud animals for copulation, striving to increase the quantity of livestock and more rationally use the steppe areas."[72] Underneath the humanitarianism of all the various proposals for transforming the steppe lurked a sort of economic statism—a continuing concern with how this distinct environmental and economic region could be made useful to the Russian Empire, heedless of its political integration.

Decrying backwardness, though, also functioned as a call from Kazak intermediaries to adapt under circumstances that had, objectively, changed significantly over the previous few decades. One Kazak, Saudaqas Shormanov, made this point as early as 1890, long before the peak of peasant resettlement to the steppe provinces. Even small peasant and Cossack settlements, as well as trade with Russians, had drastically reduced the average distance and time of Kazak pastoral migration. Moreover, Kazaks were losing their land, a situation that could only grow worse in the legal and social environment of the 1890s: "A certain quantity of suitable Kazak lands, for example, in the surroundings of the Irtysh, of Kokchetau, Baian-aul, Karkarala, Ishim, and so on, have long already been occupied by villages, and, along with this, the best sections of the remaining lands are starting to go off to the use of settlers from Russia. Poor Kazaks, because of the scantiness of the land, more or less in the near future will cease their nomadizing, against their will, which fact is proven by the present state of our population."[73] Kazak actors who chose to engage with the *KSG*, like Shormanov, believed that they were living through an era of demonstrably massive change, and that they had a responsibility to adapt. The multiple cultures in which Kazak intermediaries moved conditioned the meanings that they made of such changes. Understanding a decline or change in material conditions as a call to adapt, rather than rebel (of which the steppe had seen several instances during the 1800s) or mourn, needed subjective judgment, intellectual labor, and involvement in new cultural worlds. Nor did Kazaks agree on a single path of reform. Instead, there were polemics about how best to bring together local particularities, imperial resources, and the realities of conquest. Still, in the minds of both tsarist administrators and Kazak intermediaries, it was clear that the transfer of technologies and ideas from the metropole to the steppe would play a vital role in such adaptation. This assumption, along with the shared construction of Kazak backwardness, was the axiom from which further debates departed.

Conduits of Change

Abai's designation of Russian scholarship as "the key to the world's treasures" could have served as the unofficial motto of Kazaks who engaged with the various civilizing projects of the Siberian steppe at the end of the nineteenth century. For their part, the editors of the *KSG* were delighted at any engagement they could find; this was a sign that the civilizing project was taking root. Framing the Russian language and the achievements of Russian scholarship as conduits to a more peaceful and prosperous life only enhanced the prestige of tsarist rule on the steppe. Kazak intermediaries, in contrast, viewed the instrumental use of tsarist institutions and achievements as a means of adapting to belonging to a multiethnic empire with a single dominant nationality, while hopefully accruing material benefits along the way.

Among Kazaks, Abai was by no means an isolated voice in valorizing the Russian language and its importance for the recently conquered steppe. In 1894, lamenting the poor condition of Kazaks' traditional stock raising (in a year when the *KSG* was particularly and didactically focused on this issue), an obscure figure, Qorabai Zhapanüghlï, saw only one escape: "For all of this the sin is our ignorance and lack of knowledge of the Russian language. We need the Russian language and Russian books. From books we not only will obtain practical knowledge, but also information about the outside world and its phenomena."[74] Since the facts of conquest and rule seemed to demonstrate the material superiority of the metropole, it was necessary, it seemed to many Kazak thinkers, to use the ruling language of the empire instrumentally. Commanding it could provide access to useful information that they lacked. This was not a new idea. In a different conjunction of civilizing ideas and local initiative, Ibrai Altynsarin had planned a second volume of his *Kazak Reader* that was to "give as complete and fundamental an understanding as possible about natural history, geography, history, a little chemistry, physics, technical productions."[75] Altynsarin himself was to serve as both translator and filter in this volume, never completed, selecting and condensing what he considered the best and most useful fruits of imperial scholarship for a waiting audience, the schools under his supervision.[76] On the Siberian steppe, where bilingual education was much later to develop than in Altynsarin's Turgai province, the *KSG* was an eager supporter of state-sponsored, Russian-language education, and gladly published the work of Kazaks who appeared to support its mission.

Although Russian also had an instrumental function as the language of governance, and its proponents thought that requiring its use would produce local administrators of a better sort, its primary function was as a source of practically applicable and empirically verified information.[77] In the *KSG*, short articles, often under the generic title of "generally useful information" (*obshchepoleznye svedeniia*) taught readers lessons as seemingly trivial as methods of curing rheumatism, or as immediately practical as methods of preventing fires from breaking out in their permanent winter dwellings.[78] This useful advice was, variously, a summation of findings derived from experimental science or a write-up of the rough-and-ready methods Russian peasants used to cope with natural threats like disease and fire. If these were translated into Arabic-script Kazak in the dual-text *KSG*, the original source of the information remained abundantly clear, as did the positioning of tsarist institutions as the medium through which Kazaks ought to advance themselves. The mediation of the state language, moreover, facilitated the transfer of useful ideas from peoples in similar circumstances to Kazaks, with

Russian acting as a waystation. Thus, for example, in 1900, the newspaper published an article by a pseudonymous Kazak ("Naimanets," "of the Naiman clan"), who summarized a different article *he* had read in the capital newspaper *Sankt-Peterburgskie vedomosti* (St. Petersburg gazette) about methods of cultivating artificial hay meadows in use among the Buriats, a nomadic Siberian people of Mongolian extraction.[79] As both a medium of exchange among non-Russian peoples and an established language of scholarly communication, Kazak commentators and tsarist bureaucrats agreed that Russian had much to offer.

Just as important was the scientism of the *KSG*. In 15 years of publication, news about scholarly expeditions and new discoveries gave information about the doings of the tsarist imperial family a close run as the most frequent topic of its articles. Readers and listeners could find, next to information about governors' orders and honors given to Kazak servitors of the empire, news of the journeys of celebrated Russian explorers like Nikolai Mikhailovich Przheval'skii and Petr Kuz'mich Kozlov; accounts of the achievements of other European explorers in remote regions of the world; and recent archaeological and scientific discoveries.[80] Occasionally, such news had direct practical importance, informing subscribers how they could feed livestock in cases of extreme need, or defend themselves against epizootics (rinderpest, *chuma rogatogo skota*, being particularly terrifying). But these articles were more important in establishing an atmosphere and an attitude among readers of the *KSG*, according to which knowledge was interesting for its own sake, humanity was progressing toward ever greater scientific achievements, and metropolitan publications were the original source material for learning more about it. The idea of European science as a human endeavor dwarfed in its significance whatever intrinsic interest Kozlov's peregrinations might have had.

Rhetorically, the classic tsarist anxieties about stagnation and backwardness vis-à-vis other European great powers were actually useful in both making these arguments and securing their reception among the Kazaks toward whom they were directed. As Abai understood things, Russia served as a particularly useful example to Kazaks because they, too, had been a backward, late-developing people: "the Russians became as they are [by] learning other languages, joining world culture."[81] Only after Peter the Great opened Muscovy to the influence of western Europe was it possible for Russia to overcome centuries of stagnation, with the result that it had now become a world-class imperial power, more than strong enough to overwhelm the three Kazak hordes. Now, Russia could be to the steppe as Europe had been to Russia. Contributors to the *KSG* tended to share this developmental perspective. The example of Japan's self-strengthening under the Meiji Restoration was all the proof they required that "Asiatics" could develop under European tutelage (with China's fate in the Sino-Japanese War an object lesson in the stakes of learning correctly).[82] Indeed, stadial development made such progress a historical inevitability: "All of the advanced peoples passed through various stages in their development sequentially, before achieving their current condition."[83] The same newspaper published laudatory accounts of the gradual merger (*sliianie*) of non-Russians with Russians by means of frequent intercourse, a merger which came with their sedentarization and improvement.[84] Treating the *KSG* as a unified text, the message becomes clear: Russians possessed supreme civilizing capabilities; all peoples, including Russians, passed through developmental stages; Russians were both farther along in their development than Kazaks and the closest available "advanced" people. Accepting their tutelage made good sense.

The *KSG* also recruited a perhaps unwitting ally by regularly reprinting articles from the Bakhchiserai-based weekly newspaper *Tercüman* (The translator). Published since 1883 by the Crimean Tatar Ismail Bey Gasprinskii, founder of the reformist Jadid movement, *Tercüman* suited the needs of civilizing administrators, while Jadid ideas clearly piqued the interest of some Kazak readers.[85] Jadidism had begun as a new method of teaching literacy in the Arabic script (phonetically, rather than by rote memorization), yet it soon became associated more broadly with doctrinal adaptability and openness to worldly knowledge. These views tracked well with the *KSG*'s modernizing, didactic editorial line; both publications presented unthinking superstition as part of a complex of backward ideas that had led to Muslims' fully deserved, easily anticipated subordination by more advanced peoples.[86] Thus, when the *KSG* had column-inches to fill, it borrowed the words of *Tercüman*'s correspondents on, for example, the benefits for inorodtsy of knowing the Russian language, or the importance of supplementing religious education with secular knowledge.[87] Koranic justifications broadly in support of religious tolerance (and thus complementary to an activist, civilizing practice of imperialism) mixed with more obviously utilitarian arguments in favor of preventing the spread of infectious disease.[88] Advertisements to subscribe directly to Gasprinskii's newspaper, offering access to the views of its correspondents in a less mediated form, appeared just as did those for Russian and Siberian papers did at the end of the calendar year.[89] The "strategic alliance" that formed on the pages of the *KSG* was not only between Russian administrators and Kazak intellectuals. It entailed the overlap of perspectives on religion, ethnicity, and scholarship from around the borderlands of the Russian Empire.

Such arguments suited the developing views of even some religiously minded Kazaks. Abai, for example, noted that while traditional religious education was important, Kazaks now lived in the *dar al-harb*, where Islamic law was not in force, and thus new ways of knowing the world were needed.[90] Openness to secular learning was, moreover, doctrinally correct. After all, "it is known that Knowledge is one of the attributes of the Most-High, therefore love for knowledge is a sign of humanity and integrity."[91] Such arguments were basically consonant with the programs that Ibrai Altynsarin introduced in the Russo-Kazak schools of the Orenburg steppe. By the 1910s, some Kazak intellectuals were in conflict with the Tatar progressives who spearheaded the Jadid movement, concerned that they fundamentally misunderstood the political and economic needs of the steppe.[92] At the close of the nineteenth century, though, this was in the future, and the cause of cultural reform compatible with Islamic doctrine still trumped ethnic particularism.

It needs to be emphasized that, for administrators, making common cause with Gasprinskii's *Tercüman* was, if not a totally risky and unsanctioned move (he published, after all, with the approval of the Ministry of Internal Affairs), at least not a self-evident one. The appearance of *Tercüman* and rumors of its spread around the steppe generated an inquest about what the movement signified and the likelihood of its taking root among the Kazak population (more than a decade after excerpts from *Tercüman* had first been published in the *KSG*).[93] Outside of specific fears about *Tercüman* and Gasprinskii's character, Islamophobia remained an endemic presence in some administrative spheres. Taube and the long-serving military governor of Semipalatinsk province, Aleksandr Fedorovich Karpov (1842–after 1901), received pressure from religious authorities to seriously restrict the movement of "fanatical" Muslim travelers around the steppe. Though Karpov demurred when Taube solicited his opinion, the compromise measures he proposed still ran to opposing Kazaks' construction of mosques and schools under them.[94] Finally, just to the south of the steppe provinces, in the Turkestan Governor-Generalship, a revolt in Andijan district in May 1898, led by a Sufi spiritual leader known as the Dukchi *ishan*, prompted a sea change in administrative thinking about Islam.[95] The approximately 2,000 Muslims who rebelled, armed with swords and knives, were repulsed after a short battle. But the recently appointed governor-general of Turkestan, Sergei Mikhailovich Dukhovskoi (1838–1901), reacted sharply to the revolt, which in his view demonstrated the comprehensive failure of the earlier policy of noninterference in religious affairs.[96] He recommended active struggle, not in the form of missionary work but in the gradual subordination of independent Islamic institutions to the tsarist state and restriction of the activity of those Muslims he perceived as most dangerous.[97] Too credulous a relationship to Muslims' professions of loyalty, or letting Islam's purported "hostility to all things Christian" slip from view even for a second, threatened another Andijan.[98]

All of this was occurring as the *KSG* made common cause with one of the most prominent Muslim-run periodicals in the Russian Empire. The choice to engage with reformist Muslims, rather than persecute or ignore them, was as contingent as the choice to make any effort to civilize the apparently wild and benighted nomads of the steppe. Through the Russian language and Russian scholarship, administrators and Kazak intellectuals agreed, Kazaks would overcome their backwardness, becoming advanced, worthy parts of the empire, without violating their religious obligations.

Yet the use of tsarist institutions and knowledge did not always reflect acquiescence in the material superiority of the metropolitan center. The tsarist state's growing commitment to peasant resettlement in the 1890s added a new dimension to a long-standing polemic about the future of the steppe—could it become a new agricultural heartland for the Russian Empire, or was it better used as a hearth of animal husbandry? The answer to this question, as well as to the new question of the role Russian settlers would play in the steppe's transformation, was not self-evident. Differing perceptions of the steppe environment, its potential, and human adaptability to it fueled competing arguments about the steppe's agricultural or pastoral future. Although Russian and Kazak commentators alike could agree on the importance of "Russian science" in modernizing the steppe, in these debates, local knowledge and experience permitted the articulation of multiple arguments opposing and supporting sedentarization and colonization. The priorities of the tsarist state had not yet shifted so far as to foreclose this possibility.

Agriculture and Adaptation

The difficulty of governing a nomadic population, able to cross administrative borders, avoid taxation, and break the law with little fear of punishment, had long troubled tsarist administrators on the steppe.[99] Agriculture, moreover, stood unambiguously above pastoral nomadism on the hierarchy of stadial development, the prism through which many of them understood the world. Accordingly, for many administrators and Kazaks alike, the solution to Kazak backwardness lay in abandoning the pastoral nomadism that had been the dominant lifeway on the steppe for centuries. Kazaks could, it was argued, use Russian agronomy and the assistance of newly arrived settlers to ease their transition to agriculture. In so doing, they would live more secure and prosperous lives. In the abstract, this was an intrinsically satisfying argument. In practice, though, it depended on an idealized, and possibly untenable, conception of the steppe environment. Moving the agricultural transformation of the steppe from theory into practice required continual adaptation, and this, in turn, was a process in which knowledge moved from the bottom up every bit as much as from the top down.[100]

An obscure Russian commentator, M. Imshenetskii, devoted a long series of articles in the *KSG* early in 1891 to the material benefits that Kazaks could derive from agriculture. This was a means to social leveling, stability, and above all, personal wealth:

> Under the scepter of the Russian tsar live in Russia various peoples; among them there are many Muslims and peoples of other religions. All these people live mostly by cultivating the land, sowing various grains, such as wheat, oats, rye, millet, barley, buckwheat, peas, beans, poppies and etc. . . . If a plowman in Russia, whether Russian [*urus*] or Tatar, has two or three horses, two or three dairy cows, and ten sheep, and geese or ducks, he is considered a rich man, and he lives much better than our Kazak. His house is spacious, warm, light, he has a stove in the house. . . . The farmer's family lives warm, and full, and clean, and tidy. He is not only concerned about his existence and his family but also keeps livestock in the warmth, he is not afraid that his stock will die from ice or storms and stores up food for it for the whole winter.[101]

Here was a comprehensive solution to the various forms of backwardness that a variety of observers agreed plagued the Kazaks and their economy, if only they would learn to "use the natural wealth surrounding [them], given to [them] by God."[102] Spiritual uplift was also on the table: "agriculture refines [*oblagorazhivaet*] man and raises his intellect."[103] Imshenetskii's was the most detailed and sustained argument in favor of agriculture that appeared in the *KSG*. I quote from it at length here, though, because it neatly boils down the broader editorial line of the paper, and the benefits that its contributors thought would accrue to Kazaks if only they ceased their troublesome wandering and began to sow.

Although some Kazak contributors to the *KSG* shared Imshenetskii's perspective on the material advantages of moving to agriculture, or at least adding it to the existing pastoralism, they discerned other potential advantages as well. In particular, sowing grain recommended itself as a defense mechanism against the behavior of Russian settlers. Saudaqas Shormanov, whose observations of changes in the steppe's demographic landscape we have already seen, drew one inevitable conclusion from it: "Oh, my brothers! Would it not be better, from this point forward, to live as city people do, on places suited for it, than to be deprived now of our good quality places and remain with poor ones? Think while there is time."[104] Another Kazak correspondent lamented the seemingly endless cycle of debt and dispute into which the pastoralists around him entered, selling their land to Russians for cheap prices when poverty drove them to it at the end of a long winter, then trampling those lands en route to summer pasture. "It would be desirable," he concluded, "if these Kazaks, instead of selling their lands to the Russians, took up grain cultivation themselves."[105] Different visions of Russian settlers' cultural role on the steppe could be applied equally well to arguments in favor of sedentarization and agriculture, arguments which in all cases assumed some degree of imperial tutelage. Common ground lay in the fixity and stability that tilling the soil and caring for crops were seen to provide.

As restrictions on peasant resettlement were eased, and the railroad brought more agriculturalists from European Russia to the steppe and the provinces that surrounded it, settlers loomed, from the perspective of the *KSG*'s editorial board, as promising civilizers and logical agents of the steppe's agricultural transformation. The most programmatic statement of this argument appeared in 1896, when data about Kazak agriculturalists from nearby Turgai province was interpreted so as to attribute the lion's share of the transition to imitation of newly arrived Russian settlers:

> For the Kazaks to improve their lives, Russian influence is necessary, and it already exists. The Kazaks living near Russian settlements are beginning to live in the Russian style. In this respect, Russian settlers have a strong influence among the Kazaks. Settlers taught the Kazaks to build huts of light brick [*vozdushnogo kirpicha*], rather than of turf. . . . Now it is not a rarity to see a Kazak at a Russian mill, milling one or two sacks of wheat. One Cossack of the Burannaia station set up a water mill among Kazak settlements about 200 versts from Russian settlements, and the Kazaks now have their own flour and millet [*psheno*]. It is understandable that the Kazaks say a grateful "thank you" to this Cossack, because he saved them from difficult work at the mortar.[106]

Settlers offered superior tools and enjoyed a wealthier, more stable lifestyle than the average nomad, while their presence offered new economic opportunities. Small wonder, then, that the editors of the *KSG* claimed that the very sight of prosperous settler households was enough for enterprising nomads to "try to imitate them, and not without profit for themselves."[107] This was far from being a universally shared understanding of settlers, but for those commentators who could see the settlers of the 1890s as sources of cultural uplift, it was not just Russian science in the abstract sense, but science transformed into improved plows, seeds, and hay mowers (*senokosilki*) that would transform the steppe and its inhabitants economically.[108]

The very existence and success of settlers on the steppe, moreover, served as the best possible evidence that it was broadly suitable for agriculture. Though contributors to the *KSG* paid lip service, at times, to the idea that pastoral nomadism was a rational adaptation to life on dry grasslands, every successful attempt to farm created new evidence that the Siberian steppe did not consign its residents to eternal wandering: "The Kazaks populating the Steppe Governor-Generalship . . . occupied the best and most fertile steppes, which abundantly reward the farmer for his labor. Every year, from Russia there arrive thousands of settlers, who settle on the steppes, plow up the land, gather an abundant harvest, build log homes, and lead a full, fat [*sytuiu*] life."[109] The logical consistency of arguments in favor of agriculture depended on imagining the steppe environment to be more favorable for sowing grain than not. Steppes north of the city of Semipalatinsk were described as "very fertile in places," "possessing several of the rudiments of colonization."[110] More generally, proponents of agriculture enthused that "there is no greater wealth in the world than rich earth, heated by the warm rays of the sun," implying that the steppe did not lack for it.[111] Pastoral nomadism, meanwhile, was as likely a result of the vast spaces (*prostor*) Kazaks had occupied in an era of lower population pressure, prior to the conquest, as of natural conditions.[112] Kazaks had wandered the steppe aimlessly (so proponents of agriculture understood, or represented, the complexities of pastoral nobility) not because it made sense, but because no outside force had ever compelled them to do otherwise. Now, only laziness and ignorance prevented them from taking a step beneficial to the Russian Empire and themselves.

Even admissions that the steppe was not wholly promising for agriculture at present came to be laid at the nomads' feet. Whereas once, as even Kazak elders admitted, the steppe had been lush, wealthy, and idyllic, the situation had changed much for the worse, with scanty vegetation and insufficient surface water. The reason and the culprit were not far to seek: "Now it is not like this [*teper' ne to*]. The Kazaks, as true stock herders, destroyed almost all arboreal vegetation, and cruelly destroy what remains of it even now."[113] If human activity had ruined the steppe, then human activity could enliven it once more; unsuitable environmental conditions were not a priori evidence that the steppe could not be cultivated.

In fact, proponents of maintaining or adapting existing pastoralist praxis regularly mobilized the argument that the steppe environment was not propitious for agriculture. The extremely continental climate of the steppe held numerous dangers for grain and sparse cash crops: rapid changes from hot to cold generated killing frosts, while sparse or absent atmospheric precipitation, in bad years, caused crops to wither. Soil that could nourish fodder grasses lacked sufficient nutrients to support repeated harvests. Thus, although some enterprising Kazaks volunteered that they had taken good harvests even from bad land, it was necessary to respond to such arguments and adapt in areas where conditions seemed less favorable.[114]

Adaptations for the benefit of agriculture centered primarily on the endemic lack of moisture within the steppe. The solutions advanced ranged from the Promethean to the humble, but all depended on local expertise and local cooperation with state directives. The long-standing fixation on the role of forests in regulating climate in Russian thought meant that schemes to conserve the few existing trees on the steppe, and cultivate new ones, played an early and leading role.[115] In the very first year of the *KSG*, "preserving forests and cultivating them" led a lengthy list of measures that Kolpakovskii had taken for the agricultural development of the steppe region, a persistent concern in his more than two decades of service in Central Asia.[116] The same year, the official section of the newspaper reprinted a circular from Kolpakovskii explaining his reasoning behind such measures, undoubtedly restrictive from the perspective of a settler or Kazak in search of fuel or building material: "The climatic conditions of a country . . . stand in direct dependence on the quantity of forests which remain whole and unharmed [*utselivshikh*]. There appear droughts, want of rain, and severe winters, and the consequence of this are complete harvest failures and the complete unsuitability of the land for agricultural cultivation."[117] Kolpakovskii's good intentions proved no more practicable or successful than similar plans on the steppes of southern Russia. The other obvious method of increasing the amount of available moisture in areas receiving insufficient precipitation, artificial irrigation, had its proponents, but was also necessarily restricted in scope, for want of both the enormous capital resources needed for large-scale irrigation and, in many areas, rivers of sufficient volume and constancy.[118] What remained was to make better use of such moisture as did exist, or find ways to render the aridity of the steppe unproblematic.

As in the southern steppes of European Russia, prospective farmers searched long for drought-resistant or -tolerant crops in an effort to beat the always risky game of dry-farming. Several Kazak commentators in the *KSG*, like its editors, invested much hope in a varietal of spring wheat called *chul-bidai* (desert wheat), reputed to give a good harvest even during drought years.[119] In light of what it described as widespread Kazak interest, the editorial board offered to obtain seeds even as a comparable publication, *Turkestanskie vedomosti* (Turkestan gazette), suggested that this crop might not be a panacea for steppe agriculture.[120] Here, adaptation took the form of local interest in a varietal developed not in the metropole but a few hundred versts south, in the similar climes of Turkestan, and the success of the initiative would depend on Kazak farmers' willingness to sow it and skill in the fields. The *KSG*, in this instance, was no more than a mouthpiece and facilitator of what some Kazaks understood as local interests.

The other adaptation favored by the *KSG*'s editorial board was developed not in sophisticated metropolitan laboratories but by early agriculturalists on the steppe. These farmers were Cossacks living along the Irtysh line, long considered dubious farmers and "civilizers" at best, and the adaptation (attributed to a certain Ivan Iakovlevich Shestakov) was the *snezhnik*. Snezhniki stored up snow as it accumulated, protecting it from the action of the sun and wind (especially important on the flat, treeless steppe) and thus providing a source of extra moisture during the spring. After an initial descriptive article, the newspaper began to promote snezhniki actively: "Publishing Mr. Nesterov's article [about snezhniki], the editorial staff expresses hope that setting up snezhniki, known as yet almost exclusively in the Bel-agach steppe, will attract the attention of the Kazaks to this simple method of storing up water for summer. We hope that the invention of the Semipalatinsk Cossack, which made his native land the breadbasket of a vast region, will bring its share of good to other waterless areas, where the Kazaks would wish to apply their labor to a useful business [*poleznoe delo*]."[121] This support took on extraordinary measures for the time and place. Nesterov's instructional article was accompanied by several illustrations, an extremely rare step for the *KSG*.[122] Later in 1896, the editorial board offered to release a separate reprint of Nesterov's article to interested Kazaks free of charge, an offer it repeated in 1899.[123] The generally pro-agriculture newspaper thus staked much on the possibility of conjuring sufficient water on the steppe to make its dreams a reality. But despite the construction of Russian material superiority and the great store Russian and Kazak contributors alike set by metropolitan science, the adaptations on which it came to lean tended to derive from local experimentation and practice.[124]

Developing agricultural adaptations was both practically and rhetorically necessary. If simply sowing without taking local conditions into account failed, the material stakes were high, considering the instability many pro-agricultural observers saw in Kazak pastoralism and the very real dependence on agriculture felt by the poorest Kazaks (*zhataqs*, from the verb *zhatu*, to lie down), who lacked sufficient livestock to nomadize. More abstractly, on the success or failure of agriculture depended the authoritative claims of tsarist civilizers and pro-agriculture Kazak intellectuals, the notion that they had the right and duty to direct the economic future of the steppe, because they knew better.[125] If agriculture failed, the position of leadership to which they had appointed themselves would become unstable. They did not lack for competitors. A separate sort of scientistic argument, grounded equally, its proponents claimed, in knowledge of local conditions, dismissed large-scale agriculture as a realistic part of the steppe's future. As they imagined the steppe environment, a modified and perfected form of traditional pastoralism would better leverage the natural conditions around them. The economic future of the steppe depended on environmentally grounded arguments and adaptive practices.

Perfecting Pastoralism

The argument in favor of maintaining pastoralism as the dominant lifeway on the steppe attempted to refute the key points of the pro-agriculture argument, both disparaging the potential agents of change (Russian settlers) and offering a radically different assessment of the possibilities and limitations of the steppe biome. Still, it would be stretching the case to present this as a genuinely anti-imperial argument. It is perhaps a product of the source frame, or a reflection of the Kazak intelligentsia's quest for subjecthood and equal rights within the Russian Empire, that many arguments in favor of pastoralism emphasized that this use of the steppe would produce the greatest possible good for the empire as a whole.[126] What is less easily explained away is that advocates of pastoralism, in a variety of publications, indulged in the same rhetoric of pastoralist primitivism as did advocates of agriculture. This, in turn, left room for the same cocktail of metropolitan science and local adaptation as characterized the potential transition to agriculture. What emerges here, as in discussions of agriculture, is neither a heroic preservation of traditional lifeways in the face of an all-powerful imperial state, nor slavish submission to some sort of monolithic discourse of European science, but a different combination of local and metropolitan knowledges, legitimized by the Russian Empire's own self-representation as progressive and rational. "Russian science," in this particular social and administrative conjunction, could be made to serve a variety of outcomes.

Much the easiest argument for advocates of pastoralism to make was that the steppe was simply unsuited to large-scale grain sowing. After all, even proponents of agriculture admitted that many areas of the region had never been touched by the plow. Surely there were logical reasons for this, and therefore the lifestyle that had so long sustained Kazaks, providing many of the principles by which they ordered their lives, should not be so casually thrown away.

The first Kazak contributor to the *KSG* to make a clear and sustained argument in this line was the folklorist Mäshhur-Zhüsïp Köpeev (1857/1858 in some sources–1931).[127] Köpeev, described by one Soviet commentator as representative of the "moderate wing of clericalism," a contradictory figure vacillating between "rational" and "conservative, reactionary" attitudes, engaged in a nearly year-long polemic with pro-agriculture Kazaks.[128] In his opening salvo, he lamented the problems those around him had encountered as a result of abandoning stock-raising for agriculture. Listing a range of locations near his native Baian-aul (Pavlodar district, Semipalatinsk province) that he considered unsuitable for agriculture because of their stony soil and lack of water, he cautioned that moving unthinkingly to agriculture led only to "vain expenses and even threatened to cause disruptions to stock-raising."[129] Despite, he claimed, significant criticism from Kazaks who claimed his articles rang false, he pressed further a few weeks later, this time in a poem:

> The Kazak nomads have been stock herders
> Since ancient times
> All the wealth of the steppe people [stepniakov] is in their
>   pastures [v kocheviakh]
> For the life of nomads, stock raising is more expedient
> It is understandable that grain cultivation is also useful
> But unfortunately, among us, no one has gotten rich from it
> When I was at the Chu [River] . . .
> I more than once saw farmers
> Who wished ardently
> To live in our steppes (Sary-arka) . . .[130]

He was not, he concluded, an implacable opponent of agriculture—a potentially useful trade in the restricted areas where natural conditions permitted it. But stock raising, for nomadic Kazaks, remained more profitable and certain.

Many other Kazaks advanced such arguments in the *KSG*, with some rejecting the idea that agriculture was possible even more categorically than Köpeev had.[131] As a rule, moreover, the regional-studies publications of Semipalatinsk province tended to support this line of argument. Konshin, far and away the most productive contributor to the *PKSO*, led its first issue with a meditation on Kazak sedentarization that framed such a change as a matter of the distant future, in part because "the soil and climactic conditions of the province compel one to think that a significant part of Semipalatinsk province will, for a long time yet, be outside the area of agriculture."[132] He would make similar claims while observing small-scale Kazak irrigation works during his travels around Ust-Kamenogorsk district, published two years later, stating flatly that "There is no river, however suitable, from which canals have not been drawn. Without these agriculture on the Zaisan loess plain is unthinkable."[133] Another, anonymous contributor (X.) the same year made an argument that strongly paralleled Köpeev's—agriculture was developing, but only in very restricted areas, and could not immediately be pushed forward elsewhere.[134] Konshin, despite his radical politics, was something less than a cultural relativist. His travel notes drip with a sense of superiority to the nomads (or "wild men," *dikari*, in his words) among whom he moved, feeling distinctly uncomfortable all the while.[135] But to him and others, the steppe seemed objectively unpromising as a grain-growing region.

Left at this point, this might have seemed a bleak and hopeless picture, something out of an early travelogue or captivity narrative. If the steppe could not be made productive by agriculture, and was currently an arena of poverty and stagnant backwardness, then what exactly was it good for? Proponents of pastoralism thus went further in presenting the steppe as a uniquely favorable environment for raising large numbers of valuable animals, if only a few changes were made. The very first edition of the *Zapiski* of the new Semipalatinsk subdivision of IRGO, published in 1903, held a lengthy article by a little-known figure, B. Benkevich, who took the arguments of Konshin and X. to their logical conclusion: "The reasons for [the predominance of nomadism] consist not in some sort of addictions and sympathies of the Kazakhs, in their severe laziness, etc.; it is only a direct adaptation to the characteristics of climate, soil, vegetation, and irrigation of the steppes, the nature of which was so formed that animal husbandry and nomadism ... supply the population better or more reliably than anything else and give the possibility to successfully exploit the vast areas on which the development of agriculture would never be thinkable."[136] As so many other commentators had noted, surface water was scarce, and vegetation neither diverse nor abundant—expecting agriculture in all but extremely isolated areas was madness.[137] These steppes were not useless wastes, nor their inhabitants lazy brutes. Kazaks had seen that their environment offered tremendous possibilities for a different sort of lifeway, and, Benkevich argued, they had acted accordingly. All that was needed to see this was to stop looking at the region through the lens of sedentary agriculture.

Such a change of perspective, he noted, would also have significant profits for the empire, both in internal consumption and exports: "In Argentina animal husbandry, owing to the abundance of good places, flourishes and enriches the population. Why could the Kazak steppes not remain an animal-rearing area par excellence? Not speaking of the export of meat, it is enough to say that Russia itself needs cheap meat more and more, which it is better to have at home than import from overseas."[138] Accomplishing this undoubtedly useful feat, though, would necessitate some significant changes. Both Konshin and Benkevich believed that the roots of Kazak impoverishment lay in specific actions taken and not taken by local governors and the ministries of St. Petersburg. Benkevich, in particular, laid out a ten-step program for improving Kazak pastoralism, the vast majority of which (opening model farms, improving the availability of stud animals, etc.) demanded new investments of money, human resources, and time from the tsarist state.[139] But his first point leaps off the page by asking for a halt to an existing policy: "Significant restriction of colonization, so as to preserve pastures for animal husbandry."[140]

Criticism of peasant resettlement struck at what was, increasingly, a ministerial priority (though one not always equally shared by local administrators), and destabilized a linchpin of the pro-agriculture argument. Those settlers who appeared on the steppe were in the minds of pastoralism's advocates at best unhelpful, at worst actively harmful to Kazaks' economic interests. Settlers farmed alleged surpluses of land that, in practice, did not exist, restricting the amount of pasture available and constraining animals' freedom to graze, and Kazaks' to migrate seasonally along traditional routes.[141] Arriving to the steppe inexorably, settlers constrained nomads, pushing them off their best lands (the most productive for both agriculture and pastoralism) and into areas where life was genuinely difficult.[142] Cossack families who had sometimes established themselves over several generations derived much of their income from an exploitative relationship with the surrounding Kazaks, renting necessary lands to them and trapping them in a cycle of chronic debt.[143] And the new arrivals, rather than being prosperous and capable civilizers, were in a weak condition themselves, too busy struggling for survival to focus on any concerns other than their immediate material needs.[144] In short, settler colonization, even before its peak, in this reading both failed to deliver what it promised and militated against the coming of an equally useful, more promising future based on intensified stock raising.[145]

In the idea of intensifying and improving nomadic stock raising lay a degree of commonality with the pro-agriculture argument, a similar sense that Kazak "wandering" was seriously flawed. The KSG, despite its pro-agriculture line, also positioned itself as a space where Kazaks and Russians could discuss measures for the betterment of stock raising. In this, perhaps, can be seen the influence of the long-serving governor of Akmolinsk province, Nikolai Ivanovich Sannikov, strongly interested in the development of Kazak animal husbandry.[146] The regional-studies publications, less dialogic in format (though their authors presented themselves as intimately familiar with Kazak life, and Russophone Kazaks contributed to them), simply declared what they felt to be most necessary. The ideas they developed had significant overlap with those appearing in the KSG.

The focus of all "improving" proposals for nomadic life were based on the idea of storing hay for winter, rather than putting animals to pasture year-round (*tebenevka*). This would, it was hoped, mean stronger, healthier animals, far less susceptible to acts of God. After the severe zhŭt of 1891–92, in Turgai province (outside the Steppe Governor-Generalship), matters went as far as discussions of obligatory hay storage, at which both Kazaks and tsarist officials were presence; the *KSG* eagerly reported on the proceedings.[147] As statistical data accumulated by the late 1890s, seemingly indisputable numerical data seemed to confirm what critics of traditional pastoralism had long argued on the basis of their impressions during moments of crisis: Kazaks simply did not store enough hay for the amount of livestock they maintained.[148] Remedies emerged throughout the 1890s. Actively sowing fodder grasses, "as Russian farmers [*sel'skie khoziaeva*] do," would render more hay meadows productive, making the scarcity of fodder grasses no longer an excuse not to mow.[149] To mow the acres of hay needed to feed even a modest herd of livestock, by hand, would have demanded a massive expenditure of labor. Enter the *senokosilka*, a hay mowing machine which the *KSG* urged Kazaks to purchase, and which Benkevich urged local institutions to make available on easy, discounted terms.[150] With labor-saving technology becoming better available, and the land not inherently unsuited for it, the only possible remaining reason for Kazaks' failure to store hay, in this view, was their inherent carelessness.[151] That it was necessary to improve in this respect was a point on which proponents of pastoralism and agriculture alike could agree.[152]

The basic problem of keeping animals alive extended to questions of medicine and hygiene, as well. Correspondents to the *KSG*, alongside mass dyings from pasturage failure, were concerned that large numbers of animals were carried off by infectious diseases like rinderpest and hoof-and-mouth (*ia-shchur*).[153] Potential solutions ranged from mass education about the causes and treatments of particularly harmful diseases (paradigmatic for the *KSG*), to the introduction of special veterinary inspectors, to restricting the movement of animals to market or killing sick ones.[154] The *KSG*'s editors described the work of these veterinary inspectors as both a constant struggle against nomadic ignorance and surprisingly effective: "The nomadic population made peace with these demands [of veterinary inspectors] with difficulty. Striving to conceal the illness that appeared, so as to use the skin and meat of sick animals, they did not understand what great harm they brought themselves, their society and state. . . . We will think that the nomads and trading people are now conscious of the benefit of the measures established by the government and will not oppose, but just the opposite will help to terminate illnesses quickly, if such should appear again."[155] By introducing nomads unaware of the germ theory of disease to the harmful consequences of their behaviors, spreading fatal illnesses around the steppe, veterinary inspectors gave them a rough-and-ready understanding of the latest findings of European science.

To simply keep livestock alive was a modest, and perhaps not very exciting, goal, but tsarist observers who favored pastoralism also saw definite means to "improve" steppe livestock, in the sense of making it more saleable.[156] Descriptions of how Russian stock keepers carefully selected animals to replenish their flocks featured as early as the first year of the *KSG*—the message being, sotto voce, that Kazaks ought to consider it as well, as they were considered careless in this regard.[157] Other commentators groused that Kazaks continued to ruin the genetic weaklings in their herds once they were alive, "always liv[ing] in the moment" and taking too much milk from new mothers to fill their own bellies, harming the development of foals.[158] A Kazak, Raqïmzhan Duisembaev, calculated that it was impossible for Kazaks to make a profit from traditional stock raising, adding to the usual complaints criticism of methods of horse training that saw horses being ridden too young and too far.[159] By changing long-standing practices that had been relevant in the open steppe, Kazaks could maintain the relevance of pastoralism in changed political circumstances.

Most of these were put forward, in the *KSG* and regional-studies publications, as scientifically (or scientistically) verified measures that were certain to make an economy that was a relic of another age prosperous and useful to the empire. (Seemingly useful Kazak home remedies also occasionally found their way into print.)[160] Many, moreover, assumed significant losses of pastoral mobility, whether in returning to hay fields in time to mow or in riding young animals later, for shorter distances. Working against the spread of epizootic disease meant stricter control of migration over fairly arbitrary administrative borders. If more milk was to be given to young animals, rather than consumed by Kazaks in the form of koumiss, *airan* (a thin, yogurt-like beverage), or *qïrt* (a hard, dried cheese), the calories those staple foods provided would need to be replaced somehow, either with crops grown by Kazaks themselves or purchased from nearby merchants and farmers.

Ultimately, despite the opportunities for dialogue and the relative weakness, at times, of metropolitan knowledge, this dominant lens would prove the most significant fact of the collaboration among administrators, exiles of dubious reliability, and Kazak intellectuals on the Siberian steppe. There was no voice in favor of simply leaving Kazaks as they had been before; the fact of conquest, the steppe's incorporation into the Russian Empire, and that empire's European and global aspirations meant that this was no longer a possibility. The common consensus that Kazaks needed improvement, and improvement from without, prepared the intellectual ground for still-greater intensification of resettlement policy in later years. It was this policy that would ultimately see Kazak intellectuals go their own way.

*   *   *

Spaces of interethnic dialogue and exchange close easily when confronted with the exigencies of ethnic nationalism (expressed above all, in the steppe provinces, by colonization) and new conceptions of the national, or imperial, interest. This was the case on the entire Kazak steppe, by 1917; in 1902, we can see the first hints of that process.

Reading the *KSG* in 1901 and 1902 gives the sense of a newspaper that was slowly dying for lack of patronage. Increasing amounts of space were filled with repetitive announcements, seemingly to stretch the paper to its already thin four pages,[161] and articles from correspondents on seemingly innocuous themes were regularly rejected, a rarity before 1900.[162] The most likely cause of this shift was Taube's removal as Steppe governor-general in July 1900, as the *KSG* had flourished under him. When he was replaced by Nikolai Nikolaevich Sukhotin (1847–1918) the following year, the writing may already have been on the wall. When the editors of the *KSG* announced early in 1902 that it was to be converted to a bilingual publication devoted exclusively to agricultural issues (and thus, of much greater interest to settlers), *Sel'skokhoziaistvennyi listok* (Agricultural leaflet), this confirmed what had already been happening.[163]

Abai would pass away two years after the closure of the *KSG*, in 1904, and was immediately read by his contemporaries in Semipalatinsk province as the human avatar of the possibilities of collaboration between Russians and Kazaks. Like Altynsarin and Valikhanov before him, the multiple narratives constructed about his life in the century that followed have acquired as much historical significance as the actions of the man himself.[164]

The period between the closure of the *KSG* and the Revolution of 1905 is, as Tomohiko Uyama notes, "a 'missing link' in the history of Kazakh intellectuals."[165] We can see only tempting hints at it through what is known of the biographies of certain prominent actors and the telegrams and petitions that Kazaks gave during that tumultuous year. These, in turn, reflect a developing sense of autonomism, asking for the restriction of peasant resettlement and further rights for the Kazak language. They also, however, reflect a desire for rights within the empire and a disruption of the sedentarism-agriculture-civilization triad that tsarist and Kazak "civilizers" had so insisted on: "True—we do animal husbandry and the interests of this economy compel us to migrate . . . [but] why does animal husbandry deprive the Kazaks of electoral rights?"[166] The common ground between Kazak thinkers and the tsarist state had not yet completely disappeared, nor had Kazaks' willingness to interact with their key interlocutors on the latter's terms.

This would also prove to be the case with respect to the core issue Kazak intellectuals confronted during the last 20 years of tsarist rule, peasant resettlement.

This program was carried out in highly positivist, scientistic terms, and in this sense dovetailed nicely with the "scenario of power" presented in the *KSG* and other civilizing publications. In this sense, as in the application of objectively verified scientific findings to modernize the steppe, some Russophone Kazaks believed that this was another tsarist institution that they could work with. The next chapter shows that while at the outset they were not entirely wrong to do so, such collaboration ultimately became impossible. Within the first decade of the 1900s, the tsarist state developed a system of knowledge about the steppe that supported resettlement on an unprecedented scale and resisted any attempt to question it.

NORMING THE STEPPE

Statistical Knowledge and Tsarist
Resettlement, 1896–1917

As the tsarist state began, however hesitantly, to endorse a policy of peasant resettlement to the steppe, advocates and opponents of colonization alike sounded a note of caution. This was a caution rooted not only in fears of the unpredictable problems peasant mobility might bring about. Rather, there was real doubt about the suitability of large swaths of the steppe for agriculture, and questions also remained about how much land Kazak nomads might require for their own subsistence. In 1869, after the Steppe Commission had completed its work, Minister of Internal Affairs A. E. Timashev continued to rebuff local advocates of colonization on the grounds that "the steppe lands [have] not been made known . . . neither in terms of their quality nor of their quantity."[1] Outside of official circles, more than a decade later, questions were raised about the possibility of colonization without substantively harming Kazaks; these turned on the point that there had never been a detailed study of Kazaks' economy, no survey of lands suitable for colonization, and thus there could be no informed assessment of the impact resettlement would have on the Kazaks.[2]

When the Steppe Statute of 1891 introduced a provision allowing surplus Kazak lands (*izlishki*) to be seized for other state needs, questions about the quality and quantity of steppe land became a matter of critical state importance. When the tsarist state granted itself the right to seize surpluses, it created the legal basis on which colonization could proceed, insofar as it could be framed as a state need. But actually conducting such seizures depended on defining certain lands as surplus. This, in turn, would require attentive study of how much land

Kazaks actually needed, how much total land was available on the steppe, and of what quality. It was a daunting task, one ideally suited to what Willard Sunderland has referred to as the era of "correct colonization," orderly, scientized, and systematic.[3]

Accordingly, during the roughly 20 years (1896–1917) that comprise the resettlement era on the Kazak steppe, the tsarist state dispatched a series of costly statistical expeditions to clarify the existence of land surpluses in the region. Their progenitor, the 1896–1903 study of F. A. Shcherbina, was followed by more detailed studies of individual provinces. Shcherbina's expedition and its successors were tasked with completing an unprecedentedly thorough economic survey of the steppe provinces, supplemented by as much environmental research as possible. The end result of such studies, for each region in which they worked, was to be a norm for the amount of steppe land an average family of Kazak pastoralists required for its subsistence. This norm could then be multiplied by the total number of households in a region, and the resulting figure subtracted from the total amount of land in the region, to give the total amount of "surplus" land available for peasant resettlement without, according to the state's rhetoric, unduly constraining pastoralists.

Land norms calculated on the basis of field research satisfied many of the parties whose interests were involved in the settlement of the steppe. What better way to address doubts about the viability of colonization than with rigorous empirical study? The system of norms, in this sense, was self-justifying; norms were contrasted against the condition of relative ignorance that had come before and, representing an improvement on that condition, excluded other ways of knowing the land. Statistical expeditions, moreover, satisfied many of Kazak intermediaries' expectations. They were scientifically verified, regulated, and in principle made an effort to reckon with local particularities. Norms, moreover, were administratively easy to use. They were to act as Latourian "black boxes" in both senses of the term, bringing together diverse research elements and reducing them to one important and readily applicable piece of data.[4] Once calculated, administrators could simply take them as a given until new ones were derived. The project of creating empirically verified, expert-calculated norms of Kazak land use provided the framework, in theory, for a highly informed, nonexploitative, and mathematically perfect agricultural colonization of the steppe.

Yet these shifting norms were more political than their proponents ever publicly acknowledged. As the Russian Empire moved, in the early twentieth century, from hesitant endorsement to enthusiastic promotion of resettlement on the steppe, later statistical studies inexorably lowered the norms, freeing up more land for settlers. The rhetoric of correct, managed colonization remained intact even as ever more aggressive calculations threatened the interests of the local nomadic population. The seeming precision of the norms was sufficient to ward off serious challenges to them, based on other epistemologies, other conceptions of what it would mean to know the steppe thoroughly. Neither arguments against the norms, nor attempts to revise them, could dispense with the idea that economic and environmental knowledge, of one sort or another, was the best and most appropriate tool to manage colonization. The norms had both the appearance of dispassionate, quantitative thoroughness and, particularly from 1906 on, substantial institutional backing.[5] Thus they endured long after it became clear that statistical knowledge, converted into norms, served administrative convenience and resettlement far more than it protected local interests.

First Steps: Toward the Shcherbina Expedition

The drive to regulate peasant settlement on the steppe was, in part, the recognition of a fait accompli. Regardless of the state's sanction, thousands of irregular migrants had streamed into Siberia and the steppe, especially after the drought and famine of 1891–1892.[6] But it is likely that the tsarist state would not have acquiesced to settlers' willful behavior so easily if settlement had not also been well aligned with new political and economic goals. Indeed, expanding and promoting resettlement, rather than simply making peace with the deeds of irregular settlers, was much in accordance with two of the signal traits of the late Russian Empire—the broad shift to integrative, Russifying policies that characterized the reigns of both Alexander III and Nicholas II and the push for economic modernization that typified the decade-long tenure of Sergei Iul'evich Witte as minister of finance. Slavic peasants, in the most positive reading, were understood to carry out a civilizing mission and increase the economic productivity of the steppe, while also exerting a positive cultural influence on the pastoralists who lived there; the presence of a large Slavic population close to the all-too-permeable frontier with China also promised, for some, greater military security.[7] Achieving these desirable outcomes, though, demanded regulation in the form of laws, institutions, and knowledge.[8]

In the spring of 1895, some of the Russian Empire's brightest statistical minds met under the auspices of the Siberian Railroad Committee and the Ministry of Agriculture to discuss the form that knowledge useful to the cause of resettlement would take. They concluded that, to correctly decide the matter of the possibility of populating the steppe provinces with peasant settlers, "It is necessary, first of all, to define first which of the lands which are part of the steppe provinces cannot be used otherwise than by means of nomadic stock raising, and second, what kinds of land precisely, and of what size, are necessary so as to guarantee the nomads the possibility to keep their livestock year-round . . . only a correct decision on these questions can give, therefore, a solid foundation to ascertain the size and location of sections which can be confiscated from Kazaks' use without impoverishing them."[9] Such an approach would secure the rights of Kazak nomads under the Steppe Statute, keep them useful to the empire—since their nomadism extracted value from scrubland in a way that Russian peasants never could—and regulate state and peasant behavior. An initial, expansive plan called for three years of environmental and economic study of the steppe provinces, including the oases of Semirech'e, for the princely sum of 229,800 rubles.[10] The program that emerged, with less formal environmental study and an emphasis on economic research, still cost 29,000 rubles annually, a substantial commitment, in which the idea of land norms figured from the very earliest stages.[11]

In turning to a costly, long-term statistical expedition to regulate peasant colonization, the men of the 1895 commission were acting at the nexus of attitudes and intellectual trends within and outside of the Russian Empire. The idea of establishing a norm of land sufficient for a household's survival, and of expropriating surplus land above that norm to other purposes, dated to the 1860s, and initially pertained to the problem of allocating land to recently emancipated peasants.[12] The statistical work of local self-government organizations (zemstvos), moreover, was fundamentally connected to the detailed study of the consumption patterns and land use of rural people.[13] A prominent member of the 1895 commission, Aleksandr Arkad'evich Kaufman, produced studies of settler communities in western Siberia that were heavily premised on the idea that empirical statistical knowledge of the land and inhabitants of the Russian Empire, in the proper hands, would result in objectively superior policies; much the same can be said of the later work of Witte's Special Conference on the Needs of Agriculture.[14] After 1905, with the Resettlement Administration moved to the control of the interventionist Main Administration of Land Management and Agriculture (GUZiZ), land norms were at the center of what the historian Peter Holquist has described as this organization's "technocratic ethos," the idea that complete information could foster the maximally efficient use of land and human capital throughout the empire.[15] The Expedition for Research of the Steppe Provinces, the main fruit of the meetings of 1895, was thus one particular manifestation of a broader drive to quantify and regulate the land and people of the Russian Empire.[16]

The idea of norming the steppe, moreover, of using statistics to organize settlement and regulate the movement of settlers and steppe pastoralists alike, was part of a global set of best practices for colonization at the turn of the twentieth century. The Resettlement Administration in particular was heavily involved in the exchange of information and expertise with other colonial powers.[17] The sources of such information were myriad. Thick and scholarly journals described and extolled, on the basis of press reports and personal observation, resettlement practices from Canada to China, comparing them favorably with the disorganization purportedly endemic in Russian colonization.[18] The library of the Resettlement Administration held not only materials pertaining to the Russian borderlands but also the most current German and French works on internal and external colonization.[19] The specific manifestations of statistically informed approaches to purportedly rational, scientific colonization varied among and within empires. In German East Africa (consisting of present-day Burundi, Rwanda, and Tanzania), four times the amount of land presently cultivated by locals was set aside as "native reserve," legally ineligible for acquisition as crown land.[20] In the Maghreb (Algeria, Tunisia, and Morocco), the French created a range of "permanent [scientific] institutions to facilitate exploitation" of the territory, including peasant settlement, devoted to the training of land surveyors and meteorological and astronomical observation; these surveys facilitated the issuance of land titles to settlers without any protection for indigenous communal lands.[21] In the United States, the reservation system for indigenous people entailed expropriation and forced migration that few imperial Russian decision makers countenanced, but development schemes involving natives had a strongly quantitative bent; the Dawes Act of 1887, moreover, provided for the surveying of reservation lands, allotment of a fixed quantity of land for individuals, and expropriation of the remainder for settlers.[22] The rhetoric and broad mission of the Expedition for Research of the Steppe Provinces and its successors were thus firmly ensconced on a global spectrum of positivist, scientist ways of thinking about and managing colonization.

Still, both the institutional and political settings in which the expedition and its successors took place were unique to the Russian Empire. In particular, the state of the statistical art in Russia emerged from a context, the zemstvos, which had a long and fraught relationship with other organs of the tsarist state. Thus the interests and priorities of tsarist statisticians were not perfectly aligned with advocates of colonization in St. Petersburg. Quantification held the potential to regulate both a population and a state whose officials, especially at the provincial and district levels, were frequently derided as acting in an "arbitrary" fashion.[23] Numbers, as part of broader narratives about land use, development, and the natural environment, had a politics of their own even as they gave the appearance of indisputable certainty.[24]

The Shcherbina Expedition: Paternalism or Technocracy?

Early in the planning process of the Expedition for Research of the Steppe Provinces, its planners focused on recruiting Fedor Andreevich Shcherbina, son of a Kuban Cossack priest, to conduct the research.[25] It was, on the face of things, a logical choice. During his years working with the zemstvo of Voronezh province, in southwestern Russia, Shcherbina had pioneered the "budget" method of studying the peasant economy, focusing on the financial intakes and outlays of individual households in minute detail to understand their requirements in food and land and their position in the local economy.[26] Such practical experience and demonstrated expertise had prepared him well to perform analogous tasks on the Kazak steppe. The research techniques his expedition employed involved the compilation of budgets for a few Kazak households, the juxtaposition of these budgets against less precise mass data, and the computation of norms that erred on the more cautious side after this comparison.[27] The expedition was also of a piece with the fundamental idea of the budget method, that economic phenomena were best studied in correspondence with the specifics of local modes of production and social conditions.[28]

In another sense, though, Shcherbina was a highly unusual choice to manage an affair of significant state importance. In his youth, he was exiled for four years (1877–1880) to remote Vologda province for his involvement in Populist circles in Odessa.[29] Even after the term of his exile, he had only regained permission to travel to Moscow in 1891.[30] Later, as a member of the Kuban' Rada (assembly) during the Revolutions of 1917 and Russian Civil War, Shcherbina was involved with an institution that expressed views of Cossack and Ukrainian rights and privileges strikingly similar to those espoused for Kazaks by members of the Russophone Kazak intelligentsia. Two such Kazaks, Älikhan Bökeikhanov and Zhaqïp-Mirza Aqbaev, participated in Shcherbina's expedition.

Other participants in the expedition, though by no means all, were similarly (in the bureaucratic vernacular of the day) politically "unreliable." Timofei Ivanovich Sedel'nikov, a statistician working under Shcherbina, would later be expelled from state service for his public opposition to resettlement on the steppe.[31] Lev Karlovich Chermak, working as manager of research in Shcherbina's absence, was under secret (*neglasnyi*) police observation while the expedition carried out its work. In 1903 he and several other several other members of the expedition were briefly arrested for possession of antigovernmental literature; this in turn led to the dispersal of the expedition's Omsk bureau and its removal to St. Petersburg for further development of its statistics.[32] All of this is to suggest that there were multiple ways of thinking about imperialism, land use, and group identity in the late Russian Empire, and among members of the Shcherbina Expedition in particular. Such difference and multiplicity lent ambivalence and uncertainty to its intended transformation of the steppe into settler colonial space.[33]

Shcherbina and his assistants were selected because they were experts on statistics, not on pastoralism or grasslands. Thus, before they set off to Omsk in May 1896, they conducted a thorough review of the available scholarship on the region.[34] The understandings of steppe life that permeate Shcherbina's later reports, further supported by personal observations, represent a view of the possibilities of resettlement every bit as mixed as that corpus of scholarship was.

On one hand, Peter Rottier is entirely correct to note that Shcherbina "saw a virtue in the sedentarization of the nomads," and a pro-resettlement narrative emerges clearly from the 13 volumes his expedition published.[35] The potted histories of each steppe district that Shcherbina wrote were evolutionary, even teleological, proceeding from a chaotic "epoch of raids and rough seizures by strong neighbors" before Russian suzerainty to the destruction of the old, feudal order of things under the Provisional Statute of 1868, representing a new period of life in the steppe provinces.[36] Overwhelmingly, Shcherbina ascribed positive values to this change, the last phase of which included the presence of Russian settlers. Such evolution, in turn, was complexly interwoven with perceived civilizational hierarchies. The notion of sedentarism's inevitable triumph went hand in hand with promoting it as a superior way of life; pastoral nomadism was doomed, Shcherbina and his co-editors agreed, because of a set of specific failings on its part with respect to sedentary agriculture. Drawing a stark picture of life among mobile and semisedentary pastoralists made the agricultural future seem more hopeful in comparison. The author of one appendix described the hygienic conditions of Kazak winter dwellings in terms lurid enough to justify classing their inhabitants as "half-wild men" (*polu-dikari*): "The linens are for the most part not washed and not changed; small children look like some kind of half-dressed ragamuffins; especially unpresentable is the clothing of the women: summer half-dresses or half-shirts, impossibly dirty."[37] Kazaks' economy, mostly based on animal husbandry, was depicted as similarly disordered and in need of improvement, producing scrawny stock unsuited to the demands of the market because of the nomads' near-axiomatic laziness and unwillingness to take anything more than their surroundings readily provided.[38] In contrast to this, Russian settlers brought useful technology to an apparently benighted region, permitting agriculture without irrigation, deeply plowed furrows, and security against inclement weather, as well as an exemplary work ethic.[39] In sum, as Shcherbina put it in his description of the settler heartland of Kustanai district, "[The settler] brings with him to the steppes culture, labor, knowledge, new forms of economy, and a wider stream of production."[40] Asked to find land for settlers, Shcherbina provided at the same time a strong argument for permitting them into the steppe provinces en masse.

Similarly gloomy rhetoric was characteristic of educated Russian observers hoping to modernize the peasantry of European Russia at the fin-de-siècle. The collected works of Witte's Special Conference on the Needs of Agriculture (in which Shcherbina himself participated for Voronezh province) are a catalogue of complaints about peasant primitivism, filth, and immorality.[41] However, it is important to draw a distinction between the dim views that modernizing administrators held of the Slavic peasantry and the stereotyped ideas concerning pastoralist life that characterized much of the Shcherbina Expedition's materials and their successors.[42] First, such descriptions were not identically negative. The same peasant who was drunk, shiftless, immoral, and hostile to change in Tambov province was still preferable, for advocates of resettlement, to the backwards nomads who populated the steppe. Shcherbina's juxtaposition of purported Slavic peasant and Kazak work ethics draws this into sharp focus. Settlers may not have been ideal colonizers but, for many, they won the comparison with the indigenous population of the steppe. Second, while it is true that negative perceptions of both groups, grounded in ethnographic and statistical research, played significant roles in efforts to "modernize" their lives from without, the nature of this transformation was drastically different in the steppe provinces. The recommendations ensuing from the Special Conference involved education, technology transfer, and changing forms of land use, as well as resettlement from land-poor areas; while these were also a part of the proposed transformation of the Kazak steppe, in the latter region they were inseparable from peasant colonization and a legal regime that enabled the estrangement of land from pastoralists in its service.[43] Narratives positing the inefficiency, immorality, and ignorance of rural people are common to states pursuing transformative agendas in the countryside.[44] Transformations come in all varieties, though. If peasant settlement on the steppe was part of the same impulse as empire-wide rural reform, its manifestation there was uniquely colonial.

At the same time, the Shcherbina Expedition's collective uncertainty about resettlement extended well beyond the grudging endorsement of Kazak pastoralism expressed in the initial planning meetings. The introduction to volume seven of the expedition's works neatly summarized its ambiguous relationship to settler colonization:

It is impossible to look at [the change in nomadic lifeways] either from the indifferent view of historical perspective, or from the narrowly economic viewpoint of the nomad. In the first case it would mean to sacrifice to a theoretical view the blood interests of the population, in the second to close our eyes to reality. . . . While the Kazak herder and his herd still exist, we must take all measures so as to not allow his age-old historically developed forms of economy to collapse at once, all of a sudden. This would be a true national tragedy.[45]

An alternative narrative emerged in the Shcherbina Expedition's materials to justify a cautious approach to the construction of norms. This narrative was based on two fundamental points. First, despite optimistic projections of the steppe's future under Russian colonization (views that the expedition's personnel mostly shared), the observable effects of colonization on individual Kazaks in the short term were destructive. Shcherbina and his co-authors argued that as a result of Russian settlement, in some areas, Kazak landlessness was becoming a serious problem, "the same thing as the absence of one's own field land for a farmer," and the arrival of settlers drove rental prices for land higher than Kazaks could pay.[46] In Pavlodar district, the expedition characterized settler colonization of the Irtysh River valley as a "still more unforgiving [*bezposhchadnyi*] enemy" of the Kazaks than the earlier establishment of Cossack pickets in the region, since this new class would be less likely to rent out lands they needed; in Omsk district some Kazaks were "already completely crowded out."[47] Though authorship within the Shcherbina Expedition's materials is frequently nebulous, it is difficult not to see the influence of the budding autonomist Bökeikhanov on such rhetoric, particularly because he is known to have contributed to the volume on Pavlodar district. Colonization might have had long-term benefits in the future, but only if pursued in a way that would not ruin the indigenous population of the steppe in the near term.

Second, because of the unique properties of the steppe biome, sedentary agriculture was not everywhere unambiguously superior to mobile pastoralism as a form of economic organization. Rather, according to this counternarrative, mobile pastoralism offered distinct advantages in the steppe milieu, and therefore needed to be preserved. This was true, for example, in the notoriously inhospitable wastes of southern Atbasar district: "[In the Hungry Steppe], perhaps, is expressed most brightly the quality of the Kazak nomad, knowing how to use the scantiest and most modest vegetation of the steppe, as in Atbasar district. The Kazak is the best and most desirable manager [*khoziain*] in the steppe semidesert."[48] Similarly, in some parts of Karkaralinsk district, agriculture was weakly developed as a result of unreliable precipitation and frequent frosts, but the region was "in fortunate conditions" with respect to winter pasturage of live-stock.[49] Settler colonization, then, did not lead to change in economic lifeways as straightforwardly as Shcherbina and his co-authors argued elsewhere in their materials, nor was it necessarily desirable that the entirety of the steppe provinces be devoted to cultivation. Although environmental study played a secondary role in the statisticians' activities, they grouped the land of individual districts roughly according to their soils, water supply, and vegetation. The inevitable conclusion of such study, as the initial planning meetings had suggested, was that pastoral-ism had a serious future even after peasant settlement.

The final product of such ambivalence about the steppe environment and the potential violation of Kazaks' lives resettlement entailed was land norms that were knowingly, and significantly, elevated. Shcherbina's caution mani-fested itself in erring on the more prosperous side in determining what con-stituted an "average" Kazak household (thus increasing the size of the average land allotment); classifying pasture land according to its quality (so that Kazaks would not be allotted an apparently sufficient, but factually useless, amount of land); and in raising norms of livestock and land above a figure Shcherbina already considered high.[50] Using average budget data from families consid-ered to be well-off, Shcherbina calculated that although 16 units of livestock (in translation to a horse, based on fodder consumption) would satisfy such a family, the norm should be raised to 24, a figure then considered in accor-dance with the productivity of pastures to determine a local land norm.[51] As a result of such caution, or even deliberate inflation, late in 1901, Shcherbina concluded a presentation to a group of statisticians skeptical of his methodol-ogy with a sense of "complete moral satisfaction." As he explained, "owing to the work of the expedition, there once and for all was laid a boundary for the seizure of land from Kazaks with little land and there were given such land norms as would completely secure the economic life of the nomad. With obser-vation in this form of the core interests of the local population the surpluses of land, suitable for colonizing goals, were real surpluses."[52] Shcherbina's norms left, in some cases, on bad pasture, more than 500 desiatinas (1,350 acres) of pastureland to a single Kazak household. Furthermore, the Ministry of Agri-culture and State Properties instituted, in the interest of caution, a 25 percent increase to any norm Shcherbina calculated, and Governor-General of the Steppe Baron Maksim Antonovich Taube instructed surveyors to seize from Kazaks not "the whole surplus of land counted, [but] part of it, about a third."[53] Both the results Shcherbina and his colleagues produced and the bureaucratic milieu in which they were put to use thus combined a technocratic emphasis on abstract quantification with a paternalistic, cautious attitude toward the use of their calculations.

It is impossible to come to a single conclusion about why Shcherbina's norms were so—outlandishly, according to some later observers—high. The products of a diverse authorial collective, they satisfied multiple sets of interests. For advocates of minority rights like Bökeikhanov, they were likely superior to imagined alternatives. Hesitant local governors saw a useful gradualism that would protect the lives of the nomads under their care, or, more cynically, ensure order and steady tax revenues.[54] Shcherbina himself, beyond his leftist and autonomist views, saw in them a temporary expedient that could win over local opposition to any sort of state interference in Kazak affairs—when the Kazak pastoral economy evolved as he expected it would, they could be reduced.[55] The Shcherbina norms, in short, were the product of a moment in the history of tsarist resettlement when regulation was a greater priority than mass colonization.

At the same time, Shcherbina's own materials made different, stronger truth claims. Previously, he claimed, the Steppe Governor-Generalship had belonged "to the ranks of borderlands little known and insufficiently studied with respect to economics. Printed sources about this area are very few in number; they contain information which is poor in mass and only somewhat systematized."[56] His own research, in contrast, was distinguished by sheer number of personnel it boasted (totaling 40 men at various ranks, divided into independent subgroups); by its careful choice of "intelligent" translators from the local Kazak population; and by its rigorous definition of land use as practiced, rather than as imagined by artificial administrative divisions (the canton and village).[57] Consequently, Shcherbina boasted, his expedition had managed to both definitively establish the actual forms of Kazak land use and derive a set of land norms that secured both the interests of the pastoralist population and "the possibility of properly established colonization in the region."[58]

Such competing claims about the nature of Shcherbina's research created, during and after its publication, a set of norms that was open to two contradictory interpretations. Shcherbina's norms were simultaneously based on unprecedentedly thorough and precise research and self-consciously incorrect. As the issue of peasant resettlement to the steppe provinces became more heavily politicized after 1900, both the "true" and "false" norms had an afterlife in the public sphere and administrative circles alike, as they served the purposes of advocates and opponents of resettlement.

Cracks in the Armor

Although Shcherbina asked for, and received, full control over statistical research on the steppe, he was not permitted to carry the work out without being accountable to the organizations that had sent him. Audits of his results by qualified experts called the truth claims of his research into question, but could not fully dispense with the idea of norming as an efficient and sufficiently accurate means of allotting steppe land.

A. A. Kaufman, the dean of tsarist statisticians in resettlement affairs and questions concerning the peasant commune, and a participant in the organizational meetings of 1895, was Shcherbina's first professional critic. During an audit of Shcherbina's work during the expedition's second summer of operations, 1897, Kaufman found much to criticize. Where Shcherbina saw advantages in the extensive participation of local Kazaks in the expedition, Kaufman saw an additional danger: "As to the registrars, such were, as it seems, exclusively Kazaks still in school [*uchashchiesia*], and the household interviews were done, therefore, directly in Kazak. In general this was very advantageous for the success of the work, but this circumstance had too its unfavorable side, that it deprived—at least to a certain degree—managers of parties and subparties of the possibility of looking out for the regularity and precision of asking questions which have first-rate importance in the matter of household registration."[59] The household surveys on which the expedition relied for its norms were thus subject to doubt, putting the entire enterprise on a shaky foundation, though Kaufman added the caveat that these data remained superior to any previously collected. He had graver doubts, however, about the methods the expedition had employed to divide the steppe into smaller and more coherent units of analysis. The borders among various communes (*obshchinno-aul'nye gruppy*, "commune-village groups," in the original) did not appear to be accurate when verified by lower-ranking officials of the Resettlement Administration; the "natural-historical groups" by which the expedition classified lands of different quality were, he argued, arbitrary and useless, since they did not correspond to the ways Kazak communities disposed of land.[60] Thus, while they appeared to ensure a high degree of accuracy, Shcherbina's figures in fact complicated the reallocation of land to the state colonizing fund in a way that benefitted neither Kazaks nor settlers.[61] Moreover, because of the hurried nature of the expedition's work, fundamental questions remained unanswered—where precisely were suitable sites for peasant settlement located, and which resources were they equipped with?[62]

None of these concerns, coming from such a prominent authority, could be brushed off lightly. At the same time, though, none of them destroyed the norm-and-surplus system of land allotment. Kaufman provided methodological critiques and hinted that Shcherbina's norms were unduly generous to the Kazaks, but all of his recommendations took the form of modifications to an already established, fundamentally desirable procedure. Kaufman argued, in short, for a more accurate and practical set of land norms, more attuned to the needs of peasant colonization, not for their abolition. Deeply concerned with administrative arbitrariness, but also firmly convinced of the precedence of settler interests over Kazaks' if the two came into conflict, Kaufman viewed the creation of revised norms as a means of securing both priorities.[63] His claim that overly high norms would slow and impede the formation of settler sections, though, hinted that the calm consensus around the idea of norming the steppe would not last forever.[64]

Kaufman's criticism prompted a further investigation of the Shcherbina Expedition's methods on the part of the Ministry of Agriculture, which sent a second auditor, E. A. Smirnov, to the steppe provinces in 1899.[65] Smirnov's report combined acknowledgment of Kaufman's fine-grained methodological critiques with a practical attitude toward the means and time that any statistical study realistically had at its disposal. He acknowledged certain of Kaufman's technical criticisms to be as accurate as they were impossible to correct.[66] Similarly, Smirnov dismissed as ultimately inconsequential Kaufman's major concerns with the way the expedition had divided the steppe into communes and natural-historical regions. Communes, he became convinced during his visit, actually existed in many cases, and while the natural-historical regions were indeed unnatural and unfounded, it was unlikely that the expedition "would really have done better" to use another approach.[67] At any rate, perfect precision was not necessary at this stage. The expedition's data were still better than any that had previously been available, and its task was only to give approximate indications, to indicate those lands whose status as surplus to Kazaks' use was beyond any doubt.[68] While this left open the possibility that, in the future, such approximations would no longer serve the empire's interests, it was in context an argument for moderation and caution in norming the steppe. The realities of undergovernance in the Russian borderlands necessitated a colonization that was mathematically *good*, rather than perfect, and awareness of this fact meant, for Smirnov, that some methodological imprecision was acceptable.[69] Better some regulation, in the end, than none at all.

At the same time, Smirnov fully accepted Kaufman's view that the lack of a set of locally specific norms for hay consumption by Kazak livestock constituted a serious deficiency in the expedition's work, attempted to calculate one himself, and urged that such calculations play a role in later statistical research.[70] This, like the critique advanced by Kaufman, was an argument against the specific activities of the Shcherbina Expedition that fell firmly within the disciplinary matrix of zemstvo statistics and "correct colonization."[71] It was, if anything, a call for greater attention to the particularities of the local, greater empirical rigor, and greater correspondence between statistical methods and observable human behavior. But recognition of the impossibility of realizing this vision with a single, hurried expedition led Smirnov to recommend larger margins of error in the implementation of norms by local resettlement parties.[72] Correct colonization was at this stage an ideal, rather than an absolute fact, and awareness of the uncertainty behind even good numbers militated against their uncritical application. Leaving the details to be filled in at a later time by land-allotment bureaucrats, though, while it offered the possibility to reckon more precisely with local conditions, also removed the brake on land seizure that the Shcherbina norms were meant to represent.[73]

Ultimately, many of the gravest concerns raised by the early practices of the Expedition for Research of the Steppe Provinces were quickly addressed. Topographers were drafted to reduce the uncertainty about the precise extent and area of commune groups and natural-historical regions, while a meeting with officers of the "provisional parties" (*vremennaia partiia*) responsible for measuring off land for settlers seems to have smoothed over some of the difficulties of implementing the expedition's recommendations.[74] Moreover, both Smirnov and Kaufman were willing to write off the initial mistakes Shcherbina's team made as results of their unfamiliarity with the local landscape—they were not likely to be repeated. The project thus moved forward without significant contestation, fine-tuned and better aligned with its seemingly contradictory goals of protecting Kazak interests and allotting land to settlers, but with the idea of norming the steppe as yet fundamentally unchallenged. But officially establishing that the Shcherbina norms were no more than a flawed estimate of actual patterns of land use would have unanticipated long-term consequences.

Only some years later would more fundamental criticism emerge. Its source was Sedel'nikov, a Cossack of the Orenburg Host trained as a surveyor (*zemlemer*) at Ufa who participated both in Shcherbina's expedition and in studies of the steppe province of Ural'sk (outside Shcherbina's purview) in 1904–1905. He deployed this experience to establish his expertise at the outset of a vicious attack, in 1905, on state-sponsored colonization in *Battle for Land on the Kazak Steppe*.[75]

Sedel'nikov did not go so far as to reject the colonization of the steppe in principle. In his mind the Kazak steppe was indeed, as stipulated in the Steppe Statute, state property.[76] Seizing land on the basis of this law was, though, a conditional proposition, and the appropriate conditions had not been observed. Specifically, he noted,

> According to the first article of the surveying [*mezhevykh*] laws, surveying has two fundamental goals: (1) "to make known the quantity of lands and specific types of land [*ugodii*], all in general, and in particular those belonging to the Treasury," and (2) "to support the tranquility of the owners by establishment of regular and undoubted borders of land ownership." Have the lands of the Kazak steppe been made known? Do those institutions, in whose hands has been until now all observation

of the land organization [*zemleustroistvo*] of the nomadic population know the quantity of land on the steppe?[77]

Sedel'nikov's answer to both of these questions was firmly in the negative. His entire critique of resettlement as practiced was based on the purported inconsistency and inaccuracy of the informational apparatus that supported it, especially of the Shcherbina norms, and the illegality of any seizures of land prior to completely securing the needs of the Kazak population not in theory, but in fact. By working with a "normal" household instead of accounting for all the diversity and dynamism of the Kazak economy, and by making further calculations on the basis of a livestock norm (for Kokshetau district) that everyone admitted was flawed, Shcherbina, Sedel'nikov argued, had built all of his land norms on sand—they were little better than a guess.[78] The imprecision of the norms combined with the inexperience, ignorance, and single-minded determination to set up settlers characteristic of provisional parties under the Resettlement Administration to systematically disadvantage Kazaks, depriving them of their best lands without recompense.[79] The only solution was to do what the government should have been doing since 1891: carry out a truly extensive and precise survey of steppe lands, which would, over time, put the Russian Empire on the one possible path to a just fulfillment of its colonization program.[80]

Sedel'nikov thus went much further than earlier statisticians critical of Shcherbina had been willing to go. The impulse that motivated him, however, was much the same—Shcherbina's norms did not even live up to the modest claims they made. The pace of colonization needed to be slowed; the hard and time-consuming work the law demanded prior to land redistribution actually needed to be done. This approach, rather than Shcherbina's, could give Kazaks the secure and sufficient land allotment to which they were entitled, while maintaining the steppe's status as state property, so that the "dark and ignorant mass of the steppe population" would remain protected from itself.[81] But as Sedel'nikov spoke, the politics of resettlement were in the midst of a fundamental change—one that made speed, rather than caution, the top priority.

New Priorities, New Paths

By 1904, a broad consensus had developed in St. Petersburg about the desirability and necessity of peasant resettlement to the steppe provinces and Siberia. For Witte, this had long been part of a larger program of economic modernization. But fearing agrarian disorders within the empire's core provinces, Witte's nemesis, Minister of Internal Affairs V. K. Plehve, also came to endorse mass resettlement; his ministry compiled several proposals to this end, examined at a special conference under Kulomzin early in 1904.[82] After the Revolution of 1905, the new prime minister, P. A. Stolypin, made mass peasant resettlement a state priority for reasons dear to Witte and the now-dead Plehve alike—as a means both of housing the surplus agrarian population of central Russia and of increasing the economic productivity of areas considered to be poorly used by the colonized population or simply vacant.[83] Stolypin thus lavished attention on the reformed Resettlement Administration, moved under the auspices of the highly technocratic GUZiZ from the less interventionist Ministry of Internal Affairs in 1905.[84] The Shcherbina norms were well-suited to a paternalist, limited program of resettlement, and the demands placed on them had been relatively limited. But by 1906, moving vastly more settlers to the steppe provinces than before had been presented as an economic (and, for the Stolypin government, political) necessity.

Clearly, the modernizing tsarist state needed a larger land fund, increasing the "colonizing capacity" (*emkost'*) of regions targeted for resettlement. There was more than one way to do this, but all of them involved rethinking the informational and legal basis on which resettlement had taken place until this time.

Chief among these, on the basis of existing procedures, was lowering such norms as already existed, creating a larger surplus from which to form settler sections. The original target for such reductions was Akmolinsk province. Akmolinsk was chosen for the same reason, when the Resettlement Administration organized repeat (*povtornoe*) research in 1907, as Shcherbina had started there in 1896—the rich humus, multiple rivers, and abundant forests of its northern half made it very attractive to Slavic settlers, who did not have to change their accustomed methods of farming to survive there. The man tapped to lead this research was V. K. Kuznetsov, an experienced zemstvo statistician and an established authority on questions of colonization inside and outside of Russia.[85] His mandate, though, and the results the Resettlement Administration expected him to deliver, differed enormously from what Shcherbina had been asked to do. Kuznetsov's paymasters billed the caution that had been a virtue a decade before as a fatal flaw:

> When the Shcherbina Expedition derived [its] land norms, it did not take the conditions of the Kazak agricultural economy into the calculation, nor did it develop hay-mowing norms for the Kazak nomadic economy. Further, it took an inflated figure for the average quantity of livestock belonging to a tent-household, in comparison with the amount of livestock found by the mass count and the budget data. . . . An addition to these norms, which were already very exaggerated . . . still further distances their size as calculated from what is really necessary, and definitively ruins the final conclusion with respect to statistics.

> Therefore, at present it is especially necessary to call for repeat research of Kokchetau district [in Akmolinsk province] with the goal of introducing greater precision to the question of land norms for the Kazak population, and bringing these norms into closer correspondence with the actual requirements of the Kazak population.[86]

Shcherbina's caution, and the further safeguards that both local and central administrators instituted in their awareness of the flaws of his data, provided ample basis for downward revisions. Kuznetsov's task, without carrying out any new environmental research, was to make those revisions. Since the Resettlement Administration assumed, with Shcherbina, that peasant resettlement drove the intensification of the Kazak economy, Kuznetsov could make corrections in that light as well—Kazak farmers needed less land than they had as nomads, and he would work accordingly.[87] There was more surplus land to be invented on the steppe, and Kuznetsov was the first of several statisticians asked to deliver it.

There was another, more permanent way of maximizing the productivity of steppe land that, under imperial eyes, lay useless under the unpredictable wanderings of feckless nomads. This was *zemleustroistvo*—the reorganization of land use, providing Kazaks with a fixed amount of land and freeing the rest up for settlers. The norm-and-surplus system left a standard amount of state land in nomads' long-term use; over time, the norms would be revised and the state, as owner of the steppe, would take more of its own land back, reallocating it to settlers. Zemleustroistvo, on the other hand, offered to sedentary or sedentarizing Kazaks a smaller amount of land on conditions of permanent use, bringing their land use to its possible minimum at a single stroke. The initiative to investigate the possibilities of zemleustroistvo came from Stolypin and the main administrator of land management and agriculture, Prince B. A. Vasil'chikov, at the end of 1906, not out of any interest in Kazak rights, but out of a hope to promote further economic intensification and create new space for settler sections: "The government, by presentation of boundless land areas [to nomads], should not artificially support their nomadic way of life at the expense of the landless Russian peasantry."[88] Moreover, officials within the Resettlement Administration claimed, Shcherbina's own data proved beyond doubt that Kazaks themselves profited from colonization; in this view (characteristic of the Stolypin era) the main problem Kazaks faced was insecurity of land use as a consequence of repeated seizures of "surpluses."[89] Thus, at the two ministers' mutual request, an interdepartmental meeting packed with officers from GUZiZ formed under the chairmanship of Deputy Minister of Internal Affairs A. I. Lykoshin during the spring of 1907 to discuss the terms under which such land reorganization might occur.[90]

Many positive signs pointed in the direction of transitioning to the zem-leustroistvo system. It was well aligned with high-level administrative priorities and supported by favorable economic data. Moreover, as Sedel'nikov had already pointed out, the norm-and-surplus system was on shaky legal ground at best; the Lykoshin conference found that "the law does not contain sufficiently definite provisions about the order in which lands should be acknowledged as surplus for the nomads. The consequence of this is that resettlement officers are accused of arbitrary behavior, which serves as the main subject of the Kazaks' numer-ous complaints."[91] But as much as they might have wanted to, the members of this conference could not overcome significant practical obstacles to bringing zemleustroistvo about. The majority of Kazaks remained maddeningly nomadic, using a broad range of small patches of land over the course of the year on the basis of usufruct rights; how could surveyors attach all these scraps of land to them in a logical, permanent way?[92] Still worse, even the results of the Shcher-bina Expedition—now accepted as modest and flawed—had been obtained at great expense. Qualified surveyors and statisticians were in short supply. Thus it was impossible to avoid the conclusion that "to place the zemleustroistvo of the Kazaks first in line would mean to delay the Russian colonization of the steppe provinces for many years," even as up to 60,000 settlers remained landless and more were arriving every month.[93] Norms would have to remain in force, with the understanding that the dated, overly generous Shcherbina norms would be gradually phased out as the Resettlement Administration carried out new research (like Kuznetsov's).[94] Over the following decade, zemleustroistvo of the Kazak population would be more frequently invoked as desirable than actually practiced.

One final method of increasing the Russian Empire's store of surplus, easily colonized lands remained: opening areas that had formerly been closed for reset-tlement. This particularly concerned Turkestan, where the governor-general, A. B. Vrevskii, had ordered a ban on peasant settlement in 1896, applied to Semirech'e on its return to the jurisdiction of the governor-generalship in 1898.[95] From the perspective of the generally paternalist military administrators to whom Turke-stan was entrusted, this made good sense. They held a low opinion of Slavic migrants, feared the disorders that a large influx of them might cause, and insisted that the economic interests of the local population (Kazaks, Kyrgyz, and seden-tary "Sarts") be recognized.[96] But from a colonizing perspective, the exclusion of Semirech'e in particular was a grave error. Abundant in lush vegetation and fresh water, it was paradise in comparison to the arid steppes on which Russian settlers were forced to settle, and its huge expanses contained untold productive forces awaiting their proper exploitation.[97] This belief in Semirech'e's potential led to the lifting of the resettlement ban temporarily in 1905, and permanently in 1910, at the same time as thousands of irregular migrants flocked to a region rumored to be an "El Dorado [*zolotoe dno*]" for agriculture.[98] If setting up settlers on new land was an administrator's first priority, it was blindingly obvious that the use of Semirech'e had to be maximized.

Administrative politics, undergovernance, and the materiality of Semirech'e's environment, very different from the dry grasslands to the north of it, made this much trickier than anticipated. Between 1905 and 1909, Semirech'e was the venue for a serious crisis within the norm-and-surplus system of colonization. Land norms ultimately survived the highest-level challenge they ever received, but the Resettlement Administration was not wholly allowed to get its own way. En route to a compromise, the squabbling institutions involved lobbed competing perceptions of past and present research, imbued with competing understandings of the land and economy of Semirech'e, at one another.

The Crisis of the Norm-and-Surplus System: Semirech'e, 1905–1909

Once Semirech'e was opened for peasant settlement, it stood to reason that the norm-and-surplus system would be applied there as well. The system had worked well enough in other steppe provinces, and Semirech'e, unlike the rest of Turkestan, fell under the jurisdiction of the Steppe Statute. Thus there was a legal basis for the seizure of surplus lands against the norm there as well. But whereas the northern steppe provinces had undergone years of extravagantly funded statistical research before the largest wave of settlers hit them, useful data about the land and population of Semirech'e was sorely lacking. The exigencies of the situation required the construction of land norms without the informational background that usually supported them.

At the forefront of this effort was Sergei Nikolaevich Veletskii (1864–??), a native of Poltava province in east-central Ukraine and, like Shcherbina, an experienced zemstvo statistician, best known for publishing a lengthy reference work concerning the history and methodology of the discipline.[99] Beginning service in his home province, he subsequently (1896–1899) took up a position in Ufa province leading statistical research of its peasant population.[100] Moving thereafter to the steppe provinces, he worked there in the offices of the Resettlement Administration, and was involved in the local (Omsk) division of IRGO and Akmolinsk's provincial branch of the Witte Committee.[101] He was then appointed manager of the Semirech'e resettlement region shortly after the Revolution of 1905, replacing the politically suspect bureaucrat who had previously occupied the position.[102]

On his transfer to Semirech'e, Veletskii found himself in a difficult situation. His work in the steppe had been characterized by a degree of caution with respect to the local population; though he insisted on the necessity of Kazaks' transition to more intensive economic forms, he also was cognizant of the need to allot land to the local population before seizing surpluses.[103] But now, in complicated circumstances, he was flailing. In the event of conflict between settler and local interests, he was firmly on the side of the former. Colonization was opposed, he argued to Governor-General N. I. Grodekov, by people who placed the interests of the borderlands above those of the state as a whole, subscribing to the slogans "Turkestan for the Turkestanis," or "Semirech'e for its residents [*dlia semirekov*]," "whereas it, being a component part of Russia, should be primarily for the Russians [*russkie*]."[104] Whether out of ideology or a sense of professional obligation, Veletskii did what he felt he had to; he calculated actionable land norms at lightning speed, and of a size that would permit a large number of settlers to seize and settle on surplus lands.

Unable to take the years a thorough economic and environmental survey would have required, Veletskii cut corners. Since time was of the essence, he and his statistical assistant, Voronkov, restricted themselves, in only a few townships assumed to be representative, to a simplified method (*anketnoe issledovanie*) of establishing the needs of a normal and typical Kazak household.[105] Without qualified naturalists, or time to let them work, he relied on the work of the local statistical committee and publications by scholars like P. P. Semenov-Tian-Shanskii and I. V. Mushketov to establish the different natural-historical regions of the province—where pasture and soil were good, and where they were poor.[106] He was frank with his superiors about the constraints he worked under and their consequences; he was unable to make even the limited sort of truth claims Shcherbina and his colleagues did. The norms he presented in 1907 ranged from 40 to 82 desiatinas (108–222 acres), depending on the quality of the land—much lower than in the other steppe provinces owing to the shorter migrations and greater interest in agriculture of Semirech'e's nomads.[107] Still, there was one fundamental claim that pervaded all of the struggles Veletskii would participate in over the two years that followed. If he had erred, Veletskii claimed, it had been exclusively on the high side; the norms he presented were *maximal*, and would only be reduced as the land and people of Semirech'e were better known.[108] Thus there was no danger in immediately applying them to the formation of settler sections.

Veletskii's memoranda on these "maximal" norms, a century later, give the impression of protesting too much. But he had serious reasons for insisting on his authority and the basic applicability of his norms. Neither the district chiefs of Semirech'e province nor the powerful chancery of the Turkestan governor-general looked favorably on peasant resettlement, and by criticizing Veletskii and his work, they found what seemed to be an effective means of slowing it or stopping it altogether. Without the norms, the whole enterprise as conceived in 1907 would have to fail.

Such opposition to Veletskii took two forms. First, several district chiefs attempted to leverage their own long experience working in their counties to create their own norms; a Johnny-come-lately like Veletskii could not hope to know the land as well as they.[109] But Voronkov dealt with these amateurish attempts easily enough at meetings early in 1908.[110] Harder to dismiss were attempts, on the part of Grodekov's chancery officials, to deploy what I would term the "idea of norming" against the norms that Veletskii had actually calculated. The head of the chancery, Vladimir Andreevich Mustafin, attacked the epistemological basis of Veletskii's work directly. Semenov and Mushketov, he contended, whose work was so important to Veletskii's natural-historical regions, had not even been in Semirech'e for several decades, and organizing the mass colonization of the region was not among their scholarly tasks.[111] Rather, the Expedition for Research of the Steppe Provinces was an example of the seriousness, and caution, with which it was necessary to approach the problem: "If as the basis of work in defining norms it were possible to accept scientific research, reconnaissance and et cetera., then in the steppe region all this was done [i.e., before the expedition –I. C.], however the government found it necessary to command there the whole Shcherbina Expedition, costing millions of rubles and working for several years. What is more, it is impossible on the basis of such flimsy [*legkie*] data to determine the fate of the nomads of Semirech'e, which sharply differs from the steppe region."[112] Grodekov, on the basis of his chancery's recommendations, fretted that haste and bad information risked harming the Kazaks, and that the reduced norms Veletskii proposed amounted to forcing, rather than encouraging sedentarization.[113] Rather than accepting a norm that, *pace* Veletskii's claims, seemed low, he recommended that norms be artificially raised by 25 percent in accordance with a Ministry of Agriculture circular of 1901.[114] A series of meetings during the early months of 1908 does not seem to have changed his mind. Semirech'e's military governor lent further support to the application of the 25 percent addition to the norms, and while Grodekov grudgingly approved them, he imposed a set of onerous conditions for resettlement officers to fulfill and declared them temporary, applicable only to settlers already in the province.[115] All this was much to Veletskii's chagrin, as he believed that it prevented him from carrying out his service obligations. He therefore composed a series of increasingly strident memoranda to officials in Turkestan and St. Petersburg in opposition to what he viewed as local officials' obstructionism. Unfortunately for Veletskii, legally speaking, the governor-general remained the highest authority in Turkestan, directly entrusted with executing the will of the tsar; he would be a formidable obstacle to overcome.

So the matter stood in the spring of 1908. To cut this Gordian knot, significant changes were in the offing, all of which spoke to the favor the Resettlement Administration and its technocratic ethos enjoyed at the time. Grodekov, a military man with a long service record in Turkestan, resigned unexpectedly. In the historian Alexander Morrison's judgment, this surprise move was mostly the result of pressure from pro-colonization officials, who "forced [Grodekov] out."[116] But Grodekov's erstwhile replacement, P. I. Mishchenko, proved no more tractable on this score than Grodekov himself had been, and continued to protest strongly against mass resettlement at the nomads' expense.[117]

Still more significantly, in June 1908, largely in response to the conflict between military and resettlement authorities, Nicholas II ordered a senatorial inquest into Turkestan's affairs. Responsibility for the investigation fell to Count Konstantin Konstantinovich von der Pahlen (1861–1923), scion of an old and well-established family of Baltic German nobles. Officially, Pahlen was provided with a mandate to investigate the feasibility of extending civilian government to the region; in particular, "his principal brief was to remove the obstacles which an outdated military bureaucracy was placing in the way of increased Russian colonization in the region."[118] Though no statistician, as a trained lawyer and experienced manager of his family's gargantuan estate in Livland province (present-day Estonia and Latvia), he brought a firm commitment to legality and a certain degree of expertise in agricultural affairs (especially in stock raising) to the work.[119] Within two weeks of Nicholas's order to undertake the audit, Pahlen had assembled a cohort of young officials to aid his fact-finding mission and departed for Tashkent.[120]

Though the answers he was expected to provide were clear, Pahlen, at the end of a year's work, came to conclusions fundamentally opposed to those his paymasters desired, attacking the practice of colonization in the steppes of Semirech'e (and oasis areas of Turkestan) as well as the idea at its core—the calculation of land norms to render legal the seizure of lands from Kazak pastoralists.

Pahlen could not have been mistaken for an opponent of imperialism or colonization. The faintly Victorian echoes of his pointed statement of Russia's historic civilizing mission in Central Asia were well within the mainstream of his era: "To leave each to his own, to introduce the tribes of Turkestan to the circle of Christian cultured understandings and forms of life, to raise the wealth of the krai by raising its productive forces, to create of it a rich Russian colony and not a poor backwater [*derevnia*]—this is the only goal worthy of Russian power and corresponding both to the needs of the center and to local interests."[121] The thrust of his voluminous reports, as it concerned resettlement affairs, was simply that colonization as it had been practiced by Veletskii and other officials of the Resettlement Administration detracted from this goal, ruining the prestige of the Russian Empire among its less civilized subjects.

In three different regions—Semirech'e, formerly a part of the Steppe Governor-Generalship and dominated by Kazaks of the Great Horde; Turkestan proper, with an Uzbek and "Sart" population with a long tradition of irrigation-based agriculture; and Transcaspia (modern-day Turkmenistan), recently conquered and containing vast deserts—Pahlen uncovered administrative chaos and poverty. A year of research led him to a stinging conclusion: "Every ruble expended from the State Treasury to support resettlement as currently practiced goes not to the state's benefit but to the preparation, in the near future, of an agrarian crisis in the borderlands."[122] Some of the criticism in a report that Morrison argues, on the basis of earlier drafts stored in the central imperial archives, was toned down significantly, related to the practice of colonization as managed by corrupt officials and carried out by shiftless, rapacious settlers.[123] The irregular migrants, he argued (in comparison to earlier experiments of colonization, carried out by small groups of hand-picked peasants), arrived in the region with no resources and used the land badly; they were drunk, ridden with syphilis, and unwilling to work to better themselves.[124] As a result, "on the most fertile soil of Semirech'e, where, because of the diversity of natural conditions and with the wide spread of artificial irrigation, many branches of intensive economy could successfully flourish, the most extensive economy is done by Russian settlers, with preservation of all of those methods which led to such grievous consequences in European Russia."[125] Nor were the officials of the local filial of the Resettlement Administration to Pahlen's liking. Both corrupt and politically unreliable, he found, these men, particularly the infamous Veletskii, regularly undercompensated Kazaks for land seized from their use, lined their pockets with state funds allocated for resettlement, and made massive grants of land to city dwellers who never thought of cultivating it themselves.[126] All of this happened, he claimed, against the wishes, and despite the best efforts, of provincial governors and district chiefs. In all of this, Pahlen echoed the complaints of the old Turkestan hands whose opposition to colonization had motivated the audit to begin with. He had not been supposed, however, to take their side. But the corruption of resettlement bureaucrats and the mass estrangement of lands worked with success by the local population offended both his sense of justice (informed in equal measure by legal training and devout Lutheranism) and his pragmatic concern with the success of Russian imperialism in Central Asia.

If Pahlen had stopped here, it is very likely that his report would have been perceived as unthreatening, or at least not damning. The movement of peasants without permission, in one form or another, had been a concern for the Russian state as long as it had existed; for provincial administrators to treat their positions as sinecures was also less than novel. These were superficial phenomena, matters that could have been corrected by a vigorous house-cleaning or written off as inevitable hiccups in any large, state-driven undertaking. But Pahlen struck at the heart of colonization as the Resettlement Administration wished to practice it—at the norms. Curiously, though, his was not a fully fledged argument against the idea of rational [*planomernaia*] colonization but a sustained case that the veneer of objective truth with which norms were equipped concealed the fundamental *irrationality* that was at their core.[127] He mocked the pretensions of Veletskii and his subordinates in unthinkingly applying Shcherbina's system of norms to Semirech'e, without further local research and without any consideration of the economic and natural-historical differences between the lush foothills of this region and the grasslands of Semipalatinsk and Akmolinsk provinces.[128] The scanty reconnaissance data on which this decision was based, he argued, "[did] not merit any trust whatsoever"; the abstract use of norms, disconnected from reality, harmed both colonization (by protecting land suitable for agriculture for mobile pastoralism) and the local population (by violating its property rights to land it developed and depended on for its livelihood).[129] His disdain for the exercise came through most clearly in his memoirs, rather than the official report, in a much-cited passage:

> [Resettlement officials] would divide it [the land], split it up, give to each man toiling on the soil a parcel of land, in accordance with abstract formulae. On paper and in theory nothing could be simpler. These magic formulae were to be derived from statistical research which would show the exact number of acres needed by a "toiler" in any given district (smaller administrative units were considered unreliable as regards data) in order to be able to follow the latest scientific methods of husbandry with the means at his disposal. . . . The following reasoning was then applied. Here is a district belonging to the tsar: it contains X number of hectares and is inhabited by Y number of nomads. As each nomad is entitled to 30 hectares, the total amount of land due to them is Y multiplied by 30. Deduct that figure from the total acreage of the area and you have a balance N which should be handed over to the settlers.
>
> Q. E. D.[130]

The official report, though, was significantly more sanguine about the collection and application of statistical knowledge. Pahlen had some praise for statistical parties that had taken to their work conscientiously and well, although limited resources had prevented them from surveying large areas.[131] Moreover, he expressed a distinct preference for colonization of the sort the Shcherbina Expedition represented on the steppe, based on years of work by experienced budget statisticians, over the sketchy numbers calculated hurriedly [*na spekh*] by the Semirech'e branch of the Resettlement Administration.[132]

This surprisingly ambivalent attitude toward scientific colonization on the part of arguably the most famous opponent of land norms is borne out by a closer look at the argumentation Pahlen employed in his official report. Norms, he argued, said nothing about the characteristics of land in the state fund for colonization, rendering its rational use impossible.[133] As a result, the colonizing capacity of Semirech'e continued to be drastically overstated.[134] Pahlen thus constructed an argument against norms, so central to the Resettlement Administration's view of the colonial landscape, in the scientistic language of that very administration. Norms did not rationalize colonization, but concealed its irrationality. He deeply desired that colonization take place on the basis of detailed knowledge of local environments and conditions of land use. In practice, though, norms had become a dangerous shortcut whose poor construction and unthinking application benefitted no one but the bureaucrats who calculated them and passed them up the chain to St. Petersburg. To oppose them was, paradoxically, to stand on the side of scientific integrity and to defend the empire.

Pahlen and his retinue returned to St. Petersburg in the summer of 1909 and immediately set to drafting their report, a wide-ranging analysis treating resettlement affairs, education, and tax law among other topics, printed by an official publishing house the following year. What is striking and telling about all of this, though, is what did *not* happen next. Famously, the reports of the Pahlen Commission, published in 18 thick volumes with appendixes, were left to gather dust. Pahlen's recommendations with respect to administrative reform were received negatively at a conference devoted to revising the legal codes for Turkestan in 1911.[135] Aleksandr Vasil'evich Krivoshein (1857–1921), the newly-appointed head of GUZiZ, simply ignored the criticisms contained in Pahlen's report on settler affairs, while his successor as head of the Resettlement Administration, Grigorii Viacheslavovich Glinka (1862–1934), passionately rejected criticism of his organization on the floor of the Duma based on the Pahlen report.[136] The obstructionist (from Krivoshein's point of view) Mishchenko found himself replaced after barely a year by a new governor-general, A. V. Samsonov, who would act as "the compliant executor of Russian national interests" in Turkestan until his death during World War I.[137]

Yet if the Pahlen episode was a victory for norms, it was not a victory for Veletskii (although the man Pahlen called a "revolutionary turncoat" remained affiliated with the Resettlement Administration for several more years).[138] The same year as Pahlen's criticism was emphatically rejected, a new statistical expedition under P. P. Rumiantsev began to study Semirech'e according to a new program—allotting land for hay mowing, agriculture, and pastoral nomadism to Kazaks. This strategy was closely aligned with Rumiantsev's own view that, while the "future belong[ed]" to agricultural sedentarism, the Kazak economy of Semirech'e was presently mixed, so land allotments of multiple types were needed.[139]

Rumiantsev's results made a mockery of Veletskii's confident claims that the norms he had hurriedly calculated were maximal, and only likely to be revised downward in the future. These "maximal" norms ranged from 40 to 82 desiatinas; how maximal they actually were can be seen from Table 5.1, compiled according to several tables in Rumiantsev's reports.[140]

Virtually all were substantially higher than anything Veletskii calculated, at times by up to 50 percent. It is difficult not to see this as a balancing of the interests not only of nomads and settlers, but of the interventionist tendencies of the Resettlement Administration and the paternalist old hands who, in their posts as district chiefs, still had a role to play in setting up settlers. But the problems that Pahlen had diagnosed with the system of norms—their abstraction from reality and actual patterns of land use—would remain chronic.

TABLE 5.1   Land norms for Semirech'e calculated by P. P. Rumiantsev

LEPSINSK		KOPAL		DZHARKENT	
REGION	DESIATINAS	REGION	DESIATINAS	REGION	DESIATINAS
II	38	II	80	III	89
V	39	III	63	II	93
III	42	IV	68	VI	94
IV	52	V	70	VIII	103
VI	60	VI	85	XI	103
VIII	66			VII	105
IX	70			X	112
VII	71			V	115
				IX	129

New Norms for a New Era

Still more unfortunately for the nomads, the results of Rumiantsev's research were not typical. The Rumiantsev norms revised work that had been carried out hurriedly and poorly, breathing some life into the fundamentally flawed system of norming and ensuring that, at least rhetorically, it would live up to its promises. Worse occurred in regions more consistently targeted for resettlement, where the case could be made that the Shcherbina norms had been unnecessarily solicitous of the interests of the local population. Here the imperatives were different: not to create a compromise between interventionism and paternalism, but to maximize the estrangement of lands from Kazaks in settlers' favor. New norms emerged to pursue this goal, with calculations meant to prove that Shcherbina had not simply been working at a different stage of resettlement policy, but objectively *wrong* about the steppe, its land, and economy—and that the new, drastically reduced norms, freeing up much more land for settlers, were objectively *right*.

The most egregious downward revision took place in Akmolinsk province under V. K. Kuznetsov. As he had been directed, when he began work in 1907, Kuznetsov billed his work as an attempt to get to grips with the changes in the steppe economy that resettlement had already wrought and, crucially, to define new land norms in accordance with these changes:

> Repeat research on the Kazak economy in Akmolinsk province was undertaken with the goal of reexamination of norms of Kazak land use and bringing them into greater correspondence with the current position and conditions of this economy. These norms were established according to the data of the statistical expedition done under the statistician Shcherbina in 1896–1901 [1903—*sic*]. They were calculated exclusively for the maintenance and development of nomadic stock raising and thus everywhere were defined in very large sizes, reaching 400 and more desiatinas for an average Kazak household. Meanwhile, quickly changing in recent years under the influence of significant resettlement, the economic conditions of the Kazak steppe have introduced substantial changes to the primitive Kazak economy.[141]

It was no longer necessary to protect pastoral nomadism if this lifeway could be shown to have already had its day in the steppe provinces. Proving this would, in turn, provide a significantly larger land fund in accordance with the "strongly developed" [*razrosshikhsia*] demands of resettlement.[142] Rhetorically, then, the case for the new Kuznetsov norms depended on an intertwined pair of arguments: first, that the new data was objectively superior (more accurate and calculated more rigorously) than those of the Shcherbina Expedition; second, that the economic and demographic change resettlement had created on the steppe had proceeded so far, and so rapidly, as to be irreversible. In the five volumes (one for each district of the province) he edited, Kuznetsov aggressively pressed both of these claims, with significant consequences for the Kazak population of Akmolinsk province.

Pastoral nomadism, in Kuznetsov's view, both was and had to be fading from existence in the steppe provinces. Resettlement had profoundly and irrevocably changed the environmental conditions on which this lifestyle depended:

> The times have passed when nomads' herds wandered the steppes freely and unopposed, and were fed by fodder year round. Now the nomad is placed within limits [*v ramki*] and along with this, in places, already within quite close limits. The former vastness of the steppes has ceased to be, and passage to the available free lands is difficult—everywhere settlers have appeared, a mass of settlements has been set up. All has passed and changed, and there is "no road to what has passed away irretrievably." In place of the former careless existence and lying about [*lezhan'ia na boku*], the time of concern and work has arrived. The modern Kazak has to think, and trouble himself, and work. The gradually compressed circle of nomadic freedom, with internal obstacles for use even of that restricted area, involuntarily engendered thoughts about how to live, how to feed livestock, for which there is not enough fodder year-round.[143]

This was, for Kuznetsov, a transition with exclusively positive implications. He repeatedly cited a decline in the number of poor Kazak households and proportionate increase in middling and rich households as evidence that the arrival of settlers had been accompanied by a widespread increase in Kazaks' well-being.[144] Settlers were a necessary condition of this general flourishing, he argued, in several ways: they provided a commercial market for Kazaks' livestock, turning stock raising into a profit-making enterprise, and facilitated progress in agriculture and stock raising by their good examples and the physical transfer of technology into Kazak hands.[145] Kazaks turning to more intensive forms of cultivation with the encouragement of resettlement, in turn, both formed larger, more densely populated settlements and grew ever more distant from the "clan principle" [*rodovoe nachalo*] that had formerly governed their lives.[146] In both respects, they grew more governable and more legible to the state. Further, he argued, Kazaks eagerly welcomed Russian culture and expressed a desire to learn the dominant language of the empire with all possible speed.[147] With much good land still bereft of settlers, these benefits were most likely, if anything, to multiply in the future.

Much of this overlapped significantly with both the "pro-settlement" strain of the Shcherbina Expedition's materials and the views of peasant resettlement's loudest advocates. Kuznetsov went further than Shcherbina ever dared, though, by positing an absolute limit to the potential scope of Kazak stock raising, even if intensified, rationalized, and carried out under sedentary conditions. The reasons for this were simple enough—any district, or any subregion of a district, held a finite amount of hay-mowing lands, some of them needed for the survival of peasant settlers. Sedentarization would permit the keeping of more livestock than before, but the number of animals kept would ultimately collide with the carrying capacity of steppe land; indeed, this had already occurred in Akmolinsk district, with disastrous consequences for the thin, sickly livestock there.[148] For Kuznetsov to formulate the problem this way was significant in two ways. First, when read against his assessments of agriculture and trade among Kazaks in the province, this limitation made it unclear how Kazaks were to survive at all. Stock raising was limited; agriculture, while it "had a future," was also profoundly limited by climactic and soil conditions; and the development of trade, owing to a lack of culture and literacy among the nomads, remained a long way in the future.[149] Second, it naturalized the presence of settlers in the province, portraying them as part of the conditions with which Kazaks would have to reckon in the future and indicating the priority of settler interests over Kazak in no uncertain terms. There was no further question of balancing the two—mowing lands could be allotted to settlers or foster the growth of local stock raising, and beyond the amount required to secure locals' existence in their current state, Kuznetsov endorsed the former alternative.

Kuznetsov had a clear mandate to produce data and recommendations different from those generated by the first Expedition for Research of the Steppe Provinces, but given the disciplinary similarities between his own approach and Shcherbina's, he had to make an effort to prove that he was more correct than his predecessor. This he accomplished by both repeatedly proclaiming his adherence to the "scientific method" embodied by Shcherbina and highlighting moments at which his predecessor's work had fallen short of that standard.[150] These methodological deficiencies included drastically underestimating the productivity of pastureland per unit area (and thus overestimating how much land nomads needed); applying household budget data across district lines (thus failing to account for local conditions); and failing to account for the diversity of the Kazak economy (i.e., its partial transition to intensive agriculture).[151] All of these failings, combined with the obvious improvement in Kazaks' lives that ten years of resettlement had engendered, justified, in Kuznetsov's view, a radical reduction of norms and expansion of the state land fund for colonization. In Petropavlovsk district alone, the size of the state land fund more than doubled, from 738,603 desiatinas according to Shcherbina to 1,583,362 by Kuznetsov's calculations.[152] Norms of Kazak land use were invariably reduced by at least 50 percent and, in some cases, by more than 300 percent. They were accepted with little fuss.[153] The governor of neighboring Semipalatinsk province, A. N. Troinitskii, even argued that Kuznetsov's revisions there had not gone far enough.[154]

The primary problem with Kuznetsov's truth claims was that they were not actually true. Certain of his claims bear so little scrutiny that they lead one to suspect that he set out to prove a hypothesis that was determined and accepted in advance of the receipt of data. Although every volume of the Kuznetsov expedition's materials began with the claim that the Kazak population of Akmolinsk province was living better and more prosperously in the wake of peasant resettlement than it had before, budget data from Kokshetau district contradicted this assertion directly. These budgets showed drastic declines in Kazaks' food consumption: 8.1 percent in grain, 21.5 percent in fat, 35.4 percent in milk, and a shocking 61.6 percent in meat.[155] Such a precipitous drop in the quantity and caloric density of the average diet hardly demonstrates an improvement in well-being. While Kuznetsov's argument that the change in grain consumption was explicable because of the small sample size budgets provided may merit consideration, his treatment of the numbers for meat consumption represents an obvious case of massaging data. On the basis of small differences in livestock weight and mass data, he conjured an increase in meat consumption (86.2 percent, i.e., from three poods, eight pounds to six poods) greater than the original decrease.[156] Similarly, he repeatedly claimed that all parts of the Kazak population had been seized with the urge to take up agriculture even as his own data showed that only 20 percent of the population sowed any grain at all (Akmolinsk district) or that the total sown area of a region had actually decreased since 1896 (Atbasar district).[157] But busy administrators hardly had the time or the expertise to look deeply enough into figures that were, after all, meant to be applied with minimal fuss. Kuznetsov's norms looked correct; the consensus that mass resettlement was a state priority was clear enough; therefore, Kuznetsov's norms were correct.

Census data offer a telling picture of the scope of resettlement on the steppe, enabled by a new construction of statistical knowledge that supported ever-larger land seizures from the local population. Between 1893 and 1912, according to the Resettlement Administration's own figures, Akmolinsk province alone received more than 320,000 "male souls" (over 600,000 in all); the total figure for the steppe provinces (including Semirech'e, but excluding Syr-Darya) was over one million.[158] When state priorities and statistical expertise were aligned, they moved settlers in great numbers and with little delay. The very efficacy of the revised norms in providing both a legalistic and scientistic basis for expropriating land from nomads who were imagined to be using it wastefully ensured that they could never be effectively challenged. It took more than a decade of bureaucratic squabbling and obscure methodological disputes, but the Russian Empire ultimately arrived at a way of knowing the land and people of the steppe that served a new conception of the state interest there both at the time and into the future. In this respect, the relationship between statistical knowledge and imperial power on the steppe in this era was entirely uncomplicated.

Kazak intermediaries did not immediately realize that this policy change spelled the end of the unequal but shared project of governance and development described in earlier chapters. Indeed, although records are scanty, statistical research on the steppe provinces could not have succeeded without them, a point that Shcherbina himself conceded. The fact of their participation implies the existence of common interests between these intermediaries and resettlement statisticians during the early years of the resettlement era, interests broadly similar to those of Ibrai Altynsarin or contributors to *Kirgizskaia stepnaia gazeta*. After 1906, it was clear how far the tsarist state and its intermediaries had parted ways. For a state that thought it knew enough, the knowledge of local intermediaries could be dispensed with—particularly if it led to inconvenient conclusions. At the same time, the seemingly inexorable growth of a Slavic peasant population on land that Kazak intermediaries considered the Fatherland, the *ata meken*, was antithetical to what these men considered to be the best interests of their land and people. In contesting the change, they would seek to make use of the outward rigor and objectivity of earlier, more paternalist versions of the land norms. In this respect, the relationship between statistical knowledge and imperial power looks rather more ambiguous; the knowledge that the tsarist state produced, in its multiple generations, allowed for peasant colonization to be both implemented and disputed.

The parting of ways with respect to statistics is significant of a larger trend in Kazaks' engagement with the institutions and programs of the Russian Empire. Until the early twentieth century, discursive and institutional space existed for Kazaks to deploy their own expertise and shape the vision and articulation of imperial policy on the steppe. But the space closed as top-down economic modernization through resettlement became a higher priority than stability and gradualism. Both peasant resettlement and its expansion were historically contingent and contested policies. The closure of the space in which Kazak intermediaries sought, with varying degrees of success, to influence the terms on which they were ruled, was nothing inevitable. It was the product of an important and impactful decision that might have been taken differently, had different ways of viewing the steppe and its inhabitants been prioritized. The effects of its closure, though, were no less lasting for that. The ultimate failure of the once-promising exchange between Kazak intermediaries and the tsarist state, and the paths that were open to elite and nonelite Kazaks as a result, are the subject of our final chapter.

A DOUBLE FAILURE

Epistemology and the Crisis of a
Settler Colonial Empire

Rushing to complete his appointed tasks for the backbreaking summer work period in August 1916, a Russian resettlement worker, Dolgushin, could hardly have imagined that his career and life were soon to come to a grisly end. When rumors of a violent rebellion of *Kirgizy* near his work site in Vernyi district of Semirech'e province began to spread, his two local assistants begged him to flee.[1] But Dolgushin remained at work, reasoning "that he had offended none of the local Kirgizy, and thus they should not kill him."[2] He ought to have listened. By the time he agreed to go, it was too late. An armed crowd murdered him and took the topographers assisting him captive.[3]

The death of a relatively humble agent of the Russian Empire's resettlement program in the violence that seized Central Asia at the end of 1916 signifies the failure of that policy from the perspective of Kazaks and other Central Asians whose lands were subject to estrangement and reallocation to Slavic settlers. Despite the system of norms and other legal safeguards, resettlement disrupted traditional lifeways; it was not pleasant to be the object of technocratic change. But to truly understand why this violence flared up, and why, in the main, local intellectuals sided against the rebels, we need to look at a series of political decisions taken by the tsarist state over the previous decade.

The reforms that followed the Revolution of 1905, on the steppe as elsewhere, saw anticipation and excitement give way to disappointment. The calling and rapid dispersal of two representative bodies, the first and second State Dumas, followed by Petr Arkad'evich Stolypin's electoral coup of June 3, 1907, demonstrated that effective representative government was incommensurate with autocracy—at least as Nicholas II understood it. Stolypin's agrarian reforms, building on the earlier work of Sergei Iul'evich Witte, promoted the individualization of land use and large-scale resettlement to the east side of the Urals, including the steppe provinces. These two points of the Stolypin reforms aimed to orient rural production toward the market and increase the productivity of lands wasted by thoughtless adherence to traditional economic forms. They generated a broad range of critical responses from politicians, intellectuals, and the humbler people they affected most. When Stolypin's famous "20 years of internal and external peace" failed to ensue, so too did any hope of saving the Romanov dynasty.

Particularly on the Kazak steppe, the issues of land and representation were deeply connected. Though other issues (including the "woman question" and discussion of the status of Muslim institutions) had their place, it would not be an exaggeration to say that these were the two key issues of the Kazak-language periodical press for the majority of its prerevolutionary life. Of these, the land question raised by resettlement and its effects was undoubtedly at the forefront of most minds, but this proved inseparable from the issue of political representation. The new electoral law pronounced on June 3, 1907, created this connection. While transforming the Duma into a more reliably conservative, Russian-nationalist, and pliant representative body, it did not grant even token representation to the provinces of the steppe and Central Asia.[4] That laws enabling expanded, accelerated peasant resettlement were discussed and issued outside of the hearing of natives of the steppe, unable even to present their case, grated. But it also provided a convenient rhetorical stick with which to beat an unpopular government, a variation on "no taxation without representation" more than a century later and half a world away. This was not simply the angry rhetoric of a disenfranchised population, publishing in a language few other subjects of the empire understood. It was also presented on the floor of the Duma by those remaining deputies who were sympathetic to the Kazak cause, as in this heated exchange during a discussion of the Resettlement Administration's budget.

> KHAS-MAMEDOV: Thus, in the name of justice, humanitarianism, and the eternal rights of the Kazak population to land and its use, the settler movement to Kirgizia [i.e., the steppe provinces –I. C.] should be quickly ceased.
> BEREZOVSKII: That will never happen.
> KHAS-MAMEDOV: It is easy for you to say, deciding the fate of the Kazak population, which is even deprived of representation in the Duma.[5]

The connection between resettlement and representation, though, went beyond the rhetorical. The corpus of knowledge about the steppe and its inhabitants that

Russian scholars and administrators had accrued over the previous 70 years, and which around the turn of the twentieth century they augmented with particular alacrity, played a critical role in debates about resettlement and political representation alike. In many respects, though, the role this knowledge played was not straightforward. When making determinations about the steppe environment, and how much of the region was truly surplus to nomads' requirements, resettlement statistics offered tsarist bureaucrats a range of competing solutions, despite the patina of empiricist rigor with which they were equipped. Rather, seemingly objective data about the soil and climate of the steppe could be used—or misused—to support a wide range of arguments about the proper course of settlement. Evolutionary understandings of pastoral nomadism as a lower stage of civilization, through which all peoples would necessarily pass, clashed with environmental determinism in discussions of Kazaks' civilizational aptitudes. Competing schools of thought about Islam and its compatibility with an empire where dynastic and national principles were growing ever harder to separate only further complicated the picture.

From the perspective of both ordinary Kazaks and intellectuals, between 1905 and 1917, key decision makers in the Russian Empire made the wrong choices in every one of these debates. Their experience of direct Russian rule over the previous decades suggested a coping strategy, namely, demonstrating to their erstwhile interlocutors that they had it wrong—that Kazaks were, for example, both eminently civilizable and currently at a level deserving of political representation. This time, though, the expectations of these intermediate figures were disappointed. Resettlement was too crucial to the economic modernization of the Russian Empire and the resolution of European Russia's "agrarian question" to be delayed or reined in. A small, reliable electorate was too dear to the political stability that Nicholas prized, after burning his hand on the first two Dumas, to be tinkered with in difficult times. Political participation would have to occur ad hoc, with no guarantee of a hearing—an unstable situation.

Throughout the Russian Empire, the cataclysm of World War I—a massive strain on human resources, administration, and material—functioned as a test of years of halting reforms and occasional parleys with a developing civil society. In hindsight, it is abundantly clear that the Romanov dynasty did not pass this test. The specific manifestation of its failure in the disenfranchised provinces of Central Asia, though, should be considered as fundamentally epistemological. On June 25, 1916, Nicholas II ordered thousands of adult male inorodtsy to appear for service as manual laborers in the *tyl*, the rear of the imperial army. He did so despite sound advice to the contrary from Kazak intermediaries, and without any mention of a quid pro quo, in terms of land rights or political representation.[6] The tsar commanded, and his people were to follow. The violence that carried away Dolgushin, thousands of settlers, and tens of thousands of Kazaks and other Central Asians flared up as a result. Resettlement had created such grievances in Kazak society that conflict was likely to ensue at some point. In the conflagration of 1916, the draft was the spark, land politics the fuel, and the explosion that occurred depended on the presence of both factors. Members of the intelligentsia took the side of the tsarist state because of their own expectations and associations with military service, which they associated with their own visions for the future. They did not fundamentally disagree with the rebels' basic grievances.

Epistemological Foundations of Resettlement (or, For a Moment the Lie Becomes Truth)

To simply proceed with a program of colonization at random or in contradiction to good data would have been sharply at variance with the practices of the tsarist Resettlement Administration, particularly in the more activist guise it assumed after 1905. Peter Holquist has argued that officials within the Resettlement Administration saw colonization as, in part, "a state-directed endeavor to maximize the human and productive resources of the empire as a whole, by matching available territory with the population and its productive capacity."[7] Their "technocratic ethos" required nothing less than thorough assessments of the land and the use to which its occupants put it. Chapter 5 shows the expenses of money and time the tsarist state was willing to incur to obtain the data legally necessary to expropriate nomads. What occurred after 1905 was subtler and more interesting: the selection of seemingly objective data, outside of its original context, to justify policy changes. It is probably unknowable, and at any rate unimportant, if this was a cynical ploy to seize as much land as possible over multiple objections or the product of a naively positivist faith in statisticians' findings. The fact remains that whatever their motivations, officers of the Resettlement Administration and their superiors presented propositions of limited applicability as facts strong enough to dismiss any criticism they faced.

In promoting the seizure of land surpluses, it was first necessary to prove that the land being taken was indeed surplus to indigenous requirements, and that losing it presented no great trouble for the expropriated. Here, divorced from the context in which they had emerged, land norms took on a new and unexpected form—demagoguery. Perhaps we need not take too seriously the statements of Duma deputies only vaguely familiar with resettlement affairs that each Kazak household held 500 desiatinas (1,350 acres) of land,[8] or that a total of 225 million desiatinas lay ready for use in the steppes.[9] These were massively incorrect readings of the available data, and by themselves do not indicate that anyone with the power to make decisions about resettlement or agrarian reform took such views seriously. Aleksandr Vasil'evich Krivoshein, main administrator of land management and agriculture (and thus the immediate supervisor of the Resettlement Administration), had such power. In his hands, such rhetoric served to justify his organization's actions and promote its colonizing agenda.

In the fall of 1908, Nicholas forwarded to Krivoshein a telegram from a Kazak, Shaimardan Koshchegulov, claiming to represent the population of Kokchetau district, Akmolinsk province, and petitioning the tsar to cease resettlement to the steppe provinces until the Duma clarified Kazaks' land rights.[10] The tsar, following the appropriate formalities, forwarded the message to Krivoshein for a response. The latter noted that "the Kazaks' land supply, in the majority of cases, is defined at 150–300 desiatinas [405–810 acres] per household," and thus there could be no question of their impoverishment.[11] If Kazaks were displeased, it was only because a few rich stock herders, oppressing poor, seminomadic farmers, needed more land than the norm to keep their massive enterprises running.[12] Implicit here was a comparison with the plots that Slavic agriculturalists worked, never more than 15 desiatinas per male household member on settler plots, and sometimes drastically smaller than that in the land-poor provinces of the Central Black Earth Region. Out of context, it beggared belief that some families could survive on only a few acres, while others found a thousand insufficient for their needs. Never mind the exigencies of seasonal migration, or that the truly extraordinary allotments were on practically uninhabitable land. The sheer size of the numbers seemed to speak for itself. As Krivoshein summarized the matter when returning the petition without further movement, "the work [of the Resettlement Administration] . . . is furnished with substantial guarantees of the Kazaks' interests."[13]

Still more useful, from the perspective of GUZiZ's production-oriented mission, and the civilizing claims associated with compelling nomads to settle on the land, was to demonstrate that resettlement was actually beneficial for local Kazaks, despite their ungrateful complaining. In 1905, the manager of resettlement affairs in Ural-Turgai region, L. N. Tsabel', took up the question of colonization's influence on indigenous people in a single canton of Kustanai district, Turgai province, long a key destination of the settler movement. Tsabel's findings were highly encouraging, from the perspective of a resettlement official. The area that Kazaks sowed to grain was growing even as the average amount of livestock per household remained stable; hay storage was on the rise, and few animals died during periodic zhŭts; meat consumption was up by 21 percent.[14] All this in a mere seven years between the moment that Fedor Andreevich Shcherbina had first surveyed the canton and Tsabel's arrival. As the author who developed and published Tsabel's data in what was effectively the trade publication of the Resettlement Administration, *Voprosy kolonizatsii* (Questions of Colonization), exulted:

> All the comparisons for these two years [1898 and 1905] lead one to the conclusion that the economy of the Kazaks of Arakaragai canton is developing and growing stronger. By this are sufficiently contradicted all fears that the Kazak economy will find its downfall in agriculture, and that the introduction of a Russian element there will compel the accustomed herder to reduce his herd. . . . Reality has shown something else: the archaic form of economy is replaced by a new one, more intensive, and the wealth of the land is used more completely.[15]

This was a well-supported statement for a single canton, a unit of territory juridically unable to exceed 2,000 tents, or approximately 10,000 people, from the Resettlement Administration's civilizing, production-oriented perspective. *Voprosy kolonizatsii* further claimed that, isolated from centers of trade, the canton was not in "any kind of especially favorable conditions."[16] But this is a statement that can be questioned. Kustanai district had long attracted settlers precisely because conditions there seemed more favorable for sedentary agriculture than the alternatives. Arakaragai canton, in particular, held one of two government forest plots in a district where a shortage of timber was the main obstacle to building and heating permanent dwellings.[17] Relative to many areas to which settlers could be directed, and where they and Kazak nomads struggled to adapt to one another, conditions in Arakaragai were very good indeed.

This did not stop administrators from making generalizations on the basis of Tsabel's case study. In the summer of 1908, sixty deputies of the Third Duma submitted a draft law that would have given Kazaks and other natives of Central Asia substantial additional legal protections when having their lands seized, and satisfied their land needs before resettlement could continue.[18] The sixty deputies hoped that prioritizing Kazaks' zemleustroistvo (the reorganization and fixing of their land use) over resettlement would offer them a degree of protection. It was also a hot topic of discussion at GUZiZ between 1907 and 1909.[19] But Krivoshein disagreed that zemleustroistvo was urgently necessary for Kazaks' well-being and survival. Lamenting the deputies' "completely false" characterization of his organization's activity on the steppe in a note to Stolypin, he stated confidently that "the history of the settlement [*zaseleniia*] of the steppe shows that the establishment of settlers in the steppe provinces called forth the development among the Kazaks of agriculture and cultured stock raising. If in this one can see an important factor toward the change of economic and life [*bytovykh*] forms, in any case, there is no basis to assert that the influence of this factor harmfully affects the economic position of the Kazaks."[20] Krivoshein's words were based exclusively on research conducted in Arakaragai and one other (Saroisk) canton of Kustanai district, and his numbers came only from Arakaragai. They were apparently convincing. Stolypin hastened to reassure his close colleague that the Council of Ministers "completely agreed with your considerations concerning this matter."[21] Nothing more came of this "plan of the 60." As in the case of the land norms, the statistically verified truth, out of context, was strong enough to overcome what Kazaks presented as their experiences of resettlement, and what oppositionally minded scholars claimed were the major deficiencies of the program.

All of these interest groups had a good deal to say on the matter. Specialists in agriculture on the political Left criticized state resettlement policy strongly, though not out of any great respect for Kazaks' land rights.[22] The right to estrange Kazaks' surplus land for state needs was written clearly enough in law, as the liberal statistician Aleksandr Arkad'evich Kaufman stated in response to the arguments of a Kazak liberal, Zhihansha Seidalin.[23] Rather, these critiques focused more on the practice of resettlement and its apparently limited prospects for resolving the agrarian question in European Russia—although the latter was a parodied, extreme view of resettlement's place in the Stolypin program. Kaufman, an extraordinarily prolific author, led the charge. He tartly summarized his view of the matter soon after the passage of a law of June 6,1904, granting rights of free resettlement: "there are and will not be tens of millions of desiatinas of land," and hence, despite the apparent enormity of Siberia and the steppe provinces, resettlement could never resolve the agrarian question.[24] His reasons for thinking so emerged compactly in a pamphlet issued the following year, confrontationally titled *Pereselenie: Mechty i deistvitel'nost'* (Resettlement: Dreams and reality). Here, he noted that of the entire land fund of the Empire, only the Kazak steppe was suitable for further colonization, and even this "settler El Dorado" could only be relied on in isolated areas in the north.[25] Other regions (especially Turkestan) needed costly irrigation before they could be made productive, particularly because of what he presented as the inherent conservatism of the Russian peasant, unwilling to adapt to new natural conditions.[26] In combination with pessimism about the land and settlers that other agronomists expressed, we can see a critique of resettlement coming from the tsarist Left that might be called conditional environmental determinism, that is, that under Russia's specific cultural and political conditions, settlers were unlikely to overcome the harsh conditions in their new places of residence.[27] Cultural work thus came to be the most important matter, and resettlement to represent something of a red herring.

Kaufman's name, data, and the basic contours of his argument found their way to the Duma floor during both its first and second sessions.[28] Evidently, the Resettlement Administration felt enough public pressure to respond directly to the critiques. In an article whose title made its target unambiguously clear, "Deistvitel'nost', a ne mechty" (Reality, and not dreams), A. B. Uspenskii argued that the steppe provinces still had available huge quantities of first-rate land, which gave a larger harvest than typical of European Russia.[29] Further research promised only to expand an already-sizable land fund. As to the question of water, artificial irrigation was possible everywhere, and rain-fed (*bogarnye*) lands already showed serious promise without expending the cost and time that new canals required.[30] By 1914, rather than backing off such claims, Resettlement Administration publications continued to insist on the viability of rain-fed lands in Semirech'e.[31] One researcher would go still further, taking on perhaps the one belief that proponents and opponents of resettlement shared: that south of approximately the 48th parallel, the climate and soil were so poor that agricultural colonization was impossible. This, he argued, was a completely unstudied proposition in many areas, and meanwhile, on the basis of his personal observations, there was reason to believe that at least selective, limited colonization was possible.[32] In short, Resettlement Administration scholars had developed data that sufficed, in their minds, to reject any sort of environmentally grounded criticism from other agronomists and statisticians.

Though Kazak intellectuals and politicians were more willing than Kaufman and his ilk to question the legal basis of resettlement, their involvement in statistical expeditions and the scientistic claims of resettlement officials gave them the opportunity to attack the epistemological basis of resettlement as well.[33] If this was not a politics of total resistance, it had the advantages of continuity with their actions prior to 1905, and provided engagement with a parliamentary system that most hoped would remain viable.

The man able to embrace this approach with the most credibility, owing to his experience in resettlement expeditions and high-level technical training, was Älikhan Bökeikhanov. In a strident, mocking tone, Bökeikhanov turned to the printed word, chiefly the Petersburg publication *Sibirskie voprosy* (Siberian Questions) after the dissolution of the First Duma deprived him of that platform.[34] His articles, much like Kaufman's, were intended to highlight the failure of what he termed "chancery colonization," which he claimed was divorced from physical reality.[35] Russian settlers, he noted, were cast into environmental conditions that offered little hope of survival, whether because of sparse and capricious participation on the steppe or the Herculean labor required to clear thick coniferous forest (*urman*) from Siberia, making them "proletarians" rather than real colonizers.[36] Any civilizing claims the Resettlement Administration could make were thus null and void. Meanwhile, claims about the size of the remaining land fund on the steppe were fabulous in the literal sense, the result of baseless speculation, as when the governor-general of the steppe, Ivan Pavlovich Nadarov, wished to move a group of Kazaks from good agricultural land to deserts south of the 48th parallel: "'About' 12 million desiatinas south of the 48th parallel were calculated by the local branch of the resettlement organization according to the methods of the central Resettlement Administration. . . . For [such people] the lack of any sort of instrumental survey of the southern part of the Kazak lands does not present any kind of obstacle: they will give its size in desiatinas, for this Nadarov's resolution is enough. Is it worth reckoning with a survey, when such a rich idea has entered the general's head?"[37] Such critiques both undercut the most utopian dreams of advocates of resettlement and gave the lie to the often-voiced idea that the interests of the local population were completely protected when estranging their lands for settler villages.

With respect to the key tool of the Resettlement Administration, land norms, Bökeikhanov was ambivalent. In the more aggressive context signified by the free settlement law of 1904 and Stolypin's rise in 1906, the more cautious Shcherbina norms, on which he had worked, seemed at minimum a useful guarantee against further incursions.[38] Thus he insisted on recognizing the cautious figures that the Shcherbina Expedition had calculated and preserving the 25 percent increase to these norms that had been ordered by the Ministry of Agriculture in 1901. Criticizing the policy of resettlement, he deployed the Shcherbina norms rhetorically as an absolute and incontrovertible requirement for Kazak life: "Of the group of Kazaks, the complaints of whom reached Gen. Nadarov's conference, it turns out that more than two-thirds are left without the Shcherbina norm."[39] Vasilii Kuznetsov, in turn, he of the low and possibly falsified norms, was Bökeikhanov's particular bête noire among statisticians. In a Kazak-language publication, discussing Kuznetsov's drastic revision downward of the Shcherbina-Chermak norms in Semipalatinsk province, he resorted to language that was, even for him, colorful: Kuznetsov's norms were simply a "lie" (*ötïrïk*) that "cut off the Kazaks' nose" (*qazaqtï pŭshtitïp*), "caus[ing] the Kazaks' inheritance to be castrated [*qazaghïnïng enshïsïn qaita pïshtïrdï*]."[40]

For all his research, experience, and rhetoric, Bökeikhanov's increasingly heated tone indicates how little success his approach met with. Faced with closed epistemological ranks, no longer in the employ of the Resettlement Administration, and legally excluded from parliament, the Kazaks' most viable critic of Russian colonization was no more than a voice in the wilderness.

Concern about resettlement was not exclusively (or even primarily) the province of elites, nor were the Duma and periodical press the only venues in which grievances were aired. The petitions of Kazaks affected by land seizures provide an alternative view of resettlement's consequences for those whose lives it disrupted, one that leads to similar conclusions. An unfortunate group of Kazaks of Semipalatinsk province, mistakenly included in a new sedentary

canton (Kazaks commonly petitioned to form such cantons in response to settler incursions) complained that they did not wish to become sedentary peasants "because of the absolute impossibility, according to the local particularities of daily life, to adapt ourselves to the conditions of sedentary life."[41] Others
complained of being subjected to violence by new settlers and resettlement
officials alike.[42] Bökeikhanov dutifully publicized cases of seizure without
appropriate compensation for immovable property or for purposes contrary
to those stated in the laws on resettlement.[43] Using the rights that remained to
them as subjects, Kazaks who came out on the losing side of resettlement and
its ripple effects were not shy about letting the tsarist state know about their
experiences.

Of course, one should not be overly credulous with petitions, since Kazaks
and their trusted representatives crafted them to obtain the return of estranged
land, or at least compensation for it. We should expect petitioners' claims to
be presented in the most lachrymose terms possible. And it is clear that some
Kazaks, less committed to pastoral nomadism, cited their poverty in order to
gain access to land to farm or to gain control of lands in disputes within a canton or district.[44] Still, complaints like these show internal consistency and track
well with the more frank assessments of the practices of resettlement auditors
made before and after the 1916 revolt.[45] If some Kazaks successfully adapted to
resettlement, making careers with the extensive new bureaucracy that formed
around them or taking to agriculture or trade, many others lost good land
and valuable property as a result of the seizure, or experienced violence or
humiliation during and after settlers' arrival.[46] For all of this, the best indications we have point to a still-greater restructuring of pastoralist lifeways,
along archetypically high-modernist lines, had tsarist rule endured past World
War I. A proposal within the Resettlement Administration, originating from
Semirech'e, spoke of Kazaks' "complete and forcible" (*sploshnoe, prinuditel'noe*)
zemleustroistvo as a means of both serving their needs and creating a vast
new surplus for settlers.[47] Outside of that formidably technocratic institution,
a 1911 conference in Semipalatinsk province proposed forming a separate,
all-Kazak and -nomadic province in the center of the steppe, unsuitable for
agriculture, leaving behind provinces better-suited for the needs of settlers
and Kazak agriculturalists, a proposal that representatives of the Provisional
Government, some years later, found worthy of further attention.[48] In short,
despite a range of arguments against it from high and low, by the 1910s a range
of tsarist institutions had developed a combination of political priorities and
confidence in its knowledge that made resettlement (and, concurrently, Kazak
sedentarization) impossible to roll back. In so doing, they had also created the
economic and demographic preconditions for a rebellion.

Progress, Citizenship, and the Third of June System

Kazaks' window to present their grievances about how they were being governed, in which resettlement played a crucial role, as juridically equal participants in the imperial political system, was short-lived. Stolypin's parliamentary coup of June 3, 1907, closed it, and despite Kazaks' spirited and creative attempts to find new means of political engagement, it remained so down to 1917. It seems unlikely that Stolypin and Nicholas II, hoping to create a more compliant Duma that would ease their top-down reforms, consciously intended to create a grievance among the empire's Central Asian population—or, at least, that they considered the risk serious or significant. Still, it is inconceivable that the decision to exclude the steppe and Central Asia was taken totally at random. Despite the emphasis on creating a parliament more "Russian in spirit," the manifesto that dissolved the Second Duma and called for new elections made provisions for at least the token representation of national minority groups; the exception was "those border areas of the state where the population has not attained an adequate level of citizenship, [where] elections to the State Duma must temporarily be brought to an end."[49] This is veiled, circumspect language, difficult to penetrate. Reading scholarly and administrative texts against one another, and comparing groups who received token representation with those excluded entirely, draws the veil back: Central Asia and the steppe were excluded because the combination there of pastoral mobility and Islam made the region seem both underdeveloped and threatening.

If, as the historian Paul Werth has noted, one of the consequences of the Caucasian wars was a new wave of Islamophobia in the Russian Empire, the Andijan rebellion of 1898 raised its tenor to a new level of hysteria.[50] Exploring the paranoid rumor mongering that took place after the uprising, the historian Alexander Morrison has correctly noted that it "cast a very long shadow over Turkestan officialdom's view of Islam," sowing paranoia and hostility among administrators and settlers for years to come.[51] With significant assistance from the serving orientalist Vladimir Petrovich Nalivkin, the new governor-general of Turkestan, Sergei Mikhailovich Dukhovskoi, argued in a special report, *Islam v Turkestane* (Islam in Turkestan), that the uprising proved the failure of the tsarist state's non-interventionist religious policy there.[52] (In correspondence with his direct superiors at the Ministry of War, he would be even blunter: Turkestan, he claimed, was the only imperial borderland where the religious affairs of inorodtsy were not under some form of supervision, with results that had now been confirmed as dangerous.)[53] He recommended a program of study and active observation of Turkestani Islam and Muslims, particularly of Sufism, which seemed particularly unknown and dangerous.[54]

The ripple effects of this moment of panic, confirming all the worst fears of earlier Islamophobes, were significant, and not limited to Turkestan's borders. It is true that the Dukhovskoi program did not receive the reception in St. Petersburg that he might have hoped. On one hand, the Department of Religious Affairs of Foreign Faiths under the MVD rejected both his proposals and the continuation of ignorirovanie.[55] The powerful Minister of Finance Witte systematically rejected the arguments that Andijan was a symptom of a larger social ill and that any principle other than tolerance could serve as the basis of state religious policy.[56] On the other hand, officials on the spot and higher up connected with the Ministry of War tended to strongly support Dukhovskoi's view of the Andijan events. Investigators both blamed "Muslim fanaticism" for the uprising and proposed aggressive measures directed against a deeper danger, the further Islamicization of steppe Kazaks.[57] High officials in the Ministry of War insisted that all governmental organs needed to clarify that they would not tolerate "that the religion confessed by the natives follows political goals."[58] These fears did not decline in the years that followed Andijan.[59]

Moreover, one of the most concrete products of Dukhovskoi's brief rule in Turkestan, the *Sbornik materialov po musul'manstvu* (Collection of materials on Islam), presented as facts useful for governance the most stridently anti-Islamic views available. A volume on the hajj, for example, leaned on the work of the notoriously hysterical Mikhail Alekseevich Miropiev, a missionary graduate of the Kazan' Theological Academy.[60] Miropiev's fears with respect to Islam were as deep as they were extensive. As the historian Mark Batunskii summarizes it, "he fear[ed] not only the strengthening of Islam among its eternal confessors, not only the extension of the process of Islamicization to 'pagans,' but also the possibility of if not the entire, of course, Russian people, then likely that vast majority of its representatives whom fate had cast to various national borderlands, going off onto a 'false path.'"[61] This was not the place to look for a dispassionate analysis of the problems Islam presented to contemporary Russian life. Beyond his role as a reference in the *Sbornik*, Miropiev played a visible role in the list of materials that Dukhovskoi recommended for distribution to chanceries and libraries as references.[62] This list doubles as a handy reference guide to the most paranoid anti-Islamic works and thinkers of the Russian Empire, for example, Aleksandr Agronomov's work on *jihad*.[63] It bore the heavy stamp of the Kazan' Theological Academy: it contained numerous issues of the Kazan'-published *Missionerskii protivomusul'manskii sbornik* (Missionary anti-Muslim digest), described by the historial Robert Geraci as "consist[ing] of polemical articles to aid clergy in converting Muslims or persuading apostates to return to the church"; as well as translations and commentaries on the Koran by a Kazan' professor, Gordii Semenovich Sablukov, whose work a student described as "a primary source not only for comprehending Muhammadanism [*sic*], but also for combating it."[64] Dukhovskoi's commitment to this particular framing meant the spread of dubiously founded fears of pan-Islamism and the implacable hostility of Islam to Orthodox Christianity around Turkestan's administrative circles. When 25 copies of the *Sbornik* made their way to the governor-general of the Steppe, Maksim Antonovich Taube (also a recipient of *Islam in Turkestan*), such views spread there as well—Taube dutifully forwarded them to his district chiefs.[65] At the broadest cultural level, it is possible to accept the argument of the historian David Schimmelpenninck van der Oye that "neither fear nor contempt dominated" imperial Russian views of Islam over the broad sweep of the nineteenth century.[66] But among colonial officials, especially in this case, a fearful and contemptuous branch of tsarist orientology predominated.

The circulation of these materials, in turn, abetted the articulation of deeply obnoxious policies at the local level in the two decades that followed Andijan, even quite far from the site of the uprising. Refracted through the prism of paranoia, a mass Kazak petition of 1905 that requested equal rights of representation in the forthcoming parliament became something quite different.[67] Despite the assurances of his subordinates, Semipalatinsk's military governor, Aleksandr Semenovich Galkin, declared the petition impermissible on the grounds that "it is impossible to be sure that among the Kazaks there are not people with evil intentions, willing to, for the sake of personal profits, call forth disorders in the steppe on the basis of religious fanaticism," in which the governor-general of the Steppe, Nikolai Nikaolevich Sukhotin, supported him.[68] In this case, what Kazak subjects understood as their lawful and reasonable requests were transformed, because of administrators' understanding of Islam, into more threatening actions than they were in reality.[69] Under a still more aggressively Russocentric governor, Aleksandr Nikolaevich Troinitskii, involvement with this petition figured into the trumped-up charges that would see one important activist member of the Kazak intelligentsia, Akhmet Baitürsïnov, imprisoned.[70] At the same time, much-resented older policies had little chance of being changed in this environment. Fears of creeping Tatarization and Islamicization during the 1860s had led Orenburg's governor-general, Nikolai Kryzhanovskii, to remove the steppe from the jurisdiction of the Orenburg Muslim Spiritual Assembly.[71] For observant Kazaks, this represented a serious constraint on their freedom of conscience and a major grievance against the tsarist state; redressing it was a matter of first-rate importance.[72] But the desired reform was never forthcoming. Kazaks were thus Muslim enough to be targets of suspicion, but not so Muslim that fears of radicalizing influences from without completely disappeared.

These were the major indignities. There were also smaller ones. Urban Muslims' modest efforts to open reading rooms and charitable societies found insurmountable administrative obstacles.[73] Semirech'e's provincial board [*obshchee prisutstvie*] concerning associations repeatedly rejected the efforts of Muslims from the small city of Kopal to form a charitable society, in decisions that had only panic as their least common denominator:

> The provincial board on matters concerning associations finds that the charter contains points which are completely impermissible, like, for example, on the establishment of meetings with participation of non-association members "for popularization" of "elective rights", about awarding the society of the right to add *ziakat* to its funds, or about the right of local representatives "to accept statements or petitions from the needy," since the realization of these points, under certain conditions, and considering the existence [*pri nalichii*] of article 3, which does not restrict the member of the association by title or status, nor even by religious confession, can threaten social tranquility. Therefore the board resolves to refuse to support of the charter of the Society of Kopal Muslim Progressives, as requested by its founders.[74]

The Muslims (predominantly Tatars, apparently) of Przheval'sk, another small city in Semirech'e, did get their library, but soon found themselves targets of spurious rumors that the library was in fact a site for political meetings.[75] Even displays of patriotism with the outbreak of World War I were not necessarily above suspicion; as one district chief in Semipalatinsk province wrote, "In the sincerity of [local Muslims'] elevated patriotic feeling I, on the basis of my observations over the course of 17 years of police service, do not believe."[76] After the turn of the century, overblown fear of pan-Islamism, pan-Turkism, and suspicion of the loyalty of Muslim subjects were not incidental features of tsarist rule in the steppe provinces and Central Asia. It would have been difficult for a devout subject not to collide with such views in one form or another.

Despite Stolypin's superficial commitment to a policy of religious tolerance after the Revolution of 1905 (one that always offered more to Orthodox Christians than other confessional groups), it is clear that pan-Islamic paranoia came to influence his thinking as well. Beyond the vagueness of discourse, the historian Dmitrii Arapov has identified one likely agent in Stolypin's concrete articulation of such views, the ethnographer-turned-administrator Aleksei Nikolaevich Kharuzin, director of the Department of Religious Affairs of Foreign Faiths between 1908 and 1911.[77] By 1911, Stolypin raged against the inroads that pan-Islamism had allegedly made in all parts of the empire populated by Muslims and demanded "strictly unified and systematic" action against the "onslaught of Islam."[78] Undoubtedly, some of Stolypin's more strident rhetoric on this point should be attributed to his pragmatic shift toward conservative nationalism in the wake of the Naval Staffs crisis of 1909.[79] A generic sort of Russian national-ism (informed, among other factors, by Islamophobia) was already at the core of the Third of June coup. After 1909, the hegemonic position of such ideas made a future rapprochement unlikely. All the while, the limitations of religious toler-ance and the inexorable spread of exaggerated fears of political Islam at lower levels of governance militated against Muslims' participation in politics below the imperial level, as well.

In short, to be a Muslim and a subject of the Russian Empire after the fin-de-siècle was to be, at some level, a target of suspicion and a problem to be solved. But the largely urban Muslims of the Caucasus and Volga River basin (to say nothing of Poles and Jews, equally likely sources of antigovernmental conspiracy in imperial eyes) retained minimal representation in the Third and Fourth Dumas, a distinction of which Kazak commentators were all too aware. To fully account for the exclusion of the steppe and Central Asia from this empire-wide representative body, it is necessary to consider a second factor, views of nomadism.

This book has already dealt with the complex of stereotypes associated with pastoral nomads, in Russian thought, over the broad sweep of the nineteenth century—the dirt, the smells, the loose morals, the near-childlike trust and animal ignorance. More important than rehashing these views again is to note that they remained current after the turn of the century. This was, for the most part, not racial theorizing that held that the difference between nomads and more civilized, advanced peoples was inherent and permanent. Ample evidence seemed to suggest that Kazaks, in particular, had long-term developmental potential.[80] But, in a microcosm of the Russian Empire's fundamental problem in dealing with its inorodtsy—the constantly moving target for promotion to the ranks of ordinary subjects—they had not yet, it was thought, reached that level.[81] The very policy of peasant resettlement assumed the need to raise the cul-tural level of the steppe and promote its more efficient use by seizing it from its inhabitants, or transforming them. Even experts affiliated with the Resettlement Administration who were relatively cautious about mass resettlement associated a host of negative traits with nomadic society. For example, P. P. Rumiantsev, who revised Veletskii's land norms for Semirech'e, closely linked mobility and a lack of civil development in a major work, while citing Levshin heavily.[82] Orest Shkapskii, a "supporter of the land rights of the Kyrgyz" who left the Semirech'e branch of the Resettlement Agency in disgrace in 1906, connected pastoralism among the Kyrgyz with the exploitation of ordinary people by elites because of the indefiniteness of land claims he associated with it.[83] Meanwhile, *Aziatskaia Rossiia*, the Resettlement Administration's "masterwork" and the closest thing to an official statement on the matter, described the "idleness" of pastoralist men and derided Kazakhs' belief in the power of sorcerers.[84] To drive home the point that this was, in the main, an ignorant people whose development lay long in the future, the contributor of this volume's ethnographic sketch, I. P. Poddubnyi, borrowed words straight from the pen of the doctor and anthropologist V. D. Tronov two decades earlier: "The Kazakh stands on a low level of development, his fantasy is poor, forms are little poetic: the Kazakh thus, for example, praises [*vospevaet*] nature: 'what a mountain, what a valley! In this valley one could pasture a thousand horses, on this mountain one could pasture a thousand sheep.'"[85] A range of views on resettlement converged, if nothing else, on the principle that nomadism was a backward way of life, and nomads themselves rough and uncultured.

On the level of politics, beyond the occasional stridency of Turkestani and Kazak deputies in the first two Dumas, and pan-Islamist fears difficult to disentangle from the facts of ethnicity and geography, language issues likely played a role in the construction of the region's political immaturity. Rural cantons had serious difficulty coming up with plausible candidates as electors who both satisfied their own wishes and the basic requirement of proficiency in Russian.[86] In response to such concerns, administrators in Semirech'e could only underline their insistence that their subordinates "should not back down on the requirement that electors select people knowing Russian."[87] Thus, beyond the negative stereotypes associated with pastoralist lifeways, Kazaks and Central Asians found the failings of a long-neglected system of native schools laid at their feet.

During the last years of the Russian Empire, to be a Muslim was damning enough. To be a Muslim and a pastoralist was to be doubly ungovernable. There were, assuredly, other ways of thinking about both of these categories, but the conjunction lasted as long as the empire did. A later minister of internal affairs, Nikolai Alekseevich Maklakov, responded firmly to a petition to re-examine the electoral laws in 1914:

> I consider equally impossible, too, the restoration of representation in the State Duma from the population of the following provinces: Akmolinsk, Semipalatinsk, Ural'sk, Turgai, Semirech'e, Transcaspian, Samarkand, Syr-Darya, and Fergana, the multiracial [*raznoplemennoe*] population of which provinces cannot be yet considered, at present, sufficiently prepared for participation in the legislative work of the state, which was proven with complete clarity by the experience of elections according to the law of December 11, 1905.[88]

Both in failing to satisfy, or even acknowledge, what members of the Kazak intelligentsia considered to be their reasonable aspirations, and in closing what might have been a useful conduit between the Kazak population's representatives and the upper levels of the state, such intransigence had tragic consequences. Here, as in the case of resettlement, late tsarist scholarship provided a range of answers to questions of governance. Happenstance and the competing priorities of a struggling autocracy saw the wrong ones come to the fore.

"Worthy . . . of the Title of Citizens of Great Russia": Adapting to Resettlement and Disenfranchisement

If the nascent Kazak intelligentsia considered the presence of Russian settlers on the steppe and absence of political representation to be fundamental problems, their responses were largely grounded in the intellectual and political world that nearly two centuries of imperial rule had created. New claims on lands that Kazaks understood as ancestral prompted attempts to both modernize economically and make maximally successful counterclaims on the land.[89] These same measures would raise Kazaks' civilizational level, making them worthy participants in imperial institutions.[90] In debating among themselves how best to respond to the shocks of resettlement, Kazak thinkers displayed a range of responses to metropolitan thought and diverse understandings of the potential of their environment. Such understandings proved as instrumentally useful in intra-Kazak polemics as they had when engaging with tsarist administrators. But there was still a basic willingness to work within imperial institutions and accept the "civilizing" arguments of their interlocutors, as long as Kazaks were permitted to make their own way there.[91]

The behavior of the Kazak intelligentsia in the wake of Central Asia's disenfranchisement, and with ever more settlers flowing into the region, was in part pragmatic and political, devoted to realizing short-term goals. The two most important Kazak-language periodical organs of the 1910s, the Troitsk-based journal *Ai-qap* (1911–1915) and Orenburg-based newspaper *Qazaq* (1913–1918), agreed if nothing else that Kazaks' absence from the Duma was both a symbolic and a practical blow.[92] The members of the Muslim fraction who continued to sit in the Third Duma had little understanding of Kazaks' life conditions and thus did not know which laws would favor or harm them.[93] Thus it was necessary to struggle by all possible means to right the wrong. In 1912, a group of Kazaks including Akhmet Baitürsïnov hatched a plan to sneak a deputy into the Duma via the position reserved for the

Muslims of the city of Orenburg, a city outside the steppe provinces proper but very much within their orbit.[94] The boundaries of the steppe provinces were not the end of the world for traders and intellectuals, and this was a canny strategy of working around the late tsarist state's territorialization of backwardness, although it ultimately failed. Subsequently, efforts focused on a time-honored tool of the weakest subjects of the Russian state, the petition.[95] Later, a Kazak representative would be appointed to the Muslim fraction in St. Petersburg/Petrograd to develop draft laws and strategize.[96] This choice first fell on Bökeikhanov. By the end of 1916, as the amount of pressing business increased, the law student Mustafa Shoqaev also began to serve.[97] From a practical perspective, members of the Kazak intelligentsia were prepared to argue that they were no worse, and no less deserving of rights, than other subjects of the Russian Empire.[98] When conventional paths to representation were closed, they, for the most part, attempted to forge new ones rather than dispensing with the system entirely.

The withdrawal of rights of representation in the Duma and the ever-growing number of settlers on the steppe also played well into the Kazak intelligentsia's long-standing politics of admonition. This had been the fundamental point of Abai's *Qarasözder*: Kazaks had allowed themselves to be left behind thanks to laziness and ignorance. In the resettlement era, so members of the intelligentsia scolded their imagined audience, evidence that this was the case was only mounting. In 1909, Mïrzhaqïp Dŭlatov (1885–1935), a poet and publicist originally trained as a teacher, published a collection of poems titled *Oian Qazaq!* (Awake, Kazak!), explicitly hoping to rouse a dormant population from its slumber and oppose Russian colonization.[99] Baqïtzhan Qarataev, in a 1910 letter to Bökeikhanov, described the Kazakh people's "ignorance and nomadic lack of culture" as a threat to its existence equal to that presented by resettlement bureaucrats.[100] Bökeikhanov, for his part, glossed the electoral law of June 3, 1907, thus: "The Kazak people is ignorant, and unsuitable for the Duma, it was said."[101] Such statements came with an implicit question that members of the intelligentsia addressed head-on, though their responses differed wildly: how could the Kazak people become less ignorant, and more suitable? How could they become skillful (*önerlï*) or, as one anonymous commentator put it, "worthy . . . of the title of citizens of Great Russia, our beloved Motherland [*Otan*]?"[102]

Ai-qap and *Qazaq* pursued, in the main, two lines in answering these questions, each mixing environmental determinism and social evolutionism in different measures. These may be distinguished even though there was some overlap between them, and neither publication completely rejected sedentarism.[103] The time of nomadism had passed, owing to political circumstances and natural laws.

This did not mean, however, that there was consensus about which *kind* of sedentarism best suited the Kazaks and their land. The *Ai-qap* group tended to favor the near-abandonment of stock raising, with a very strong role for agriculture, while the *Qazaq* group argued instead for sedentary, intensified, and commercially oriented animal husbandry. If the final goal of self-strengthening through learning and settling on the land was similar, these authors' understandings of local environments differed wildly.

The *Ai-qap* group, in general, showed itself to be less concerned with the quality of the land per se than with disassociating Kazakness from pastoral nomadism. All around the edges of the steppe, one contributor to the journal argued, Kazaks were discovering a range of trades outside of traditional stock raising, only possible through totally abandoning pastoral mobility: "If I look at the Kazaks of Kokand, I see Kazaks who have become owners of huge gardens, have begun to sow rice and cotton, who are living very well. In Astrakhan, they live by fishing on the coast, in Troitsk, Atbasar, Petropavl, Omsk, Semei, Zarechnyi, and Qaraötkel the Kazaks live by trading [*saudagershīlīk*]; our youths who have studied, I see, work as clerks, translators, scribes, secretaries, teachers, medical assistants, doctors, lawyers, judges, and engineers."[104] Similarly, a later pseudonymous commentator (under the pen name *Qazaqemes*—"not a Kazak") argued that Kazaks had always been characterized by economic diversity, with some sowing, some raising livestock, some migrating, some not.[105] Thus becoming sedentary and cultivating grain would not necessarily be alien to Kazakhs' historical experience. Rather, considering Kazaks as a part of universal history, they would have to sedentarize. Everywhere, when population density increased, people settled on the land. Why would Kazaks be any different?[106]

The benefits to be gained from such an immediate transition, further, were described as vast. The first and most obvious was prosperity. Like the official *Kirgizskaia stepnaia gazeta* before it, *Ai-qap* publicized cases of successful transitions to agriculture, as among Kazaks living on the Baraba steppe of western Siberia. Having taken good land, these Kazaks were able to market an agricultural surplus and sell copious amounts of hay during the zhŭt years that threatened their nomadic neighbors. They checked the other key box for intellectuals of the age, too, by reinvesting their profits in religious and educational institutions. It was, all in all, a "very pleasing thing to hear [*qulaq süisinerlīk īs*]."[107]

Kazaks' failure to extract maximum value from their surroundings, rather "surviving on the back of the land and water," positioned them, for adherents of the *Ai-qap* line, as among the least cultured subjects of the Russian Empire.[108] Sedentarizing, and using European science to arrive at the necessary methods of making agriculture work in the steppe environment, would both raise the overall level of culture and create opportunities for still further development. And this, in turn, would provide fabulous returns in the long run. A single desiatina of land, one anonymous author argued, could easily yield 50 to 100 rubles every year under properly managed agriculture.[109] Kazaks who found themselves with a less reliable or more meager income from their stock raising, despite the apparent vastness of their herds, ought to think carefully about their next steps. This, too, was an argument with little consideration of parts of the steppe that might be less propitious for agriculture; the same author ended his article with a confident statement that "our farmers will make it known that our land is indeed gold."[110]

Finally, sedentarism with an emphasis on agriculture offered distinct political advantages, according to the *Ai-qap* line. Gaining the zemstvo (and, thus, gaining legal equality with the core provinces of the empire)—a local government institution offering a degree of local control over education, medical care, and other affairs—was a crucial goal for the Kazak intelligentsia by the 1910s.[111] But, an unsigned piece noted, caricaturing their opponents' views, an institution mostly designed for the rural administration of peasants could only function if Kazaks were sedentary: "The zemstvo is a good thing. But in order to use the zemstvo it is necessary for the people to be sedentary. *Qazaq* is saying to be nomadic."[112] Sedentarization thus offered both political advantages and a clear means of cultural uplift. Moreover, it offered a fixed claim to land that nomadism, with ever-decreasing land norms and the stipulation that nomads' surpluses could be seized, did not. Zemleustroistvo as sedentary, guaranteeing 15 desiatinas of land per male soul, promised at least a limit to the seizures.[113] In a context where peasants were arriving on the steppe, driving Kazaks off to the worst parts of the steppe, and impoverishing them, closing ranks and sedentarizing guaranteed survival.[114]

The opponents of the *Ai-qap* line, many of them affiliated with *Qazaq* after 1913, found such views to be laughably optimistic and ill founded, for several reasons. First, the pro-agriculture group's simplistic equation of agriculture and higher culture fell apart on closer inspection. As an anonymous piece in *Qazaq* early in 1914 noted, "If you want to be cultured, raising livestock will not stop it [*mal baghudïng toqtaulïghï zhoq*]".[115] The following year, in the same paper, Bökeikhanov cited the Arabic language as an example of the level of culture a stock-raising people could achieve, and Switzerland and Australia as countries combining animal husbandry and efficient economic organization; though the Bashkirs and Tatars had turned to agriculture before the Kazaks, he further argued, they had not achieved any more than the latter.[116] This being the case, agriculture's role in cultural uplift generally, and as a means of achieving equality within the Russian Empire in particular, was open to serious doubt.

This was just as well, supporters of the *Qazaq* line claimed, because there was very little evidence that much of the steppe could ever be made suitable for agriculture, and a great deal of scientific evidence that suggested the opposite. Dŭlatov had already presented this side of the argument when attempting to stimulate discussion in *Ai-qap* in 1911: "The Kazak people has never said, I will nomadize, it nomadizes in dependence [*qarap*] on the climactic conditions of the land. Man is the slave of the climactic conditions of the land where he lives. The land where the Kazak lives is unsuited to agriculture."[117] *Qazaq* ran in several directions with this fundamental principle. Just as *Ai-qap* trumpeted the achievements of successful farmers, *Qazaq* ran articles depicting the transition to farming in a gloomier light: without the promised aid from tsarist administrators, for example, the unfortunate Kazaks of Mengdïqara canton, in the settler-heavy northern steppe, quickly learned that "it is impossible to survive by sowing grain."[118] Faced with an administration that would not let them return to nomadism, their future was uncertain. More generally, the prominent statistician and agronomist Konstantin Antonovich Verner, who served in the Steppe Governor-Generalship in the early 1890s, had declared the steppe only suitable for pastoral stock herders.[119] Another professor, cited only as "Bogdanov," apparently argued that "the Kazak steppe cannot be grain-sowing land."[120] What had the proponents of sedentary agriculture to offer in response? Only good intentions and the unfounded claims of a few Tatars who "do not know the Kazak land question well."[121] Both empirical and subjective evidence suggested that the *Ai-qap* camp could not deliver what it promised.

The showpiece of the *Qazaq* line was a massive article serialized in 1915 and 1916, "Sharualïq özgerïsï" ("Economic Change"). This, in its first stages, was a guided tour through the classics of European political economy (bearing a particularly strong influence from Friedrich List), theories of globalization, and social evolutionist thought.[122] By the time its author turned to conditions on the steppe proper, he had drawn the following conclusions: "natural conditions, population density, and the transition to trades and crafts [*sheberlïk*]: these are the first-rank reasons why an economy changes."[123] Although 1915 ended with more questions than answers, it was clear that the author had been strongly influenced by ideas of environmental determinism—if not in questions of national character, then at least in the sense that the environment placed firm limits on a people's economic choices:

> According to what we know, to be sedentary, various conditions must be favorable. After saying that these conditions are available on Kazak land, phrases like "culture will come to a sedentary people" and "if you sow, grain will grow [*ekseng egïn shïghadï*]" are often heard. With sowing,

will grain continue to grow? For grain to grow, is it only necessary to sow, are there no other conditions? First, for grain to grow it is necessary for the soil to be suitable. On sand and saline soil [*solonchak*], nothing will grow. Second, there must be moisture within the soil. If there is no moisture, grain will not come from the dry soil. Third, warm air is needed. In cold earth grain, again, will not grow.[124]

In the specific case of the steppe, "the question of Kazaks sedentarizing or not is like this problem of sowing grain. Before sowing it is necessary to know whether or not the necessary conditions are present."[125] The author thus positioned himself as an honest broker sorting through all the data at hand—the steppe was environmentally diverse, and some Kazaks had already settled on the land, so it was vital to know how well they lived, and if sedentary Kazaks did better in some areas than others.[126] The following year, he began to break down the data, with help from books published by the Resettlement Administration, particularly the work of Fedor Andreevich Shcherbina (much derided in the Resettlement Administration proper by that time). The conclusion he drew from these first, cautious studies was pessimistic: "In Turgai province, out of 43 million desiatinas, 28 million seem unsuitable for grain sowing. This is two-thirds of the province's land."[127] Particularly with the more promising sowing land going over to peasant settlers, settling and doing agriculture represented only a limited solution at best.

In fact, the *Qazaq* line had never been, as opponents parodied it, an utter rejection of sedentarism, nor a continued validation of the dark and feudal past. Baitŭrsïnov, a key early contributor to *Ai-qap* who later became "the soul of *Qazaq*,"[128] and who evinced a cautious attitude towards sedentarization, neatly summarized this intermediate position early on: "The advice to sedentarize [*qala salu degen söz*] was not said to all Kazaks, it was said to Kazaks who sow grain and have good land [*kün körerlïk zherĭ*]."[129] Already in the days of the *KSG*, there had been few Kazak thinkers willing to defend pastoralism as it had been in the distant past. It was too associated with risk, poverty, and internal misrule to have a serious future. Economic and demographic pressures on the Kazaks had only gotten worse since the *KSG* was shuttered early in 1902. An urgent question thus arose: if not farming, then what?

The answer here, too, lay in the way that authors who held the *Qazaq* line thought about their surrounding environment. The steppe, as they described it, was not merely bad agricultural land, but *good* stock-raising land. "Because the land is stock-raising land," an article in *Qazaq* argued, "there is no way not to raise stock there."[130] The same piece noted that stock raising leveraged skills that Kazaks already had: "What the Kazaks know is how to raise stock, badly plow, do trade, other than this they have no trades or arts."[131] Rather, the models that Bökeikhanov, in particular, looked to were Switzerland and Australia. In the former, on small amounts of bad land, sedentary people raised small amounts of well-bred livestock, whose products sold for high prices abroad. In the latter, perhaps most similar to the steppe with its huge amounts of open grassland, sedentary people raised comparatively large amounts of sheep, whose high quality secured it a market as far away as St. Petersburg.[132] The trick, then, was to reduce the total amount of livestock kept, figure out what the market wanted, and improve its quality accordingly. Peoples in similar conditions to Kazaks had proven that it was possible to do so. Then, the long-term benefits of sedentarism could accrue without pursuing a course that was unlikely to succeed. Just as important, making claims on the larger amounts of land (double what was needed for agriculture) needed even for intensive stock raising would serve an important political goal, putting more of the precious *ata meken* (Fatherland) in Kazak hands and restricting its availability to settlers.[133] That GUZiZ would never have considered a zemleustroistvo that saw Kazaks receive more land per soul than settlers was beside the point when an idea seemed both politically desirable and environmentally plausible. Kazaks could remain a valuable part of the Russian Empire, improve themselves, and keep more of their land.

The debate among adherents of the *Ai-qap* and *Qazaq* lines was not complete when a new issue, the outbreak of World War I and its creeping influence on the steppe, pushed it to the back burner. Neither course had gained serious traction at higher levels of administration, one because it ran contrary to what was considered the higher state goal of peasant resettlement, the other because local resettlement bureaus could barely get new Russian migrants settled on new lands, let alone nomads.[134] Nor, with the rejection of further petitions for Duma representation, and the growing pan-Islamist threat that the outbreak of war with the Ottoman Empire seemed to augur, had Central Asians succeeded in regaining the political rights they coveted. The tensions of disenfranchisement and expropriation remained unresolved when the all-consuming claims of World War I reached the steppe provinces.

Things Fall Apart: War and Rebellion

Historians may disagree on the matter of when exactly humans began to fight total wars, but it is indisputable that World War I, with its mass mobilizations and fusion of war and politics, was a total conflict for all combatants.[135] This

presaged difficulty in the Russian Empire: how was it possible to evenly mobi-
lize this patchwork of special rights, privileges, and obligations? Some of the
empire's inorodtsy had long been exempt from the duty to offer troops for
long-term service or, after the military reforms of 1874, from universal conscription.[136] This was both a privilege that came as a condition of submitting
to the Russian Empire and, viewed through another lens, a barrier to full imperial citizenship—a point driven home by the exclusion of some of these same
inorodtsy from the Duma.[137] Mobilizing the steppe and Central Asia, when the
moment came, laid bare the contradictions of tsarist rule there. On one hand, in
a vacuum, it looked to some Kazaks, as well as other Muslims within the empire,
like an opportunity: to acculturate to the other peoples of the empire, as well as
to develop stronger claims on land and political rights.[138] On the other, it was
an unprecedented claim on the lives and work of imperial subjects who had
developed a long list of grievances over the previous two decades of resettlement, to be implemented through a stereotypically weak state apparatus. When
a rebellion ensued on the heels of a draft order of June 25, 1916, it was equally
the product of a botched mobilization and the economic disruptions of 20 years
of resettlement. Both of these, in turn, were rooted in the hegemonic ideas tsarist administrators had come to hold about the steppe, and the decisions they
made on that basis.

In the early stages of the war, those regions of the Russian Empire that were
exempt from conscription paid significantly increased taxes in kind and in
cash as their contribution to the war effort.[139] This arrangement suited tsarist
administrators well, both because meat, wool, and cash were in high demand
for an enormous army and because many inorodtsy, "especially in Central Asia
and the Caucasus, were not considered ready for assimilation, at least with
regards to military conscription and service."[140] However, as combatants' initial
hopes for a quick, victorious war were extinguished, and in particular in the
wake of reverses that Russia suffered on the Eastern Front during 1915, the wisdom of a universal exemption became open to question. Already, during the fall
of 1915, the Ministry of War solicited the Ministry of Internal Affairs' opinion
on a proposal to draft various inorodtsy, and the pages of *Qazaq* buzzed with
newspaper reports about different ministries' opinions on the matter.[141] The
arguments against deployed the accustomed old stereotypes about Kazaks' low
cultural level, and specific concerns about their ability to understand Russian-
speaking commanders. Some arguments in favor employed a different set of
stereotypes—Kazaks as a warrior people—while GUZiZ and Muslim newspapers argued, respectively, that Kazaks were already somewhat Russianized, not
the savages they had once been, and that military service would only further
acculturate them. The editors of *Qazaq*, at this stage, were laconic: "Kazaks

agreed [*könĭp bergen*] to be identical with other peoples with respect to Russia. Therefore, the Kazaks will not refuse military service."[142] They asked only for careful consideration of the mechanics of the draft, so as to avoid complications. But 1915 brought no firm decision among the ministries of St. Petersburg, nor any consensus among Kazaks who were left to imagine what form military service might take, if or when it came. As with respect to the land question some years earlier, while the state pursued its own course, the Kazak press attempted to solicit correspondence from a range of perspectives. These perspectives show that the draft, for the Kazak intelligentsia, was associated with both potential problems and high aspirations.

Support for providing troops was not universal even among the literate, educated people who wrote to *Qazaq* (not a representative sample under the best of circumstances). One correspondent turned the discourses of civilization by which Kazaks had been politically excluded on their heads. The lack of attention the tsarist state had paid to local schools meant that Kazaks were, indeed, unprepared for military service at present; with preparation offered by schools and the zemstvo, they might be able to serve at some future time, but at present "The Kazak people will not refuse the government's order, but does not wish soldiers to be taken during this war."[143] The consensus, though, seems to have fallen on the desirability of mounted Cossack service. There were good reasons to expect this to align with state priorities. The first administrative discussions of Kazak military service, in the early 1880s, had turned entirely on cavalry service, as "incomparably easier for the natives than in the infantry."[144] Kazaks who advocated, or at least considered it unwise to resist, military service advanced similar arguments. Cossacks' way of life was already familiar to Kazaks, because Cossack settlements had long existed on the steppe, and Kazaks themselves learned to ride horses at a very young age—if taken as Cossacks, they would be good soldiers, and the government would have successfully leveraged local skills to its own advantage.[145] It also promised the most comfortable transition to military life for a population unaccustomed to such service: "An [infantry] soldier's movement is on foot, and they live in a barrack. A cavalryman goes on horse and also lives in a barrack, a Cossack serves on horse and lives at home (only leaves home during a war). There is also the greater size of the Cossacks' land share [*sĭbagha*]."[146] Getting hold of more of the *ata meken* than the 15 desiatinas offered to peasant infantry, indeed, was another persistent argument in favor of mounted Cossack service. Infantry service would place less land in Kazak hands, perhaps not even enough for stock raising.[147] The few arguments in favor of infantry service, focusing on sedentary agriculture alone as a path to culture, paled in comparison to this consensus.[148]

As these discussions evolved during 1916, it became clear that, despite the rhetoric of good and obedient subjecthood, several Kazak thinkers had begun to think of contributing to the war effort in terms of a quid pro quo. That service as soldiers would permit claims on the land was obvious enough, according to the general laws of the Russian Empire. Breaking an arrangement more than a century old, however, in providing troops seemed an extraordinary circumstance, and a moment where political demands could be successfully pressed. One hesitant advocate of military service, Akhmet Zhantalin, thought it self-evident that "if soldiers are taken from the Kazaks, so that the condition of their daily life will not bear serious harm, measures must be taken, with more privileges than for peoples who have long been accustomed to having soldiers taken."[149] But the matter went beyond special accommodations. Zhantalin also argued that Kazak representatives should "ask for representation in the Duma [deputattïq sŭrau]" and for the "introduction of the zemstvo and general education [zhalpï oqu]."[150] Kazaks and other Central Asians had been held to be unfit for political representation or military service. Now, if suited for the latter, it stood to reason that they were also qualified to do the former. After the draft order, members of the Kazak intelligentsia extended this instrumental view of the war effort beyond those who were actually called, directing the public's attention to a coming age of freedom and equality after the war's victorious end. It was necessary for them to remain calm and return to the fields, since "this war too will end. At that time everyone will value service [ärkim qïzmetïn baghalar]. At that time those who were not at the sowing or plowing will not be able to pretend to land. If we say we want to claim equality and justice, we must first think carefully. One good turn deserves another [almaqtïng da salmaghï bar]."[151] In a total war, on the steppe as elsewhere, empire and subjects were making new claims on each other. Service would be an opportunity for Kazaks, but it was obligatory for them at least to carry out their end of the bargain.

In the Kazak-language press, the lack of a deputy to the Duma, a representative who could publicly present Kazaks' wishes, conditions, and requirements, rankled deeply. In fact, the tsarist government worked on the mobilization, as it so often did, through informal channels, pressing a few well-known and vetted inorodtsy for their recommendations on the draft. These men, despite their suspect politics in the post-1905 era, were archetypical intermediaries of a multiethnic empire, Kazaks educated in bilingual schools with significant service experience. The Semirech'e-based engineer Mŭkhametzhan Tïnïshbaev, according to his own testimony, was first asked to prepare a report on this topic in September 1915.[152] Early the following year, Baitŭrsïnov and Bökeikhanov were part of a three-man deputation to St. Petersburg with a similar purpose.[153] The recommendations these men made were similar, and echoed the consensus on the pages of *Qazaq*: Kazaks could be drafted, preferably for cavalry service, in exchange for land and only after verification of the metrical books (records of births and deaths—this would ensure an orderly and accurate conscription).[154] That this advocacy seemed to be going poorly was among the direct inspirations for the formation of a more sophisticated political organization, a bureau reporting to the Duma's Muslim fraction.[155] The bottom line, though was that conscription could work as long as the state reckoned with local conditions, of which these intermediaries presented themselves as the best interpreters.

In almost every way imaginable, this did not come off. The exigencies of total war, the contradictory nature of the dying autocracy, and long-held stereotypes about the proper way to rule "Asiatics" combined to produce a mobilization out of the Kazak intelligentsia's nightmares.[156] The call, when it came on June 25, 1916, was for labor behind the front lines of the army. If this perhaps lacked the risks of active combat on the Eastern Front, it also lacked the potential rewards, and indeed, Nicholas II's order made no promises of any rights to be gained in the future, while subjecting recruits to strict martial discipline.[157] The order came down during the middle of the summer, when crops were in the fields and nomads were on the move. The surprising order, requiring rapid fulfillment, allowed no time to bring the metrical books into order. This created broad space for abuse on the part of lower-level Kazak administrators (or accusations of abuse, which amounted to the same thing). In some areas, even awareness that the draft was going badly seemed no excuse to stop it; bowing to necessity in this way, administrators thought, would be an unforgivable display of weakness before the natives.[158] The requisition of inorodtsy would continue, regardless of the consequences.

Some leading elders (*aqsaqals*) were quick to declare their readiness to serve, and despite administrative suspicions to the contrary, the editors of *Qazaq* supported the mobilization as much as the tsarist state could have wished.[159] But the overall effects of the ill-taken draft order were frightful, culminating in the Central Asian revolt of 1916. As the draft order was implemented, riots seized cities and large towns during the month of July, and unrest quickly spread to the nomadic Kazaks, Kyrgyz, and Turkmen during August. Different scholars have estimated that between 2,000 and 10,000 Russians, mostly settlers, were killed during these revolts, and between 100,000 and 200,000 pastoralists perished during reprisals on the part of settlers and the colonial administration.[160]

Although it is clear that the botched draft order was the proximal cause of the revolt, and the course of the revolt varied significantly in different areas, the evidence suggests that for many Central Asians, it was peasant resettlement on the norm-and-surplus system that created long-standing grievances. Such is the conclusion of the most rigorous account of the revolt that we have for Semirech'e, the work of Jörn Happel.[161] It squares well with contemporaries' observations. Tïnïshbaev, for example, reported of one instance that he considered it significant that "the first two people killed were settlement bureaucrats, from the institution that laid the foundation of the Kazaks' dissatisfaction."[162] One specific case of massive violence emerged from a district of Semirech'e where it had long been known that the presence of settlers put an untenable strain on scarce water resources.[163] Attacks on peasants also took place further north, in Akmolinsk province, although both here and in Semipalatinsk the scope of the revolt was far smaller than in Semirech'e.[164] The majority of administrative opinion here blamed the clumsy implementation of the draft order for resistance, although at least one official considered the presence of settlers to be the root cause.[165] In the case of Turgai province, where a revolt under the leadership of Amangeldi Imanov continued into 1917, the historian Tomohiko Uyama accords to the pressures of colonialism a role alongside the "hasty and careless way the ukase was issued and implemented," while also noting the importance of Islam in stimulating resistance.[166] Resettlement played a significant role, alongside other local factors, in provoking and shaping the Central Asian Revolt. GUZiZ and the Resettlement Administration might have known better, but chose not to.

As the repressive apparatus of the tsarist state made itself felt in putting down the revolt, the exhortations of Dŭlatov, Baitŭrsïnov, and Bökeikhanov began to take on a rather different tone. On one hand, they continued to invoke the idea that Kazaks were subjects of the empire, just like other nationalities who had fought, and needed to fulfill the responsibilities this entailed. But as reports of massacres piled up, their core message was that Kazaks should comply with the labor requisition as a means of self-protection.[167] Their readiness to cooperate, if only to secure the well-being of Kazaks who had been called up, extended to recruiting bilingual Kazaks to assist worker brigades and obtaining provisions for recruits.[168] The long-term effect of the revolt and its suppression, though, was to reveal with finality the impossibility of finding a rapprochement with Nicholas II's government. Their input about the implementation of the conscription order had apparently been ignored, and their aspirations to earn equality before the law through service seemed remote.[169]

Worse still would probably have been to come. Gen. Aleksei Nikolaevich Kuropatkin, who had been sent to Turkestan to handle the implementation of the draft order, understood the stakes of the revolt clearly and proposed a draconian punishment:

It is necessary that the native population learns definitively that the spilling of Russian blood is punishable not only by the execution of those directly guilty but also taking of land from natives who turned out unworthy to own it, as was done with those guilty of the Andijan rebellion. This principle, decisively carried out with each flare-up from the native population, resulting in the shedding of Russian blood, should compel the sensible part of the population to refrain from attempts to struggle against Russian power by force of arms.[170]

The day after Kuropatkin filed his report, the population of St. Petersburg— Petrograd, during the war—flooded its streets demanding bread. One week after that, Nicholas II—now simply Nikolai Aleksandrovich Romanov—abdicated the throne. With the exception of Turgai province, the revolt had been put down, and the intelligentsia remained deeply willing to make common cause with a government that promised land and representation, as evidenced in a statement that many signed early in March: "The Kazaks now need to organize for the support of the new structure and new government. It is necessary to work in contact with all nationalities, supporting the new structure. The Kazaks should prepare for the Constituent Assembly and select worthy candidates. . . . Hurry to discuss the agrarian question. Our slogan is 'democratic republic' and land to whomever extracts income from it by animal husbandry and agriculture."[171] But there were few to mourn what they now understood as "the old government's various sorts of evil, violence, and shame [zorlïq]."[172] As in the core provinces of the empire, space for cooperation between the public, at its various levels, and the monarchy had irreversibly disappeared.

Within a year of the February Revolution, in a move that had long been prefigured, the liberal faction of the Kazak intelligentsia had broken with the liberal Kadet party. Bökeikhanov attributed the split to Kadets' prioritization of Russian issues and opposition to national autonomy.[173] Subsequently, many among the Kazak intelligentsia were instrumental in forming an ephemeral anti-Bolshevik republic called the Alash Autonomy.[174] By the end of the Russian Civil War, they had little choice but to negotiate with their former opponents; shortly after the final victory of Soviet arms, the Alash Autonomy was disbanded in August 1920, and replaced by the "Kirgiz" Autonomous Socialist Soviet Republic. This decision was to prove personally unfortunate for Baitŭrsïnov, Bökeikhanov, and other members of the Kazak intelligentsia whose death dates of 1937 and 1938 testify mutely to their fate under Soviet power, shot as "bourgeois nationalists" and "enemies of the people."[175] The mass famine brought on by collectivization and sedentarization of Kazak pastoralists during the First Five-Year Plan indicates that, whatever long-term benefits urbanization, expanded education, and public health campaigns might have brought the average Kazak, there were serious costs to this decision for the bulk of the population as well.[176] After the turbulent restoration of power during the 1920s, Soviet officials knew the land and population of the steppe more thoroughly, and had more coercive force at their disposal, than did their tsarist counterparts. Both of these factors helped them to realize their vision of governance. The incomplete knowledge according to which the Russian Empire ruled Central Asia and the voluminous data backing Soviet administration there came to lend themselves equally well to misrule. The common denominator was the certainty with which a pair of aggressively modernizing states chose to apply them. In both cases, ultimately, other ways of knowing were set aside, and with them, the roles that intermediaries could play were circumscribed.

Conclusion

A strikingly common formulation among Kazak intermediaries of the long nineteenth century was that the Kazak steppe and its inhabitants were in a "transitional state." Arguing for the implementation of his educational reforms to the tsarist administrator V. V. Katarinskii, for example, Ibrai Altynsarin wrote that "the [Kazak] people, being now in a transitional state, requires some sort of moral food; and it receives this food, out of necessity, from ignorant hands, eats it up rather greedily and ruins its healthy body."[1] Even those intermediaries who did not explicitly use the rhetoric of a "transitional state" (*perekhodnoe sostoianie*) were concerned, in some way, with the steppe's process of becoming something else. Usually, in their view, this entailed its becoming something better than it had previously been. These narratives of progress and transition varied substantially on the basis of time, place, and personal experience. For some Kazaks, the source of their problems lay in a moral crisis, while for others, the fundamental issue was a failure of economic modernization; the route forward, for some, lay in Europeanization, while for others, it was to be found in the spread of a purified, modernist Islam. The Russian conquest had been a major event in the history of the steppe, a mark of a backwardness that was to be overcome, and the main task was to determine how best to overcome it.

For tsarist administrators, the Kazak steppe was also long in the process of becoming something new. Their visions of how it and its inhabitants might benefit the empire varied: it might be a second grain-growing center for the empire or a center of intensified, market-oriented stock raising. Bringing either goal to fruition might involve a concerted effort at education and civilizational uplift, the mass settlement of peasant colonizers, or simply the eternal vigilance of military rule. One thing was clear: once the steppe became an internal borderland, rather than a frontier, it would need to change somehow. The savagery that tsarist administrators thought they saw there, perhaps acceptable at the edge of the empire, was unacceptable now that the region seemed closer to the core. On this, in the main, tsarist administrators and scholars and their Kazak interlocutors could agree. Moreover, both sides' vision of the steppe's future involved some sort of role for the tsarist state; the fait accompli of the conquest was something for Kazaks to work with, rather than actively attempt to overthrow. But for decades, the specifics of this transition were subject to dispute, and much more was said than done, because of tsarist administrators' fundamental ignorance of the geography and ethnography of the region they were asked to govern.[2] Thus the Provisional Statute of 1868, the result of a dedicated study tour of experts, was essentially and consciously a guess at what the future of governance on the steppe might look like, a two-year experiment that ultimately lasted more than two decades. While bringing Kazaks closer to imperial institutions, thus setting in motion pressures to become sedentary, it also contained several provisions protecting their pastoral nomadic lifestyle.[3] It endorsed a "traditional" system of customary law that had never been successfully codified. The Provisional Statute was the product of the "known unknowns" of steppe life, to be modified as experience filled in gaps in scholarly and administrative knowledge.

In the fluid world the Provisional Statute made, with governance subject to constant revision and the whims of lower-level administrators, Kazaks found that presenting themselves to the tsarist state as knowledgeable insiders could work to their benefit.[4] This was particularly the case because no single consensus existed among tsarist administrators about which policies toward the steppe best served local interests and the empire as a whole. Thus in Turgai province, in the Orenburg steppe, Altynsarin, the product of an earlier generation of schools for natives, used the authority his local expertise conferred to advance a moral-educational program that cobbled together multiple tsarist administrative practices in a new way. Doing so both helped Altynsarin to make a career and advance the region where he was born in the direction he thought most likely to succeed, granting him a measure of authority both among Kazaks and in administrative circles. Kazaks needed both material and moral progress, he thought, and his actions demonstrated his belief that the tsarist state offered a promising means of affecting it. If, in this respect, Altynsarin shared the assumptions of administrative interlocutors more powerful than he, and on whose patronage he depended, the specifics of this "progress" were up for negotiation on the basis of local conditions. These policies, in turn, made a material difference in the lives of the

Kazaks who were their objects. Altynsarin's insider status, combined with his understandings of Kazakness and the local environment, helped him to cobble together one way forward out of many, rather than submitting to an undifferentiated, all-powerful imperial regime.

By the 1890s, several things had changed, but most of them did not prove sufficient to doom the uneven dialogue between tsarist administrators and Kazak intermediaries. St. Petersburg began to shed its hesitancy about peasant mobility, promulgating the Resettlement Act of 1889 (which designated state land as free land available for settlement) and, in 1896, organizing the Resettlement Administration to give more structure to peasant movement to the steppe (and Siberia). The Steppe Statute of 1891 (effective in 1893) drew Kazaks closer than ever to the bureaucratic structures of the state and contained the legal architecture for peasant settlement on land Kazaks had held. In all, the tsarist state was developing greater unity of purpose on the steppe, favoring policies directed toward active intervention in Kazaks' lives, sedentarization, and the development of agriculture. But at this early, experimental stage, there remained space for give-and-take. Provincial governors, distrustful of settlers and wary of disrupting their Kazak subjects' lives too suddenly, were sometimes skeptical of both resettlement and agriculture. Nor were Kazaks, at least those who recorded their opinions, unanimous on the matter. Some advocated progress through agriculture, as a means of achieving economic stability and cultural development that were apparently impossible under pastoral nomadism, while others believed that modified animal husbandry best leveraged local conditions, local expertise, and the resources that belonging to a vast empire provided. Both sides of this debate were able to draw on what they presented as their own local knowledge and the authority of "Russian science." Neither the materialist assumptions of the civilizing telos, nor metropolitan expertise, nor the views of local actors led to a single vision of the steppe's future.

When mass peasant resettlement became the sine qua non of tsarist policy on the steppe, rather than an experiment or one priority among many, the space for dialogue between tsarist administrators and Kazak intermediaries began to close. Some of these Kazaks had been prepared enough to make their peace with limited, tightly regulated resettlement. Such a program, based on rigorous statistical and environmental surveys, offered a means of controlling settlement; it was the best escape from a worsening situation. But as rapid resettlement at any cost became a high-level state priority, it became clear that Kazaks would lose more land, with greater disruption to their lifeways, than the men who had appointed themselves their representatives could countenance. Rapid resettlement and expropriation, too, were based on environmental and statistical surveys, but now the numbers served a new regulatory purpose, and tsarist statisticians carried out calculations that were aggressive in the best case, fudged in the worst. The tsarist state's growing confidence in its own knowledge of the steppe, after the turn of the twentieth century, did not manifest in policies that Kazaks favored.

The exigencies of metropolitan politics intersected with the most pernicious fruits of tsarist orientology to worsen the situation. In the summer of 1907, an intractable Duma was prorogued, replaced by one constituted under new electoral laws strongly favoring the dominant nationality of the Russian Empire. Much-exaggerated fears of Turkic and Muslim revanchism and irredentism made it unlikely that Central Asia and the Kazak steppe would regain representation. Thus Kazaks lost a platform to directly and publicly express their concerns to representatives from around the empire, while the tsarist state lost the opportunity to hear these grievances (though there is no guarantee they would have been taken seriously). In the summer of 1916, these two strands, expropriation and disenfranchisement, intersected with deadly consequences. Resettlement fueled the resentments of the masses of Kazaks and Kyrgyz who rebelled against the draft order of June 1916, while the intermediaries on whom the state had formerly depended were unable to argue successfully for a different, arguably better implementation of the draft order. In both respects, this represented an epistemological failure. Political considerations led tsarist officials to set aside ways of knowing the steppe and its inhabitants that argued against the disastrous policies they pursued.

Dependent as it was on the whims of an autocratic state and its servitors, the space that Kazak intermediaries made within the scholarly and bureaucratic world of the Russian Empire was always vulnerable. As the knowledge they and others gathered found new, sometimes unexpected uses, and as still others refuted it, the common ground they had previously found with scholars and administrators began to disappear. In the Kazak steppe, as in other European colonial empires, what the Russian Empire knew about the region and its inhabitants was an important part of the consolidation, maintenance, and transformation of its rule. Ironically, though, the moment when tsarist administrators believed themselves to know the most about the steppe was the moment of greatest existential threat to imperial rule. When bureaucrats and intermediaries could envision many transitional states, they combined local and metropolitan knowledge in idiosyncratic ways to advance their views. When the forces of autocracy and bureaucracy threw their weight behind a single transition, with positive certainty that the course they pursued was correct, neither local knowledge nor the alternative visions of the future it fostered could be heard. The shame of this outcome lies precisely in its contingency.

Notes

The following abbreviations are used in the notes:

Archives

d.	delo (file)
f.	fond (collection)
l., ll.	list, listy (page, pages)
ob.	oborot (verso)
op.	opis' (register)
RGIA	Rossiiskii gosudarstvennyi istoricheskii arkhiv
RGVIA	Rossiiskii gosudarstvennyi voenno-istoricheskii arkhiv
sv.	sviazka (bundle)
TsGARK	Tsentral'nyi gosudarstvennyi arkhiv Respubliki Kazakhstana

Publications

IIRGO	*Izvestiia Imperatorskogo russkogo geograficheskogo obshchestva*
KKhAO	*Kirgizskoe khoziaistvo v Akmolinskoi oblasti*
KSG	*Kirgizskaia stepnaia gazeta*
MPKZ	*Materialy po kirgizskomu zemlepol'zovaniiu*
MSb	*Morskoi sbornik*
PKSO	*Pamiatnaia knizhka Semipalatinskoi oblasti*
PSZ	*Polnoe sobranie zakonov Rossiiskoi imperii*
SOGD	*Gosudarstvennaia duma: Stenograficheskie otchety*
SSCV	*Ch. Ch. Valikhanov: Sobranie sochinenii v piati tomakh*
SSIA	*Sobranie sochinenii Ibraia Altynsarina*
TSb	*Turkestanskii sbornik*
VSb	*Voennyi sbornik*
ZhMNP	*Zhurnal Ministerstva narodnogo prosveshcheniia*
ZIRGO	*Zapiski Imperatorskogo russkogo geograficheskogo obshchestva*
ZOrIRGO	*Zapiski Orenburgskogo otdela Imperatorskogo russkogo geograficheskogo obshchestva*
ZSP	*Zapiski Semipalatinskogo pod"otdela Zapadno-Sibirskogo otdeleniia Imperatorskogo russkogo geograficheskogo obshchestva*

INTRODUCTION

1. RGVIA f. 400, op. 1, d. 211, l. 1 (Main Administration of Irregular Troops to Main Staff, January 5, 1870). Title of file: "O nauchnoi rabote Fedchenko i dr. o Turkestane."

2. See, e.g., David W. Darrow, "The Politics of Numbers: Zemstvo Land Assessment and the Conceptualization of Russia's Rural Economy," *Russian Review* 59, no. 1 (2000): 52–75, particularly the sections on taxation and statistics (59–68).

3. Here I am using "knowledge" in a sense distinct from "information," referring to organized and taxonomized material rather than data at a low level of conceptual definition. In this I am following C. A. Bayly, *Empire and Information: Intelligence Gathering and Social Communication in India, 1780–1870* (New York, 1996).

4. Alexander Morrison, "'Applied Orientalism' in British India and Tsarist Turkestan," *Comparative Studies in Society and History* 51, no. 3 (2009): 619–647.

5. Bayly, 349. On the mutual (and occasionally productive) misunderstandings this ignorance engendered in steppe diplomacy, see especially the work of Michael Khodarkovsky: *Where Two Worlds Met: The Russian State and the Kalmyk Nomads, 1600–1771* (Ithaca, 1992); and *Russia's Steppe Frontier: The Making of a Colonial Empire, 1500–1800* (Bloomington, 2002).

6. See, e.g., Michael Adas, *Machines as the Measure of Men: Science, Technology, and Ideologies of Western Dominance* (Ithaca, 1989).

7. Alvin I. Goldman, "Why Social Epistemology Is *Real* Epistemology," in *Social Epistemology*, ed. Adrian Haddock, Alan Millar, and Duncan Pritchard (New York, 2010), 1–29. Goldman dismisses poststructuralist approaches as "revisionism" (3), outside the ken of traditional epistemology.

8. Ian Hacking, *The Social Construction of What?* (Cambridge, MA, 1999), 68–99. In Hacking's reading, Thomas Kuhn, for example, is an archconstructivist in all three senses.

9. Edward W. Said, *Orientalism* (1978; New York, 2003).

10. This despite a spirited early argument by Adeeb Khalid, "Russian History and the Debate over Orientalism," *Kritika: Explorations in Russian and Eurasian History* 1, no. 4 (2000): 691–699. The consensus lies among the following works: Nathaniel Knight, "Grigor'ev in Orenburg, 1851–1862: Russian Orientalism in the Service of Empire?" *Slavic Review* 59, no. 1 (2000): 74–100; David Schimmelpenninck van der Oye, *Russian Orientalism: Asia in the Russian Mind from Peter the Great to Emigration* (New Haven, 2010); Vera Tolz, *Russia's Own Orient: The Politics of Identity and Oriental Studies in the Late Imperial and Early Soviet Periods* (Oxford, 2011).

11. Suzanne Marchand, *German Orientalism in the Age of Empire: Religion, Race, and Scholarship* (Cambridge, 2009); Loïc Charles and Paul Cheney, "The Colonial Machine Dismantled: Knowledge and Empire in the French Atlantic," *Past and Present* 219 (2013): 127–163.

12. For a rather skeptical reading of the New Criticism and its lack of concern with authorial intention, see Terry Eagleton, *Literary Theory: An Introduction*, 2nd ed. (Minneapolis, 1996), 40–44; and Bruno Latour, *Science in Action: How to Follow Scientists and Engineers Through Society* (Cambridge, MA, 1987), 35.

13. Bernard Cohn, *Colonialism and Its Forms of Knowledge: The British in India* (Princeton, 1996), 4–5.

14. Cohn, 4, 21.

15. Bayly, 143.

16. Ibid., 3–9, 179 (quotation).

17. Benjamin Lawrance, Emily Lynn Osborn, and Richard L. Roberts, "Introduction," in *Intermediaries, Interpreters, and Clerks: African Employees in the Making of Colonial Africa*, ed. Benjamin Lawrance, Emily Lynn Osborn, and Richard L. Roberts (Madison, 2006), 30.

18. This expression is originally Christian Teichmann's (personal conversation).

19. Yuriy Malikov, *Tsars, Cossacks, and Nomads: The Formation of a Borderland Culture in Northern Kazakhstan in the 18th and 19th Centuries* (Berlin, 2011). Compare the argument of Thomas Barrett, *At the Edge of Empire: The Terek Cossacks and the North Caucasus Frontier, 1700–1860* (Boulder, 1999).

20. Alexander Morrison, "'Nechto eroticheskoe,' 'courir après l'ombre'?—Logistical Imperatives and the Fall of Tashkent, 1859–1865," *Central Asian Survey* 33, no. 2 (2014): 165.

21. On the okrug prikazy, see Martha Brill Olcott, *The Kazakhs*, 2nd ed. (Stanford, 1995), 59. Virginia Martin (80–83), in an emic study of land relations in the Siberian steppe, treats 1822 as a watershed in terms of tsarist administrative intervention on the

steppe. See Martin, "Kazakh Chinggisids, Land, and Political Power in the Nineteenth Century: A Case Study of Syrymbet," *Central Asian Survey* 29, no. 1 (2010): 79–102.

22. On non-Kazak intermediaries on the steppe, see Gulmira Sultangalieva, "The Russian Empire and the Intermediary Role of Tatars in Kazakhstan: The Politics of Cooperation and Rejection," in *Asiatic Russia: Imperial Power in Regional and International Contexts*, ed. Tomohiko Uyama (New York, 2011), 52–79.

23. Alida C. Metcalf, *Go-Betweens and the Colonization of Brazil, 1500–1600* (Austin, 2005), 9–13.

24. Paul Werth, *At the Margins of Orthodoxy: Mission, Governance, and Confessional Politics in Russia's Volga-Kama Region, 1827–1905* (Ithaca, 2002), 7.

25. Ibid., italics in text.

26. Robert Geraci, *Window on the East: National and Imperial Identities in Late Tsarist Russia* (Ithaca, 2001).

27. For an excellent study of how, in one context, diverse local ways of thinking became compatible with a reactionary, nation-state paradigm, see Faith Hillis, *Children of Rus': Right-Bank Ukraine and the Invention of a Russian Nation* (Ithaca, 2013).

28. For a similar formulation with respect to the Resettlement Administration, subordinated to GUZiZ after 1905, see Peter Holquist, "'In Accord with State Interests and the People's Wishes': The Technocratic Ethos of Imperial Russia's Resettlement Administration," *Slavic Review* 69, no. 1 (2010): 151–179. On tsarist institutional cultures more broadly, see especially Alfred Rieber, "Bureaucratic Politics in Imperial Russia," *Social Science History* 2, no. 4 (1978): 399–413.

29. Nicholas Dirks, "Colonial Histories and Native Informants: Biography of an Archive," in *Orientalism and the Postcolonial Predicament: Perspectives on South Asia*, ed. Carol Breckenridge and Peter van der Veer (Philadelphia, 1993), 279–313.

30. Geoffrey Hosking, *The Russian Constitutional Experiment: Government and Duma, 1907–1914* (Cambridge, 1973), 14–55.

31. Marina Mogil'ner, in *Homo Imperii: Istoriia fizicheskoi antropologii v Rossii* (Moscow, 2008) has described tsarist physical anthropology in Kuhnian terms as paradigmatic rather than monolithic, i.e., characterized by significant diversity of thought within a narrow set of scholarly practices. This would also be an apt characterization of the disciplines of ethnography and orientology in this setting. See also Thomas S. Kuhn, *The Structure of Scientific Revolutions* (Chicago, 1962).

32. This characterization of Kazak autonomism is drawn from Peter Rottier's excellent dissertation, "Creating the Kazak Nation: The Intelligentsia's Quest for Acceptance in the Russian Empire, 1905–1920" (PhD diss., University of Wisconsin, 2005), a highly constructivist account of the movement. Marginally less constructivist (seeking sources of ethnic solidarity in the precolonial era) is Steven Sabol, *Russian Colonization and the Genesis of Kazak National Consciousness* (New York, 2003); closer to the primordialist end of the spectrum is Kemal Karpat, "The Roots of Kazakh Nationalism: Ethnicity, Islam, or Land?" in *In a Collapsing Empire: Underdevelopment, Ethnic Conflicts, and Nationalisms in the Soviet Union*, ed. Marco Buttino (Milan, 1993), 313–333. R. Charles Weller, *Rethinking Kazakh and Central Asian Nationhood: A Challenge to Prevailing Western Views* (Los Angeles, 2006) strikes a deeply primordialist tone in its defense of ethnonationalism against "western modernist" ideas.

33. Bayly, 348–350.

34. Ü. Subkhanberdina et al., ed., *"Qazaq" gazetï* (Almaty, 1998), "Zor özgerïs," 366–368.

35. A full recounting of the period between 1917 and 1920 is well outside the ken of this work. However, Älikhan Bökeikhanov's recounting of his grievances against the liberal Kadet party, "Men kadet partiiasïnan nege shïqtïm?" focusing on Kadets' prioritization of ethnic Russian issues and opposition to national autonomy, gives some sense of the complexity of the time. See R. N. Nurgaliev, ed., *Älikhan Bökeikhan: Tangdamalï/izbrannoe* (Almaty, 1995), 414.

36. Virginia Martin, *Law and Custom on the Steppe: The Kazakhs of the Middle Horde and Russian Colonialism in the Nineteenth Century* (Richmond, 2001), 160.

37. Austin Jersild, *Orientalism and Empire: North Caucasus Mountain Peoples and the Georgian Frontier, 1845–1917* (Montreal, 2003); Robert Crews, *For Prophet and Tsar: Islam and Empire in Russia and Central Asia* (Cambridge, MA, 2006).

38. On the centrality of scientistic rhetoric in another colonial context, see Gyan Prakash, *Another Reason: Science and the Imagination of India* (Princeton, 1999).

39. David Scott, *Conscripts of Modernity: The Tragedy of Colonial Enlightenment* (Durham, 2004).

40. Partha Chatterjee, *Nationalist Thought and the Colonial World: A Derivative Discourse?* (London, 1986), 38.

41. Partha Chatterjee, *The Nation and Its Fragments: Colonial and Postcolonial Histories* (Princeton, 1993), 13 (quotation), 6.

42. The classic thesis on collaboration and imperialism is Ronald Robinson, "Non-European Foundations of European Imperialism: Sketch for a Theory of Collaboration," in *Studies in the Theory of Imperialism*, ed. E. R. J. Owen and Robert Sutcliffe (London, 1972), 117–142.

43. On Russia as a European state, but not a Western one, see Vera Tolz, "Russia and the West," in *A History of Russian Thought*, ed. W. Leatherbarrow and D. Offord (Cambridge, 2010), 179–216; on the unfamiliarity of steppe environments for observers more accustomed to forests, David Moon, "The Russian Academy of Sciences Expeditions to the Steppes in the Late Eighteenth Century," *Slavonic and East European Review* 88, no. 1–2 (2010): 204–236.

44. Ann Laura Stoler, *Along the Archival Grain: Epistemic Anxieties and Colonial Common Sense* (Princeton, 2009), 17–53.

45. Tony Ballantyne, "Archive, Discipline, State: Power and Knowledge in South Asian Historiography," *New Zealand Journal of Asian Studies* 3, no. 1 (2001): 87–105. See also, for the French case, George R. Trumbull IV, *An Empire of Facts: Colonial Power, Cultural Knowledge, and Islam in Algeria, 1870–1914* (New York, 2009).

46. The most sustained attempt at comparative history in the Central Asian context is Alexander Morrison, *Russian Rule in Samarkand, 1868–1910: A Comparison with British India* (Oxford, 2008), reviewed very skeptically by Adeeb Khalid, *Slavic Review* 69, no. 1 (2010): 242–243. Consider also the reception of Willard Sunderland, *Taming the Wild Field: Colonization and Empire on the Russian Steppe* (Ithaca, 2004). An actively hostile response is Igor Grachev and Pavel Rykin, "A European's View of Asiatic History," trans. Catriona Kelly, *Forum for Anthropology and Culture* 1 (2004): 395–401. Alexander Morrison's defense of Sunderland, "What Is 'Colonisation'? An Alternative View of *Taming the Wild Field*," *Forum for Anthropology and Culture* 1 (2004): 402–415, strikes a similar tone to my arguments in this subsection.

47. As in, e.g., E. A. Glushchenko, *Rossiia v Srednei Azii: Zavoevaniia i preobrazovaniia* (Moscow, 2010).

48. Alexander Etkind, *Internal Colonization: Russia's Imperial Experience* (Cambridge, 2011).

49. Compare Willard Sunderland, "The Ministry of Asiatic Russia: The Colonial Office That Never Was but Might Have Been," *Slavic Review* 69, no. 1 (2010): 120–150.

50. The direct methodological inspiration for this is Mark Bassin's meta-geographical approach to Siberian history. See Bassin, *Imperial Visions: Nationalist Imagination and Geographical Expansion in the Russian Far East 1840–1865* (Cambridge, 1999).

51. This is an adaptation of a phrase from Jane Burbank and Frederick Cooper, *Empires in World History: Power and the Politics of Difference* (Princeton, 2010), 3–8.

52. In a different context, Willard Sunderland has described this as the era of "correct colonization." See Sunderland, *Taming*, 177.

1. SEEING LIKE A HALF-BLIND STATE

1. See, inter alia, Adeeb Khalid, *The Politics of Muslim Cultural Reform: Jadidism in Central Asia* (Berkeley, 1998); Virginia Martin, *Law and Custom in the Steppe: The Kazakhs of the Middle Horde and Russian Colonialism in the Nineteenth Century* (Richmond, 2001); Steven Sabol, *Russian Colonialism and the Genesis of Kazak National Consciousness* (New York, 2003); Jeff Sahadeo, *Russian Colonial Society in Tashkent, 1865–1923* (Bloomington, 2007); and Ali Iğmen, *Speaking Soviet with an Accent: Culture and Power in Kyrgyzstan* (Pittsburgh, 2012).

2. A. F. Gumbol'dt, *Tsentral'naia Aziia: Izsledovaniia o tsepiakh gor i po sravnitel'noi klimatologii*, trans. P. I. Borozdich, ed. D. N. Anuchin (1843; Moscow, 1915), 140.

3. L. F. Kostenko, *Sredniaia Aziia i vodvoreniia v nei russkoi grazhdanstvennosti* (St. Petersburg, 1870). For biographical data on Kostenko and other military men I rely on M. K. Baskhanov, *Russkie voennye vostokovedy do 1917 goda* (Moscow, 2005).

4. A. N. Kharuzin, *Bibliograficheskii ukazatel' statei, kasaiushchikhsia etnografii kirgizov i karakirgizov* (Moscow, 1891).

5. Bruno Latour, *Science in Action: How to Follow Scientists and Engineers through Society* (Cambridge, MA, 1987), 40–41.

6. David Moon, "The Russian Academy of Sciences Expeditions to the Steppes in the Late Eighteenth Century," *Slavonic and East European Review* 88, nos. 1–2 (2010): 204–236 (here 206–209).

7. These petitions for subjecthood gave rise to the unfortunate Soviet myth of the "voluntary entry" of these lands into the Russian Empire, with little attention paid to the conflict these petitions immediately engendered, or the resistance that tsarist rule faced thereafter. See, e.g., T. Zh. Shoinbaev, *Dobrovol'noe vkhozhdenie kazakhskikh zemel' v sostav Rossii* (Alma-Ata, 1982).

8. L. S. Semenov, *Puteshestvie Afanasiia Nikitina* (Moscow, 1980).

9. Valerie Kivelson, *Cartographies of Tsardom: The Land and Its Meanings in Seventeenth-Century Russia* (Ithaca, 2006), 19 (quotation); A. I. Maksheev, *Opisanie nizov'ev Syr-Dar'i* (St. Petersburg, 1856), 2–5.

10. Kivelson, 184–187, plate 28.

11. Alton Donnelly, *The Russian Conquest of Bashkiria, 1552–1740: A Case Study of Imperialism* (New Haven, 1968), 64–81.

12. Iu. N. Smirnov, *Orenburgskaia ekspeditsiia (komissiia) i prisoedinenie Zavol'zhia k Rossii v 30–40-e gg. XVIII veka* (Samara, 1997), 24–25, 28 (quotation).

13. On Rychkov, see M. G. Novlianskaia, "Nauchnye raboty Orenburgskoi ekspeditsii," *Trudy Instituta istorii estestvoznaniia i tekhniki* 27 (1959): 26–43 (here 29); and Alexander Vucinich, *Science in Russian Culture: A History to 1860* (Stanford, 1963), 170–171.

14. P. I. Rychkov, *Topografiia Orenburgskoi gubernii* (1762; Orenburg, 1887); Rychkov, *Istoriia Orenburgskaia (1730–1750)* (1759; Orenburg, 1896).

15. On the rise of "modern Russian territoriality" (53) as embodied by these expeditions, as well as the work of regional scholars like Rychkov, see Willard Sunderland, "Imperial Space: Territorial Thought and Practice in the Eighteenth Century," in *Russian Empire: Space, People, Power, 1700–1930*, ed. Jane Burbank, Mark von Hagen, and Anatolyi Remnev (Bloomington, 2007), 33–66.

16. Vucinich, 150–151; see also V. I. Vernadskii, *Trudy po istorii nauki v Rossii* (Moscow, 1988), 215–216; and A. K. Sytin, "'Rossiiskaia flora' Petra Simona Pallasa," in *Estestvennaia istoriia v Rossii (Ocherki razvitiia estestvoznaniia v Rossii v XVIII veke)*, ed. E. I. Kolchinskii, A. K. Sytin, and G. I. Smagina (St. Petersburg, 2004), 106–129. On the contradictions between nationalism and scholarly cosmopolitanism in Pallas's Russian career, see Ryan T. Jones, "Peter Simon Pallas, Siberia, and the European Republic of Letters," *Studies in the History of Biology* 3, no. 3 (2011): 55–67.

17. My discussion of systematization draws on Susan Faye Cannon's notion of "Humboldtian," i.e., comparative and theoretical, science, as developed in Michael Dettelbach, "Humboldtian Science," in *Cultures of Natural History*, ed. Nicholas Jardine, James A. Secord, and E. C. Spary (New York, 1996), 287–304. The work of, e.g., the Swedish academician Johann Peter Falck did not see Russian translation until 1824 (Falck himself had committed suicide fifty years earlier). See *Polnoe sobranie uchenykh puteshestvii po Rossii, izdavaemoe Imperatorskoiu Akademieiu nauk, po predlozheniiu eia prezidenta: S primechaniiami, iz"iasneniiami, i dopolneniiami,* vol. 6: *Zapiski puteshestviia Akademika Fal'ka* (St. Petersburg, 1824).

18. V. A. Obruchev, *Istoriia geologicheskogo issledovaniia Sibiri: Period vtoroi (1801–1850 gody)* (Leningrad, 1933), 22–30. Shangin also compiled a herbarium and gathered material on the genealogy of Kazak clans, though this material remained (and remains) unpublished. See A. V. Postnikov, *Stanovlenie rubezhei Rossii v Tsentral'noi i Srednei Azii (XVIII–XIX vv.): Rol' istoriko-geograficheskikh issledovanii i kartografirovaniia. Monografiia v dokumentakh* (Moscow, 2007), 160.

19. E. K. Meiendorf, *Puteshestviie iz Orenburga v Bukharu* (Moscow, 1975), 20. Meiendorf was part of an embassy to Bukhara under A. S. Negri, whose officers produced two noteworthy maps (Postnikov, 161–168).

20. Levshin describes his research process in A. I. Levshin, *Opisanie kirgiz-kazach'ikh, ili kirgiz-kaisatskikh, ord i stepei,* pt. 1: *Izvestiia geograficheskiia* (St. Petersburg, 1832), iv–vi.

21. Multiple observers acknowledged that Kazaks themselves did not recognize the term "kirgiz" when it was applied to them. See, e.g., Khristofor Bardanes, "Kirgizskaia, ili kazatskaia, khorografiia," in *Istoriia Kazakhstana v russkikh istochnikakh XVI–XX vekov,* vol. 4: *Pervye istoriko-etnograficheskie opisaniia kazakhskikh zemel': XVIII vek,* ed. I. V. Erofeeva (Almaty, 2007), 93.

22. N. P. Rychkov, *Dnevnye zapiski puteshestviia Kapitana Nikolaia Rychkova v kirgis-kaisatskoi stepe, 1771 godu* (St. Petersburg, 1772), 43, 67, 87–88.

23. For one such hypothesis, see P. I. Rychkov, "Nizhaishee predstavlenie o sostoianii kirgiz-kaisatskikh ord i o sposobakh k privedeniiu ikh k spokoinomu prebyvaniiu i ko ispolneniiu poddanicheskikh dolzhnostei," in Erofeeva, 4:196. For the consensus view, see I. G. Georgi, *Opisanie vsiekh obitaiushchikh v rossiiskom gosudarstve narodov: ikh zhiteiskikh obriadov, obyknovenii, odezhd, zhilishch, uprazhnenii, zabav, veroispovedanii i drugikh dostopamiatnostei. Tvorenie, za n"skol'ko let pred sim na Nemetskom iazyke Ioganna Gottliba Georgi, v perevode na Rossiiski iazyk ves'ma vo mnogom izpravlennoe i v nov' sochinennoe,* 4 pts. (St. Petersburg, 1799), 120.

24. Georgi, 119. See also V. Ia. Butanaev and Iu. S. Khudiakov, *Istoriia Eniseiskikh kyrgyzov* (Abakan, 2000), 189–192.

25. Petr Rychkov, for example, attributes this characterization of the Kirgiz to Müller. See Rychkov, *Topografiia,* 93–95. On Müller, see Han Vermuelen, *Before Boas: The Genesis of Ethnography and Ethnology in the German Enlightenment* (Lincoln, 2015), 131–218.

26. A. I. Levshin, *Opisanie kirgiz-kazach'ikh, ili kirgiz-kaisatskikh, ord i stepei,* pt. 2: *Istoricheskie izvestiia* (St. Petersburg, 1832), 30.

27. Ibid., 39–46.

28. Ibid., 55–57.

29. Ibid., 55.

30. Compare the argument of Alexander Morrison, "Writing the Russian Conquest of Central Asia," unpublished article ms. I am grateful to Prof. Morrison for providing an advance copy of his work.

31. See, e.g., Levshin, 2:223–231.

32. On the multiple misunderstandings between Russians and the nomadic peoples with whom they came into contact during the early modern era, see Michael Khodarkov-

sky, *Where Two Worlds Met: The Russian State and the Kalmyk Nomads, 1600–1771* (Ithaca, 1992).

33. Levshin, 2:157–158.

34. I. G. Andreev, *Opisanie Srednei ordy kirgiz-kaisakov* (1795–96; Almaty, 1998), 43.

35. On salaries, see ibid., 42–43; on fortifications, see Rychkov, *Topografiia*, 105–106. This formulation echoes arguments that Bruce Grant has made for the conquest of the Caucasus. See Grant, *The Captive and the Gift: Cultural Histories of Sovereignty in Russia and the Caucasus* (Ithaca, 2009). It also remained the standard version of events more than a century after Abulkhair's submission. See V. V. Vel'iaminov-Zernov, *Istoricheskie izvestiia o Kirgiz-kaisakakh i snosheniiakh Rossii s Sredneiu Azieiu so vremeni konchiny Abul-Khair khana (1748–1765 g.)*, vol. 1 (Ufa, 1853).

36. Levshin, 2:291–298.

37. Meiendorf, 42–43.

38. Ibid.

39. The diary of Kutlu-Mukhammed Tevkelev's mission to the Small Horde in the early 1730s, for example, contains multiple mentions of narrowly escaped violent death. See "Zhurnal bytnosti v Kirgiz-kaisatskoi orde perevodchika Mametia Tevkeleva (1731–1733 gg.)," in *Istoriia Kazakhstana v russkikh istochnikakh XVI–XX vekov*, vol. 3: *Zhurnaly i sluzhebnye zapiski diplomata A. I. Tevkeleva po istorii i etnografii Kazakhstana (1731–1759 gg.)*, ed. I. V. Erofeeva (Almaty, 2005).

40. Alan Bodger, "The Kazakhs and the Pugachev Uprising in Russia, 1773–1775" (Bloomington, 1988), 13; Michael Khodarkovsky, *Russia's Steppe Frontier: The Making of a Colonial Empire, 1500–1800* (Bloomington, 2002), 173–174. Paul Avrich, *Russian Rebels, 1600–1800* (New York, 1976), 195, asserts that some Kazaks were part of Pugachev's "large if motley army."

41. Rychkov, "Nizhaishee," 208–209.

42. Levshin, 2:275–276.

43. A. I. Levshin, *Opisanie ord i stepei kazakhov* (1832; Pavlodar: EKO, 2005), 164. For a similar argument, see E. I. Blankennagel', *Zamechaniia maiora Blankennagelia vposledstvie poezdki ego iz Orenburga v Khivu v 1793–94 godakh: Izdany, s ob''iasneniiami, V. V. Grigor'evym* (St. Petersburg, 1858), 8–9.

44. Rychkov, *Topografiia*, 112–113.

45. Levshin, *Opisanie kazakhov*, 147–148.

46. Pallas, for one, noted in the late eighteenth century that "as the Kazaks are not very skillful in trade, and take during exchange [*pri promene*] many bad goods and all sorts of trifles, Russian merchants get a great profit from them" (352). See P. S. Pallas, *Puteshestvie po raznym provintsiiam Rossiiskoi imperii*, pt. 1 (St. Petersburg, 1773); on state revenues see, e.g., Levshin, *Opisanie kazakhov*, 148–149, 157–158. Rychkov, *Topografiia*, 227, claims more than 50,000 rubles in customs duties were being collected annually at Orenburg by 1754.

47. E. Kaidalov, "Karavan-zapiski vo vremia pokhoda v Bukhariiu rossiiskogo karavana pod voinskim prikrytiem v 1824 i 1825 godakh," *TSb* 270, is a dramatic narrative of attacks on a caravan by Khivan forces. See 45 and 115–116 on the role of Kazak assistants within the caravan. On the tsarist merchantry's fears of travel on the steppe, see Kaidalov, 10; and S. Russov, "Puteshestvie iz Orenburga v Khivu samarskogo kuptsa Rukavkina v 1733 [sic: 1753] godu s priobshcheniem raznykh izvestii o Khive s otdalennykh vremen donynye," *TSb* 386:59a.

48. [S. B. Bronevskii], "Zapiski General-Maiora Bronevskogo o Kirgiz-Kaisakakh srednei Ordy (okonchanie)," *Otechestvennye zapiski* 124, ch. 43 (1830): 194–285 (here 235–236); see also Scott C. Levi, *The Indian Diaspora in Central Asia and Its Trade, 1550–1900* (Boston, 2002), 233–241.

49. Willard Sunderland, *Taming the Wild Field: Colonization and Empire on the Russian Steppe* (Ithaca, 2004); David Moon, *The Plough That Broke the Steppes: Agriculture and Environment on Russia's Grasslands, 1700–1914* (Oxford, 2013).

50. Khristofor Bardanes, "Dopolnenie pervoe: Poezdka Khristofora Bardanesa v Kirgizskuiu step', po predporucheniiu Akademika Fal'ka," in *Polnoe sobranie uchenykh puteshestvii po Rossii, izdavaemoe Imperatorskoiu Akademieiu Nauk, po predlozheniiu eia prezidenta: S primechaniiami, iz"iasneniiami, i dopolneniiami*, vol. 7: *Zakliuchaiushchii v sebe dopolnitel'nye stat'i k Zapiskam Puteshesviia Akademika Fal'ka* (St. Petersburg, 1825), 46–47.

51. Bardanes, "Khorografiia," 94.

52. On the Ural/Yaik, see *Pol'noe sobranie uchenykh puteshestvii*, 6:218; on the Irtysh, see Bardanes, "Khorografiia," 95–96.

53. This artificial division of Eurasia has been most thoroughly criticized by Martin W. Lewis and Kären E. Wigen, *The Myth of Continents: A Critique of Metageography* (Berkeley, 1997), 27–28.

54. Rychkov, *Topografiia*, 7; Levshin, *Opisanie kirgiz-kazach'ikh ord*, 1:3.

55. Levshin, *Opisanie kirgiz-kazach'ikh ord*, 1:4.

56. Ibid., 1–2.

57. N. V. Khanykov, *O naselenii kirgizskikh stepei, zanimaemykh vnutrenneiu i maloiu ordami* (St. Petersburg, 1844), 26. This piece, an attempt to apply the population theories of Malthus, Quetelet, and others to a "wild tribe," remained unfinished. The basic source on Khanykov's career is N. A. Khalfin and E. F. Rassadina, *N. V. Khanykov—vostokoved i diplomat* (Moscow, 1977).

58. G. [sic] Gaverdovskii, "Obshchee obozrenie mestopolozheniia Kirgiz-Kaisatskoi stepi (izvlechenie iz Zapisok G. Gaverdovskogo)," *Sibirskii vestnik*, pt. 3, bk. 13 (1823): 43–60 (here 43–44). For biographical data on Gaverdovskii, see I. V. Erofeeva, ed., *Istoriia Kazakhstana v russkikh istochnikakh XVI–XX vekov*, vol. 5: *Pervye istoriko-etnograficheskie opisaniia kazakhskikh zemel': Pervaia polovina XIX veka* (Almaty, 2007), 5–14.

59. Levshin, *Opisanie kirgiz-kazach'ikh ord*, 1:14–36.

60. Ibid., 14–15.

61. See, e.g., Andreev, 48; Filipp Nazarov, *Zapiski o nekotorykh narodakh i zemliakh srednei chasti Azii* (St. Petersburg, 1821), 4; and Khanykov, 13–15. Bardanes frequently employed the "infertile" language—see Bardanes, "Dopolnenie," 14, 19, 21.

62. N. P. Rychkov, "Dnevnye zapiski," 78–79; [I. P. Shangin], "Izvlechenie iz opisaniia ekspeditsii, byvshei v Kirgizskuiu step' v 1816 g," *Sibirskii vestnik*, pt. 9 (1820): 1–40 (here 6–7); Al'fons Iagmin, *Kirgiz-kaisatskiia stepi i ikh zhiteli* (St. Petersburg, 1845), 18–19.

63. Gaverdovskii, 36–37; Khanykov, 15.

64. Levshin, *Opisanie kirgiz-kazach'ikh ord*, 1:39–40, lists several river basins in the northern steppe as "suitable for grain cultivation."

65. Bardanes noted the potential utility of the steppe for Kazaks (see "Khorografiia," 119, 135) but also had a dim view of the region as a whole. See "Dopolnenie," 4: "On May 11 we traveled across open, mostly clayey steppe, overgrown with low reeds and covered in small, scanty patches of saline soil and salt-tolerant [*solianymi*] vegetation."

66. Bronevskii, 237–238.

67. P. I. Rychkov, "Istoricheskii ekstrakt o kirgiz-kaisatskom narode, sochinennoi pri orenburgskikh pogranichnykh delakh po orderam ego siiatel'stva general-anshefa i vsekh rossiiskikh orderov kavalera grafa petra Ivanovicha Panina," in Erofeeva, 4:230.

68. Levshin, *Opisanie kirgiz-kazach'ikh ord*, 1:125–126.

69. Khanykov fretted that "approximately three-quarters" of the Orenburg steppe was without irrigation (28).

70. Levshin, *Opisanie kirgiz-kazach'ikh ord*, 1:21.

71. C.f. Rychkov, *Topografiia*, 145–152, for descriptions of the Aral and Caspian; Bardanes, "Khorografiia," 98–100, on Balkhash; and Rychkov, *Topografiia*, 154–55, on major salt lakes. The salt lakes of the west Siberian plain, though not unknown, remained without serious study until almost the end of the nineteenth century. See L. Berg, V. Elpat'evskii, and P. Ignatov, *O solenykh ozerakh Omskogo uezda* (St. Petersburg, 1899).

72. Levshin, *Opisanie kirgiz-kazach'ikh ord*, 1:106–07. Levshin's fantasies were based on inaccurate, or incomplete, information: he hoped that the Syr did not form shoals (*otmeli*), during hot times, which made it impossible to travel by ship, because of the profits that commerce along it would provide if it did not, and because other sources suggested that it was "in general navigable."

73. Meiendorf, 66 (he gives an extraordinary, but unlikely, temperature of 49 degrees Reaumur—142 Fahrenheit!—during the summer of 1821); Levshin, *Opisanie kirgiz-kazach'ikh ord*, 1:6–11; Khanykov, 56–60.

74. Meiendorf, 66; Iagmin, 5. Contrast these with fears about the "very unhealthy" (520) marshy and saline surroundings of Gur'ev-gorodok, present-day Atyrau, Kazakhstan. See [I. I. Lepekhin], *Dnevnie zapiski puteshestviia doktora i akademii nauk ad"iunkta Ivana Lepekhina po raznym provintsiiam rossiiskago gosudarstva, 1768 i 1769 godu*, pt. 1 (St. Petersburg, 1795).

75. Levshin, *Opisanie kazakhov*, 21; Khanykov, 4.

76. Gaverdovskii, 43.

77. Khanykov, 53–55.

78. Khanykov, 32. He was also (37) interested in revising the work of Humboldt, who had attempted similar calculations after his 1829 visit but, Khanykov argued, sampled atypical years.

79. Ibid., 38–41.

80. A. Golubev, *O srednei godichnoi temperature i sostoianii barometra v ukreplenii Vernom* (St. Petersburg, 1860).

81. For attempts to cultivate, see Rychkov, *Topografiia*, 257; for speculation, see, e.g., Pallas, 1:445–446.

82. James Scott, *The Art of Not Being Governed: An Anarchist History of Upland Southeast Asia* (New Haven, 2009), 6.

83. Levshin, *Opisanie kazakhov*, 5.

84. Tevkelev, "Izvestie o kirgiz-kaisatskom narode, i kak onye v razdelenii, i o zemliakh, na kotorykh oni kachuiut, i k kakim narodom te zemle prilezhat, i v chem ikh udobstvie i torgi sostoiat, to zhachit nizhe sego," in Erofeeva, 3:389 (30,000 per horde); Rychkov, "Nizhaishee," 200 (20,000, up to 30,000, in the Small Horde); Andreev, 68 (about 70,000 in the Middle Horde). For estimates of united strength see anon. (likely G. I. Spasskii), "Kirgiz-Kaisaki bol'shoi, srednei i maloi ordy: Istoricheskoe vvedenie o Kirgiz-Kaisakakh," *Sibirskii vestnik*, pt. 10 (1820): 141–164 (here 142); Petr Rychkov, "Kratkoe opisanie o kirgis-kaisakakh, 1795 g.," in Erofeeva, 4:267.

85. Levshin, *Opisanie kazakhov*, 155.

86. Rychkov, *Topografiia*, 198–199, 208–209. In neither passage does Rychkov indicate that these numbers were exceptional. According to Georgi (126), even the "very simplest" herder would have owned more than 200 animals.

87. For Pallas (1:568–569), Kazaks were both "all prosperous" and lived in better dwellings than a comparable nomadic people, the Kalmyks. Indications of poverty and stratification are e.g. at Bronevskii, 219; and Meiendorf, 38.

88. Khanykov, 56.

89. Rychkov, "Nizhaishee," 195. I am grateful to Michael Hancock-Parmer (personal conversation) for the idea that tsarist administrators saw Kazaks as more fixed in place than had historically been the case.

90. Rychkov, *Topografiia*, 97–103, offers detailed descriptions for both the Small and Middle Hordes.

91. Rychkov, "Nizhaishee," 201.

92. Levshin, *Opisanie kazakhov*, 12.

93. Ibid., 63, 155.

94. On ancestral attachments to winter camps, and the underlying order to seasonal migration ("no one occupies another's place"), see Bronevskii, 74–75.

95. For the rhetoric of ignorance and "natural laws," see Rychkov, "Kratkoe opisanie," 268; for the Islamic interpretation, Meiendorf, 41.

96. Anon. (likely Spasskii), "Kirgiz-Kaisaki," 130–131; Levshin, *Opisanie kirgiz-kazach'ikh ord*, 3:170–178.

97. On the legal culture that emerged from this interface of imperial knowledge and Kazak practices, see Martin, *Law and Custom*.

98. Rychkov, "Kratkoe opisanie," 268; Bronevskii, 79–80 (worst in summer); Khanykov, 59 (worst in fall).

99. Meiendorf, 41–42; Levshin, *Opisanie kirgiz-kazach'ikh ord*, 2:241–242; Levshin, *Opisanie kazakhov*, 127.

100. For "natural law" language, see also Georgi, x, 125; compare Jean-Jacques Rousseau, "Discourse on the Origin and Foundations of Inequality among Men," *The Essential Writings of Rousseau*, trans. Peter Constantine (New York, 2013), 5–87 (especially 58–59); see also commentary in Patrick Riley, ed., *The Cambridge Companion to Rousseau* (New York, 2001), 19–20. On another (non-Rousseauvian) reading of the state of nature and its decline, see Anthony Pagden, *The Fall of Natural Man: The American Indian and the Origins of Comparative Ethnology* (New York: Cambridge, 1982).

101. On divide-and-rule, see Rychkov, "Nizhaishee," 205–206; on the regulation of baranta, see Tevkelev, "Ekstrakt brigadira Tevkeleva v bytnost' evo v Orskoi kreposti o dvukh kirgis-kaisatskikh Srednei i Menshei ordakh po mnogim s kirgistsami razgovoram," in Erofeeva, 3:311. On the tensions between tsarist and Kazak understandings of baranta, and Kazak adaptations of this practice in a new legal context, see Virginia Martin, "Barïmta: Nomadic Custom, Imperial Crime," in *Russia's Orient: Imperial Borderlands and Peoples, 1700–1917*, ed. Daniel Brower and Edward Lazzerini (Bloomington, 2001), 249–270.

102. Levshin, *Opisanie kirgiz-kazach'ikh ord*, 3:156, 167–169; G. S. Sultangalieva, ed., *Kazakhskie chinovniki na sluzhbe Rossiiskoi imperii: Sbornik dokumentov i materialov* (Almaty, 2013), 4–5.

103. Levshin, *Opisanie kazakhov*, 49–50. This fits well with Ricarda Vulpius's observation that, by the end of the eighteenth century, Russian elites had "adopted a feeling of civilizational superiority towards non-Russian subjects" (27). See Vulpius, "The Russian Empire's Civilizing Mission in the Eighteenth Century: A Comparative Perspective," in *Asiatic Russia: Imperial Power in Regional and International Contexts*, ed. Tomohiko Uyama (New York, 2012), 13–31.

104. Khanykov, 24.

105. Levshin, for example, explicitly invoked this sort of thinking; see *Opisanie kazakhov*, 123–124, 136–137; see also Georgi, ix–x. For one Enlightenment-era developmental scheme (with pastoralism the second stage of ten), see Antoine-Nicolas de Condorcet, *Sketch for a Historical Picture of the Progress of the Human Mind*, trans. June Barraclough (London, 1955); see also commentary in Edward Goodell, *The Noble Philosopher: Condorcet and the Enlightenment* (Buffalo, 1994), 209–223.

106. Iagmin, 41–42.

107. Compare Levshin, *Opisanie kazakhov*, 92: "Neither their way of life, nor morals, nor religion permit the Kazaks to be educated [*obrazovannymi*]."

108. Levshin, *Opisanie kazakhov*, 100, expresses grudging respect for some Kazak medicinal practices; for a less relativist (and more common) view see Andreev, 61; Shangin, 155; and Iagmin, 63, 68–69.

109. Robert Crews, *For Prophet and Tsar: Islam and Empire in Russia and Central Asia* (Cambridge, MA, 2006), 31–91.

110. Georgi, 140; Levshin, *Opisanie kazakhov*, 40.

111. On rituals, see inter alia Bardanes, "Khorografiia," 179 (though Levshin, *Opisanie kazakhov*, 40, disputed that Kazaks regularly engaged in ritual washing); Bronevskii, 196; and Georgi, 133; on prejudice, see Levshin, *Opisanie kazakhov*, 39, 109.

112. Nikolai Rychkov, "Dnevnye zapiski," 30–31. On the role of "enlightenment" (variously understood) in early tsarist observers' creation of an ethnographic Other, see Yuri Slezkine, "Naturalists versus Nations: Eighteenth-Century Russian Scholars Confront Ethnic Diversity," in Brower and Lazzerini, *Russia's Orient*, 27–57 (especially 39–45).

113. Shangin, 141 (quotation), 144.

114. Bardanes, "Khorografiia," 114–115; Pallas, 1:566–567.

115. Levshin, *Opisanie kazakhov*, 57–60.

116. On hospitality, see Pallas, 1:566–567; on gender relations, see Bronevskii, 85–86.

117. Ibid. Much later in the nineteenth century, the ethnographer Aleksei Nikolaevich Kharuzin would attempt, on the basis of "impartial" (207) judgment, to mold two centuries of contradictory observations into a single conclusive definition of Kazaks' national character. See Kharuzin, *Kirgizy Bukeevskoi Ordy (antropologo-etnologicheskii ocherk*, no. 1) (Moscow, 1889),

118. Levshin, *Opisanie kazakhov*, 123–124.

119. Bronevskii, 72; see also Meiendorf, 38.

120. Nikolai Rychkov, "Dnevnye zapiski," 58.

121. Rychkov, *Topografiia*, 100–101; Andreev, 77; Spasskii, 182–183.

122. For the balance among environment, climate, government, and civil order in the life of a population, see Khanykov, 3–4.

123. Levshin, *Opisanie kazakhov*, 21.

124. Ibid., 23–24.

125. For route data, see Levshin, *Opisanie kirgiz-kazach'ikh ord*, 1:180–201; see also James Hevia, *The Imperial Security State: British Colonial Knowledge and Empire-Building in Asia* (New York, 2012), 73–106.

126. W. Bruce Lincoln, *In the Vanguard of Reform: Russia's Enlightened Bureaucrats, 1825–1861* (DeKalb, 1982), 91–101.

2. INFORMATION REVOLUTION AND ADMINISTRATIVE REFORM, CA. 1845–1868

1. N. I. Krasovskii, ed., *Materialy dlia statistiki i geografii Rossii, sobrannye ofitserami General'nogo Shtaba: Oblast' Sibirskikh kirgizov*, pt. 1 (St. Petersburg, 1868), 260.

2. RGIA f. 1291, op. 81, d. 233 (1856), ll. 92ob.–93, "Otchet Orenburgskoi Pogranichnoi Kommissii po upravleniiu Zaural'skimi Kirgizami Orenburgskogo vedomstva i Shkoloi dlia kirgizskikh detei za 1857 god."

3. The authors of the Turkestan Statute of 1867, for example, justified their decisions largely on the basis that a new administrative system would increase the empire's tax revenues. See RGVIA f. 400, op. 1, d. 101, ll. 163–164, "Obshchee soobrazhenie po proektu Polozheniia Turkestanskogo General-Gubernatorstva." Title of file: "Ob obrazovanii novogo Turkestanskogo general-gubernatorstva, i o preobrazovaniiakh v Zapadno-Sibirskom i Orenburgskom voennykh okrugakh."

4. My approach in this chapter is particularly inspired by Alexander Morrison, "Applied Orientalism in British India and Tsarist Turkestan," *Comparative Studies in*

Society and History 51, no. 3 (2009): 619–647; for a different view of the question, see Nathaniel Knight, "Grigor'ev in Orenburg, 1851–1862: Russian Orientalism in the Service of Empire?" *Slavic Review* 59, no. 1 (2000): 74–100.

5. The standard Russian work on IRGO remains L. S. Berg, *Vsesoiuznoe geograficheskoe obshchestvo za 100 let* (Moscow, 1946); see also Nathaniel Knight, "Constructing the Science of Nationality: Ethnography in Mid-19th-Century Russia" (PhD diss., Columbia University, 1995), along with several articles; and Joseph Bradley, *Voluntary Associations in Tsarist Russia: Science, Patriotism, and Civil Society* (Cambridge, MA, 2009), 86–127.

6. For this idea in the context of the British Empire, see Felix Driver, *Geography Militant: Cultures of Exploration and Empire* (Malden, MA, 2001), 21, 24–48.

7. "Osnovanie v S. Peterburge Russkago geograficheskago obshchestva i zaniatiia ego s sentiabria 1845 po mai 1846 g.," *ZIRGO* 1 (1846): 25.

8. See especially W. Bruce Lincoln, *In the Vanguard of Reform: Russia's Enlightened Bureaucrats, 1825–1861* (DeKalb, 1986). Scott C. Matsushita Bailey also makes a connection between pre-reform attitudes and Central Eurasian exploration in his dissertation, "Travel, Science, and Empire: The Russian Geographical Society's Expeditions to Central Eurasia, 1845–1905" (PhD diss., University of Hawaii, 2008), 1–2.

9. RGIA f. 853, op. 1, d. 5, ll. 6–11, "Vypiska iz Zhurnala Soveta Imperatorskogo Russkogo Geograficheskogo Obshchestva 10-go marta 1851 goda," forwarded from Ia. Khanykov to V. V. Grigor'ev, April 17, 1851. Title of file: "Perepiska Soveta Geograficheskogo ob-va s V. V. Grigor'evym po voprosu ob izdanii perevoda nekotorykh chastei zemlevedeniia (geografii)." Publications included, inter alia, *Zemlevedenie Azii Karla Rittera*, pt. 1: *Obshchee vvedenie i vostochnaia okraina Azii*, trans. P. P. Semenov-Tian-Shanskii (St. Petersburg, 1856).

10. Lincoln, 136.

11. A. L—., "Glavnye osnovaniia voennoi statistiki i voenno-statisticheskie trudy General'nogo Shtaba," *VSb*, no. 1 (1861): 228–233.

12. Ibid., 239–241.

13. On the institutional culture of the tsarist General Staff, see David Rich, *The Tsar's Colonels: Professionalism, Strategy, and Subversion in Late Imperial Russia* (Cambridge, MA, 1998); and Alex Marshall, *The Russian General Staff and Asia, 1800–1917* (London, 2006).

14. V. Grigor'ev, "O russkikh interesakh v podvlastnykh nam osedlykh stranakh Srednei Azii (pis'ma k redaktoru 'Moskvy')," *TSb*, 1:107–129.

15. RGIA f. 1291, op. 82, d. 5a, ll. 1–1ob., Miliutin to Valuev, February 13, 1865, and 2–2ob., presentation of Valuev to Council of State, February 1865. Title of file: "Po vysochaishemu poveleniiu. O komandirovanii v Kirgizskiia stepi osoboi kommissii dlia izucheniia byta kirgizov . . ."

16. Ibid., l. 1ob.

17. Ibid., ll. 8ob.–9, Miliutin to Valuev, April 5, 1865.

18. Ibid., l. 21, Miliutin to Valuev, April 28, 1865.

19. Ibid., l. 26, Miliutin to Valuev, May 3, 1865; l. 21, Miliutin to Valuev, April 28, 1865.

20. Ibid., l. 18, Valuev to Miliutin, April 16, 1865.

21. Ibid., ll. 43–48ob., Miliutin to Alexander II, June 5, 1865.

22. Ibid., l. 10, Miliutin to Valuev, April 5, 1865.

23. Ibid., l. 68, Girs to Valuev, July 17, 1865.

24. Compare, e.g., the journey of Alexander I to Bessarabia to support a new statute for local administration of a mostly unknown new territory. See, e.g., A. Kushko, Viktor Taki, and Oleg Grom, *Bessarabiia v sostave Rossiiskoi imperii* (Moscow, 2012), 70–97. Other classic examples (to reform an existing territorial unit) include the revisions of Turkestan by F. K. Girs in 1882 and K. K. von der Pahlen in 1908.

25. RGIA f. 1291, op. 82, d. 5a (1865), ll. 66–66ob., Miliutin to Valuev, June 23, 1865; 67–67ob., Valuev to Miliutin, July 3, 1865.

26. A. K. Geins, *Sobranie literaturnykh trudov A. K. Geinsa*, vol. 1 (St. Petersburg, 1897), "Dnevnik 1865 goda: puteshestvie po kirgizskim stepiam," 208, 251.

27. RGIA f. 1291, op. 82, d. 5a (1865), ll. 71–73ob., Girs to Valuev, February 1, 1866.

28. A. K. Geins, *Sobranie literaturnykh trudov A. K. Geinsa*, vol. 2 (St. Petersburg, 1898), "Dnevnik 1866 goda: puteshestvie v Turkestan," 3.

29. For a series of criticisms of the management of Turkestan oblast, ruled with great difficulty from Orenburg, more than a thousand miles away, see, e.g., RGVIA f. 400, op. 1, d. 101, ll. 6–11, April 11, 1867.

30. RGIA f. 1291, op. 82, d. 5a (1865), l. 93, Miliutin to Valuev, June 3, 1867.

31. Ibid., l. 94, Miliutin to MVD, September 23, 1867. See also L. L. Meier, ed., *Materialy dlia geografii i statistiki Rossii, sobrannye ofitserami General'nogo Shtaba: Kirgizskaia step' Orenburgskogo vedomstva* (St. Petersburg, 1865).

32. RGIA f. 1291, op. 82, d. 5a (1865), ll. 83–84, Kryzhanovskii to Valuev, March 9, 1867; 86ob.–87, Valuev to Miliutin, March 18, 1867.

33. RGVIA f. 400, op. 1, d. 120, l. 4, Girs to Miliutin, 1 January 1868.

34. Dov Yaroshevski has argued that, by the Alexandrine era, grazhdanstvennost' connoted civil order and citizenship as reflected by participation in reformed public institutions; Austin Jersild has rightly noted, however, that for many colonial officials (in the Caucasian provinces, in the case he treats) it came with a sense of obligation and responsibility to the colonial state, rather than rights. See Dov Yaroshevski, "Empire and Citizenship," and Austin Jersild, "From Savagery to Citizenship: Caucasian Mountaineers and Muslims in the Russian Empire," both in *Russia's Orient: Imperial Borderlands and Peoples, 1700–1917*, ed. Daniel Brower and Edward Lazzerini (Bloomington, 2001), 58–79, 101–114.

35. On the difficulties of counting and taxing nomads, see Iu. Iuzhakov, "Nashi priobreteniia v Srednei Azii," *TSb*, 5:127–128.

36. *Voenno-statisticheskoe obozrenie zemli Kirgiz-Kaisakov Vnutrennoi (Bukeevskoi) i Zaural'skoi (Maloi) Ordy Orenburgskogo vedomstva: Po rekognistsirovkam i materialam sobrannym na meste, sostavleno ober-kvartirmeisterom Orenburgskogo korpusa Gen. Shtaba Col. Blarambergom* (n.p.: 1848), 91. On conflicting understandings of horse theft in tsarist courts, see Virginia Martin, "Barïmta: Nomadic Custom, Imperial Crime," in Brower and Lazzerini, 249–270.

37. RGIA f. 1291, op. 82, d. 9 (1858), ll. 6ob.–7ob. (a later summary of Perovskii's correspondence with officials at the Ministry of Foreign Affairs, Karl Nesselrode and Konstantin Konstantinovich Rodofinikin). Title of file: "O razvitii zemlepashestva mezhdu Kirgizami Orenburgskogo vedomstva."

38. See, e.g., criticism of Speranskii's good intentions, but ignorance of local conditions, in establishing direct rule at Geins, 1:209.

39. Krasovskii, 1:146.

40. Idarov, "Kirgizskaia step' Sibirskogo vedomstva i novouchrezhdennaia v nei Semipalatinskaia oblast'," *TSb*, 398:50–50a.

41. N. N. Dlusskaia, "Zapiski N. G. Zalesova, soobshchennye N. N. Dlusskoi," *Russkaia starina* 34, no. 7 (1903): 21.

42. RGIA f. 1291, op. 82, d. 9 (1858), ll. 10ob.–11, Memorandum of Katenin to Minister of Foreign Affairs A. M. Gorchakov, March 4, 1859.

43. Ibid., ll. 12–13.

44. RGIA f. 1291, op. 82, d. 6 (1859), l. 73ob., note by Katenin, "Zapiska o peredache Kirgizov Maloi Ordy v vedomstvo Ministerstva Vnutrennykh Del," undated, likely March 1859. Title of file: "O peredache upravleniia kirgizami Maloi Ordy ili step'iu Zaural'skikh

kirgizov iz vedomstva Ministerstva inostrannykh del v Ministerstvo vnutrennikh del, s pereimenovaniem v Oblast' kirgizov orenburgskikh."

45. For biographical data on Meier, see E. S. Syzdykova, *Rossiiskie voennye i Kazakhstan: voprosy sotsial'no-politicheskoi i ekonomicheskoi istorii Kazakhstana XVIII–XIX vv. v trudakh ofitserov General'nogo shtaba Rossii* (Moscow, 2005), 48.

46. Meier, *Materialy*, 99.

47. Ibid., 102, 105, 114–115.

48. Ibid., 247.

49. Ibid., 121–122.

50. Meier, "Del'ta reki Syr-Dar'i i eia otnoshenie k Rossii," *MSb* 55, no. 9 (1861): 144–155; Meier, "Aral'skaia flotiliia v otnoshenii k sredne-aziatskoi torgovle," *MSb* 60, no. 7 (1862): 109–134.

51. Meier, "Aral'skaia flotiliia," 129–130.

52. RGIA f. 1291, op. 82, d. 23 (1866), l. 2, register of the Main Administration of Western Siberia, 20–21 October 1866. Title of file: "O vodvoreniii russkikh zemledel'tsev v Kirgizskoi stepi Sibirskogo vedomstva."

53. Ibid., ll. 3–4.

54. Virginia Martin, *Law and Custom in the Steppe: The Kazakhs of the Middle Horde and Russian Colonialism in the Nineteenth Century* (Richmond, 2001), 34.

55. *Polozhenie ob upravlenii Orenburgskimi kirgizami* (St. Petersburg, 1844), 18–19 (articles 56–63).

56. Ibid., 20 (article 65).

57. *PSZ*, series 1, vol. 38 (1822–23), no. 29127. The numbers in brackets refer to specific articles of the statute.

58. Martin, *Law and Custom*, 43.

59. RGIA f. 1291, op. 82, d. 6 (1847), ll. 33–34, Katenin to Minister of Foreign Affairs A. M. Gorchakov, January 26, 1859. Title of file: "Ob izmenenii poriadka suda nad Kirgizami Zaural'skoi Ordy."

60. Ibid., ll. 35–36; see also a separate note summarizing the reform process, ll. 93–93ob., April 22, 1861.

61. Ibid., ll. 37–40ob.

62. Ibid., ll. 52–52ob., Panin to Gorchakov, March 1, 1859; ll. 53–57, Bludov to Gorchakov, March 22, 1859.

63. Ibid., ll. 184ob.–185ob.

64. Ibid., ll. 194–201.

65. Ibid., ll. 206–206ob., Valuev to Kryzhanovskii, September 21, 1865.

66. TsGA RK f. 345, op. 1, d. 807, l. 2, May 13, 1863. Title of file: "Delo o preobrazovanii suda v kazakhskoi stepi."

67. See, e.g., ibid., ll. 25–26, conclusions of assembly of biys of Kokshetau okrug, May 31, 1863.

68. According to Valikhanov's own testimony, the administration of Western Siberia was aware of his views; see *SSCV*, 5:161 (letter of Valikhanov to K. K. Gutkovskii, April 3, 1864). In 1860–1861 Valikhanov lived in St. Petersburg, working for the General Staff and the Asiatic Department of the Ministry of Foreign Affairs; see Makbal Musina and Boris Tikhomirov, *Chokan Valikhanov v Sankt-Peterburge* (St. Petersburg, 2009), 5–11. While living in St. Petersburg, he frequently attended meetings of IRGO and the Free Economic Society. See N. P. Ivlev, "Pobornik prosveshcheniia: novoe o Chokane," *Prostor*, no. 10 (1993): 224–228.

69. Ch. Ch. Valikhanov, "Zapiska o sudebnoi reforme," in *Ch. Ch. Valikhanov: Etnograficheskoe nasledie kazakhov*, ed. Zh. O. Artykbaev (Astana, 2007), 134.

70. Ibid., 144.

71. On the importance of local conditions (with citation to John Stuart Mill), see ibid., 122.

72. I. I. Zavalishin, *Opisanie Zapadnoi Sibiri*, vol. 3: *Sibirsko-Kirgizskaia step'* (Moscow, 1867), 63–64.

73. M. I. Veniukov, "Ocherki Zailiiskogo kraia i Prichuiskoi strany" (n.p.: 1861), 86.

74. P. I. Nebol'sin, *Rasskazy proezzhago* (St. Petersburg, 1854), 303; P. P. Semenov-Tian-Shanskii, *Puteshestvie v Tian'-Shan' v 1856–7 gg.* (Moscow, 1946), 154–55.

75. Martin, *Law and Custom*, 45

76. For one such attempt at a collection, see G. Zagriazhskii, "Iuridicheskie obychai Kirgiz i o narodnom sude u kochevogo naseleniia Turkestanskogo kraia, po obychnomu pravu (zan)," in *Materialy dlia statistiki Turkestanskogo kraia*, no. 4, ed. N. Maev (St. Petersburg, 1876), 150–202.

77. Marginalia indicate that the MVD's summary of correspondence on Katenin's legal reform was forwarded to the chairman of the Steppe Commission, F. K. Girs. See RGIA f. 1291, op. 82, d. 6 (1847), l. 101.

78. On *dvoeverie* and its implications for the nineteenth-century intellectuals who argued for its existence, see Eve Levin, "Dvoeverie and Popular Religion," in *Seeking God: The Recovery of Religious Identity in Orthodox Russia, Ukraine, and Georgia*, ed. Stephen K. Batalden (DeKalb, 1993), 31–52.

79. For this argument, see above all Robert Crews, *For Prophet and Tsar: Islam and Empire in Russia and Central Asia* (Cambridge, MA, 2006). Even the cooptation of Islamic institutions was accompanied by a degree of Islamophobia, or at least concern about the divided loyalties of Muslim subjects, in some areas. See, e.g., Kelly A. O'Neill, "Between Submission and Subversion: The Incorporation of the Crimean Khanate into the Russian Empire, 1783–1853" (PhD diss., Harvard University, 2006), 35–91.

80. In this connection, see especially the work of Allen Frank, e.g., *Muslim Religious Institutions in Imperial Russia: The Islamic World of Novouzensk District and the Kazakh Inner Horde, 1780–1910* (Boston, 2001); and Pavel Shablei, "Akhun Siradzh ad-din Saifulla al-Kyzyl"iari u kazakhov Sibirskogo vedomstva: Islamskaia biografiia v imperskom kontekste," *Ab Imperio*, no. 1 (2012): 175–208.

81. Devin DeWeese, *Islamization and Native Religion in the Golden Horde: Baba Tükles and Conversion to Islam in Historical and Epic Tradition* (State College, 1994).

82. Meier, *Materialy*, 228.

83. Krasovskii, 1:391.

84. P. I. Pashino, "Turkestanskii krai v 1866 g.: Putevye zametki," *TSb*, 14:56.

85. Here I am inspired by Bruno Latour's discussion of the ways in which scholarly texts are constructed to withstand critique. See Latour, *Science in Action: How to Follow Scientists and Engineers through Society* (Cambridge, MA, 1987), 45–60.

86. RGIA f. 821, op. 8, d. 594, ll. 31–31ob., "Izvlechenie iz otcheta General-Ad"iutanta Kryzhanovskogo po upravleniiu Orenburgskim kraem s fevralia 1865 do marta 1866." Title of file: "Preobrazovanie magometanskikh dukhovnykh uchrezhdenii (Otchet Orenburgskogo General-Gubernatora. Mery protiv rasprostraneniia islamizma)."

87. Ibid., ll. 33ob.–34ob.

88. Ibid., l. 26ob., MVD Department of General Affairs to MVD Department of Religious Affairs of Foreign Faiths, July 22, 1866.

89. Ibid., ll. 43ob.–46, ll. 48–49ob., Kryzhanovskii to Valuev, January 31, 1867.

90. Ibid., l. 48.

91. This increased anti-Islamic sentiment tracks with the Russian Empire's broad shift from a dynastic to a national model and, more specifically, with the Caucasian war against Shamil in the 1850s. See Paul Werth, *At the Margins of Orthodoxy: Mission, Governance, and Confessional Politics in Russia's Volga-Kama Region, 1827–1905* (Ithaca, 2002), 181.

92. RGIA f. 821, op. 8, d. 594., ll. 55–63ob., Valuev to Kryzhanovskii, May 22, 1867; ll. 94–98, Timashev to Kryzhanovskii, June 15, 1868.

93. Valuev attempted to solicit the views of Governor-General of Novorossiisk and Bessarabia P. E. Kotsebue on Kryzhanovskii's proposal (ibid., ll. 53–54).

94. On Valikhanov, see above; Babadzhanov was the recipient of a silver medal from IRGO, and apparently the first Kazak to be so honored. See N. P. Ivlev, "Vvedenie: Zabytyi etnograf iz Naryn-peskov," *Khodzha Mukhammed-Salikh Babadzhanov: Sochineniia (sbornik statei 1861–1871 gg.)*, ed. N. P. Ivlev (Almaty, 1996), 23.

95. Artykbaev, *Etnograficheskoe nasledie*, 109 ("O musul'manstve v stepi").

96. Ibid., "Sledy shamanstva u kirgizov," 68–98.

97. *SSCV*, 1:198–199 ("Zamechaniia na tret'iu chast' opisaniia kirgiz kazach'ikh ord [A. I. Levshina]").

98. See Artykbaev, "O musul'manstve v stepi," for a claim that Islam and its proponents "cannot help the Russian or any other Christian government" (111).

99. Ibid., 114.

100. Zh. O. Artykbaev, ed., *Khodzha Mukhammed Salikh Babadzhanov: Etnografiia kazakhov Bukeevskoi ordy* (Astana, 2007), "Zametki kirgiza o kirgizakh," 79–80; on khojas, see Frank, 278–281.

101. Artykbaev, "Zametki kirgiza," 81–83, 85–86.

102. Ibid., 81, 87–88, 90.

103. The articles on forest regulation, for example, were inspired by the failure of the prevailing system in European Russia. See RGIA f. 1291, op. 82, d. 5c (1865), ll. 111ob.–112, "Ob"iasnitel'naia zapiska k proektu polozheniia ob upravlenii v Priural'skoi, Turgaiskoi, Akmolinsk, i Semipalatinskoi oblastei."

104. RGIA f. 1291, op. 82, d. 5c, ll. 10–10ob.

105. RGVIA f. 400, op. 1, d. 71, ll. 2–9ob. Title of file: "Soobrazheniia general-maiora Gutkovskogo i polkovnika Geinsa po administrativnomu ustroistvu kirgizskoi stepi," July 2, 1866.

106. RGVIA f. 400, op. 1, d. 63, ll. 198–220ob. Title of file: "Po otzyvu komanduiushchogo voiskami Orenburgskogo okruga o novom polozhenii dlia Turkestanskoi oblasti i o naznachenii pomoshchnikom voennogo gubernatora Turkestanskoi oblasti general-maiora Vorontsova-Dashkova." Though undated and unsigned, this note's contents are consonant with proposals Kryzhanovskii made elsewhere, and it likely belongs to him. The phrase in quotation marks is an allusion to Richard Robbins, *The Tsar's Viceroys: Russian Provincial Governors in the Last Years of the Empire* (Ithaca, 1987).

107. Daniel Brower, *Turkestan and the Fate of the Russian Empire* (New York, 2003), 27–35, argues for a division between "strong-arm" military rule and the civil development advocated by Girs and others; in light of evidence presented in this chapter, this argument seems an oversimplification. For fears about unification, see RGIA f. 1291, op. 82, d. 5a (1865), ll. 177–178, "Svod ob"iasnenii na zamechaniia Ministerstva Vnutrennykh Del, po proektu Polozheniia ob upravlenii Stepnymi oblastiami Orenburgskogo kraia i Zapadnoi Sibiri."

108. On administrative anxieties about unifying Kazaks under a single statute, see Martin, *Law and Custom*, 55.

109. RGVIA f. 400, op. 1, d. 63, ll. 98ob.–99ob., Girs to Miliutin, January 30, 1867; d. 77, ll. 10–10ob., Duhamel to Miliutin, 13 September 1866.

110. RGIA f. 1291, op. 82, d. 5c, ll. 90ob.–91. The summary of this committee's report uses both Russian terms which may be translated to English as "property," *vladenie* (holding) and *sobstvennost'* (proprietary ownership).

111. Ibid.

112. Ibid., ll. 91–93; Geins, 2:103.

113. RGIA f. 1291, op. 82, d. 5c, ll. 94ob.–95.

114. Ibid., ll. 96–96ob.; *Vremennoe polozhenie ob upravlenii v oblastiakh Ural'skoi, Tur-gaiskoi, Akmolinskoi, i Semipalatinskoi* (n.d.), 28 (article 217).

115. RGIA f. 1291, op. 82, d. 5c, ll. 104–105.

116. Ibid., l. 103ob.

117. Ibid.

118. Ibid., ll. 107–107ob.

119. Ibid., l. 104. This caution echoes the views of the Western Siberian administrators who proposed peasant colonization in 1866.

120. RGVIA f. 400, op. 1, d. 120, ll. 182ob.–183ob., A. A. Zelenoi to Miliutin, February 20, 1868.

121. Geins, 2:69–70, 104, 110.

122. Ibid., 104.

123. RGIA f. 1291, op. 82, d. 5c, ll. 42–42ob.

124. Ibid., ll. 57–58ob.

125. Ibid., ll. 52ob.–53.

126. Ibid., l. 53.

127. RGVIA f. 400, op. 1, d. 120, ll. 304ob.–305, Butkov to Miliutin, March 15, 1868.

128. Ibid., ll. 188–188ob., Asiatic Department of the MID to Miliutin, February 23, 1868.

129. Ibid., l. 189.

130. *Vremennoe polozhenie*, 15 (article 94, with notes).

131. Geins, 1:211–12, mentions no disagreements on this issue.

132. RGIA f. 1291, op. 82, d. 5c, l. 118.

133. Ibid., l. 119–120ob.

134. Ibid., l. 124.

135. Ibid., ll. 126–131ob.

136. Ibid., ll. 133–148.

137. Ibid., ll. 141–141ob.

138. RGIA f. 1291, op. 82, d. 5a, ll. 116–126ob., Khrushchov to Miliutin, February 20, 1868; ibid., l. 154, undated.

139. See, e.g., I. F. Babkov, *Vospominaniia o moei sluzhbe v Zapadnoi Sibiri 1859–1875 gg.: Razgranichenie s Zapadnym Kitaem 1869 g.* (St. Petersburg, 1912), 313–316.

140. RGVIA f. 400, op. 1, d. 120, ll. 550–550ob., "Zamechaniia Chlena Gosudarstvennogo Soveta Levshina po proektu polozheniia ob upravlenii v stepnykh oblastiakh Orenburg-skogo i Zapadno-Sibirskogo General-Gubernatorstv," July 13, 1868.

141. Ibid., l. 549.

142. Ibid., ll. 548–548ob.

143. Ibid., 550ob.

144. Ibid., l. 554, "Izvlechenie iz pis'ma Deistvitel'nogo Statskogo Sovetnika Khanykova, iz Parizha, ot 30-go iiunia 1868 g."

145. Ibid., ll. 554ob., 555, 553.

146. Ibid., ll. 555ob.–556.

147. RGIA f. 1291, op. 82, d. 5a, ll. 252ob.–253, "Vozrazheniia protiv zamechanii Chlena Gos Soveta Levshina po proektu Polozheniia ob upravlenii v stephnykh oblastiakh Oren-burgskogo i Zapadno-Sibirskogo General-gubernatorstv.'" D. A. Miliutin forwarded this copy to A. E. Timashev on September 27, 1868; per RGVIA f. 400, op. 1, d. 120, l. 552ob., members of the Steppe Commission composed this note and presented it to the chief of the General Staff, F. L. Geiden, on September 23.

148. RGIA f. 1291, op. 82, d. 5a, l. 249ob., "Vozrazheniia protiv zamechanii Levshina."

149. Ibid., l. 248ob.

150. See, e.g., Geins, 2 (appendix):47, "Ob"iasnitel'naia zapiska k polozheniiu i shtatam voenno-narodnogo upravleniia Semirechenskoi i Syr-Dar'inskoi oblasti"; RGIA f. 1291, op. 82, d. 5c, ll. 63–63ob.

151. RGIA f. 1291, op. 82, d. 5a, ll. 220ob.–221ob., extract from registers of meetings of the Committee of Ministers, October 22, 1868.

3. AN IMPERIAL BIOGRAPHY

1. The end of RGIA f. 1291, op. 82, d. 5a (1865), is a rich source for official perspectives on the history of this rebellion. See, e.g., the reports from Kryzhanovskii to Timashev at ll. 379–384, August 20, 1869; and 390–396ob., October 28, 1869).

2. See especially the tragicomic history of Sary-su district in southern Akmolinsk province: RGIA f. 1291, op. 82, d. 6 (1869). Title of file: "Ob otkrytii v Akmolinskoi oblasti piatogo uezda na reke Sary-Su."

3. RGVIA f. 400, op. 1, d. 259, l. 63, "Instruktsiia volostnym upraviteliam i aul'nym starshinam." From revisions proposed for Akmolinsk and Semipalatinsk oblasts, March 5, 1871. Title of file: "O rassmotrenii proekta polozheniia ob upravlenii oblastiami Akmolinskoi i Semipalatinskoi, predstavlennogo general-gubernatorom Zapadnoi Sibiri."

4. The basic source (though with only one citation to Altynsarin's collected works) on Altynsarin's life in English is Isabelle Kreindler, "Ibrahim Altynsarin, Nikolai Il'minskii, and the Kazakh National Awakening," *Central Asian Survey* 2 (1983): 99–116.

5. For this approach to the history of empires, see David Lambert and Alan Lester, *Colonial Lives across the British Empire: Imperial Careering in the Long Nineteenth Century* (New York, 2006); also see the chapter devoted to the Khakass ethnographer Nikolai Katanov in Robert Geraci, *Window on the East: National and Imperial Identities in Late Tsarist Russia* (Ithaca, 2001), 309–341.

6. For the "class enemy" interpretation, see S. D. Asfendiarov, *Istoriia Kazakhstana s drevneishikh vremen* (Alma-Ata, 1935), cited in Lowell Tillett, *The Great Friendship: Soviet Historians on the Non-Russian Nationalities* (Chapel Hill, 1969), 389–390; for the "democratic enlightener" interpretation, see E. B. Bekmakhanov, *Sobranie sochinenii*, 7 vols., vol. 4: *Istoriia Kazakstana (uchebnik i uchebnye posobiia)* (1959; Pavlodar, 2005), 370; for the proto-nationalist interpretation, see M. K. Kozybaev, ed., *Istoriia Kazakstana s drevneishikh vremen do nashikh dnei*, 5 vols., vol. 3 (Almaty, 2000), 535.

7. On the changing narratives surrounding Altynsarin's life, see G. G. Kosach, "Ibragim Altynsarin: Chelovek v potoke vremeni," *Vestnik Evrazii*, no. 1–2 (1998): 110–130.

8. Jane Burbank and Frederick Cooper, *Empires in World History: Power and the Politics of Difference* (Princeton, 2010), 3–8 ("imperial repertoires").

9. Frederick Cooper, *Colonialism in Question: Theory, Knowledge, History* (Berkeley, 2005), 21. Cooper challenges, e.g., Dipesh Chakrabarty, *Provincializing Europe: Postcolonial Thought and Historical Difference* (Princeton, 2000) and Walter Mignolo, *Local Histories/Global Designs: Coloniality, Subaltern Knowledges, and Border Thinking* (Princeton, 2000). The critique of the oppressive power of the colonizer's discourse that has been most influential in the contemporary Western academy is that of Frantz Fanon, e.g., *Black Skin, White Masks*, trans. Charles Lam Markmann (New York, 1967).

10. My use of "groupness" here is a nod to the argument of Frederick Cooper and Rogers Brubaker that speaking in terms of "identity" when the very bounds and existence of such are in flux and contestation is to beg the question; see Brubaker and Cooper, "Identity," in Cooper, *Colonialism in Question*, 59–90. Compare Altynsarin's blend of loyal service to a dynastic empire and active participation in projects of ethnic and linguistic differentiation to, e.g., Christine Philliou's account of the Ottoman *phanariot* administrator Stephanos Vogorides, *Biography of an Empire: Governing Ottomans in an Age of Revolution* (Berkeley, 2011).

11. K. Beisembiev, *Iz istorii obshchestvennoi mysli Kazakhstana vtoroi poloviny XIX veka* (Alma-Ata, 1957), 133.

12. *SSIA*, 1:9.

13. For documents pertaining to this administrative conflict, which mainly concerned the appropriate curriculum for the school and occupations of its graduates (local authorities favored a broader spectrum of both), see the appendix to N. I. Il'minskii, *Vospominaniia ob I. A. Altynsarine* (Kazan', 1891), 8, 42–43.

14. A. V. Vasil'ev, *Istoricheskii ocherk russkogo obrazovaniia v Turgaiskoi oblasti i sovremennoe ego sostoianie* (Orenburg, 1896), 44–47; Il'minskii, *Vospominaniia*, 86–91 (appendix).

15. Il'minskii, *Vospominaniia*, 76 (appendix), journal presentation of Orenburg Frontier Commission of August 9, 1850.

16. RGIA f. 1291, op. 81, d. 233 (1856), ll. 74ob.–75, "Spisok vospitannikov Shkoly kirgizskikh detei, uchrezhdennoi pri Orenburgskoi Pogranichnoi Kommisii, s oboznacheniem chisla ballov, poluchennykh kazhdym iz nikh, srednim chislom, v techenii 1856 goda." Title of file: "Otchet Orenburgskoi pogranichnoi kommissii po upravleniiu Zaural'skimi kirgizami Orenburgskogo vedomstva i shkoloi dlia kirgizskikh detei."

17. *SSIA*, 1:14.

18. On Grigor'ev's service in this region, see also Nathaniel Knight, "Grigor'ev in Orenburg, 1851–1862: Russian Orientalism in the Service of Empire?" *Slavic Review* 59, no. 1 (2000): 74–100.

19. On Il'minskii's career, see Robert Geraci, *Window on the East: National and Imperial Identities in Late Tsarist Russia* (Ithaca, 2001), especially 47–85; and Wayne Dowler, *Classroom and Empire: The Politics of Schooling Russia's Eastern Nationalities* (Montreal, 2001), 41–61.

20. Il'minskii, *Vospominaniia*, 21.

21. Ibid.

22. TsGA RK f. 4, op. 1, d. 2953, sv. 424, ll. 2–3, May 31, 1860, indicates that Altynsarin was to serve, due to lack of personnel, both as a translator and as a teacher of Russian in the fortress in exchange for an augmented salary. Title of file: "O naznachenii zauriadkhorunzhego Altynsarina perevodchikom Orenburgskogo ukrepleniia."

23. Il'minskii, *Vospominaniia*, 98–99 (appendix). Reprint of a presentation to the Governor-General of Orenburg and Samara, October 9, 1859.

24. For the anti-Tatar language, see Grigor'ev's memorandum to Bezak in Il'minskii, *Vospominaniia*, 136–37 (appendix), letter of January 16, 1861.

25. He complains, retrospectively, of this in a letter to Il'minskii dated March 16, 1864. See *SSIA*, 3:25.

26. TsGA RK f. 4, op. 1, d. 2953, sv. 424, l. 21, August 14, 1861; and l. 25 July 23, 1862.

27. Ibid., ll. 51–51ob., Altynsarin to Ladyzhenskii, October 26, 1863.

28. Dowler, 38. Bakhtiarov's involvement suggests the importance of locals in co-creating linguistic knowledge even before Altynsarin's administrative rise; compare Kapil Raj, *Relocating Modern Science: Circulation and the Construction of Knowledge in South Asia and Europe, 1650–1900* (New York, 2007), especially chap. 5 (159–180).

29. Il'minskii, *Vospominaniia*, 30.

30. A. V. Remnev, "Iazyk i alfavit v imperskoi politike v kazakhskoi stepi (vtoraia polovina XIX veka)," in *Imperskie i natsional'nye modeli upravleniia: Rossiiskii i evropeiskii opyt*, ed. A. O. Chubar'ian (Moscow, 2007), 206–207; Il'minskii, *Vospominaniia*, 30–32.

31. Xavier Hallez, "Petite histoire des dictionnaires kazakh-russes (1861–2002): Parmi les alphabets arabe, latin, et cyrillique," *Cahiers d'Asie centrale*, nos. 11/12 (2004): 291–316; V. V. Grigor'ev, "O peredache zvukov kirgizskogo iazyka bukvami russkoi azbuki (pis'mo k N. I. Il'minskomu)" (Kazan', 1862).

32. Il'minskii, "O primenenii russkogo alfavita k inorodcheskim iazykam," in *Nikolai Ivanovich Il'minskii: Izbrannye mesta iz pedagogicheskikh sochinenii, nekotorye svedeniia o ego deiatel'nosti i o poslednykh dniakh ego zhizni* (Kazan', 1892), 5.

33. Here and throughout I accept the argument that historians should use the term "Russification" with greater historicity and caution. See, e.g., Aleksei Miller, "Russifikatsiia: klassifitsirovat' i poniat'," *Ab Imperio*, no. 2 (2002): 133–148. For a focused examination of the meanings of Russification in a specific colonial context, see Ilya Vinkovetsky, *Russian America: An Overseas Colony of a Continental Empire, 1804–1867* (New York, 2011). For Vinkovetsky, Russification/*russifikatsiia* proper is "an aggressive and coordinated government policy aimed at cultural transformation," exclusive to the western borderlands of the empire, while Russianization/*obrusenie* is an interactive cultural process aimed at making "[non-Russians] more like the Russians in specific characteristics" (96).

34. Tomohiko Uyama, "A Particularist Empire: The Russian Policies of Christianization and Military Conscription in Central Asia," in *Empire, Islam, and Politics in Central Eurasia*, ed. Uyama (Sapporo, 2007), 23–63.

35. Daniel R. Brower, *Turkestan and the Fate of the Russian Empire* (New York, 2003), 30–31; for this policy in comparative perspective, see Alexander S. Morrison, *Russian Rule in Samarkand, 1868–1910: A Comparison with British India* (New York, 2008), 55–58, 84.

36. Brower, 69.

37. "K voprosu ob ustroistve uchilishch dlia inorodcheskikh detei Kazanskogo uchebnogo okruga," *ZhMNP* 134 (1867): 75–96.

38. Ibid., 89. The intermediate religious forms described in Vicente Rafael's discussion of conversion in the Philippines, *Contracting Colonialism: Translation and Christian Conversion in Tagalog Society under Early Spanish Rule* (Ithaca, 1988) suggest that such fears were not totally unfounded; also compare Paul W. Werth, "Big Candles and 'Internal Conversion': The Mari Animist Reformation and Its Russian Appropriations," in *Of Religion and Empire: Missions, Conversion, and Tolerance in Tsarist Russia*, ed. Robert Geraci and Michael Khodarkovsky (Ithaca, 2001), 144–172.

39. "K voprosu ob ustroistve," 91. Italics in text.

40. Ibid., 92.

41. M. Miropiev, "Kakie glavnye printsipy dolzhny byt' polozheny v osnovu obrazovaniia russkikh inorodtsev-musul'man? Rech' proiznesennaia na godichnom akte Turkestanskoi uchitel'skoi seminarii, 30-go avgusta 1882 g., prepodavatelem seminarii M. A. Miropievym," *TSb*, 361:144b–145b.

42. N. Ostroumov, "Kharakteristika religiozno-nravstennoi zhizni musul'man preimushchestvenno Srednei Azii," *TSb*, 329:51.

43. Dowler, 17.

44. Knight, "Grigor'ev," 95.

45. Gulmira Sultangalieva, "The Russian Empire and the Intermediary Role of Tatars in Kazakstan: The Politics of Cooperation and Rejection," in *Asiatic Russia: Imperial Power in Regional and International Contexts*, ed. Tomohiko Uyama (New York, 2012), 58–62. The Tatar population of Orenburg varied between 12 and 24 percent of the city's total during the late imperial era; see G. G. Kosach, *Gorod na styke dvukh kontinentov: Orenburgskoe tatarskoe men'shinstvo i gosudarstvo* (Moscow, 1998), 42.

46. RGIA f. 1291, op. 82, d. 5c (1865), ll. 118–148.

47. Kazaks were considered inorodtsy in both the formal sense (an estate of unassimilated people not subject to the general laws of the Russian Empire) and the informal sense of "non-Christian, eastern 'others'" (185). On the conceptual shifts around this term, see John Slocum, "Who, and When, Were the *Inorodtsy*? The Evolution of the Category of 'Aliens' in Imperial Russia," *Russian Review* 57, no. 2 (1998): 173–190. For the script debate after the turn of the century, see, e.g., Ü. Subkhanberdina et al., qŭr., *Qazaq gazetĭ* (Almaty, 1998), 165, "Shkoldargha ana tĭlĭmen oqu" (1915).

48. *SSIA*, 3:30–31 (letter to N. I. Il'minskii, August 31, 1871).

49. *SSIA*, 3:14 (letter to N. I. Il'minskii, January 19, 1861).

50. N. A. Kryzhanovskii, "Rech', proiznesennaia pokrovitelem Orenburgskogo otdela pri otkrytii otdela," *ZOrIRGO* 1 (1870): 25–26. Speech of January 14, 1868.

51. Ibid., 17.

52. I. Altynsarin, "Ocherk obychaev, pri svatovstve i svad'be, u kirgizov Orenburgskogo vedomstva," *ZOrIRGO* 1 (1870): 101.

53. Ibid., 104.

54. For example, Krasovskii, *Materialy dlia geografii i statistiki Rossiiskoi imperii: Oblast' Sibirskikh kirgizov* (St. Petersburg, 1868), 2:60–61, describes Kazak guesting and feasts at weddings and funerals as a negative influence on stock raising second only to mutual raiding (baranta). Other ethnographers sought, like Altynsarin, not to exoticize what they observed in such rituals but to understand the logic behind them, e.g., A. N. Kharuzin, *Kirgizy bukeevskoi ordy (antropologo-etnograficheskii ocherk)* (Moscow, 1889), 1:107–108.

55. Altynsarin, "Svatovstve," 103–104.

56. Ibid., 108–109, 116.

57. V. N. Plotnikov, "Zametki na stat'iu g. Altynsarina 'Ocherk Kirgizskikh obychaev pri svatovstve i svad'be,'" *ZOrIRGO* 1 (1870): 122, italics added.

58. Vasil'ev, 66.

59. *SSIA*, 3:168–212; 212 also displays a document that presents Altynsarin as the "acting judge" (*imeiushchii dolzhnost'*) of Turgai district.

60. *Vremennoe polozhenie ob upravlenii v oblastiakh Ural'skoi, Turgaiskoi, Akmolinskoi i Semipalatinskoi* (n.d.), 38.

61. Vasil'ev, 77–78; the proposal about the teachers' school was made in 1870 and the one pertaining to mobile schools in 1871.

62. Ibid., 80.

63. Ibid., 82–84, indicates that even after Kazak schools were moved to the jurisdiction of the Ministry of Education, their annual allotment remained at 3,465 rubles; collections from the Kazak population, though, at 7–10 kopecks per household, formed a capital of more than 26,000 rubles by the end of the decade.

64. The Russo-Kazak primary school in the city of Turgai could boast only nine students in 1874. See *SSIA*, 3:211. Altynsarin contributed to this report.

65. Special regulations for Tatar, Bashkir, and Kazak schools explicitly extended this law to the steppe provinces in 1874. See Dowler, 131.

66. Il'minskii, *Vospominaniia*, 161, "Mnenie po voprosu o merakh dlia obrazovaniia kirgizov" (March 30, 1870).

67. Gulmira Sultangalieva, "Kazakhskoe chinovnichestva [*sic*] Orenburgskogo vedomstva: Formirovanie i napravlenie deiatel'nosti (XIX)," *Acta Slavica Iaponica* 27 (2009): 86.

68. Dowler, 4–5, has articulated this point clearly with respect to education; Altynsarin's career, though, indicates the connections of this multiplicity with equally diverse views of economic development and steppe ecology.

69. Il'minskii, *Vospominaniia*, 163.

70. *SSIA*, 3:31–32 (letter to Il'minskii, August 31, 1871).

71. Il'minskii, *Vospominaniia*, 35–36.

72. Il'minskii reports asking Altynsarin's permission to recommend him to Tolstoi in *Vospominaniia*, 38–39; Iakovlev endorsed the promotion in a letter to Il'minskii (*SSIA*, 3:253–54) of January 10, 1877.

73. *Khrestomatiia* is directly translated "chrestomathy," a selection of literary passages used in teaching foreign languages. I use "reader" as a less clumsy means of communicating this meaning. For the second edition, see Ibrahim Altynsarin, *Kirgizskaia khrestomatiia*, 2nd ed. (Orenburg, 1906), iii.

74. Dowler, 41–61; *SSIA*, 2:38–39 ("O vremennom polozhenii ob upravlenii v stepnykh oblastiakh"). The editors of Altynsarin's collected works, confusingly, list this document

under the year 1868, but it cannot have been written before 1882, as their own footnotes attest.

75. Paul'son's reader is I. I. Paul'son, *Kniga dlia chteniia i prakticheskikh uprazhnenii v russkom iazyke: Uchebnoe posobie dlia narodnykh uchilishch* (Moscow, 1872). On Paul'son's progressive methodologies in zemstvo schools, see Ben Eklof, *Russian Peasant Schools: Officialdom, Village Culture, and Popular Pedagogy, 1861–1914* (Berkeley, 1986), 77. On the sources of the *Khrestomatiia*, see *SSIA*, 1:342.

76. These three stories can be found in the original Kazak in the *Khrestomatiia* on 10, 49–53, and 39, respectively; Russian translations are in *SSIA*, 1:146, 98–102, and 140.

77. Altynsarin, *Khrestomatiia*, viii–x; *SSIA*, 1:54–55.

78. *SSIA*, 2:158–59 ("O sostoianii uchebnoi chasti v Turgaiskoi oblasti za 1882 g."), contains a proposal that graduates of the two-class schools be allowed to teach in cantonal schools (at least until the opening of a special teachers' seminary for Kazaks), along with holding other public offices (*obshchestvennye dolzhnosti*).

79. For a reprint, see Zh. O. Artykbaev, ed., *Ïbïrai Altïnsarin: Etnografiialïq ocherkter zhäne auïz ädebiet ülgïleri* (Astana, 2007).

80. Compare the conflict among local lexical variations in creating a standard Turkmen language in the early days of the Turkmen SSR, described in Adrienne Edgar, *Tribal Nation: The Making of Soviet Turkmenistan* (Princeton, 2004), especially chap. 5.

81. Altynsarin, *Khrestomatiia*, vii (*dadandïq*), 3 (*patsa*), 6 (*keshkentai*); for the dialect reference, see Sh. Sarïbaev and E. Nŭrmaghambetov, eds., *Qazaq tïlïnïng dialektologiialïq sözdïgï* (Almaty, 1996), 1:155. A yet more explicit attempt to impose lexical discipline on the Kazak language was made by an obscure figure named Ish-Mukhammed Bukin, who published a lengthy Kazak-Russian dictionary at Tashkent in 1883. See discussion at Steven Sabol, *Russian Colonization and the Genesis of Kazak National Consciousness* (New York, 2003), 60.

82. In *SSIA*, 1:23 (letter to Il'minskii, sometime in 1862), Altynsarin argues that it is not harmful to employ Tatar (or Arabic, or Persian) loan words when the Kazak language lacks a suitable equivalent.

83. Altynsarin, *Khrestomatiia*, iii.

84. Ibid., iv.

85. Ibid.

86. *SSIA*, 2:107 ("Kirgizskaia gazeta, god pervyi" [January 1880]).

87. *SSIA*, 2:193 ("Zapiski na imia voennogo gubernatora Turgaiskoi obl., 'O vvedenii professial'no-tekhnicheskogo obucheniia v dvukhklassnykh russko-kazakhskikh shkolakh'" [27 September 1884]). *Sblizhenie* is distinct from *sliianie*, the complete merging of peoples.

88. *SSIA*, 3:108 (letter to N. I. Il'minskii, September 30, 1884).

89. Though Il'minskii's primary interest as a missionary was preventing apostasy among converts to Orthodoxy, he also, in 1869, proposed introducing Orthodox education to Central Asian Muslims, a proposal that was roundly rejected. See Uyama, "Particularist," 30.

90. Tomohiko Uyama translates this title as *Norms of Islam* (101); I would propose "buttress" or "rock" of Islam as other possible translations of *tŭtqa*. See Uyama, "The Changing Religious Orientation of Qazaq Intellectuals in the Tsarist Period: Shari'a, Secularism, and Ethics," in *Islam, Society, and States across the Qazaq Steppe (18th–Early 20th Centuries)*, ed. Niccolò Pianciola and Paolo Sartori (Vienna, 2013), 95–115.

91. A. Seidïmbekov, ed., *Mŭsïlmanshïlïqtïng tŭtqasï* (Almaty, 1991).

92. *SSIA*, 3:77 (letter to N. I. Il'minskii, September 12, 1882).

93. Ibid., 78.

94. *SSIA*, 2:116–117 ("Ushur"). The essay on *zaket* ("O ziakate," 2:118–124) is more laconic and concerned with the proper fulfillment of an important obligation.

95. Robert Crews, *For Prophet and Tsar: Islam and Empire in Russia and Central Asia* (Cambridge, MA, 2006), 192–240, emphasizes tsarist efforts to direct Kazaks away from Islam, with the assistance of local collaborators. Altynsarin's modest successes indicate both the diversity of administrative views and the possibility of multiple directions for collaboration between tsarist officials and Kazaks. In this sense, my data is a much better fit for the conditional model of religious tolerance offered in Paul Werth, *The Tsar's Foreign Faiths: Toleration and the Fate of Religious Freedom in Imperial Russia* (New York, 2014).

96. *SSIA*, 3:79–80.

97. Seidĭmbekov, 9–10.

98. Ibid.

99. Compare the discussion of the Uniate and Catholic Churches in the work of Theodore Weeks, e.g., "Between Rome and Tsargrad: The Uniate Church in Imperial Russia," in Geraci and Khodarkovsky, 70–91; also his *Nation and State in Late Imperial Russia: Nationalism and Russification on the Western Frontier, 1863–1914* (DeKalb, 1996). By contrast, Jeffrey Veidlinger notes that Zionism benefited from relative noninterference by tsarist officials until the adoption of a program of broad reform goals within the Russian Empire in 1907. See Veidlinger, *Jewish Public Culture in the Late Russian Empire* (Bloomington, 2009), 115–118.

100. See Adeeb Khalid, *The Politics of Muslim Cultural Reform: Jadidism in Central Asia* (Berkeley, 1999), 210–213, for discussion of the production of educational materials in "Turkestan Turkic" by the reformist Muslims in Central Asia after the turn of the twentieth century.

101. This discussion of the content, as opposed to the form, of religious ritual echoes Boris Uspenskii's semiotic analysis of the rise of Old Belief in seventeenth-century Muscovy. See Uspenskii, "The Schism and Cultural Conflict in the Seventeenth Century," in *Seeking God: The Recovery of Religious Identity in Orthodox Russia, Ukraine, and Georgia*, ed. Stephen K. Batalden (DeKalb, 1993), 106–133.

102. *SSIA*, 2:177 ("Predstavlenie popechiteliu Orenburgskogo uchebnogo okruga ob otkrytii shkol v Turgaiskoi oblasti" [October 5, 1883]); in this presentation, supported by the military governor of the province, Altynsarin argues that giving graduates of the two-class school rights to state service would both be useful to understaffed canton and district administrations and increase the local population's interest in the schools.

103. *SSIA*, 3:47–48 (letter to N. I. Il'minskii, November 25, 1879).

104. See, e.g., *SSIA*, 3:63–64 (letter to N. I. Il'minskii, October 4, 1881).

105. On building materials, see *SSIA*, 2:143–144, where Altynsarin lists the availability of good timber (a rare commodity on the steppe) in close proximity as one of the necessary preconditions for constructing a school building.

106. *SSIA*, 2:187 ("O sostoianii narodnykh shkol Turgaiskoi oblasti za 1883 g."). Altynsarin may have meant by this that pork was excluded from his boarders' diets; the daily menu he described included plentiful bread, tea, and kasha—none of which were exactly traditional Kazak foods.

107. *SSIA*, 3:259 (concerning schools in Iletsk district) lists expenditures for six dozen plates, 30 knives, spoons and forks, a tablecloth, several thousand napkins, and 25 iron bedframes; for expenditures for boarders' linens and outerwear, see *SSIA*, 3:288 ("Spravka o sostoianii uchilishchnogo fonda v Turgaiskoi oblasti za 1884–1886 gg").

108. *SSIA*, 2:137 ("Otchet o sostoianii kazakhskikh shkol Turgaiskoi obl. za 1880 g.").

109. RGVIA f. 400, op. 1, d. 498, l. 19, Sovet Glavnogo upravleniiia Zapadnoi Sibiri, "O kolonizatsii v Kirgizskoi stepi," November 29, 1874. Title of file: "O kolonizatsii okrugov Sibirskogo i Turkestanskogo."

110. Ibid., ll. 5ob.–6, Kaznakov to A. E. Timashev, January 20, 1876.

111. *SSIA*, 2:99–100 ("Po povodu goloda v kirgizskoi stepi").

112. Ibid.

113. Ibid.

114. Ibid., 102.

115. *SSIA*, 2:98–99 ("O dzhute (gololeditse)").

116. *SSIA*, 2:86 ("Ob oroshaemom zemledelii v Turgaiskoi oblasti").

117. *SSIA*, 2:70–71 ("Sostoianie zemledeliia, senokosheniia i skotovodstva Turgaiskogo uezda za 1872 g").

118. *SSIA*, 2:102 ("Po povodu goloda").

119. Ibid., 99–101.

120. Ibid., 103.

121. Ibid., 105. Compare here discussions of *metis* in James C. Scott, *Seeing Like a State: How Certain Schemes to Improve the Human Condition Have Failed* (New Haven, 1998).

122. See, e.g., TsGA RK f. 393, op. 1, d. 6, sv. 2, ll. 31–32, report of chief of Akmolinsk district to military governor M. A. Liventsov, December 2, 1883. Title of file: "Raporty uezdnykh nachal'nikov i perepiska s kantseliariei Stepnogo general-gubernatora ob obuchenii v internatakh kazakhskikh mal'chikov i devochek remeslam i sel'skomu khoziaistvu."

123. *SSIA*, 2:154 ("Popechiteliu Orenburgskogo uchebnogo okruga V. N. Daliu ob otkrytii v gor. Turgae remeslennoi shkoly, ob obuchenii devushek-kazashek" [January 20, 1882]); for provisions for study of Russian (at the two-class school, until a teacher could be found) see *SSIA*, 2:152 ("Proekt ustroistva nachal'noi remeslennoi shkoly v gor. Turgae" [January 20, 1882]).

124. *SSIA*, 2:193 ("Zapiska na imia voennogo gubernatora Turgaiskoi obl., 'O vvedenii professial'no-tekhnicheskogo obucheniia v dvukhklassnykh russko-kazakhskikh shkolakh'" [September 27, 1884]).

125. Ibid., 194.

126. Ibid., 196.

127. Ibid., 195–196, 157 ("O sostoianii uchebnoi chasti Turgaiskoi oblasti za 1882 g.," January 12, 1883). The latter plan was realized with the establishment of a special school for girls, focusing on handiwork, at Irgiz in 1888; see *SSIA*, 3:141–142 (letter to V. V. Katarinskii, November 5, 1888).

128. See, e.g., the lengthy descriptions of Kazakh women's production of felt and reed mats in P. Makovetskii, "Iurta (letnee zhilishche kirgiz)" (Omsk, 1893), especially 7–10.

129. Analogous discussions of the supervision and professionalization of domestic tasks have usually focused on issues of gender rather than ethnicity. See, e.g., Laura Downs, *Manufacturing Inequality: Gender Division in the French and British Metalworking Industries, 1914–1939* (Ithaca, 1995); and Anna Kuxhausen, "Raising the Nation: Medicine, Morality and *Vospitanie* in Eighteenth-Century Russia" (PhD diss., University of Michigan, 2006). I thank Valerie Kivelson for directing me to this literature.

130. *SSIA*, 2:175 ("Ob otkrytii volostnykh shkol v Turgaiskoi obl." [October 3, 1883]).

131. *SSIA*, 2:163–64 ("O sostoianii uchebnoi chasti Turgaiskoi oblasti za 1882 g."). Report dated January 12, 1883.

132. RGIA f. 1291, op. 82, d. 28 (1882), ll. 30–34, V. Il'in to Minister of Internal Affairs D. A. Tolstoi, "Zapiska ob ustroistve obshchestvennogo upravleniia u kirgizov," October 31, 1883. Title of file: "Po predlozheniiam Turgaiskogo oblastnogo nachal'stva ob izmeneniiakh v deistvuiuschem Vremennom Polozhenii 1868 g. ob upravlenii v stepnykh oblastiakh."

133. The *zar zaman* bards still await a scholarly treatment as something more than déclassé feudal ideologues. See, e.g., I. T. Diusenbaev, ed., *Istoriia kazakhskoi literatury*, 3 vols., vol. 2: *Dorevoliutsionnaia kazakhskaia literatura* (Alma-Ata, 1979); and T. G. Winner, *The Oral Art and Literature of the Kazaks of Russian Central Asia* (Durham, 1958).

134. RGIA f. 1291, op. 82, d. 28 (1882), ll. 40–44. Some lines within this poem make it clear that it cannot have been composed prior to 1880.

135. Ibid., l. 29.

136. Ibid., l. 14, "Donesenie po predmetu razsmtoreniia proekta polozheniia ob upravlenii Turgaiskoi oblast'iu, sostavlennogo mestnym Voennym Gubernatorom," March 2, 1883.

137. Ibid., ll. 54ob.–55ob., Golitsyn to D. A. Tolstoi, May 14, 1884.

138. *PSZ*, series 3, vol. 11 (1891), no. 7574, articles 55–86. The Steppe Statute envisioned slightly more flexibility with respect to village and canton boundaries, as Il'in had recommended, but preserved all of the institutions he recommended against.

139. On Catholicism, see Allen Sinel, *The Classroom and the Chancellery: State Educational Reform in Russia under Count Dmitry Tolstoy* (Cambridge, MA, 1973), 50–51.

140. N. I. Il'minskii, *Pis'ma N. I. Il'minskogo k ober-prokuratoru Sviateishego sinoda Konstantinu Petrovichu Pobedonostsevu* (Kazan', 1895), 52–53, 63–64, also cited in Dowler, 159–60. On Jadidism, see especially Khalid, *Politics*; also Edward Lazzerini, "Beyond Renewal: The Jadid Response to Pressure for Change in the Modern Age," in *Muslims of Central Asia: Expressions of Identity and Change*, ed. Jo-Ann Gross (Durham, 1992), 151–66.

141. This fear and relative ignorance of what Jadidism actually represented were part of yet another informational crisis for Russian orientalism; see TsGA RK f. 64, op. 1, d. 5620, sv. 357, "O progressivnom dvizhenii sredi tatarskogo naseleniia Rossii," for panicked correspondence to this point from 1900 to 1902. Very likely, the particularities of the Jadid movement—connections with Istanbul, the Crimean Tatar roots of its founder, Ismail Bey Gasprinskii, and retention of the Arabic language—would have been more disquieting for Il'minskii than anything Altynsarin put forward.

142. Robert Geraci, "Going Abroad or Going to Russia? Orthodox Missionaries in the Kazak Steppe, 1881–1917," in Geraci and Khodarkovsky, 274–310. See TsGA RK f. 15, op. 1, d. 108, "Delo ob otvode uchastka zemli Dolonskomu stanu Kirgizskoi dukhovnoi missii," for the difficulties one missionary, the priest Nikol'skii, encountered in securing land allotments for his small flock of converts.

143. *SSIA*, 2:294–295 ("Rasporiazhenie voennogo gubernatora Turgaiskoi obl. inspektoru shkol I. Altynsarinu o vvedenii prepodavaniia zakonov musul'manskoi religii v russko-kazakhskikh shkolakh" [August 12, 1881]).

144. Ibid., 294.

145. On the notorious anti-Islamic division of the Kazan' Theological Academy, see Geraci, *Window*, 54–61.

146. Dowler, 142.

147. *SSIA*, 2:234–235 ("Zapiski o kirgizskikh volostnykh shkolakh" [1886]).

148. Ibid., 238–239.

149. T. Tazhibaev, *Prosveshchenie i shkoly Kazakhstana vo vtoroi polovine XIX veka* (Alma-Ata, 1962), 175–177.

150. *SSIA*, 3:137–138 (letter to N. I. Il'minskii, September 1888). There is conflicting information in this respect; Vasil'ev, 95–97, shows four cantonal schools open by the end of 1887, one more in 1888, and two more in 1891.

151. *SSIA*, 3:237–238 ("Smeta na soderzhanie volostnoi shkoly v Turgaiskoi obl." [June 25, 1887]).

152. Vasil'ev, 98. See TsGA RK f. 64, op. 1, sv. 206, d. 3177, ll. 2–6, Barabash memorandum to Steppe Governor-General Taube, December 8, 1894, for a history of the mobile village schools. The file, "Materialy ob uchrezhdenii v stepnykh oblastiakh aul'nykh kirgizskikh shkol," also holds correspondence about the use of such schools in the other steppe provinces.

153. Scott Richard Lyons, *X-Marks: Native Signatures of Assent* (Minneapolis, 2010).

4. THE KEY TO THE WORLD'S TREASURES

1. Abai Kunanbaev, *Qara söz: Poemalar/Kniga slov: Poemy*, ed. and trans. K. Serikbaeva and R. Seisenbaev (Alma-Ata, 1992), 186 (no. 25). This is a dual-text (Russian-Kazak) edition; although I consulted both versions, and the *Qarasözder* were originally set down in Kazak, my translations come from the Russian except where noted. *Qarasözder* is literally translated as *Black Words*, although *Book of Words* or *Words of Admonition* are the more common translations. On Abai's ancestry, see Zhanuzak Kasymbaev, *Starshii sultan Kunanbai Oskenbaev i ego okruzhenie*, 2nd ed. (Almaty, 2004), 66.

2. Ronald Robinson, "Non-European Foundations of European Imperialism: Sketch for a Theory of Collaboration," in *Studies in the Theory of Imperialism*, ed. E. R. J. Owen and Robert Sutcliffe (London, 1972), 117–142.

3. Thanks to Julia Fein for reminding me that *kraevedenie* would have been an anachronism in the nineteenth century. Tomohiko Uyama's reading of the *KSG* as an interactive, collaborative enterprise among Kazak intellectuals and tsarist administrators is basically consonant with my interpretation. Nor do I disagree with his contention that this official organ was important in creating a broader consciousness of Kazak community and awareness of Kazaks' place within the empire. My intervention is simply different: moving away from an identity-centered paradigm to understand the different ways Kazaks and administrators thought the steppe might progress. See Uyama, "A Strategic Alliance between Kazak Intellectuals and Russian Administrators: Imagined Communities in *Dala Walayatining Gazeti* (1888–1902)," in *The Construction and Deconstruction of National Histories in Slavic Eurasia*, ed. Hayashi Tadayuki (Sapporo, 2003), 237–259.

4. On the tsarist civilizing mission on the steppe in comparative perspective, see Steven Sabol, "Comparing American and Russian Internal Colonization: The 'Touch of Civilisation' on the Sioux and Kazakhs," *Western Historical Quarterly* 43 (2012): 29–51.

5. I. T. Diusenbaev, ed., *Istoriia kazakhskoi literatury*, 3 vols., vol. 2: *Dorevoliutsionnaia kazakhskaia literatura* (Alma-Ata, 1979) 57. See also K. Beisembiev, *Ideino-politicheskie techeniia v Kazakhstane kontsa XIX–nachala XX veka* (Alma-Ata, 1961). The only substantive English-language treatment of these bards makes similar claims that they, especially Shortanbai, sought salvation in "the return to the tribal patriarchal society of the past" (96). See T. G. Winner, *The Oral Art and Literature of the Kazakhs of Russian Central Asia* (Durham, 1958).

6. Diusenbaev, 59.

7. M. M. Magauin, ed., *Poety Kazakhstana* (Leningrad, 1978), 253.

8. S. Däuitov, *Zar zaman: Zhïr-tolghaular* (Almaty, 1993), 111.

9. Däuitov, 112.

10. This was a frequently repeated theme in *KSG*—see Kushenev, "Neudavshaiasia popytka otkryt' shkolu," *KSG*, May 26, 1896, for criticism of Kazaks' ignorance in failing to open a Russo-Kazak school, among a host of other citations.

11. "Shkola pri mecheti," *KSG*, March 19, 1895.

12. T. T. Tazhibaev, *Prosveshchenie i shkoly Kazakhstana vo vtoroi polovine XIX veka* (Alma-Ata, 1962), 276–277.

13. Daniel Brower, *Turkestan and the Fate of the Russian Empire* (New York, 2003).

14. Anon., "Po voprosu ob obrazovanii kirgizov," in *Dala ualaiatïnïng gazetï: Adam, qogham, tabighat, 1888–1902*, ed. Ü. Subkhanberdina (Almaty, 1994), 474.

15. Partha Chatterjee, *The Black Hole of Empire: History of a Global Practice of Power* (Princeton, 2012), 185–263.

16. Marina Mogil'ner, in *Homo Imperii: A History of Physical Anthropology in Russia* (Lincoln, 2013), 10–11, offers four distinct paradigms of tsarist physical anthropology: a liberal paradigm centered around Moscow University, a medical paradigm based

in Kazan', a failed racial paradigm centered around Kiev University, and the "colonial anthropology" of St. Petersburg University.

17. The Russian edition of Mogil'ner's book mentions Zeland, in passing, as a member of the Petersburg school (and, hence, as part of the paradigm of colonial anthropology). See Mogil'ner, *Homo imperii: Istoriia fizicheskoi antropologii v Rossii (XIX–nachalo XX vv.)* (Moscow, 2008), 134.

18. V. D. Tronov, "Materialy po antropologii i etnologii kirgiz," *ZIRGO po otdeleniiu etnografii* 17, no. 2 (1891): 54, 63.

19. Ibid., 60.

20. N. Zeland, *Kirgizy—etnograficheskii ocherk* (Semipalatinsk, 1885), 19, 25, 20.

21. Zeland, 71–72.

22. Untitled, *KSG*, January 1, 1888. Canton-level administrators were required to subscribe to the newspaper and thus received a reduced rate.

23. Ibid.

24. Ibid.

25. See, e.g., TsGA RK f. 64, op. 1, d. 5378, ll. 1–2 (January 17, 1890) for a complaint from Minister of Internal Affairs Ivan Nikolaevich Durnovo to Taube about publishing the work of the notoriously Russophobic historian Arminius Vambery in *KSG*. Title of file: "Pis'mo MVD po delam pechati ob izdanii v Akmolinskikh oblastnykh vedomostiakh osobogo 'pribavleniia' na russkom i kirgizskom iazykakh dlia oznakomleniia mestnykh kirgiz s pravitel'stvennymi rasporiazheniiami."

26. On the uses and limitations of the *KSG* as a primary source, see Q. Atabaev, *Qazaq baspasözï: Qazaqstan tarikhïnïng derek közï (1870–1918)* (Almaty, 2000), 87–91.

27. On the range of the Semipalatinsk committee's occupations within a given year see, e.g., TsGA RK f. 460, op. 1, d. 54, sv. 4, l. 2, "Otchet Semipalatinskogo statisticheskogo komiteta za 1899 g," undated.

28. Publication of the *PKSO* continued, apparently, until 1913, but long-form articles disappear almost entirely after 1902.

29. V. A. Berdinskikh, *Uezdnye istoriki: Russkaia provintsial'naia istoriografiia* (Moscow, 2003), 32–33 (on the influence of Populism on regional studies within European Russia); Catherine Evtuhov, *Portrait of a Russian Province: Economy, Society, and Civilization in Nineteenth-Century Nizhnii Novgorod* (Pittsburgh, 2011). In a review essay on the various regional-studies traditions, Susan Smith-Peter refers to the "overlapping and sometimes clashing networks of meaning that connect and divide provinces" (839). See Smith-Peter, "Bringing the Provinces into Focus: Subnational Spaces in the Recent Historiography of Russia," *Kritika: Explorations in Russian and Eurasian History* 12, no. 4 (2011): 835–848.

30. The most famous depiction of this materialism is the character of Evgenii Bazarov in Ivan Turgenev's *Fathers and Sons*. The expression "small-deeds liberalism" (14–15) is drawn from George Fischer, *Russian Liberalism: From Gentry to Intelligentsia* (Cambridge, MA, 1958).

31. V. Z. Galiev, *Ssyl'nye revoliutsionery v Kazakhstane (vtoraia polovina XIX veka)* (Alma-Ata, 1978).

32. On liberal justifications for western European imperialism, see Jennifer Pitts, *A Turn to Empire: The Rise of Imperial Liberalism in Britain and France* (Princeton, 2005).

33. Gulnara Khabizhanova, E. Zh. Valikhanov, and Andrei Krivkov, *Russkaia demokraticheskaia intelligentsiia v Kazakhstane (vtoraia polovina XIX–nachalo XX vv.)* (Moscow, 2003), 77. Khabizhanova and her co-authors—unfortunately, without a reference—attribute this displeasure to the Semipalatinsk Statistical Committee's "truthful and objective illumination of several economic and political problems of the steppe from the position of the interests of the core population."

34. TsGA RK f. 460, op. 1, d. 54, l. 1ob.

35. A. Bökeikhanov, "Iz perepiski khana Srednei kirgizskoi ordy Bukeia i ego potom-kov," *PKSO* (1901): 1–17.

36. V. Ivanov, "O kirgizskoi osedlosti," in Subkhanberdina, *Dala*, 657.

37. I. I. Kraft, "Unichtozhenie rabstva v kirgizskoi stepi," in Subkhanberdina, *Dala*, 708–709.

38. For the multiple discourses surrounding existential threats to these groups, see Yuri Slezkine, *Arctic Mirrors: Russia and the Small Peoples of the North* (Ithaca, 1994), 116–120.

39. Adeeb Khalid, *The Politics of Muslim Cultural Reform: Jadidism in Central Asia* (Berkeley, 1998); Peter Rottier, "Creating the Kazak Nation: The Intelligentsia's Quest for Acceptance in the Russian Empire, 1905–1920" (PhD diss., University of Wisconsin, 2005). Uyama, "Strategic" (247) describes native administrators as the "common opponents" of Kazak and Russian contributors to the *KSG*.

40. *Qarasözder*, 10. The Russian translation adds two qualifiers—"enlightened and knowledgeable [*prosveshchennye i znatnye*] Russians"—which are absent from the Kazakh text.

41. On Soviet historiography concerning non-Russian nationalities in this vein, see Lowell Tillett, *The Great Friendship: Soviet Historians on the Non-Russian Nationalities* (Chapel Hill, 1969).

42. Äbish Zhirenchin, *Abai zhäne orïstïng ülï revoliutsiiashïl demokrattarï* (Almaty, 1957), 187.

43. Älikhan Bökeikhanov, "Abai Kunanbaev—nekrolog," *ZSP* 3 (1907): 4.

44. Abai was personally acquainted with the arbitrariness of some administrators in Semipalatinsk oblast, having faced, among other things, a spurious investigation for bribery in 1877 (see TsGA RK f. 15, op. 1, d. 2047, sv. 108, especially ll. 20–25, "Ob obrazovanii volostei Semipalatinskogo uezda") and equally ill-grounded accusations in 1903 of collaboration and correspondence with Shaimerden Koshchygulov, a purportedly anti-Russian mullah from Kokshetau (Petropavlovsk, according to some sources) district. See Kasymbaev, 86–93, on this incident.

45. Donald Treadgold, *The Great Siberian Migration: Government and Peasant in Resettlement from Emancipation to the First World War* (Princeton, 1957), 76–78. Treadgold did not benefit from access to Russian archives but is particularly strong on legal aspects of the resettlement movement. The other key Western monograph on the topic, with some central archival support, is Francois-Xavier Coquin, *La Sibérie: Peuplement et immigration paysanne au 19e siècle* (Paris: Institut d'études slaves, 1969), but this volume does not touch Central Asia or the steppe. A useful *longue durée* sketch focused on environmental factors is Ihor Stebelsky, "The Frontier in Central Asia," in *Studies in Russian Historical Geography*, ed. James H. Bater and R. A. French (London, 1983), 1:143–173.

46. Treadgold, 78–79.

47. *Vremennoe polozhenie ob upravlenii v oblastiakh Ural'skoi, Turgaiskoi, Akmolinskoi, i Semipalatinskoi*, article 210. Article 238 makes the same rule for forests in the steppe provinces. For surpluses under the Steppe Statute, see *PSZ*, series 3, vol. 11 (1891), no. 7574, article 120 with note. Ekaterina Pravilova argues (116–125) that in the borderlands of the Russian Empire, tsarist officials felt less politically constrained to respect individual property rights, instead embracing a statist view of property justified by ideas of the public interest. See Pravilova, *A Public Empire: Property and the Quest for the Common Good in Imperial Russia* (Princeton 2014).

48. Treadgold, 120–121.

49. Anon, "Odin iz voprosov mestnogo upravleniia," in Subkhanberdina, *Dala*, 75–76. For specific complaints see e.g. a discussion of precolonial slavery, M.T., "Osvobozhdenie rabov v kirgizskoi stepi," *KSG*, November 12, 1895; and a history of eighteenth-century Kazak raids on the Russian border, borrowed from the *Eparkhial'nye vedomosti* (Diocesan gazette)

of Tobol'sk province, "Iz istorii kirgizskikh nabegov," *KSG*, July 23, 1900. This latter feature would continue to occupy column inches throughout 1901.

50. On horse theft, see, e.g., the memorandum of Taube to Akmolinsk military governor Nikolai Ivanovich Sannikov, June 16, 1892, published in *KSG*, July 3, 1892; Diusenbaev, "Kak unichtozhit' sredi kirgizov konokradstvo," *KSG*, October 20, 1896; on corruption, see "Kopchik," "Material k kharakteristike biiskikh reshenii," *KSG*, May 7, 1900; Anon., "Pered vyborami," *KSG*, April 29, 1901.

51. V.D., "Kirgizy v tsarstvovanie Imperatora Aleksandra II," *KSG*, August 30, 1898.

52. Here I adapt Richard Wortman's term for the specific manifestations of deep-seated political narratives ("myths," in Wortman's term) under individual rulers. See Wortman, *Scenarios of Power: Myth and Ceremony in Russian Monarchy*, 2 vols. (Princeton, 1995–2000).

53. Anon., "V chem vred dlia zhizni," *KSG*, April 9, 1895. On medicine as a "cultural force" intended to have a "civilizing influence" (115), see Anna Afanas'eva, "'Osvobodit' . . . ot shaitanov i sharlatanov': Diskursy i praktiki Rossiiskoi meditsiny v Kazakhskoi stepi v XIX veke," *Ab Imperio*, no. 4 (2008): 113–150.

54. A. P—v, "Kak lechat baksy," *KSG*, May 19, 1896; Anon., "Raznye izvestiia," *KSG*, July 18, 1899. Compare the discussion in Paula Michaels, *Curative Powers: Medicine and Empire in Stalin's Central Asia* (Pittsburgh, 2003).

55. R. Diusembaev, "Sueveriia u nashikh kirgizov," *KSG*, January 14, 1896.

56. Cathy A. Frierson, *Peasant Icons: Representations of Rural People in Late Nineteenth-Century Russia* (New York, 1993); Laura Engelstein, "Morality and the Wooden Spoon: Russian Doctors View Syphilis, Social Class, and Sexual Behavior, 1890–1905," *Representations* 14 (1986): 169–208.

57. Asylqozha Qurmanbaev, "Neskol'ko slov o bespechnosti kirgizov," in Subkhanberdina, *Dala*, 288.

58. Konshin, N. Ia., "Zametka ob odnom kirgizskom dzhute," *ZSP* 2 (1905): 1–17.

59. Compare the argument of Cathy A. Frierson in *All Russia Is Burning! A Cultural History of Fire and Arson in Late Imperial Russia* (Seattle, 2002).

60. O. A. Shkapskii, "Nekotoryia dannyia dlia osveshcheniia kirgizskogo voprosa," *Russkaia mysl'* 1897, no. 7 (1897): 36.

61. On migration as a response, see Musa Chormanov, "Kazakhskie narodnye obychai," republished in *Musa Chormanov: Kazakhskie narodnye obychai*, ed. E. M. Aryn (Pavlodar, 2005), 9–10. On physical removal, see Chormanov, "O skotovodstve u kirgizov Zapadnoi Sibiri," in Aryn, 20–21.

62. [A. Perepletnikov], *Materialy po obsledovaniiu khoziaistva i zemlepol'zovaniia kirgiz Semipalatinskoi oblasti*, vol. 1: *Pavlodarskii uezd*; no. 2 (*tekst*): *Povtornoe obsledovanie 1910 g.* (St. Petersburg, 1913), 28–29.

63. Michel Foucault, "Governmentality," in *The Foucault Effect: Studies in Governmentality*, ed. Graham Burchell, Colin Gordon, and Peter Miller (Chicago, 1991), 87–104.

64. On microcredit institutions, all with similar statutes necessitating documentation by tsarist institutions, see inter alia RGIA f. 1291, op. 82, d. 1 (1873), "Ob utverzhdenii proekta ustava ssudnoi kassy dlia kirgizov Semipalatinskoi oblasti" and RGIA f. 1291, op. 82, d. 26 (1879), "Ob uchrezhdenii ssudnoi kassy dlia kirgizov Akmolinskoi oblasti."

65. Anon., "Mestnye izvestiia," *KSG*, June 12, 1892.

66. Richard Robbins, *Famine in Russia, 1891–92: The Imperial Government Responds to a Crisis* (New York, 1975).

67. Anon., "Konevodstvo i konnozavodstvo v Turgaiskoi oblasti," *KSG*, July 5, 1891.

68. On wolves, see V. Mikhailov, "Besedy o skotovodstve (IV)," *KSG*, March 13, 1894.

69. Anon., "Konevodstvo i konnozavodstvo," inter alia.

70. RGVIA f. 400, op. 1, d. 1077, ll. 7ob.–9ob. (2 May 1886, presented to N. N. Obruchev, head of the Main Staff). Title of file: "Vsepoddanneishii otchet Stepnogo

general-gubernatora o glavneishikh meropriiatiiakh k blagoustroistvu stepnogo kraia." Rather less sensibly, Kolpakovskii fretted that speculators were already buying up Kazak horses and selling them to the Austrian army. On tsarist goals for developing Kazak horses, and the way these conflicted with local priorities, see Carole Ferret, "Des chevaux pour l'empire," *Cahiers d'Asie Centrale* 17–18 (2009): 211–253.

71. V. Mikhailov, "Besedy o skotovodstve (III)," *KSG*, February 6, 1894. On the building of the Trans-Siberian Railroad, see Steven Marks, *Road to Power: The Trans-Siberian Railroad and the Colonization of Asian Russia, 1850–1917* (Ithaca, 1991).

72. Bruce Grant, *The Captive and the Gift: Cultural Histories of Sovereignty in Russia and the Caucasus* (Ithaca, 2009); Anon, "Sibirskaia zheleznaia doroga," *KSG*, December 4, 1894. Taube would go as far as awarding medals to Kazaks who regularly produced high-quality horses; see TsGA RK f. 64, op. 1, d. 823, sv. 57, "Delo o nagrazhdenii kirgizov medalami za uspeshnoe vedenie konevodstva v Stepnom krae."

73. S. Sh., "O mestnostiakh stoianki kirgizov," in Subkhanberdina, *Dala*, 127.

74. Qorabai Zhapanŭghlï, "Neobkhodimost' prosveshcheniia," in Subkhanberdina, *Dala*, 352.

75. *SSIA*, 3:60 (Altynsarin to V. V. Katarinskii, April 7, 1880).

76. For example, he would later seek out the work of Aleksei Levshin and the orientalist Vladimir Vel'iaminov-Zernov (1830–1904) to complete the historical section of this second volume. See *SSIA*, 3:108–109 (Altynsarin to N. I. Il'minskii, September 30, 1884).

77. For concern about improving local administrators, see, e.g., Subkhanberdina, *Dala*, 76–77 (1888); and S.A., "Korrespondentsiia. Dzharkentskii uezd," *KSG*, March 4, 1901; on the equivalency among civilization, progress, and the idea of Europe in another of the Russian Empire's Central Asian possessions, Turkestan, see Jeff Sahadeo, *Russian Colonial Society in Tashkent, 1865–1923* (Bloomington, 2007).

78. On rheumatism, see Anon., "Obshchepoleznye svedeniia," *KSG*, January 11, 1891; on fire prevention, see Anon, "Ogneupornye postroiki," *KSG*, November 30, 1890.

79. Naimanets, "Oroshenie lugov u buriat," *KSG*, April 9, 1900.

80. Anon., "Novoe puteshestvie N. M. Przheval'skogo," *KSG*, September 9, 1888; Anon., "Sredneaziatskaia ekspeditsiia," *KSG*, December 19–26, 1899; M. T., "Novyi podvig dlia nauki," *KSG*, July 13, 1897; Anon., "Redkostnoe arkheologicheskoe otkrytie," *KSG*, April 29, 1901; S.L., "Sposob kormleniia skota drevesnymi vetvami," *KSG*, October 21, 1900.

81. *Qarasözder*, 185.

82. Anon., "Kirgizy, stremites' k prosveshcheniiu," in Subkhanberdina, *Dala*, 434–435.

83. Dinmukhamet Sultangazin, "Mysli o budushchem," in Subkhanberdina, *Dala*, 296–297.

84. Anon., "Aidashinskie inorodtsy," *KSG*, October 7, 1900.

85. On Gasprinskii in his Crimean context, see Edward J. Lazzerini, "Local Accommodation and Resistance to Colonialism in Nineteenth-Century Crimea," in *Russia's Orient: Imperial Borderlands and Peoples, 1700–1917*, ed. Daniel Brower and Lazzerini (Bloomington, 2001), 169–187; on Jadidism outside Crimea see Khalid, *Politics*.

86. Consider Anon., "Izuverstvo fanatika," *KSG*, June 15, 1897, a report that dozens of women in Tehran were buried alive when a bathhouse collapsed on them because a local *mujtahid* claimed men could not be permitted to see their naked bodies.

87. *KSG*, April 12, 1891; Anon., "Raznye izvestiia," *KSG*, January 1, 1893. Reprint of correspondence by an "Akhmed-Safa Sabitov" of Kazan'.

88. Anon., "Sblizhenie narodov," *KSG*, March 18, 1901; Anon., "O kholere i predokhranenii ot neia," *KSG*, August 7–21, 1891.

89. *KSG*, December 14, 1890.

90. *Qarasözder*, 186.

91. *Qarasözder*, 215.

92. This is not to deny the importance of Jadid ideas in the views of this generation. See, e.g., Steven Sabol, *Russian Colonization and the Genesis of Kazak National Consciousness* (New York, 2003), 67 (on Mukhamedzhan Seralin).

93. TsGA RK f. 64, op. 1, d. 5620, sv. 357, "O progressivnom dvizhenii sredi tatarskogo naseleniia Rossii"; TsGA RK f. 369, op. 1, d. 780, sv. 185, "O literaturno-obshchestvennom i natsionalno-religiozno dvizhenii sredi kazakhskogo naseleniia."

94. TsGA RK f. 64, op. 1, d. 3155, sv. 204, ll. 5–7 (Bishop Makarii to Taube, January 7, 1893), 2–4ob. (Karpov to Taube, March 4, 1893). Title of file: "Delo po pis'mu episkopa Tomskogo i Semipalatinskogo o vospreshchenii raz"ezdov po kirgizskoi stepi tataram, bukhartsam i turkam, v vidakh ustraneniia propagandy Islama."

95. For investigation of this revolt, its causes, and possible future outbreaks see TsGA RK f. 64, op. 1, d. 881, sv. 59, "Materialy o vosstanii musul'man v Andizhane."

96. Hisao Komatsu, "The Andijan Uprising Reconsidered," in *Muslim Societies: Historical and Comparative Perspectives,* ed. Tsugitaka Sato (London, 2004), 29–61; Bakhtiyar Babadzhanov, "Andizhanskoe vosstanie 1898 goda i 'Musul'manskii vopros' v Turkestane (vzgliady 'kolonizatorov' i 'kolonizirovannykh')," *Ab Imperio,* no. 2 (2009): 155–200.

97. TsGA RK f. 64, op. 1, d. 5578, sv. 355, ll. 8, 10–11. Title of file: "Doklad Turkestanskogo general-gubernatora Dukhovskogo ob Islame v Turkestane."

98. Ibid., ll. 3ob., 8ob.

99. An interesting case study of the effects of modern state regimes on nomadic populations is Nazif Shahrani, *The Kirghiz and Wakhi of Afghanistan: Adaptation to Closed Frontiers* (Seattle, 1979).

100. Pey-Yi Chu, in her work on permafrost science in Eastern Siberia, defines adaptation as "a fraught but ever-present and ongoing process of responding to dynamic constraints presented by the environment," a definition I am borrowing in this section. See Chu, "Encounters with Permafrost: The Rhetoric of Conquest and Practices of Adaptation in the Soviet Union," unpublished article ms.

101. M. Imshenetskii, "Nesmetnoe bogatstvo, sokryvaemoe v kirgizskoi stepi," *KSG,* January 1–February 1, March 1, 1891. This quotation from January 1.

102. Ibid., February 1, 1891.

103. Ibid., March 1, 1891.

104. S. Sh., "O mestnostiakh."

105. Gamkhorov, "Iz Pavlodarskogo uezda," in Subkhanberdina, *Dala,* 191.

106. Anon., "Kirgizy-zemledel'tsy Turgaiskoi oblasti," *KSG,* December 15, 1896.

107. Anon., "Ob otkrytii skladov zemledel'cheskikh orudii v Petropavlovske i Atbasare," *KSG,* August 23, 1898.

108. A. V. Remnev and N. G. Suvorova, "'Obrusenie' aziatskikh okrain Rossiiskoi imperii: Optimizm i pessimizm russkoi kolonizatsii," *Istoricheskie zapiski* 11 (2008): 132–179.

109. I., "O kirgizskoi osedlosti," *KSG,* May 9–16, 1899.

110. Anon., "Belogach (ocherk)," in Subkhanberdina, *Dala,* 54–55.

111. Imshenetskii, "Nesmetnoe," quotation from February 1.

112. Anon., "O neobkhodimosti razvitiia zemledeliia sredi kirgizskogo naseleniia," in Subkhanberdina, *Dala,* 313–314.

113. Anon., "'Nezabytoe' proshloe i nastoiashchee kirgizov—ocherki," *KSG,* July 17–October 2, 1892. This quotation from July 17. This line of thinking strongly parallels the myth of environmental degradation in the Maghreb uncovered in Diana Davis, *Resurrecting the Granary of Rome: Environmental History and French Colonial Expansion in North Africa* (Athens, 2007).

114. See, e.g., T. Kabekov, "Korrespondentsiia iz Tarbogataiskikh gor," *KSG,* April 14, 1896, a report of successful grain cultivation in a mountainous area along the border with

China. In general, the *KSG* eagerly published letters from Kazaks indicating that they had successfully sown and harvested crops.

115. David Moon magisterially explains the evolution of modern pedology in the wake of this earlier concern in *The Plough That Broke the Steppes: Agriculture and Environment on Russia's Grasslands, 1700–1914* (Oxford, 2013).

116. Anon., "O razvitii pchelovodstva v stepnom general gubernatorstve," *KSG*, March 4, 1888.

117. *KSG*, February 5, 1888. Circular of December 8, 1887.

118. For proponents of irrigation, see, e.g., I. L. Iavorskii, "Sredniaia Aziia: Kul'turnye uspekhi i zadacha v nei Rossii," *TSb* 443:145a–147a; and Shkapskii, "Nekotoryia dannyia." The best work on Central Asian irrigation projects is Maya Peterson, "Technologies of Rule: Water, Power, and the Modernization of Central Asia, 1867–1941" (PhD diss., Harvard University, 2011).

119. See, e.g., A. Kurmanbaev, "K voprosu o chul-bidae," *KSG*, June 5, 1894. Discussion of the adaptability of "chul wheat" is also in Mark Alfred Carleton, *The Small Grains* (New York, 1920), 168. "Chul" ("cho'l," in modern Uzbek) refers to a desert or barren place— I thank Maya Peterson for the reminder. Less publicized than chul-bidai, but a source of similar hopes, was a varietal of spring wheat called *kara-bugdai* (literally, "black wheat"). See Anon., "Iarovaia pshenitsa 'kara-bugdai,'" *KSG*, August 28, 1892.

120. On obtaining seeds, see *KSG*, March 13, 1894. Skepticism from *Turkestanskie vedomosti* was addressed in Kurmanbaev, "K voprosu."

121. For the descriptive article, see Ia. Nesterov, "Kak mozhno dobyvat' vodu v bezvodnykh stepiakh (ustroistvo snezhnikov)," *KSG*, November 3, 1896; for promotion, see Anon., untitled, *KSG*, November 10, 1896. The Bel'-Agach steppe is a slightly elevated region north of the city of Semipalatinsk. See "Bel'-agachskaia step'," Sibirskaia Sovetskaia Entsiklopediia—1929 god, http://45f.ru/sse/bel-agachskaya-step-bel-agach-derevya-na-perevale/.

122. Ia. Nesterov, "Kak mozhno dobyvat' vodu v bezvodnykh stepiakh (ustroistvo snezhnikov)," *KSG*, November 10, 1896. Other than portraits of imperial family members or advertisements, I saw only one other illustrated article in a 15-year print run.

123. Anon., "Ob"iavleniia ot redaktsii," *KSG*, November 17, 1896; Anon., "Kak dobyt' vodu v bezvodnoi stepi," *KSG*, November 28, 1899.

124. Other methods that Moon mentions for adapting agriculture to the dry, treeless steppe, most notably the labor-intensive practice of black fallowing (*chernyi par*, Moon, 263–268), do not appear on the pages of the *KSG*. This is likely because they had simply not been tested locally yet. By the 1910s, manuals for settlers to the steppe mention a broader array of adaptive practices. See, e.g., N. Matveev, ed., *Khodokam i pereselentsam, napraviaiushchimsia v Kustanaiskii uezd Turgaiskoi oblasti v 1914 godu (nastavleniia, opisanie raiona i uchastkov)*, 4th ed. (Poltava, 1914), 10–12.

125. This argument about intellectuals and authority draws on and parallels Khalid, *Politics* (with explicit invocation of Bourdieu's idea of cultural capital), and Rottier, "Creating."

126. This is the central, and to my reading accurate, argument of Rottier, "Creating."

127. Short biographical data (90) is in Tomohiko Uyama, "The Geography of Civilizations: A Spatial Analysis of the Kazakh Intelligentsia's Activities, from the Mid-Nineteenth to the Early Twentieth Century," in *Regions: A Prism to View the Slavic-Eurasian World*, ed. Kimitaka Matsuzato (Sapporo, 2000), 70–99.

128. Beisembiev, *Ideino-politicheskie*, especially 199–241 (quotations from 199 and 241, respectively).

129. Iu. Köpeev, "Korrespondentsiia iz Baian-aula," *KSG*, April 27, 1890.

130. The sharpest criticism of Köpeev appeared later in 1890, e.g., Maten Botbaev, untitled poem, *KSG*, August 3, 1890. For Köpeev's poem, see Iu. Köpeev, untitled, *KSG*, June 8, 1890.

131. For example, K. Zhapanov, "Kochevye stoibishcha" (*KSG*, August 20, 1895) noted that his native Pavlodar district had very few suitable places for grain cultivation; Makash Tulemysov (*KSG*, June 5, 1894) made an argument favoring pastoralism based on both tradition and environmental conditions, and received a response from the *KSG*'s editors that this was simply not true. See Anon., "Eshche raz o preimushchestvakh zemledel'cheskogo khoziaistva," *KSG*, June 5, 1894).

132. N. Ia. Konshin, "K voprosu o perekhode kirgiz Semipalatinskoi oblasti v osedloe sostoianie," *PKSO* (1898): 48–50 (quotation from 48).

133. N. Ia. Konshin, "Po Ust'kamenogorskomu uezdu. Putevye zametki," *PKSO* (1900): 44.

134. X., "Zemledelie i khlebnaia proizvoditel'nost' Semipalatinskoi oblasti," *PKSO* (1898): 17.

135. For "wild men," see Konshin, "K voprosu," 34; for discomfort, see Konshin, "Po Ust'kamenogorskomu uezdu," 36.

136. B. Benkevich, "Kirgizskoe stepnoe skotovodstvo i mery k ego uluchsheniiu," *ZSP* 1 (1903): 1.

137. Ibid., 2–3.

138. Ibid., 6–7.

139. Ibid., 22–24.

140. Ibid.

141. Ibid., 8.

142. Konshin, "K voprosu," 39.

143. N. Ia. Konshin, "Ocherki ekonomicheskogo byta kirgiz Semipalatinskogo oblasti," *PKSO* (1901): 179–181.

144. Konshin, "K voprosu," 49.

145. Interestingly, such criticisms are broadly similar to the best-known administrative critique of mass resettlement: K. K. Pahlen, *Otchet po revizii Turkestanskogo kraia, proizvedennoi po VYSOCHAISHCHEMU poveleniiu*, vol. 6: *Pereselencheskoe delo* (St. Petersburg, 1910).

146. See, e.g., a reprint of his circular to district chiefs and veterinary doctors following an inspection tour of the province in *KSG*, February 12–19, 1893.

147. Anon., "Raznye izvestiia," *KSG*, March 19, 1893.

148. A. K., "O sostoianii skotovodstva v Akmolinskoi oblasti," *KSG*, January 3–April 18, 1899. This citation from January 17.

149. Il'ia I. Ivanov, "Korrespondentsiia," *KSG*, April 12, 1891.

150. Anon., "O vazhnosti zavedenii v kirgizskikh khoziaistvakh senokosilok i konnykh grabel," *KSG*, February 6, 1900; Benkevich, 24.

151. Anon., "Po povodu pozdnei vesny," *KSG*, March 22, 1898.

152. Iu. Köpeev, "Korrespondentsiia iz Baian-aula," *KSG*, August 10, 1890.

153. Anon., "O bor'be s upadkom skotovodstva," *KSG*, December 7, 1890.

154. On education, see ibid.; on veterinary inspectors, see Anon., "Khronika," *KSG*, October 16, 1892; on restricted movement, see Anon., "Nuzhno-li zaiavliat' o bolezni skota?" *KSG*, October 30, 1894.

155. Anon., "Khronika," *KSG*, October 16, 1892.

156. This parallels what David Spurr has described as the rhetoric of "appropriation" (28–42) in colonial discourse. See Spurr, *The Rhetoric of Empire: Colonial Discourse in Journalism, Travel Writing, and Imperial Administration* (Durham, 1993).

157. Anon., "Ovtsy v iuzhnoi polose Rossii," *KSG*, December 2–9, 1888.

158. A. Dorofeev, "Kirgizskoe skotovodstvo v Akmolinskoi oblasti," *KSG*, February 24–March 3, 1902. Quotation from March 3.

159. R. D., "Vygodno-li dlia kirgizov skotovodstvo v tom vide, v kotorom ono nakhoditsia v nastoiashchee vremia?" *KSG*, January 17–May 2, 1899. Quotation from January 31.

160. Magomet-gali Ibragimov, "Kirgizskii sposob lecheniia nekotorykh boleznei skota," *KSG*, December 21, 1890.

161. *KSG*, December 23, 1901–January 13, 1902 repeated a proclamation by Steppe Governor-General N. N. Sukhotin that Kazaks would once more be permitted to make pilgrimage to Mecca and Medina.

162. E.g. "Pochtovyi iashchik," *KSG*, April 7, 1901: "To K. Dzhapanov: Your correspondence 1. About the Chinese war; 2. About how to give petitions and 3. About the rules of the *ssudnaia kassa* will not be printed."

163. "Ob"iavlenie ot Kantseliarii Stepnogo General-Gubernatora," *KSG*, March 12, 1902.

164. Even a partial bibliography of *Abaevedenie*, Abai studies, would overwhelm this book. But see inter alia Mukhtar Auezov's somewhat romanticized historical novel, *Put' Abaia*, trans. Leonid Sobolev (Moscow, 1952), as well as specialized studies by, e.g., B. G. Gabdullin, *Eticheskie vozzreniia Abaia* (Alma-Ata, 1970); and A. Nïsanbaev, *Abaidïng dünietanïmï men filosofiiasï* (Almaty, 1995).

165. Uyama, "Strategic," 258.

166. TsGA RK f. 64, op. 1, d. 5658, ll. 10 (telegram), 17–19 (petition). Title of file: "Ob agitatsii sredi kirgiz Karkaralinskogo i Pavlodarskogo uezdov o posylke v Peterburg deputatsii dlia predstavlenii ot kirgizskogo naroda petitsii tsariu." Dina Amanzholova, the leading scholar of the Alash movement, notes, "The public revival in the [steppe] krai over the course of the first revolution in Russia stirred up the Kazak intelligentsia" (20). See D. A. Amanzholova, *Kazakhskii avtonomizm i Rossiia: Istoriia dvizheniia Alash* (Moscow, 1994).

5. NORMING THE STEPPE

1. RGIA f. 1291, op. 82, d. 23 (1866), l. 30, Timashev to Khrushchov, February 4, 1869.

2. "O kolonizatsii Turgaiskoi oblasti," *TSb* 328:137; "Vopros o zaselenii stepei i priuchenii kochevnikov k zemledeliiu," *TSb* 395:139.

3. Willard Sunderland, *Taming the Wild Field: Colonization and Empire on the Russian Steppe* (Ithaca, 2004), 183.

4. Bruno Latour, *Science in Action: How to Follow Scientists and Engineers through Society* (Cambridge, MA, 1987), 2, 131.

5. The single best study of the steppe during the resettlement era is the exhaustive S. N. Maltusynov, *Agrarnyi vopros v Kazakhstane i Gosudarstvennaia Duma, 1906–1917 gg.: Sotsiokul'turnyi podkhod* (Almaty, 2006).

6. George Demko, *The Russian Colonization of Kazakhstan, 1896–1916* (Bloomington, 1969), 52–58; for treatment of this famine in a global context, see Mike Davis, *Late Victorian Holocausts: El Niño Famines and the Making of the Third World* (New York, 2002).

7. This positive reading of the peasantry's role was not universally shared, but was one among several arguments favoring resettlement. See Willard Sunderland, "The 'Colonization Question': Visions of Colonization in Late Imperial Russia," *Jahrbücher für Geschichte Osteuropas* 48, no. 2 (2000): 210–232; and especially A. V. Remnev and N. G. Suvorova, "'Obrusenie' aziatskikh okrain Rossiiskoi imperii: Optimizm i pessimizm russkoi kolonizatsii," *Istoricheskie zapiski* 11 (2008): 132–179. A comprehensive account of imperial Russian stereotypes of the peasantry is Cathy Frierson, *Peasant Icons: Representations of Rural People in Late Nineteenth-Century Russia* (New York, 1993).

8. On institutions, see especially A. N. Kulomzin, *Vsepoddanneishii otchet Stats-Sekretaria Kulomzina po poezdke v Sibir' dlia oznakomlenii s polozheniem pereselencheskogo dela* (St. Petersburg, 1896). This critical report was the inspiration for the formation of a separate Resettlement Administration under the Ministry of Internal Affairs.

9. RGIA f. 391, op. 1, d. 205, ll. 9ob.–10ob., "Zakliucheniia Soveshchaniia 18 marta 1895 po voprosu ob izsledovanii Stepnykh oblastei." Title of file: "Ob organizatsii issledovaniia stepnykh oblastei Zapadnoi Sibiri."

10. Ibid., l. 6 (undated).

11. Ibid., ll. 42–45ob., "Zapiska v vide proekta o norme kirgizskogo nadela," April 6, 1895.

12. Local maxima of land for peasants were defined by a set of local statues, above which land could be seized as surplus and reallocated. See P. Zaionchkovskii, *The Abolition of Serfdom in Russia*, ed. and trans. Susan Wobst (Gulf Breeze, 1978), 83–87.

13. N. M. Pirumova, *Zemskaia intelligentsia i ee rol' v obshchestvennoi bor'be do nachala XX v.* (Moscow, 1986), 132.

14. A. A. Kaufman, *Khoziaistvennoe polozhenie pereselentsev vodvorennykh na kazen-nykh zemliakh Tomskoi gubernii po dannym proizvedennogo v 1894 g., po porucheniiu g. Tomskogo gubernatora, podvornogo issledovaniia*, 2 vols. (St. Petersburg, 1895); *Trudy mest-nykh komitetov o nuzhdakh sel'skokhoziaistvennoi promyshlennosti*, 59 vols. (St. Petersburg, 1903).

15. Peter Holquist, "'In Accord with State Interests and the People's Wishes': The Tech-nocratic Ideology of Imperial Russia's Resettlement Administration," *Slavic Review* 69, no. 1 (2010): 151–179.

16. The connections among mapping, measurement, and the control and cultivation of a population are inherent in Michel Foucault's concept of governmentality; see *Secu-rity, Territory, Population: Lectures at the College de France, 1977–1978*, ed. Michel Senellart, trans. Graham Burchell (New York, 2009). The most sustained effort to apply a Foucauldian framework to mapping, statistics, and imperial expansion is Matthew G. Hannah, *Govern-mentality and the Mastery of Territory in Nineteenth-Century America* (New York, 2000).

17. This fact presents serious difficulty for arguments about the exceptional or unique nature of Russian imperialism, e.g., E. A. Glushchenko, *Rossiia v Srednei Azii: Zavoevaniia i preobrazovaniia* (Moscow, 2010. A stimulating attempt to place the Resettlement Admin-istration in a global context is Willard Sunderland, "The Ministry of Asiatic Russia: The Colonial Office That Never Was but Might Have Been," *Slavic Review* 69, no. 1 (2010): 120–150; on interimperial transfers more broadly, see Martin Aust, Rikarda Vul'pius [Ricarda Vulpius], and Aleksei Miller, eds., *Imperium inter pares: Rol' transferov v istorii Rossiiskoi imperii* (Moscow, 2010).

18. A. Kokhanovskii, "Po povodu kolonizatsii v Kitae i u nas," *IIRGO* 45 (1909): 499–519; V. Kuznetsov, "Pereselentsy-zemledel'tsy v Severnoi Amerike," *Russkoe bogatstvo*, no. 8 (1900): 19–37. Kuznetsov also edited some volumes of the Shcherbina Expedition's mate-rials, and his particular role in creating land norms for the steppe is discussed in more detail below.

19. Sunderland, *Taming*, 196.

20. Philippa Söldenwagner, *Spaces of Negotiation: European Settlement and Settlers in German East Africa, 1900–1914* (Munich, 2006), 86–87.

21. Lewis Pyenson, *Civilizing Mission: Exact Sciences and French Overseas Expansion, 1830–1940* (Baltimore, 1993), 87–153 (quotation from 131); David Prochaska, *Making Algeria French: Colonialism in Bône, 1870–1920* (New York, 1990), 65–71; Diana K. Davis, *Resurrecting the Granary of Rome: Environmental History and French Colonial Expansion in North Africa* (Athens, 2007), 96–100.

22. Richard White, *The Roots of Dependency: Subsistence, Environment, and Social Change among the Choctaws, Pawnees, and Navajos* (Lincoln, 1983), 250–289; Jeffrey Ostler, *The Plains Sioux and US Colonialism from Lewis and Clark to Wounded Knee* (New York, 2004), 219–225; Leonard A. Carlson, *Indians, Bureaucrats, and Land: The Dawes Act and the Decline of Indian Farming* (Westport, 1981), 3–4.

23. David W. Darrow, "The Politics of Numbers: Statistics and the Search for a Theory of Peasant Economy in Russia, 1861–1917" (PhD diss., University of Iowa, 1996); Piru-mova, 131–41. Martine Mespoulet has described zemstvo statisticians and administrators

at the close of the nineteenth century as "allied in management" (*alliés pour gérer*). See Mespoulet, *Statistique et révolution en Russie: Un compromise impossible (1880–1930)* (Rennes, 2001), 106. On quantification and authority, see Theodore Porter, *Trust in Numbers: The Pursuit of Objectivity in Science and Public Life* (Princeton, 1996).

24. Darrow, "Politics"; David Ludden, "Orientalist Empiricism: Transformations of Colonial Knowledge," in *Orientalism and the Postcolonial Predicament: Perspectives on South Asia*, ed. Carol Breckenridge and Peter van der Veer (Philadelphia, 1993), 250–278.

25. RGIA f. 391, op. 1, d. 205, ll. 66–67, Tikheev to Shcherbina, 18 November 1895. A solid biography of Shcherbina, though offering relatively little information on Shcherbina's activities in the Kazak steppe, is S. N. Iakaev, *Fedor Andreevich Shcherbina: Vekhi zhizni i tvorchestva* (Krasnodar, 2004).

26. See especially F. A. Shcherbina, *Krest'ianskie biudzhety* (Voronezh, 1900).

27. Shcherbina also exhibited this tendency to "round up" the needs of rural people when calculating feeding norms for the Russian peasantry; see Shcherbina, "Prodovol'stvennye normy," *Russkoe bogatstvo*, no. 8 (1900): 1–19.

28. David Darrow, "The Politics of Numbers: Zemstvo Land Assessment and the Conceptualization of Russia's Rural Economy," *Russian Review* 59, no. 1 (2000): 52–75.

29. Iakaev, 17–21. On the Populist movement, see especially Franco Venturi's magisterial *Roots of Revolution: A History of the Populist and Socialist Movements in Nineteenth-Century Russia*, trans. Francis Haskell (New York, 1960). Shcherbina's turn toward leftist politics and the natural sciences parallels Laurie Manchester's argument that sons of priests (*popovichi*) in the late nineteenth century came to see their mission as secular and oriented toward service to the people (*narod*). See Manchester, *Holy Fathers, Secular Sons: Clergy, Intelligentsia, and the Modern Self in Revolutionary Russia* (DeKalb, 2008).

30. Iakaev, 42.

31. Sedel'nikov was expelled for *Bor'ba za zemliu v kirgizskoi stepi*, about which more below; on him, see also Khabizhanova, Valikhanov, and Krivkov, *Russkaia demokraticheskaia intelligentsiia*, 79. On his expulsion see *Ural'skaia istoricheskaia entsiklopediia*, http://ural.academic.ru/1760.

32. Police files concerning Chermak are at TsGA RK f. 369, op. 1, d. 839. See also T. P. Petrova, "K voprosu o sostave ekspeditsii F. A. Shcherbiny po issledovaniiu stepnykh oblastei Kazakhstana," *Izvestiia Akademii nauk Kazakhskoi SSR: Seriia obshchestvennykh nauk*, no. 4 (1980): 52–54.

33. James Ferguson and Akhil Gupta, "Spatializing States: Towards an Ethnography of Neoliberal Governmentality," *American Ethnologist* 29, no. 4 (2002): 981–1002.

34. RGIA f. 391, op. 1, d. 290, l. 23ob., I. Tikheev, "Ob issledovanii stepnykh oblastei i o raskhodakh potrebnykh na prodolzhenie etogo issledovaniia v 1897 godu," October 26, 1896. Title of file: "Ob organizatsii issledovaniia stepnykh oblastei v 1897 godu."

35. Peter Rottier, "The Kazakness of Sedentarization: Promoting Progress as Tradition in Response to the Land Problem," *Central Asian Survey* 22, no. 1 (2003): 67–81 (quotation from 70).

36. F. A. Shcherbina and E. Dobrovol'skii *MPKZ*, vol. 3: *Akmolinskaia oblast', Akmolinskii uezd* (Chernigov, 1909), 91, 93–94.

37. *MPKZ*, 1:71–2.

38. Criticism of livestock is ibid., 99; on laziness, see F. A. Shcherbina, *MPKZ*, vol. 2: *Akmolinskaia oblast', Atbasarskii uezd* (Voronezh, 1902), xxi.

39. F. A. Shcherbina and L. K. Chermak, *MPKZ*, vol. 9: *Semipalatinskaia oblast', Ust'kamenogorskii uezd* (St. Petersburg, 1905), 68; *MPKZ*, 1:139. Compare Michael Adas, *Machines as the Measure of Men: Science, Technology, and Ideologies of Western Dominance* (Ithaca, 1989).

40. *MPKZ*, 5:iv.

41. On primitivism, see V. V. Biriukovich, ed., *Svod trudov mestnykh komitetov po 49 guberniiam Evropeiskoi Rossii*, vol. 3: *Sel'skokhoziaistvennaia tekhnika* (St. Petersburg, 1903), 28, referring to Olonets province in the far north of the empire; on filth, see ibid., 43–44 (a particularly lurid description of living conditions in rural Tula province, just south of Moscow); on immorality, see S. I. Shidlovskii, ed., *Svod trudov mestnykh komitetov po 49 guberniiam Evropeiskoi Rossii*, vol. 6: *Zemel'nye zakhvaty i mezhevoe delo* (St. Petersburg, 1904), 16, 51. This immorality, in the eyes of outside observers, manifested itself particularly in lack of respect for others' rights to land use.

42. Here I argue against the interpretation offered in Alexander Etkind, *Internal Colonization: Russia's Imperial Experience* (Cambridge, 2011)—a stimulating argument, but one that runs into difficulty in a context of land seizures from and legal discrimination against non-Russians. The most sophisticated argument against applying a colonial framework to the steppe provinces in particular is A. V. Remnev, "Kolonial'nost', postkolonial'nost', i 'istoricheskaia politika' v sovremennom Kazakhstane," *Ab Imperio*, no. 1 (2011): 169–205.

43. David A. J. Macey, *Government and Peasant in Russia, 1861–1906: The Prehistory of the Stolypin Reforms* (DeKalb, 1987), 43–81. On resettlement in particular, see I. V. Sosnovskii, ed., *Svod trudov mestnykh komitetov po 49 guberniiam Evropeiskoi Rossii*, vol. 4: *Zemlevladenie* (St. Petersburg, 1904), 30–31.

44. Yanni Kotsonis, "How Peasants Became Backward: Agrarian Policy and Cooperatives in Russia, 1905–14," in *Transforming Peasants: Society, State, and the Peasantry, 1861–1930*, ed. Judith Pallot (New York, 1998), 15–36. Pallot, in the introduction to this volume (5), cites Jane Nadel-Klein, "Occidentalism as a Cottage Industry: Representing the Autochthonous 'Other' in British and Irish Rural Studies," in *Occidentalism: Images of the West*, ed. James G. Carrier (New York, 1996), 109–134, to argue that peasant backwardness is a constructed idea common to Western, industrializing societies.

45. *MPKZ*, 7:ii–iii.

46. *MPKZ*, 4:ii–iii.

47. Ibid., 90.

48. *MPKZ*, 2:xxxvi.

49. F. A. Shcherbina and L. K. Chermak, *MPKZ*, vol. 6: *Semipalatinskaia oblast', Karkaralinskii uezd* (St. Petersburg, 1905), 66, 5 (appendix).

50. F. A. Shcherbina, ed., *MPKZ*, vol. 1: *Akmolinskaia oblast', Kokchetavskii uezd* (Voronezh, 1898), 186. For retrospective criticism of some of the expedition's methodology, see T. P. Petrova, "Organizatsiia statisticheskogo obsledovaniia kazakhskikh khoziaistvo ekspeditsiei F. A. Shcherbiny," *Problemy istorii SSSR*, no. 9 (1979): 75–91.

51. Petrova, "Organizatsiia," 84; for selection criteria for budget households and the exhaustively detailed questions asked of families surveyed, see S. N. Veletskii, *Zemskaia statistika: Spravochnaia kniga po zemskoi statistike*, 2 vols. (Moscow, 1899–1900), 2:1–34. Later volumes of the expedition's work, in which Shcherbina seems to have participated less, calculated different norms, although most maintained a significant increase over the livestock norm considered truly necessary.

52. F. A. Shcherbina, "Issledovaniia stepnykh oblastei," *Trudy Imperatorskgo vol'nogo ekonomicheskogo obshchestva*, no. 4 (1902): 338.

53. RGIA f. 1291, op. 84, d. 16, l. 17ob., Taube to Korablev, manager of a group of surveyors charged with forming settler sections in Akmolinsk province, June 14, 1897.

54. For hesitation on the part of Taube and Ia. F. Barabash, governor of Turgai province, see RGIA f. 1291, op. 84, d. 16 (1897), ll. 15–15ob., Taube, June 1897, and 33ob.–34, a summary of Barabash's views by the MVD bureaucrat Savich, May 6, 1898. Title of file: "Proekt instruktsii zavedyvaiushchim Akmolinskimi vremennymi partiiami o poriadke obrazovaniia pereselencheskikh uchastkov v Akmolinskom i Kokchetavskom uezdakh."

55. RGIA f. 391, op. 1, d. 290, ll. 107ob.–108, Shcherbina to Tikheev, June 24, 1897.

56. *MPKZ*, 1:1.

57. *MPKZ*, 1:4, 13; for personnel numbers, see A. A. Kaufman, *Materialy po voprosu ob organizatsii rabot po obrazovaniiu pereselencheskikh uchastkov v stepnykh oblastiakh (iz otcheta starshago proizvoditelia rabot Kaufmana po komandirovke v Akmolinskuiu oblast' letom 1897 g.)* (St. Petersburg, 1897), 57–58.

58. *MKPZ*, 1:iii–iv.

59. Kaufman, *Materialy*, 62.

60. Ibid., 67, 81.

61. Ibid., 3.

62. Ibid., 84–86.

63. Ibid., 24.

64. Ibid., 31.

65. Smirnov, *Otchet revizora zemleustroistva Smirnova po komandirovke letom 1899 g. v Akmolinskuiu i Semipaltinskuiu oblasti* (St. Petersburg, 1899).

66. Ibid., 12.

67. Ibid., 92, 54.

68. Ibid., 11–12.

69. This emphasis on undergovernance, and on the resulting slippages between the intent and execution of colonial policies, is central to Alexander Morrison, *Russian Rule in Samarkand: A Comparison with British India* (New York, 2008); also see, for the conflicts between local and central administration this engendered, A. V. Remnev, "Stepnoe general-gubernatorstvo v imperskoi geografii vlasti," in *Aziatskaia Rossiia: Liudi i struktury imperii*, ed. N. G. Suvorova (Omsk, 2005), 163–222.

70. Smirnov, 56, 61–63.

71. For the phrase "disciplinary matrix," see Thomas Kuhn, *The Structure of Scientific Revolutions*, 2nd ed. (Chicago, 1970), 182.

72. Smirnov, 65.

73. In this sense it is possible to agree with the historian Gulnar Kendirbai's emphasis on the "arbitrary administrative rule" (1) that resettlement represented. See *Land and People: The Russian Colonization of the Kazak Steppe* (Berlin, 2002). The more interesting question, addressed below, is how such arbitrariness could occur in a context where many officials were devoted to a program defined by its *lack* of arbitrariness.

74. On topographers, see Smirnov, 42; on the meeting, which took place early in 1898, and factors motivating it, see Kaufman, *Materialy*, 95–6, 102; and Smirnov, 18.

75. T. I. Sedel'nikov, *Bor'ba za zemliu v kirgizskoi stepi: Kirgizskii zemel'nyi vopros i kolonizatsionnaia politika pravitel'stva* (St. Petersburg, 1907), 3.

76. Ibid., 38.

77. Ibid., 37.

78. Ibid., 5–6, 44–45.

79. Ibid., 49–50.

80. Ibid., 51.

81. Ibid., 19–20. The analogy here, which certain Kazak critics invited, was to the Turkic-speaking Bashkir population of the southern Urals, which had mostly sedentarized and granted the right to sell their land, with mostly negative results for themselves. See Charles Steinwedel, "How Bashkiria Became a Part of European Russia, 1762–1881," in *Russian Empire: Space, People, Power, 1700–1930*, ed. Jane Burbank, Mark von Hagen, and Anatolyi Remnev (Bloomington, 2007), 94–124.

82. Edward H. Judge, *Plehve: Repression and Reform in Imperial Russia, 1902–1904* (Syracuse, 1983), 189–191.

83. The classic statement is P. A. Stolypin and A. V. Krivoshein, *Poezdka v Sibir' i Povolzh'e* (St. Petersburg, 1911).

84. Holquist, "In Accord," 152.

85. V. K. Kuznetsov, ed., *Kustarnye promysly krest'ian Kargopol'skogo uezda Olonetskoi gubernii* (Petrozavodsk, 1902).

86. RGIA f. 391, op. 3, d. 458, ll. 2ob–3. Title of file: "Po predostavleniiu statisticheskikh materialov po obsledovaniiu kirgizskogo khoziaistva i zemlepol'zovaniia v Akmolinskoi oblasti."

87. Ibid., 3–3ob.

88. RGIA f. 1291, op. 84, d. 28a, l. 1, Stolypin to Vasil'chikov, January 10, 1907. Title of file: "Ob obrazovanii osobogo mezhduvedomstvennogo soveshchaniia dlia razrabotki glavneishikh osnovanii zemel'nogo ustroistva kirgizskogo naseleniia stepnykh oblastei. Chast' 1."

89. G. F. Chirkin, "Zemleotvodnoe delo v Kirgizskoi stepi i neobkhodimost' zemleustroistva kirgiz," *Voprosy kolonizatsii* 3 (1908): 62–66.

90. RGIA f. 1291, op. 84, d. 28a, l. 29, "Sostav soveshchaniia po voprosu o zemel'nom ustroistve kirgizskogo naseleniia stepnykh oblastei," indicates that six delegates out of fourteen came from GUZiZ.

91. Ibid., l. 93, "Zhurnal soveshchaniia o zemleustroistve kirgiz."

92. Ibid., ll. 98–98ob.

93. Ibid., ll. 96ob. (quotation), 97ob.–98.

94. Ibid., ll. 100ob.–107ob.

95. Brower, 138.

96. Jeff Sahadeo, "Progress or Peril: Migrants and Locals in Russian Tashkent, 1906–1914," in *Peopling the Russian Periphery: Borderland Colonization in Eurasian History*, ed. Nicholas B. Breyfogle, Abby M. Schrader, and Willard Sunderland (New York, 2007), 148–166. Some provincial governors in the steppe did evince concern about resettlement; thus in May 1906, the vice-governor of Akmolinsk province, A. A. Abaza, requested that the province be closed to settlement, as its land fund was used up; the response that this was impossible to permit reflects the priority given to peasant resettlement by this time. See S. N. Maltusynov, *Agrarnaia istoriia Kazakstana, konets XIX–nachalo XX vv.: Sbornik dokumentov* (Almaty, 2006), 99–100. "Sart" was an ill-defined term with shifting meanings in the scholarly and bureaucratic vernacular of the nineteenth and early twentieth centuries, often referring to all sedentary natives of Turkestan, at other times referring to exclusively Turkic-speaking sedentary people.

97. See, e.g., P. P. Rumiantsev's later paean, "Usloviia kolonizatsii Semirech'ia," *Voprosy kolonizatsii* 9 (1911): 191–225.

98. For this language, see A. L. Tregubov, "Pereselencheskoe delo v Semipalatinskoi i Semirechenskoi oblastiakh," *Voprosy kolonizatsii* 6 (1910): 166–167.

99. Veletskii, *Zemskaia*. Compilation of this work would have given Veletskii some familiarity with Shcherbina's methods even before his transfer to the steppe provinces, since it contains reproductions of the survey materials used and instructions for the completion of survey cards and budgets (2:1–34).

100. Multiple publications ensued from this effort, e.g., *Sbornik statisticheskikh svedenii po Ufimskoi gubernii* (Ufa, 1898).

101. *Otchet Imperatorskogo russkogo geograficheskogo obshchestva za 1903 g.* (St. Petersburg, 1904), 198, record of a meeting of ZSO IRGO of December 13, 1902. The same record lists Sedel'nikov as presenting a paper on the Shcherbina norms with commentary from Veletskii and Bökeikhanov, but unfortunately, I have not been able to find a record of what was actually said during these discussions.

102. On the Revolution of 1905 in Turkestan, see especially Jeff Sahadeo, *Russian Colonial Society in Tashkent, 1865–1923* (Bloomington, 2007), 108–136.

103. Maltusynov, *Sbornik*, 259 (August 6, 1905); 261 (August 22, 1905); 267 (August 23, 1905).

104. TsGA RK f. 19, op. 1, d. 41, sv. 5, l. 20ob., Veletskii's report to the Turkestan Governor-General, February 24, 1907.

105. RGIA f. 391, op. 3, d. 486, l. 7ob., "Doklad o normakh dlia obezpecheniia zemleiu kirgizskago naseleniia pri obrazovanii v Semirechenskoi oblasti pereselencheskikh uchastkov iz gosudarstvennykh zemel', sostoiashchikh v pol'zovanii kochuiushchikh po nim Kirgiz," Veletskii and Voronkov to Grodekov, 5 November 1907. Title of file: "O vremennykh normakh obezpecheniia zemleiu kirgiz Semirechenskoi oblasti i o poriadke iz"iatiia zemel' iz kirgizskogo pol'zovaniia, ch. 1."

106. Ibid., ll. 9–9ob.

107. Ibid., ll. 10–11ob.

108. Ibid., ll. 2–2ob., Veletskii to the Resettlement Administration, November 5, 1907.

109. Ibid., ll. 265ob.–267ob.

110. Ibid., ll. 268–269ob.

111. TsGA RK f. 19, op. 1, d. 39, sv. 5, l. 6ob., Report of December 29, 1907.

112. Ibid., l. 7ob.

113. Ibid., l. 13ob. (January 2, 1908).

114. Ibid., l. 11.

115. RGIA f. 391, op. 3, d. 486, ll. 270–270ob; on Grodekov's conditions, see Veletskii's complaints to the Resettlement Administration, RGIA f. 391, op. 3, d. 487, ll. 11ob.–17ob. (March 21, 1908); on temporary norms, see ibid., l. 46, A. I. Pil'ts to Resettlement Administration (May 13/15, 1908).

116. Alexander Morrison, "'Sowing the Seed of National Strife in This Alien Region': The Pahlen Report and *Pereselenie* in Turkestan, 1908–1910," *Acta Slavica Iaponica* 31 (2012): 6–7.

117. Brower, 140–143.

118. Morrison, "Sowing," 6–7.

119. Richard A. Pierce, "Introduction," *Mission to Turkestan: Being the Memoirs of Count K. K. Pahlen, 1908–1909*, trans. N. J. Couriss (New York, 1964), viii–ix. Pahlen explicitly cited his agricultural knowledge as the reason he was able to question the pretensions of Semirech'e's resettlement officials in his memoir, dictated from memory while in Finland (to which he and his family had fled after the October Revolution) in 1922. See Pahlen, *Mission*, 203–4. Though this work suffers from the nostalgia and hindsight common to all memoirs, it is also much less guarded in tone than Pahlen's official report and thus a worthwhile source concerning his own attitudes, if not a perfectly reliable register of facts.

120. Pierce, x–xi.

121. K. K. Pahlen, *Otchet po revizii Turkestanskogo kraia, proizvedennoi po VYSO-CHAISHCHEMU poveleniiu*, vol. 6: *Pereselencheskoe delo* (St. Petersburg, 1910), 419. Cited hereafter as *Pereselencheskoe delo*.

122. Pahlen, *Pereselenecheskoe delo*, 430.

123. Morrison, "Sowing," 10.

124. Pahlen, *Pereselencheskoe delo*, 15, 162.

125. Ibid., 150.

126. Ibid., 64–67, 205–208, 229.

127. This emphasis distinguishes my interpretation from Holquist, "In Accord," and Morrison, "Sowing."

128. Pahlen, *Pereselencheskoe delo*, 37–41.

129. Ibid., 42, 43, 48.

130. Pahlen, *Mission*, 191.

131. Pahlen, *Pereselencheskoe delo*, 243, for praise of the Syr-Darya provincial statistical party affiliated with the Resettlement Administration; records of this party's work are at TsGA RK, f. 33, op. 1, dd. 9 and 28.

132. Pahlen, *Pereselencheskoe delo*, 68–71.

133. Ibid., 43.

134. Ibid., 415.

135. Brower, 103–108; see also Morrison, "Sowing," 8.

136. *SOGD, tretii sozyv, sessiia chetvertaia, chast' I* (St. Petersburg, 1910), 2607–2612. Speech of December 7, 1910. In this instance the most vocal critic of Glinka and his organization was the liberal historian P. N. Miliukov (ibid., 2593–2607).

137. Brower, 144.

138. Pahlen, *Mission*, 183; for evidence of Veletskii's continuing affiliation, see S. Veletskii, "Poslednie sobytiia v Priiliiskom Kul'dzhinskom krae," *Voprosy kolonizatsii* 15 (1914): 158–189.

139. P. P. Rumiantsev, *Materialy po obsledovaniiu tuzemnogo i russkogo starozhil'cheskogo khoziaistv i zemlepol'zovaniiu v Semirechenskoi oblasti, sobrannye i razrabotnnye pod rukovodstvom P. P. Rumiantseva*, vol. 2: *Kopalskii uezd, Kirgizskoe khoziaistvo* (St. Petersburg, 1913), 89–91.

140. Adapted from P. P. Rumiantsev, *Materialy po obsledovaniiu tuzemnogo i russkogo starozhil'cheskogo khoziaistva i zemlepol'zovaniia v Semirechenskoi oblasti, sostavlennye i razrabotannye pod rukovodstvom P. P. Rumiantseva*, vol. 3: *Dzharkentskii uezd, Kirgizskoe khoziaistvo* (St. Petersburg, 1912), 400.

141. V. K. Kuznetsov, ed., *KKhAO*, vol. 1: *Kokchetavskii uezd, Povtornoe issledovanie 1907 g.* (St. Petersburg, 1909).

142. Ibid., xiii.

143. Ibid., 94.

144. For example, *KKhAO*, vol. 2: *Omskii uezd, Povtornoe issledovanie 1908 g.* (St. Petersburg, 1910), vi–vii.

145. *KKhAO*, 1:x; *KKhAO*, vol. 5: *Akmolinskii uezd, Povtornoe issledovanie 1909 g.* (St. Petersburg, 1910), viii.

146. *KKhAO*, 1:52–53; *KKhAO*, 2:vi.

147. *KKhAO*, 1:38.

148. Ibid., 112.

149. Ibid., xi, 122–123.

150. Ibid., ix–x.

151. For low estimates of productivity, see ibid., 152; and *KKhAO*, vol. 3: *Petropavlovskii uezd, Povtornoe issledovanie 1908 goda* (St. Petersburg, 1910), viii; on inattentiveness to local conditions, see *KKhAO*, 1:135; on economic diversity, see *KKhAO*, 1:126–127. On the question of economic diversity, there are tempting parallels with what Darrow describes as the "politics of numbers," fundamentally a clash between a cadastral viewpoint (favored by the Central Statistical Committee of the MVD) that assumed a uniform, unchanging peasant economy and the heterogeneous approach to peasant households pursued by zemstvo statisticians. See Darrow, "Politics," 111–118.

152. *MPKZ*, 12:17–18; *KKhAO*, 3:viii.

153. RGIA f. 391, op. 4, d. 200, ll. 84ob.–85, "Spravka k vnesennomu na utverzhdenie Soveta Ministrov raspisaniiu norm zemel'nogo obezpecheniia kirgiz Pavlodarskogo uezda, Semipalatinskoi oblasti," February 1912. Title of file: "Ob utverzhdenii norm zemel'nogo obezpecheniia kirgizov v Akmolinskom raione v 1910 g."

154. RGIA f. 1291, op. 84, d. 171 (1908), l. 9, Troinitskii, secret report to Steppe Governor-General E. O. Shmit, September 11, 1908. Title of file: "Po voprosu o neobkhodimosti i usloviiakh nemedlennogo zaseleniia Zaisanskogo i Ust'-Kamenogorskogo uezdov Semipalatinskoi oblasti russkimi pereselentsami."

155. *KKhAO*, 1:140.

156. Ibid., 141–142. A pood was equivalent to 36.11 pounds, so Kuznetsov described an increase in consumption from roughly 116 to 216 pounds per year.

157. *KKhAO*, 1:62; *KkhAO*, 4:119–120.

158. *Aziatskaia Rossiia*, vol. 1: *Liudi i poriadki za Uralom* (St. Petersburg, 1914).

6. A DOUBLE FAILURE

1. I leave the word *Kirgizy* untranslated because in this case, there are no indications in the archive of whether the speaker was referring to the ethnic group we would today call "Kazaks" or "Kyrgyz." Nor does the location of these events, the southwestern edge of Vernyi district, provide a reliable basis for guessing.

2. TsGA RK f. 19, op. 1, d. 623, sv. 79, l. 162, statement of resettlement worker Ismagul Tabyldin, August 23, 1916. Title of file: "Delo o vosstanii kazakhov v 1916 g."

3. Ibid.

4. Beyond these, only thinly populated Yakutsk province, in eastern Siberia, was specifically excluded; other regions populated by ethnic minorities saw their representation decrease.

5. *SOGD tret'ego sozyva, sessiia pervaia* (St. Petersburg, 1908), 1246. Khalil-Bek Khas-Mamedov was an Azeri member of the Muslim fraction, representing several Caucasian provinces, while his opponent, Petr Vasil'evich Berezovskii, was a rightist deputy from Volyn' province.

6. Romanov, Iu. I., ed., *Qaharlï 1916 zhyl/Groznyi 1916-i god* (Almaty, 1998), 13–14. Title of document: "Ukaz Rossiiskogo imperatora Nikolaia II 'O privlechenii muzhskogo inorodcheskogo naseleniia imperii dlia rabot po ustroistvu oboronitel'nykh sooruzhenii i voennykh soobshchenii v raione deistvuiushchei armii, a ravno dlia vsiakikh inykh neobkhodimykh dlia gosudarstevnnoi oborony rabot.'"

7. Peter Holquist, "'In Accord with State Interests and the People's Wishes': The Technocratic Ideology of Imperial Russia's Resettlement Administration," *Slavic Review* 69, no. 1 (2010): 151–179 (quotation from 156).

8. *SOGD vtorogo sozyva, sessiia pervaia*, 1509 (S. I. Kelepovskii, April 2, 1907).

9. *SOGD vtorogo sozyva, sessiia vtoraia*, 627 (P. N. Krupenskii, May 16, 1907).

10. RGIA f. 391, op. 3, d. 910, ll. 1–3, telegram from Koshchegulov addressed to Nicholas II, September 25, 1908. Title of file: "Po vsepoddanneishei telegramme kirgiza Koshchegulova o prekrashchenii russkogo pereseleniia v step'."

11. Ibid., ll. 4–4ob., report of Krivoshein to Nicholas II, October 20, 1908.

12. Ibid., ll. 5ob.–6.

13. Ibid., l. 7ob., Krivoshein to governor of Akmolinsk province, October 25, 1908.

14. Al. Uspenskii, "Vliianie kolonizatsii na kirgizskoe khoziaistvo (po dannym povtornogo izsledovaniia Arakaragaiskoi volosti, Kustanaiskogo uezda, Turgaiskoi oblasti, proizvedennogo L. N. Tsabelem)," *Voprosy kolonizatsii* 2 (1907): 35–36, 40–41.

15. Ibid., 42.

16. Ibid., 31.

17. F. Los'-Roshkovskii, *Khodokam i pereselentsam napravliaiushchimsia v Kustanaiskii uezd Turgaiskoi oblasti v 1911 godu (nastavleniia, opisanie raiona i uchastkov)* (Poltava, 1911), 6.

18. S. N. Maltusynov, *Agrarnaia istoriia Kazakhstana (konets XIX–nachalo XX v.) (sbornik dokumentov i materialov)* (Almaty, 2006), 853–857. Title of document: "Polozhenie ob uchrezhdenii zemlustroitel'nykh komissii v Akmolinskoi, Turgaiskoi, Semipalatinskoi, Ural'skoi, Semirechenskoi, Syr-Dar'inskoi i Zakaspiiskoi oblastiakh, vnesennoe v tret'iu Gosudarstvennuiu dumu (proekt 60-ti)."

19. See, e.g., G. Chirkin, "Zemleotvodnoe delo v Kirgizskoi stepi i neobkhodimost' zemleustroistva Kirgiz," *Voprosy kolonizatsii* 3 (1908): 59–79.

20. RGIA f. 391, op. 3, d. 929, ll. 20, 25, "Prilozhenie no. 7 k predstavleniiu Glavnoupravliaiushchogo zemleustroistvom i zemledeliem v Sovet ministrov ot 23 maia 1909 za

no. 17579," originally a note from Krivoshein to Stolypin, October 19, 1908. Title of file: "Perepiska o zemleustroistve kirgizov 1908–1909 gg."

21. Ibid., l. 25ob., Stolypin to Krivoshein, November 1, 1908.

22. Though Nikolai Nikolaevich Kutler, a leading Kadet thinker on the agrarian question, did express some fears for the interests of the "local" (i.e., Kazak) population on the floor of the Second Duma. See *SOGD vtorogo sozyva, sessiia pervaia*, 732 (N. N. Kutler, March 19, 1907).

23. A. A. Kaufman, "Kirgizy i Konstitutsionno-demokraticheskaia partiia," *Rech'*, March 18, 1906. Seidalin replied in "Kirgizskii vopros," *Rech'*, April 3, 1906. Thanks to Alexander Morrison for providing these references.

24. A. A. Kaufman, *Pereselenie i kolonizatsiia* (St. Petersburg, 1905), 155.

25. A. A. Kaufman, *Pereselenie: Mechty i deistvitel'nost'* (Moscow, 1906), 9–10.

26. Ibid., 10, 37.

27. For fears of failure without further assistance to settlers, see also P. Kokoulin, "Khod pereseleniia, vodvoreniia, i khoziaistvennogo ustroeniia pereselentsev v Turgaiskoi oblasti," *Voprosy kolonizatsii* 1 (1907): 220–221. O. A. Shkapskii, "Pereselentsy i agrarnyi vopros v Semirechenskoi oblasti," *Voprosy kolonizatsii* 1 (1907): 29, extended Kaufman's fears about irrigation to Semirech'e.

28. *SOGD pervogo sozyva, sessiia pervaia* (T. I. Sedel'nikov, May 4, 1906), 204; *SOGD vtorogo sozyva, sessiia pervaia* (A. L. Karavaev, March 19, 1907), 717–718.

29. Al. Uspenskii, "Deistvitel'nost', a ne mechty," *Voprosy kolonizatsii* 2 (1907): 1–28 (citation from 22–23).

30. Ibid., 23–24.

31. *Aziatskaia Rossiia*, vol. 2: *Zemlia i khoziaistvo* (St. Petersburg, 1914), 3. The author of this section was the celebrated climatologist A. I. Voeikov. On Voeikov's optimism about irrigation in relation to his views of the history of the global climate, see Deborah Coen, "Imperial Climatographies from Tyrol to Turkestan," *Osiris* 26, no. 1 (2011): 45–65 (here 51). However, K. K. Pahlen, for example, was deeply skeptical of the unproven potential of rain-fed lands, as he was of most of the Resettlement Administration's actions. See RGIA f. 391, op. 3, d. 1498, l. 19, "Predvaritel'nyi otchet o polozhenii pereselencheskogo dela v Semirech'e, sostavlennyi po dannym revizii Senatora Grafa Palena."

32. Nik. Zdravomyslov, "Prirodnye usloviia Atbasarskogo uezda i vidy na kolonizatsiiu iuzhnoi ego chasti," *Voprosy kolonizatsii* 7 (1910): 223–236.

33. In different ways: Seidalin, "Kirgizskii vopros"; and Maltusynov, 726–728 (speech of B. B. Karataev to first subcommission of the Agrarian Commission, Second State Duma, April 14, 1907).

34. By signing the Vyborg Manifesto after the dissolution of the First Duma, Bökeikhanov (along with 165 other signatories) disqualified himself from any further participation in politics. See Steven Sabol, *Russian Colonization and the Genesis of Kazak National Consciousness* (New York, 2003), 78 (on Bökeikhanov signing); and Abraham Ascher, *P. A. Stolypin: The Search for Stability in Late Imperial Russia* (Stanford, 2002), 148 (on the consequences for signatories).

35. Statistik, "Krizis kantseliarskogo pereseleniia," in *Älikhan Bökeikhan: Izbrannoe/ tangdamalï*, ed. R. N. Nurgaliev (Almaty, 1995), 273–274.

36. On precipitation, see V., "Russkie poseleniia v glubine Stepnogo kraia," in Nurgaliev, 218–237 (quotation from 223); on forest clearing, see A. Bukeikhan, "Pereselentsy v tarskikh urmanakh," in Nurgaliev, 237–242.

37. V., "Biurokraticheskaia utopiia," Nurgaliev, 275–277 (quotation from 276).

38. Donald Treadgold gives 1906 as the beginning of resettlement's "flood tide" (235) period. See Treadgold, *The Great Siberian Migration: Government and Peasant in Resettlement from Emancipation to the First World War* (Princeton, 1957).

39. Älikhan Bökeikhanov, "Kirgiz na soveshchanii stepnogo general-gubernatora," in Nurgaliev, 255.

40. Ä. Bökeikhanov, "Zhauap khat," in *Alash qozghalïsï: Qŭzhattar men materialdar zhinaghï*, ed. M. Q. Qoigeldiev (Almaty, 2004), 2:151.

41. On the formation of sedentary cantons, see, e.g., TsGA RK f. 19, op. 1, d. 545, sv. 75, ll. 16–16ob., "Dokladnaia zapiska o kirgizskom zemleustroistve v Semirechenskoi oblasti," undated and unsigned, probably 1915. Title of file: "Dokladnaia zapiska o zemleustroistve kazakhov, spisok sel i volostei Semirechenskoi oblasti"; for opposition to inclusion in such a canton, see RGIA f. 1291, op. 84, d. 56 (1915), l. 1, petition addressed to the minister of internal affairs, February 13, 1915. Title of file: "Po prosheniiu kirgiz no. 1 aula Archalinskoi volosti, Semipalatinskogo uezda i obl. Dzhilbaevykh i dr., khodataistvuiushchikh ob obratnom perechislenie ikh v kochevoe sostoianie." This petition would ultimately be rejected by the incorrect application of a procedural rule.

42. On settler violence, see RGIA f. 1291, op. 84, d. 212 (1912), ll. 1–2ob., petition addressed to the minister of internal affairs, July 7, 1912). Title of file: "Po zhalobe kirgiza no. 4 aula Cherubai-Nurinskoi vol., Akmolinskogo uezda Mussy Salykpaeva o vooruzhennom napadenii krest'ian na ikh aul"; on violent acts by resettlement officials, see TsGA RK f. 33, op. 1, d. 40, sv. 1, ll. 1–3ob., report of January 1912. Title of file: "Doklad zaveduiushchego pereselencheskim delom v Syr'-Darinskom raione o gazetnoi zametke v 'Russkom slove.'"

43. On seizures without compensation, see V., "Pereselencheskie nadely v Akmolinskoi oblasti," in Nurgaliev, 248; on seizures for inappropriate purposes, see Qïrbalasï, "Qazaqtan biurogha baratïn ökïl / Zapros," in *"Qazaq" gazetï: Alash azamattarïnïng ruhkïna baghïshtaladï*, ed. Ü. Subkhanberdina et al. (Almaty, 1998), 300.

44. On access to farmland see, e.g., TsGA RK f. 15, op. 1, d. 2315, sv. 124, l. 20, petition of Chiykebai Musafirov and Aksy Uzdembaev to the military governor of Semipalatinsk province, April 25, 1911. Title of file: "O nadelenii zimovymi stoibishchami kazakhov Kokon'skoi volosti Semipalatinskogo uezda"; on land disputes see, e.g., TsGA RK f. 15, op. 1, d. 1549, sv. 80, ll. 79ob.–80, petition of Kazaks of *starshinstvo* no. 1, Ulansk canton, to military governor of Semipalatinsk province, July 22, 1907. Title of file: "O zemel'nom spore mezhdu kazakhami Slusarinskoi volosti pervogo uchastka i Sebinskoi vtorogo uchastka Ust'-Kamenogorskogo uezda."

45. Already in 1914, one local governor warned that "unrest" occurred in some districts "because of the not-always-correct seizures of Kazak land surpluses." See TsGA RK f. 44, op. 1, d. 38202, sv. 1819, l. 9, report of Semirech'e Military Governor Mikhail Aleksandrovich Fol'baum to Turkestan governor-general, June 23, 1914). Title of file: "Po predstavleniiu g. Voennogo Gubernatora Turkestanskomu General-Gubernatoru o kirgizskom zemleustroistve."

46. For example, a Semirech'e Kazak, Satygali Sabataev, served in Veletskii's statistical party in 1906. See TsGA RK f. 44, op. 1, d. 2529, sv. 233, ll. 32, Sabataev's petition, May 25, 1906; and 79, Veletskii's recommendation, August 11, 1906. Title of file: "O komandirovanii v Semirechenskuiu oblast' partii po obrazovaniiu pereselencheskikh uchastkov." Dolgushin's assistants were also Kazaks.

47. RGIA f. 391, op. 5, d. 1786, l. 3, Semirech'e manager of resettlement affairs to Resettlement Administration, February 3, 1915. Title of file: "Organizatsionnye voprosy v Semirechenskom raione v 1915 g."

48. For the original proposal, see TsGA RK f. 15, op. 1, d. 2294, ll. 116–117, meeting register, September 15, 1911; for discussion under the Provisional Government see ibid., ll. 130–132, memorandum of Semipalatinsk province commission to Ispolkom, March 31, 1917. Title of file: "Delo ob izmenenii granits Semipalatinskoi oblasti i ee uezdov."

49. *PSZ*, series 3, vol. 27 (1907), no. 29240.

50. Werth, *At the Margins of Orthodoxy: Mission, Governance, and Confessional Politics in Russia's Volga-Kama Region, 1827–1905* (Ithaca, 2002), 181; B. M. Babadzhanov, "Andidzhanskoe vosstanie 1898 goda i 'musul'manskii vopros' v Turkestane (vzgliady 'kolonizatorov' i 'kolonizuemykh')," *Ab Imperio*, no. 2 (2009): 155–200 (here 160–161, 191–192).

51. Alexander Morrison, "Sufism, Pan-Islamism, and Information Panic: Nil Sergeevich Lykoshin and the Aftermath of the Andijan Uprising," *Past and Present* 214 (2012): 255–304 (quotation from 286).

52. TsGA RK f. 64, op. 1, d. 5578, sv. 355; on Nalivkin's role, see D. Iu. Arapov, *Imperatorskaia Rossiia i musul'manskii mir (konets XVIII–nachala XX v.): Sbornik materialov* (Moscow, 2006), 258.

53. RGIA f. 821, op. 8, d. 621, ll. 32ob.–33ob., Dukhovskoi report addressed to the minister of war, August 8, 1898). Title of file: "Ustroistvo dukhovnykh del magometan Turkestanskogo kraia."

54. Ibid., ll. 113–115.

55. Ibid., ll. 103–103ob., Department of Foreign Faiths to Main Staff, March 30, 1899.

56. "Zapiska S. Iu. Vitte po 'musul'manskomu voprosu,'" in Arapov, 244–257.

57. RGIA f. 821, op. 8, d. 621, ll. 59–67, report of Lieut.-Gen of the General Staff, Korol'kov, to Dukhovskoi, August 5, 1898). Title of note: "Otchet po razsledovaniiu obstoiatelstv vozstaniia tuzemtsev Ferganskoi oblast v mae 1898 goda."

58. TsGA RK f. 64, op. 1, d. 5578, sv. 355, ll. 32 ob.–33, Sakharov, for the War Ministry, to MVD, May 16, 1900. This rhetoric tracks well with Paul Werth's argument that in the Russian Empire, "the concept of 'religious toleration' excluded all manifestations of spirituality that could be glossed as 'political.'" (149) See Werth, *The Tsar's Foreign Faiths: Toleration and the Fate of Religious Freedom in Imperial Russia* (New York, 2014), 105–127, 149–178. At the same time, it puts pressure on Elena Campbell's statement that "secular authorities . . . did not regard the religious question as a problem of the state" (342). See E. Campbell, "The Muslim Question in Late Imperial Russia," in *Russian Empire: Space, People, Power, 1700–1930*, ed. Jane Burbank, Mark von Hagen, and Anatolyi Remnev (Bloomington, 2007), 320–347.

59. See, e.g., the worries about Pan-Islamism and the influence of the Young Turks in Central Asia expressed by Turkestan's new governor-general, Aleksandr Vasil'evich Samsonov, in 1909: RGIA f. 821, op. 8, d. 621, ll. 365–367, Samsonov to Minister of War V. A. Sukhomlinov, August 8, 1909.

60. TsGA RK f. 64, op. 1, d. 881, sv. 59, ll. 239–253. Title of file: "Materialy o vosstanii musul'man v Andizhane."

61. M. A. Batunskii, *Rossiia i Islam*, pt. 2: *Russkaia kul'tura v ee otnoshenii k Zapadu i Vostoku: Opyt istoriko-epistemologicheskoi rekonstruktsii* (Moscow, 2003), 363.

62. RGIA f. 821, op. 8, d. 621, ll. 48–49, undated, "Spisok izdanii rekomenduemykh dlia priobreteniia v biblioteki, upravleniia i kantseliarii v kachestve spravochnykh po vorposam, otnosiashchimsia do sovremennogo polozheniia musul'manstva."

63. Batunskii, 2:225–239.

64. Robert Geraci, *Window on the East: National and Imperial Identities in Late Tsarist Russia* (Ithaca, 2001), 86–87, 90.

65. For Taube's receipt, see TsGA RK f. 64, op. 1, d. 5578, sv. 355, l. 3; for distribution, see TsGA RK f. 64, op. 1, d. 881, sv. 59, ll. 210–210ob. (February 1, 1899).

66. David Schimmelpenninck van der Oye, *Russian Orientalism: Asia in the Russian Mind from Peter the Great to the Emigration* (New Haven, 2010), 238–239.

67. For the text of the petition, see TsGA RK f. 64, op. 1, d. 5658, ll. 17–19. Title of file: "Ob agitatsii sredi kirgiz Karkaralinskogo i Pavlodarskogo uezdov o posylke v Peterburg deputatsii dlia predstavlenii ot kirgizskogo naroda petitsii tsariu."

68. Ibid., ll. 1 ob., Galkin, July 19, 1905; 8, Sukhotin, July 29, 1905.

69. There are strong parallels here with processes that Christian Noack has described among the Kazan' Tatars the same year. See Noack, "Retroactively Revolting: Kazan Tatar 'Conspiracies' during the 1905 Revolution," in *The Russian Revolution of 1905: Centenary Perspectives*, ed. Jonathan D. Smele and Anthony Heywood (New York, 2005), 119–136.

70. TsGA RK f. 64, op. 1, d. 5832, ll 61–61 ob., excerpt from the Semipalatinsk newspaper *Sovremennoe slovo*, November 19, 1909. Title of file: "O vyselenii i vospreshchenii zhitel'stva v Stepnom krae kazakham Baitursynovu Akhmetu, Raimbekovu i drugim za protivopravitel'stvennye deistviia."

71. Robert Crews, *For Prophet and Tsar: Islam and Empire in Russia and Central Asia* (Cambridge, MA, 2006), 225–226. According to Kimberly Ann Powers (personal conversation), Kryzhanovskii made a similar proposal for the Inner Horde in 1872.

72. An assembly of Kazaks in June 1914 gave a statement in favor of returning the four steppe provinces to the OMDS and establishing a separate muftiate for Turkestan, including Semirech'e. See "Qazaqtardïng dïni, khŭqïk häm zher khaqïndaghï özara kengesterïnïng qorïtïndïsï," in *"Aiqap,"* ed. Ü. Subkhanberdina and S. Däuitov (Almaty, 1995), 218. Document signed by Baqïtzhan Qarataev, Zhihansha Seidalin, Serali Lapin, Dosan Amanshin, and A. Narïnbaev. See also Qarataev's speech from the same assembly, "Kenges zhiïlïsïnda Qarataevtyng söilegen dokladï," in Subkhanberdina and Däuitov, 211–213. Tomohiko Uyama has noted that the secularist direction (exemplified by Älikhan Bökeikhanov) ultimately prevailed among the Kazak intelligentsia. See Uyama, "The Changing Religious Orientation of Qazaq Religious Intellectuals in the Tsarist Period: *Shari'a*, Secularism, and Ethics," in *Islam, Society, and States across the Qazaq Steppe*, ed. Niccolò Pianciola and Paolo Sartori (Vienna, 2013), 112–113.

73. Robert Geraci has noted a similar phenomenon in the Volga region: the rise of an Islamic progressive movement stoked fears of an orientalized other among tsarist statesmen akin to those they had previously projected onto conservative clergy. See Geraci, "Russian Orientalism at an Impasse: Tsarist Education Policy and the 1910 Conference on Islam," in *Russia's Orient: Imperial Borderlands and Peoples, 1700–1917*, ed. Daniel Brower and Edward Lazzerini (Bloomington, 2001), 138–161.

74. TsGA RK f. 44, op. 1, d. 2868, sv. 263, ll. 27–27ob., register of Semirech'e provincial board on societies, July 11, 1908. Title of file: "Po khodataistvu musul'man g. Kopala ob utverzhdenii ustava Kopalskikh musulman progressistov." These petitioners would be rejected twice more in 1910, at the last instance, absurdly, because it divided off Muslims from other confessional groups—that is, for exactly the opposite reason it was initially rejected. See TsGA RK f. 44, op. 1, d. 3171, sv. 284, ll. 11ob., register of Semirech'e provincial board on societies, January 5, 1910; and 28ob.–29, register of Semirech'e provincial board on societies, June 4, 1910.

75. TsGA RK f. 44, op. 1, d. 2839, sv. 260, ll. 3–4, petition of G. A. Bogdanov, March 13, 1908; 2, report of Przheval'sk district chief to Semirech'e military governor, August 8, 1908). Title of file: "Po prosheniiu Vernenskogo meshchanina G. Bogdanova o tom, chto Prezheval'skaia musul'manskaia biblioteka chital'nia sluzhit mestom sborishcha dlia obsuzhdeniia voprosov, ne imeiushchikh otnosheniia k biblioteke."

76. TsGA RK f. 15, op. 1, d. 357, sv. 17, l. 13, top secret report of Pavlodar district chief, November 5, 1914. Title of file: "Delo o dvizhenii sredi musul'manskogo naseleniia v sviazi s pervoi imperialisticheskoi voinoi." Other district chiefs, it should be noted, were less troubled and more sanguine about what they saw than this man.

77. Arapov, 306. Kharuzin fulminated against the spread of Islam on the steppe as contrary to both Kazak customs and the spread of Orthodoxy in *Kirgizy Bukeevskoi Ordy: Antropologo-etnologicheskii ocherk* (Moscow, 1889), 1:91–103. On the Kharuzin family, which produced four distinguished ethnographers, see Nathaniel Knight, "Nikolai

Kharuzin and the Quest for a Universal Human Science: Anthropological Evolutionism and the Russian Ethnographic Tradition, 1885–1900," *Kritika: Explorations in Russian and Eurasian History* 9, no. 1 (2008): 83–111.

78. Stolypin, "O merakh protivodeistviia panislamskomu i panturanskomu (panti-urkskomu) vliianiiu sredi musul'manskogo naseleniia," in Arapov, 318–337 (quotations from 320).

79. Werth, *Tsar's Foreign Faiths*, 235–239, emphasizes this point. See also Geoffrey Hosking, *The Russian Constitutional Experiment: Government and Duma, 1907–1914* (Cambridge, 1973), 74–105.

80. See, e.g., K. N. Voitekhovskii, "Kirgizy Kustanaiskogo uezda, Turgaiskoi oblasti" (Kazan', 1910), 16.

81. John W. Slocum, "Who, What, and When Were the *Inorodtsy*? The Evolution of the Category of 'Aliens' in Imperial Russia," *Russian Review* 57, no. 2 (1998): 173–190; Andreas Kappeler, *The Russian Empire: A Multiethnic History*, trans. Alfred Clayton (Harlow, 2001), especially 168–171, 204–208; Paul Werth, "Changing Conceptions of Difference, Assimilation, and Faith in the Volga-Kama Region, 1740–1870," in *Russian Empire: Space, People, Power, 1700–1930*, 169–195.

82. P. P. Rumiantsev, *Kirgizskii narod v proshlom i nastoiashchem* (St. Petersburg, 1910), 28, 19.

83. O. A. Shkapskii, "Pereselentsy-samovol'tsy i agrarnyi vopros v Semirechenskoi oblasti" (St. Petersburg, 1906), 44. On Shkapskii, see Daniel Brower, *Turkestan and the Fate of the Russian Empire* (New York, 2003), 136–138.

84. *Aziatskaia Rossiia*, vol. 1: *Liudi i poriadki za Uralom* (St. Petersburg, 2014), 159–163. For the word "masterwork" (142), see Willard Sunderland, "The Ministry of Asiatic Russia: The Colonial Office That Never Was but Might Have Been," *Slavic Review* 69, no. 1 (2010): 120–150.

85. Ibid., 162. No quotation or citation is given, but this is a word-for-word copy of a passage in V. D. Tronov, "Materialy po antropologii i etnologii kirgiz," *ZIRGO po otdeleniiu etnografii* 17, no. 2 (1891): 60.

86. TsGA RK f. 44, op. 1, d. 2527, sv. 233, l. 259, telegram from Pishpek to Semirech'e Military Governor Mikhail Efremovich Ionov, June 17, 1906. Title of file: "Po telegramme Turkestanskogo General-Gubernatora o naznachenii novykh vyborov v Gosusarstvennuiu Dumu."

87. Ibid., l. 215, Ionov to district chief of Lepsinsk district, June 8, 1906.

88. RGIA f. 391, op. 5, d. 1063, l. 5, Maklakov to I. L. Goremykin, March 7, 1914. Title of file: "Po zakonodatel'nomu predpolozheniiu 38-mi chlenov Gosudarstvennoi Dumy o vozstanovlenii predstavitel'stva v Gos. Dume ot naseleniia stepnykh oblastei i oblastei Turkestanskogo kraia."

89. Peter Rottier, "The Kazakness of Sedentarization: Promoting Progress as Tradition in Response to the Land Problem," *Central Asian Survey* 22, no. 1 (2003): 67–81.

90. Here I agree with Rottier's central thesis that the Kazak intelligentsia sought autonomy without self-determination. See Rottier, "Creating the Kazak Nation: The Intelligentsia's Quest for Acceptance in the Russian Empire, 1905–1920" (PhD diss., University of Wisconsin, 2005).

91. This formulation draws on Ali Iğmen, *Speaking Soviet with an Accent: Culture and Power in Kyrgyzstan* (Pittsburgh, 2012).

92. E.g. Mïrzhaqïp Dŭlatov, "Gosudarstvennaia duma häm qazaq," in Subkhanberdina and Däuitov, 62–64.

93. Ibid.

94. Akhmet Baitŭrsïnov, "Qazaq häm törtïnshï duma," in Subkhanberdina and Däuitov, 118–119.

95. *Qazaq*, for example, reported on a petition to reopen the Duma given by the Kazaks of Ural'sk province on the occasion of the tercentenary of the Romanov dynasty. See Anon., "Ĭshkĭ zhangalïqtar," in Subkhanberdina et al., 17.

96. Anon., "Biurogha kĭsĭ zhĭberu," in Subkhanberdina et al., 287.

97. Anon., "Biurogha ekĭnshĭ adam qoiu," in Subkhanberdina et al., 341. On Shoqaev, see K. L. Esmaghambetov, *Älem tanïghan tŭlgha: Mustafa Shoqaidïng dünietanïmï zhäneqairatkerlĭk bolmïsï* (Almaty, 2008).

98. Recall the language of the petition thousands of Kazaks gave in 1905: "True—we do animal husbandry . . . but because of this should we be deprived of such an important and valuable political right as participation in the representative assembly [*zemskii sobor*]?" See TsGA RK f. 64, op. 1, d. 5658, l. 10.

99. Sabol, 66–67; Z. Akhmetov, "Zhanga ideialar zharïsï," in *Mĭrzhaqïp Dŭlatŭlï: Shïgharmalarï*, ed. Kh. Toikenov (Almaty, 1996), 3–18.

100. Qoigeldiev, 88–89, letter dated September 30, 1910.

101. Qïr balasï, "Üshïnshï duma häm qazaq," in Subkhanberdina et al., 27.

102. Anon., "Bĭzdĭng bŭrïnghï häm qazĭrgĭ khalĭmĭz: 'Zamanïng tülkĭ bolsa, tazï bolïp qu,'" in Subkhanberdina and Däuitov, 82.

103. This is *pace* some Soviet scholarship arguing that *Qazaq* advocated the preservation of nomadism, as summarized by Rottier, "Kazakness," 74–75, 78. See also Gulnar Kendirbai, "We Are Children of Alash . . ." *Central Asian Survey* 18, no. 1 (1999): 5–37.

104. Anon., "Bĭzdĭng bŭrïnghï . . . ," in Subkhanberdina and Däuitov, 82.

105. Qazaqemes, "Qazaqqa alalïq qaidan keldi," in Subkhanberdina and Däuitov, 172.

106. Saudaqas Shormanov, "Baianauïl zhaiïnan," in Subkhanberdina and Däuitov, 102.

107. Meiram Ĭsqaqov, "Qala bolushïlar," in Subkhanberdina and Däuitov, 201–202.

108. Ghalaldin Mamikov, "Bĭzdĭng qazaq balasïna ne qïlghanda basqa zhŭrttargha tengeluĭ khaqïnda biraz kenges," in Subkhanberdina and Däuitov, 262.

109. Bĭr kĭsĭ, "Topïraghïmïz altïn," in Subkhanberdina and Däuitov, 197.

110. Ibid., 198.

111. On the tensions between popular participation and administrative standardization in the borderlands of a nationalizing empire, as encapsulated in the zemstvo, see Theodore R. Weeks, *Nation and State in Late Imperial Russia: Nationalism and Russification on the Western Frontier, 1863–1914* (DeKalb, 1996), 131–151.

112. Anon., "Shïn sözge zhan pida," in Subkhanberdina and Däuitov, 180.

113. This was Baqïtzhan Qarataev's approach in Ural'sk province; see Qoigeldiev, 89–90.

114. Azamat Alashŭghlï (Mĭrzhaqïp Dŭlatov), "Zher mäselesi: Qazaq bolu kerek deushĭlerdïng pĭkĭrï," in Subkhanberdina and Däuitov, 83–84. This pen name translates to "Citizen Son of Alash." Alash was the name of the Kazaks' legendary common ancestor.

115. Anon., "Zher zhŭmïsïna din zhŭmïsïn qïstïrmalau," in Subkhanberdina et al., 86.

116. Bökeikhanov, "Zhauap khat," in Nurgaliev, 303.

117. Azamat Alashŭghlï, "Zher mäselesi: köshïp zhüru kerek deushĭlerdĭng pĭkĭrï," in Subkhanberdina and Däuitov, 84.

118. Mŭsa Zhanalin, "Qala boludan qaitu," in Subkhanberdina et al., 141–142.

119. Anon., "Zher zhŭmïsïna," in Subkhanberdina et al., 84. See also Bökeikhanov's obituary, "Konstantin Antonovich VERNER (Munähib—Nekrolog)," in Nurgaliev 419–420.

120. Anon., "Zher zhŭmïsïna," in Subkhanberdina et al., 84. Although, due to the lack of a citation, I have not been able to find the text the Kazak author refers to in the relevant passage, this was probably the Kiev professor of agronomy Sergei Mikhailovich Bogdanov.

121. Anon., "Qazaq häm zher mäselesi," in Subkhanberdina et al., 94. Bökeikhanov was also characteristically sharp with Tatar journalists whom he felt were speaking out of turn with respect to the land question; see A. B., "'Angdaspaghan mäsele' turasïnda," in Subkhanberdina et al., 86–87.

122. Both the six-stage model of economic development (explicitly cited) and the emphasis on the different potential of different climactic zones (*salqïn* and *ïstïk üiek*, cool and warm latitudes) are strongly Listian. See Anon., "Sharualïq özgerïsï," in Subkhanberdina et al., 246; see also Friedrich List, *The National System of Political Economy*, trans. Sampson S. Lloyd (London, 1916).

123. Anon., "Sharualïq özgerïsï," in Subkhanberdina et al., 252.

124. Ibid., 254.

125. Ibid., 255.

126. Ibid., 255–256.

127. Ibid., 265.

128. Sabol, 107.

129. Akhmet Baitŭrsïnov, "Taghï da zher zhaïïnan," in Subkhanberdina and Däuitov, 59.

130. Anon, "Zher zhŭmïsïna dïn zhŭmïsïn qïstïrmalau," in Subkhanberdina et al., 85.

131. Ibid.

132. Bökeikhanov, "Zhauap khat," in Nurgaliev, 303.

133. Anon., "Qazaq häm zher mäselesï," in Subkhanberdina et al., 93.

134. For delays in the zemleustroistvo of sedentarizing Kazaks in diverse areas, see, e.g., TsGA RK f. 33, op. 1, d. 47, sv. 5, l. 3, report of May 14, 1913; and TsGA RK f. 469, op. 1, d. 526, sv. 76, l. 147, reply to petition, November 30, 1913. Titles of files: "Doklady i proekty rabot po zemleustrostvu kazakhov v Aulie-atinskom uezde" and "Delo ob osedlom ustroistve kazakhov Semipalatinskogo uezda," respectively. The delays do not read as ideologically grounded, but rather as chronic problems of an understaffed bureaucracy.

135. David Bell, *The First Total War: Napoleon's Europe and the Birth of Warfare as We Know It* (Boston, 2007), 1–21.

136. On the 1874 reform, see Robert F. Baumann, "Universal Service Reform: Conception to Implementation, 1873–1883," in *Reforming the Tsar's Army: Military Innovation in Imperial Russia from Peter the Great to the Revolution*, ed. David Schimmelpenninck van der Oye and Bruce W. Menning (New York, 2004), 11–33.

137. As part of a broader argument about the relationship among universal conscription, nationalism, and mass violence in the Russian Empire, Joshua Sanborn has noted the difficulties of a citizenship-based model of military service in an autocratic, dynastic empire. See Sanborn, *Drafting the Russian Nation: Military Conscription, Total War, and Mass Politics, 1905–1925* (DeKalb, 2003). Alexander Morrison has ably summarized the maintenance and expansion of legal and administrative difference between the inorodtsy of Central Asia and the steppe and "imperial citizens" of the dominant nationality. See Morrison, "Metropole, Colony, and Imperial Citizenship in the Russian Empire," *Kritika: Explorations in Russian and Eurasian History* 13, no. 2 (2012): 327–364.

138. For the classic argument framing military service as a tool of cultural homogenization, see Eugen Weber, *Peasants into Frenchmen: The Modernization of Rural France, 1870–1914* (Stanford, 1976).

139. Anon., "Soghïs salïghï," in Subkhanberdina et al., 145, describes to Kazak readers their new responsibilities in comparison with other tax-paying regions.

140. Dana M. Ohren, "All the Tsar's Men: Minorities and Military Conscription in Imperial Russia, 1874–1905" (PhD diss., Indiana University, 2006), 26–27.

141. RGIA f. 1291, op. 84, d. 172 (1915), l. 1, MVD Upravlenie voinskoi povinnosti to MVD Zemskii otdel, September 29, 1915. Title of file: "O privlechenii k otbyvaniiu voinskoi povinnosti nekotorykh chastei naseleniia, osvobozhdennogo ot neia do nastoiashchego vremeni"; "Gazetalardan" (correspondence from various newspapers), "Qazaqtan soldat alu," in Subkhanberdina et al., 234–236; anon., "Qazaqtan soldat alu turalï," in Subkhanberdina et al., 236–238.

142. Anon., "Qazaqtan soldat alu turalï," in Subkhanberdina et al., 238.

143. Anon., "Soldattïq mäselesï" (opinion of Mŭstafin Maldïbaiŭghlï), in Subkhanberdina et al., 261.

144. TsGA RK f. 369, op. 1, d. 5845, sv. 659, l. 8, report of Semirech'e military governor Aleksei Iakovlevich Fride, January 13, 1883.

145. Anon., "Petrograd khatï: ne ïsteuge?" in Subkhanberdina et al., 274–275.

146. Ibid., 274.

147. Anon., "Qaisïsï paidalï?" in Subkhanberdina et al., 291–292.

148. Q. Mirza, "Äsker alsa," in Subkhanberdina et al., 285–286.

149. Anon., "Soldattyq mäselesï" (opinion of Akhmet Zhantäliŭghlï), in Subkhanberdina et al., 260.

150. Ibid.

151. Älikhan, Akhmet, and Mïrzhaqïp, "Alashtïng azamatï," in Subkhanberdina et al., 323.

152. Qoigeldiev, 201 ("Iz protokola doprosa mirovym sud'ei 4-go uchastka Cherniaevskogo u. inzhenera M. Tynyshpaeva ob istorii vzaimootnoshenii Rossiiskoi vlasti s kazakhami"). For biographical data on Tïnïshbaev, see the documents pertaining to his election to the Duma, TsGA RK f. 44, op. 1, d. 2663, ll, 185–185 ob., report of April 5, 1907. Title of file: "Delo o vyborakh v Gos. Dumu, t. III".

153. M. D., "G. Duma häm soldattïq mäselesï," in Subkhanberdina et al., 269–270.

154. Qoigeldiev, 201; Sabol, 85.

155. Anon., "Petrograd khatï: Taghï ne ïsteuge," in Subkhanberdina et al., 276–278; Anon., "Petrograd khatï: Mŭsïlman fraktsiiada," in Subkhanberdina et al., 279–281.

156. On fears of the negative consequences of displaying weakness on the borderlands, see Bahktiyar Babadzhanov, "'How Will We Appear in the Eyes of *Inovertsy* and *Inorodtsy?*' Nikolai Ostroumov on the Image and Function of Russian Power," *Central Asian Survey* 33, no. 2 (2014): 270–288.

157. RGIA f. 1291, op. 84, d. 129 (1916), ll. 8ob.–9ob., "Sobranie uzakonenii i rasporiazhenii pravitel'stva, izdavaemoe pri Pravitel'stvuiushchem senate, December 24, 1916, no. 361." Title of file: "O privlechenii inorodtsev Evropeiskoi i Aziatskoi Rossii k tylovym rabotam v deistvuiushchei armii." Unhelpfully, some proclamations *did* imply a quid pro quo. The Provisional Council of the Bukei (Inner) Horde promised, "By this your participation in the war you will obtain that attention on the part of the government, which the core population of our vast Fatherland enjoys." See Romanov, 15.

158. RGIA f. 1291, op. 84, d. 129 (1916), l. 32, "Kopiia telegrammy iz Astrakhani na imia Upravliaiushchogo Zemskim Otdelom ot 26 iiulia 1916 goda." Telegram of Astrakhan' provincial governor Ivan Nikolaevich Sokolovskii.

159. On elders, see, e.g., Romanov, 16 ("Telegramma aksakalov Poludenskoi volosti Petropavlovskogo uezda General-Gubernatoru Stepnogo kraia N. A. Sukhomlinovu o gotovnosti priniat' uchastie v tylovykh rabotakh," July 9, 1916); on the intelligentsia, see Älikhan, Akhmet, Mïrzhaqïp, "Alashtïng azamatï," in Subkhanberdina et al., 321. An investigation in August 1916 declared that "the editorial direction of *Qazaq* . . . has been the most correct." See Qoigeldiev, 172–73, "Iz doneseniia nachal'nika Orenburgskogo gubernskogo zhandarmskogo upravleniia voennomu gubernatoru Turgaiskoi oblasti o deiatel'nosti A. Baitursynova, A. Bukeikhanova i M.-Ia. Dulatova po agenturnym svedeniiam" (August 12, 1916).

160. Brower, *Turkestan*, 162; Jörn Happel, *Nomadische Lebenswelten und zarische Politik: Der Aufstand in Zentralasien 1916* (Stuttgart, 2010), 15.

161. Happel, *Nomadische Lebenswelten*, 55. Marco Buttino offers a contrasting argument. For Buttino, this was an organized and planned revolt, whose scope is best explained by the persistence of tribal structures among non-Russians, the weakness of local authority, and an escalating trend of violence provoked by the worsening economic conditions of wartime. See Buttino, *Revoliutsiia naoborot: Sredniaia Aziia mezhdu padeniem tsarskoi imperii i obrazovaniem SSSR*, trans. Nikolai Okhotin (Moscow, 2007), 58–90.

162. Qoigeldiev, 205. For similar interpretations, see Maltusynov, 1124–1140 (speech of A. F. Kerenskii, December 13, 1916); and TsGA RK f. 380, op. 1, d. 1, ll. 180–180ob., from the report of A. N. Kuropatkin to Nicholas II, February 22, 1917. Title of file: "Raport Turkestanskogo general-gubernatora, komanduiushchego voiskami Turkestanskogo voennogo okruga Kuropatkina, i drugie materialy po vosstanovleniiu kazakhov v 1916 g."

163. Alexander Morrison, "'Sowing the Seed of National Strife in This Alien Region': The Pahlen Report and *Pereselenie* in Turkestan, 1908–1910," *Acta Slavica Iaponica* 31 (2012): 1–29 (here 23–24).

164. For example, S. G. Agadzhanov et al., eds.., *Vosstanie 1916 goda v Srednei Azii i Kazakhstane: Sbornik dokumentov* (Moscow, 1960), 512. Title of document: "Telegramma predsedatelia s"ezda krest'ianskikh nachal'nikov Atbasarskogo uezda E. M. Vodiannikov voennomu gubernatoru Akmolinskoi oblasti P. N. Masal'skomu o vosstanii kazakhov v Atbasarskom uezde" (July 18, 1916).

165. Ibid., 504–506. Title of document: "Doklad chlena Soveta ministra vnutrennikh del V. F. Kondoidi upravliaiushchemu Ministerstvom vnutrennikh del A. D. Protopopovu o vosstanii v Akmolinskoi, Semipalatinskoi, i Ural'skoi oblastiakh" (December 8, 1916).

166. Tomohiko Uyama, "Two Attempts at Building a Qazaq State: The Revolt of 1916 and the Alash Movement," in *Islam in Politics in Russia and Central Asia (Early Eighteenth to Late Twentieth Centuries)*, ed. Stephane Dudoignon and Hisao Komatsu (London, 2001), 77–98 (quotation from 83).

167. Anon., "Torghai aqsaqaldarïna," in Subkhanberdina et al., 342; for an especially strong statement, see Akhmet Baitŭrsïnov, Mïrzhaqïp Dŭlatov, Seiitgazim Kädirbaev, and Mŭkhamediiar Tŭngghashin, "Torghai häm Ïrghïz uezining khalqïna," in Subkhanberdina et al., 348–349.

168. On recruitment, see Älikhan, "Mäskeu khatï," in Subkhanberdina et al., 341–342; on provisions, see Älikhan and Mustafa, "Zhŭmïsshïlar zhaïïnan (Petrograd, 29 oktiabr')," in Subkhanberdina et al., 343–344.

169. The first part of this sentence draws on Sabol, 137.

170. TsGA RK f. 380, op. 1, d. 1, l. 184 ob.

171. Qoigeldiev, 219. This statement was issued under the heading "K kirgizam, svobodnym grazhdanam obnovliaemoi Rossii" (To the Kazaks, free citizens of a renewed Russia). For continued support of the war effort, see RGIA f. 1291, op. 84, d. 50 (1917), l. 4ob., "Protokol Turgaiskogo oblastnogo kirgizskogo s"ezda s uchastiem predstavitelei oblastei Ural'skoi, Akmolinskoi, Semipalatinskoi, Syr-Dar'inskoi i Bukeevskoi ordy," proiskhodivshogo v g. Orenburge 2–8 aprelia 1917 goda." Title of file: "Protokoly i rezoliutsii Kirgizskikh i dr. inorodcheskikh i musul'manskikh s"ezdov s 2 aprelia po 15 oktiabria 1917 g."

172. Anon., "Zor özgerïs," in Subkhanberdina et al., 367.

173. Älikhan Bökeikhanov, "Men kadet partiiasïnan nege shïqtïm?" in Nurgaliev, 414.

174. Bökeikhanov was particularly vehement in this respect, equating Bolsheviks with reactionary Black Hundreds. See Nurgaliev, 414, "Pamiatka krest'ianam, rabochim i soldatam."

175. On the tensions between Soviet power and intelligentsia agendas in Central Asia, see Adeeb Khalid, *Making Uzbekistan: Nation, Empire, and Revolution in the Early USSR* (Ithaca, 2015).

176. More than a million people died on the steppe during a famine in the early 1930s. Eloquent personal testimony concerning this era can be found in Mukhamet Shayakhmetov, *The Silent Steppe: The Story of a Kazak Nomad under Stalin*, trans. Jan Butler (London, 2006). An excellent dissertation about the famine ensuing from sedentarization and collectivization of the Kazaks is Sarah Cameron, "The Hungry Steppe: Soviet Kazakhstan and the Kazakh Famine, 1921–1934" (PhD diss., Yale University, 2010). For other notable scholarship on the famine and sedentarization campaign, see Niccolò Pianciola, "Famine

in the Steppe: The Collectivization of Agriculture and the Kazak Herdsmen, 1928–1934," trans. Susan Finnel, *Cahiers du monde russe* 45, no. 1–2 (2004): 137–191; and Isabelle Ohayon, *La sédentarisation des Kazakhs dans l'URSS de Staline: Collectivization et changement social (1928–1945)* (Paris, 2006). For a sense of the contradictions involved in Soviet modernization campaigns, which juxtaposed, in the long term, improved rates of literacy and infant mortality with tremendous violence, both cultural and physical, see inter alia Paula Michaels, *Curative Powers: Medicine and Empire in Stalin's Central Asia* (Pittsburgh, 2003); and Paul Stronski, *Tashkent: Forging a Soviet City, 1930–1966* (Pittsburgh, 2010).

CONCLUSION

1. *SSIA*, 1:49–50, letter to V. V. Katarinskii (dated December 27, 1879). See also M.-S. Babadzhanov, "Zametki kirgiza o zhit'e-byt'e i uchasti ego rodichei," in Ivlev, *Khodzha Mukhammed-Salikh Babadzhanov: Sochineniia (sbornik statei 1861–1871 gg.)* (Almaty, 1996), 104–119.

2. On this issue, see also Alexander Morrison, "Russia, Khoqand, and the Search for a Natural Frontier, 1863–1865," *Ab Imperio* no. 2 (2014): 165–192.

3. Martin, *Law and Custom on the Steppe: The Kazakhs of the Middle Horde and Russian Colonialism in the Nineteenth Century* (Richmond, 2001), 133, citing N. I. Krasovskii, ed., *Materialy dlia statistiki i geografii Rossii, sobrannye ofitserami General'nogo Shtaba: Oblast' Sibirskikh kirgizov*, 3 vols. (St. Petersburg, 1868), 3:160.

4. A. K. Geins, "Motivirovannaia vremennaia instruktsiia uezdnym nachal'nikam Turgaiskoi oblasti," *Sobranie literaturnykh trudov A. K. Geinsa*, 2 (St. Petersburg, 1898), 539–540.

Bibliography

UNPUBLISHED ARCHIVAL SOURCES

Rossiiskii gosudarstvennyi istoricheskii arkhiv (Russian State Historical Archive, St. Petersburg)

f. 391, Pereselencheskoe upravlenie

f. 821, Departament dukhovnykh del inostrannykh ispovedanii Ministerstva vnutrennikh del (MVD)

f. 853, Grigor'ev, Vasilii Vasil'evich

f. 1291, Zemskii otdel MVD

Rossiiskii gosudarstvennyi voenno-istoricheskii arkhiv (Russian State Military-Historical Archive, Moscow)

f. 400 Glavnyi shtab

Tsentral'nyi gosudarstvennyi arkhiv Respubliki Kazakhstana (Central State Archive of the Republic of Kazakhstan)

f. 4, Oblastnoe pravlenie Orenburgskimi kirgizami

f. 15, Semipalatinskoe oblastnoe pravlenie

f. 19, Zaveduiushchii pereselencheskim upravleniem Semirechenskoi oblasti Glavnogo upravleniia zemleustroistva i zemledeliia

f. 33, Zaveduiushchii pereselencheskim delom v Syr-Dar'inskoi oblasti

f. 44, Semirechenskoe oblastnoe pravlenie

f. 64, Stepnoe general-gubernatorstvo

f. 345, Oblastnoe pravlenie Sibirskimi kirgizami

f. 369, Akmolinskoe oblastnoe pravlenie

f. 380, Lichnyi fond B. P. Trizny

f. 460, Semipalatinskii statisticheskii komitet MVD

f. 469, Zaveduiushchii pereselencheskim delom v Semipalatinskom raione

PUBLISHED PRIMARY SOURCES

A., S. "Korespondentsiia: Dzharkentskii uezd." *Kirgizskaia stepnaia gazeta*, March 4, 1901.

Agadzhanov, S. A., et al., eds. *Vosstanie 1916 goda v Srednei Azii i Kazakhstane: Sbornik dokumentov.* Moscow, 1960.

"Aidashinskie inorodtsy." *Kirgizskaia stepnaia gazeta*, October 7, 1900.

Altynsarin, I. *Kirgizskaia khrestomatiia.* 2nd ed. Orenburg, 1906.

——. "Ocherk obychaev, pri svatovstve i svad'be, u kirgizov Orenburgskogo vedomstva." *Zapiski Orenburgskogo otdela imperatorskogo russkogo geograficheskogo obshchestva*, no. 1 (1870): 101–116.

Andreev, I. G. *Opisanie Srednei ordy kirgiz-kaisakov.* 1795–1796. Reprint, Almaty, 1998.

Arapov, D. Iu. *Imperatorskaia Rossiia i musul'manskii mir (konets XVIII–nachala XX v.): Sbornik materialov.* Moscow, 2006.

Artykbaev, Zh. O., ed. *Ch. Ch. Valikhanov: Etnograficheskoe nasledie kazakhov.* Astana, 2007.

——. *Ïbïrai Altïnsarin: Etnografiialïq ocherkter zhäne auïz ädebiet ülgïlerï.* Astana, 2007.

——. *Khodzha Mukhammed Salikh Babadzhanov: Etnografiia kazakhov Bukeevskoi ordy.* Astana, 2007.

Aryn, E. M., ed. *Musa Chormanov: Kazakhskie narodnye obychai.* Pavlodar, 2005.

Aziatskaia Rossiia, vol. 1: *Liudi i poriadki za Uralom.* St. Petersburg, 1914.

Aziatskaia Rossiia, vol. 2: *Zemlia i khoziaistvo.* St. Petersburg, 1914.

Babkov, I. F. *Vospominaniia o moei sluzhbe v Zapadnoi Sibiri 1859–1875 gg.: Razgranichenie s Zapadnym Kitaem 1869 g.* St. Petersburg, 1912.

Benkevich, B. "Kirgizskoe stepnoe skotovodstvo i mery k ego uluchsheniiu." *Zapiski Semipalatinskogo pod"otdela Zapadno-Sibirskogo otdeleniia Imperatorskogo russkogo geograficheskogo obshchestva* 1 (1903): 1–24.

Berg, L., V. Elpat'evskii, and P. Ignatov. *O solenykh ozerakh Omskogo uezda.* St. Petersburg: Bezobrazov, 1899.

Biriukovich, V. V., ed. *Svod trudov mestnykh komitetov po 49 guberniiam Evropeiskoi Rossii*, vol. 3: *Sel'skokhoziaistvennaia tekhnika.* St. Petersburg, 1903.

Blankennagel', E. I. *Zamechaniia maiora Blankennagelia vposledstvie poezdki ego iz Orenburga v Khivu v 1793–94 godakh: Izdany, s ob"iasneniiami, V. V. Grigor'evym.* St. Petersburg, 1858.

Blaramberg, I. F. *Voenno-statisticheskoe obozrenie zemli Kirgiz-Kaisakov Vnutrennei (Bukeevskoi) i Zaural'skoi (Maloi) Ordy Orenburgskogo vedomstva: Po rekognistsirovkam i materialam sobrannym na meste, sostavleno ober-kvartirmeisterom Orenburgskogo korpusa Gen. Shtaba Col. Blarambergom.* N.p., 1848.

Bökeikhanov, Ä. "Abai Qunanbaev—nekrolog." *Zapiski Semipalatinskogo pod"otdela Zapadno-Sibirskogo otdeleniia Imperatorskogo russkogo geograficheskogo obshchestva* 3 (1907): 1–8.

——. "Iz perepiski khana Srednei kirgizskoi ordy Bukeia i ego potomkov." *Pamiatnaia knizhka Semipalatinskoi oblasti* (1901): 1–17.

Botbaev, Maten. Untitled poem. *Kirgizskaia stepnaia gazeta*, August 3, 1890.

Bronevskii, S. B. "Zapiski General-Maiora Bronevskogo o Kirgiz-Kaisakakh srednei Ordy (okonchanie)." *Otechestvennye zapiski* 124, pt. 43 (1830): 194–285.

Chirkin, G. F. "Zemleotvodnoe delo v Kirgizskoi stepi i neobkhodimost' zemleustroistva kirgiz." *Voprosy kolonizatsii* 3 (1908): 59–79.

Condorcet, Antoine-Nicolas de. *Sketch for a Historical Picture of the Progress of the Human Mind.* Trans. June Barraclough. London, 1955.

D., R. "Vygodno-li dlia kirgizov skotovodstvo v tom vide, v kotorom ono nakhoditsia vnastoiashchee vremia?" *Kirgizskaia stepnaia gazeta*, January 17–May 2, 1899.

D., V. "Kirgizy v tsarstvovanie Imperatora Aleksandra II." *Kirgizskaia stepnaia gazeta*, August 30, 1898.

Däuitov, S. *Zar zaman: Zhïr-tolghaular.* Almaty, 1993.

Diusembaev, R. "Kak unichtozhit' sredi kirgizov konokradstvo." *Kirgizskaia stepnaia gazeta*, October 20, 1896.

——. "Sueveriia u nashikh kirgizov." *Kirgizskaia stepnaia gazeta*, January 14, 1896.

Dlusskaia, N. N. "Zapiski N. G. Zalesova, soobshchennye N. N. Dlusskoi." *Russkaia starina* 34, no. 7 (1903): 21–37.

Dorofeev, A. "Kirgizskoe skotovodstvo v Akmolinskoi oblasti." *Kirgizskaia stepnaia gazeta*, February 24–March 3, 1902.

Erofeeva, I. V., ed. *Istoriia Kazakhstana v russkikh istochnikakh XVI–XX vekov*, vol. 3: *Zhurnaly i sluzhebnye zapiski diplomata A. I. Tevkeleva po istorii i etnografii Kazakhstana (1731–1759 gg.).* Almaty, 2005.

———. *Istoriia Kazakhstana v russkikh istochnikakh XVI–XX vekov*, vol. 4: *Pervye istoriko-etnograficheskie opisaniia kazakhskikh zemel', XVIII vek*. Almaty, 2007.

———. *Istoriia Kazakhstana v russkikh istochnikakh XVI–XX vekov*, vol. 5: *Pervye istoriko-etnograficheskie opisaniia kazakhskikh zemel', pervaia polovina XIX veka*. Almaty, 2007.

"Eshche raz o preimushchestvakh zemledel'cheskogo khoziaistva." *Kirgizskaia stepnaia gazeta*, June 5, 1894.

Gaverdovskii, G [sic]. "Obshchee obozrenie mestopolozheniia Kirgiz-Kaisatskoi stepi (izvlechenie iz Zapisok G. Gaverdovskogo)." *Sibirskii vestnik*, pt. 3, bk. 13 (1823): 43–60.

Geins, A. K. *Sobranie literaturnykh trudov A. K. Geinsa*. 3 vols. St. Petersburg, 1897–1899.

Georgi, I. G. *Opisanie vsekh obitaiushchikh v rossiiskom gosudarstvie narodov: Ikh zhiteiskikh obriadov, obyknovenii, odezhd, zhilishch, uprazhnenii, zabav, veroispovedanii i drugikh dostopamiatnostei. Tvorenie, za n"skol'ko let pred sim na Nemetskom iazyke Ioganna Gottliba Georgi, v perevode na Rossiiski iazyk ves'ma vo mnogom izpravlennoe i v nov' sochinennoe*. 4 vols. St. Petersburg, 1799.

Golubev, A. *O srednei godichnoi temperature i sostoianii barometra v ukreplenii Vernom*. St. Petersburg, 1860.

Gosudarstvennaia Duma: Stenograficheskie otchety. St. Petersburg, 1906–1917.

Grigor'ev, V. V. "O peredache zvukov kirgizskogo iazyka bukvami russkoi azbuki (pis'mo k N. I. Il'minskomu." Kazan', 1862.

———. "O russkikh interesakh v podvlastnykh nam osedlykh stranakh Srednei Azii (pis'ma k redaktoru 'Moskvy')." *Turkestanskii sbornik* 1: 107–129.

Gumbol'dt, A. F. *Tsentral'naia Aziia. Izsledovaniia o tsepiakh gor i po sravnitel'noi klimatologii*, edited by D. N. Anuchin. Translated by P. I. Borozdich. Moscow, 1915.

I. "O kirgizskoi osedlosti." *Kirgizskaia stepnaia gazeta*, May 9–16, 1899.

Iagmin, Al'fons. *Kirgiz-kaisatskiia stepi i ikh zhiteli*. St. Petersburg, 1845.

"Iarovaia pshenitsa 'kara-bugdai.'" *Kirgizskaia stepnaia gazeta*, August 28, 1892.

Iavorskii, I. L. "Sredniaia Aziia: Kul'turnye uspekhi i zadacha v nei Rossii." *Turkestanskii sbornik* 443:137a–155b.

Ibragimov, Magomet-gali. "Kirgizskii sposob lecheniia nekotorykh boleznei skota." *Kirgizskaia stepnaia gazeta*, December 21, 1890.

Idarov. "Kirgizskaia step' Sibirskogo vedomstva i novouchrezhdennaia v nei Semipalatinskaia oblast'." *Turkestanskii sbornik* 398:42–59a.

Il'minskii, N. I. *Pis'ma N. I. Il'minskogo k ober-prokuratoru Sviateishogo sinoda Konstantinu Petrovichu Pobedonostsevu*. Kazan', 1895.

———. *Vospominaniia ob I. A. Altynsarine*. Kazan', 1891.

Imshenetskii, M. "Nesmetnoe bogatstvo, sokryvaemoe v kirgizskoi stepi." *Kirgizskaia stepnaia gazeta*, January 1–March 1, 1891.

Iuzhakov, Iu. "Nashi priobreteniia v Srednei Azii." *Turkestanskii sbornik* 5:100–144.

Ivanov, Il'ia I. "Korrespondentsiia." *Kirgizskaia stepnaia gazeta*, April 12, 1891.

Ivlev, N. P., ed. *Khodzha Mukhammed-Salikh Babadzhanov: Sochineniia (sbornik statei 1861–1871 gg.)*. Almaty, 1996.

"Iz istorii kirgizskikh nabegov." *Kirgizskaia stepnaia gazeta*, July 23, 1900.

"Izuverstvo fanatika." *Kirgizskaia stepnaia gazeta*, June 15, 1897.

K., A. "O sostoianii skotovodstva v Akmolinskoi oblasti." *Kirgizskaia stepnaia gazeta*, January 3–April 18, 1899.

"K voprosu ob ustroistve uchilishch dlia inorodcheskikh detei Kazanskogo uchebnogo okruga." *Zhurnal Ministerstva narodnogo prosveshcheniia* 134 (1867): 75–96.

Kabekov, T. "Korrespondentsiia iz Tarbogataiskikh gor." *Kirgizskaia stepnaia gazeta*, April 14, 1896.

Kaidalov, E. "Karavan-zapiski vo vremia pokhoda v Bukhariiu rossiiskogo karavana pod voinskim prikrytiem v 1824 i 1825 godakh." *Turkestanskii sbornik* 270:1–432.

"Kak dobyt' vodu v bezvodnoi stepi." *Kirgizskaia stepnaia gazeta*, November 28, 1899.

Kaufman, A. A. *Khoziaistvennoe polozhenie pereselentsev vodvorennykh na kazennykh zemliakh Tomskoi gubernii po dannym proizvedennogo v 1894 g., po porucheniiu g. Tomskogo gubernatora, podvornogo issledovaniia.* 2 vols. St. Petersburg, 1895.

——. "Kirgizy i konstitutsionno-demokraticheskaia partiia." *Rech'*, March 18, 1906.

——. *Materialy po voprosu ob organizatsii rabot po obrazovaniiu pereselencheskikh uchastkov v stepnykh oblastiakh (iz otcheta starshago proizvoditelia rabot Kaufmana po komandirovke v Akmolinskuiu oblast' letom 1897 g.).* St. Petersburg, 1897.

——. *Pereselenie i kolonizatsiia.* St. Petersburg, 1905.

——. *Pereselenie: mechty i deistvitel'nost'.* Moscow, 1906.

Khanykov, N. V. *O naselenii kirgizskikh stepei, zanimaemykh vnutrenneiu i maloiu ordami.* St. Petersburg, 1844.

Kharuzin, A. N. *Bibliograficheskii ukazatel' statei, kasaiushchikhsia etnografii kirgizov i karakirgizov.* Moscow, 1891.

——. *Kirgizy Bukeevskoi Ordy (antropologo-etnologicheskii ocherk).* 2 vols. Moscow, 1889–1891.

"Khronika." *Kirgizskaia stepnaia gazeta*, October 16, 1892.

"Kirgiz-Kaisaki bol'shoi, srednei i maloi ordy: Istoricheskoe vvedenie o Kirgiz-Kaisakakh." *Sibirskii vestnik*, pt. 9 (1820): 71–164, 173–188.

"Kirgizy-zemledel'tsy Turgaiskoi oblasti." *Kirgizskaia stepnaia gazeta*, December 15, 1896.

Kokhanovskii, A. "Po povodu kolonizatsii v Kitae i u nas." *Izvestiia Imperatorskogo russkogo geograficheskogo obshchestva* 45 (1909): 499–519.

Kokoulin, P. "Khod pereseleniia, vodvoreniia, i khoziaistvennogo ustroeniia pereselentsev v Turgaiskoi oblasti." *Voprosy kolonizatsii* 1 (1907): 208–221.

"Konevodstvo i konnozavodstvo v Turgaiskoi oblasti." *Kirgizskaia stepnaia gazeta*, July 5, 1891.

Konshin, N. Ia. "K voprosu o perekhode kirgiz Semipalatinskoi oblasti v osedloe sostoianie." *Pamiatnaia knizhka Semipalatinskoi oblasti* (1898): 29–54.

——. "Ocherki ekonomicheskogo byta kirgiz Semipalatinskogo oblasti." *Pamiatnaia knizhka Semipalatinskoi oblasti* (1901): 1–182.

——. "Po Ust'kamenogorskomu uezdu. Putevye zametki." *Pamiatnaia knizhka Semipalatinskoi oblasti* (1900): 1–51.

——. "Zametka ob odnom kirgizskom dzhute." *Zapiski Semipalatinskogo pod"otdela Zapadno-Sibirskogo otdeleniia Imperatorskogo russkogo geograficheskogo obshchestva* 2 (1905): 1–17.

Kopchik. "Material k kharateristike biiskikh reshenii." *Kirgizskaia stepnaia gazeta*, May 7, 1900.

Köpeev, Iu. "Korrespondentsiia iz Baian-aula." *Kirgizskaia stepnaia gazeta*, April 27 and August 10, 1890.

Kostenko, L. F. *Sredniaia Aziia i vodvoreniia v nei russkoi grazhdanstvennosti.* St. Petersburg, 1870.

Krasovskii, N. I., ed. *Materialy dlia statistiki i geografii Rossii, sobrannye ofitserami General'nogo Shtaba: oblast' Sibirskikh kirgizov.* 3 vols. St. Petersburg, 1868.

Kryzhanovskii, N. A. "Rech', proiznesennaia pokrovitelem Orenburgskogo otdela pri otkrytii otdela." *Zapiski Orenburgskogo otdela Imperatorskogo russkogo geograficheskogo obshchestva* 1 (1870): 13–30.

Kulomzin, A. N. *Vsepoddanneishii otchet Stats-Sekretaria Kulomzina po poezdke v Sibir'*
  dlia oznakomlenii s polozheniem pereselencheskogo dela. St. Petersburg, 1896.
Kurmanbaev, A. "K voprosu o chul-bidae." *Kirgizskaia stepnaia gazeta*, June 5, 1894.
Kushenev. "Neudavshaiasia popytka otkryt' shkolu." *Kirgizskaia stepnaia gazeta*, May
  26, 1896.
Kuznetsov, V. "Pereselentsy-zemledel'tsy v Severnoi Amerike." *Russkoe bogatstvo*, no. 8
  (1900): 19–37.
Kuznetsov, V. K., ed. *Kirgizskoe khoziaistvo Akmolinskoi oblasti*. 5 vols. St. Petersburg,
  1909–1910.
———. *Kustarnye promysly krest'ian Kargopol'skogo uezda Olonetskoi gubernii*.
  Petrozavodsk, 1902.
L—, A. "Glavnye osnovaniia voennoi statistiki i voenno-statisticheskie trudy
  General'nogo Shtaba." *Voennyi sbornik*, no. 1 (1861): 225–252.
L., S. "Sposob kormleniia skota drevesnymi vetvami." *Kirgizskaia stepnaia gazeta*,
  October 21, 1900.
Lepekhin, I. I. *Dnevnye zapiski puteshestviia doktora i akademii nauk ad"iunkta Ivana
  Lepekhina po raznym provintsiiam rossiiskogo gosudarstva, 1768 i 1769 godu*, pt.
  1. St. Petersburg, 1795.
Levshin, A. I. *Opisanie Kirgiz-kazach'ikh, ili Kirgiz-kaisatskikh, ord i stepei*. 3 vols. St.
  Petersburg, 1832.
———. *Opisanie ord i stepei kazakhov*. 1832. Reprint, Pavlodar, 2005.
List, Friedrich. *The National System of Political Economy*. Translated by Sampson S.
  Lloyd. London, 1916.
Los'-Roshkovskii, F. *Khodokam i pereselentsam napravliaiushchimsia v Kustanaiskii
  uezd Turgaiskoi oblasti v 1911 godu (nastavleniia, opisanie raiona i uchastkov)*.
  Poltava, 1911.
Magauin, M. M., ed. *Poety Kazakhstana*. Leningrad, 1978.
Makovetskii, P. "Iurta (letnee zhilishche kirgiz)." Omsk, 1893.
Maksheev, A. I. *Opisanie nizov'ev Syr'-Dari*. St. Petersburg, 1856.
Maltusynov, S. N. *Agrarnaia istoriia Kazakstana, konets XIX–nachalo XX vv.: Sbornik
  dokumentov*. Almaty, 2006.
Margulan, A. Kh., ed. *Ch. Ch. Valikhanov: Sobranie sochinenii*. 5 vols. Alma-Ata,
  1961–1972.
Matveev, N., ed. *Khodokam i pereselentsam, napraviaiushchimsia v Kustanaiskii uezd
  Turgaiskoi oblasti v 1914 godu (nastavleniia, opisanie raiona i uchastkov)*. 4th ed.
  Poltava, 1914.
Meiendorf, E. K. *Puteshestvie iz Orenburga v Bukharu*. Reprint, Moscow, 1975.
Meier, L. L. "Aral'skaia flotiliia v otnoshenii k sredne-aziatskoi torgovle." *Morskoi
  sbornik* 60, no. 7 (1862): 109–134.
———. "Del'ta reki Syr-Dar'i i eia otnoshenie k Rossii." *Morskoi sbornik* 55, no. 9 (1861):
  144–155.
———. *Materialy dlia geografii i statisiki Rossii, sobrannye ofitserami General'nogo
  Shtaba. Kirgizskaia step' Orenburgskogo vedomstva*. St. Petersburg, 1865.
"Mestnye izvestiia." *Kirgizskaia stepnaia gazeta*, June 12, 1892.
Mikhailov, V. "Besedy o skodovodstve (III)." *Kirgizskaia stepnaia gazeta*, February 6,
  1894.
———. "Besedy o skodovodstve (IV)." *Kirgizskaia stepnaia gazeta*, March 13, 1894.
Miropiev, M. "Kakie glavnye printsipy dolzhny byt' polozheny v osnovu obrazovaniia
  russkikh inorodtsev-musul'man? Rech' proiznesennaia na godichnom akte
  Turkestanskoi uchitel'skoi seminarii, 30-go avgusta 1882 g., prepodavatelem
  seminarii M. A. Miropievym." *Turkestanskii sbornik* 361:134a–146a.

Naimanets. "Oroshenie lugov u buriat." *Kirgizskaia stepnaia gazeta*, April 9, 1900.

Nazarov, Filipp. *Zapiski o nekotorykh narodakh i zemliakh srednei chasti Azii.* St. Petersburg, 1821.

Nebol'sin, P. I. *Rasskazy proezzhago.* St. Petersburg, 1854.

Nesterov, Ia. "Kak mozhno dobyvat' vodu v bezvodnykh stepiakh (ustroistvo snezhnikov)." *Kirgizskaia stepnaia gazeta*, November 10, 1896.

"'Nezabytoe' proshloe i nastoiashchee kirgizov—ocherki." *Kirgizskaia stepnaia gazeta*, July 17–October 2, 1892.

Nikolai Ivanovich Il'minskii: Izbrannye mesta iz pedagogicheskikh sochinenii, nekotorye svedeniia o ego deiatel'nosti i o poslednykh dniakh ego zhizni. Kazan', 1892.

"Novoe puteshestvie N. M. Przheval'skogo." *Kirgizskaia stepnaia gazeta*, September 9, 1888.

Nurgaliev, R. N., ed. *Älikhan Bökeikhan: Tangdamalï/izbrannoe.* Almaty, 1995.

"Nuzhno-li zaiavliat' o bolezni skota?" *Kirgizskaia stepnaia gazeta*, October 30, 1894.

"O bor'be s upadkom skotovodstva." *Kirgizskaia stepnaia gazeta*, December 7, 1890.

"O kholere i predokhranenii ot neia." *Kirgizskaia stepnaia gazeta*, August 7–21, 1891.

"O kolonizatsii Turgaiskoi oblasti." *Turkestanskii sbornik* 328:135–137.

"O razvitii pchelovodstva v stepnom general gubernatorstve." *Kirgizskaia stepnaia gazeta*, March 4, 1888.

"O vazhnosti zavedenii v kirgizskikh khoziaistvakh senokosilok i konnykh grabel." *Kirgizskaia stepnaia gazeta*, February 6, 1900.

"Ob otkrytii skladov zemledel'cheskikh orudii v Petropavlovske i Atbasare." *Kirgizskaia stepnaia gazeta*, August 23, 1898.

"Ob''iavleniia ot redaktsii." *Kirgizskaia stepnaia gazeta*, November 17, 1896.

"Obshchepoleznye svedeniia." *Kirgizskaia stepnaia gazeta*, January 11, 1891.

"Ogneupornye postroiki." *Kirgizskaia stepnaia gazeta*, November 30, 1890.

"Osnovanie v S. Peterburge Russkago geograficheskago obshchestva i zaniatiia ego s sentiabria 1845 po mai 1846 g." *Zapiski Imperatorskogo russkogo geograficheskogo obshchestva* 1 (1846): 25–42.

Ostroumov, N. "Kharakteristika religiozno-nravstvennoi zhizni musul'man preimushchestvenno Srednei Azii." *Turkestanskii sbornik* 329:31–96.

Otchet Imperatorskogo russkogo geograficheskogo obshchestva za 1903 g. St. Petersburg, 1904.

"Ovtsy v iuzhnoi polose Rossii." *Kirgizskaia stepnaia gazeta*, December 2–9, 1888.

P—v, A. "Kak lechat baksy." *Kirgizskaia stepnaia gazeta*, May 19, 1896.

Pahlen, K. K. *Mission to Turkestan: Being the Memoirs of Count K. K. Pahlen, 1908–1909.* Translated by N. J. Couriss. New York, 1964.

——. *Otchet po revizii Turkestanskogo kraia, proizvedennoi po VYSOCHAISHCHEMU poveleniiu,* vol. 6: *Pereselencheskoe delo.* St. Petersburg, 1910.

Pallas, P. S. *Puteshestvie po raznym provintsiiam Rossiiskoi imperii,* pt. 1. St. Petersburg, 1773.

Pashino, P. I. *Turkestanskii krai v 1866 g. Putevye zametki. Turkestanskii sbornik* 14:1–184.

Paul'son, I. I. *Kniga dlia chteniia i prakticheskikh uprazhnenii v russkom iazyke: Uchebnoe posobie dlia narodnykh uchilishch.* Moscow, 1872.

"Pered vyborami." *Kirgizskaia stepnaia gazeta*, April 29, 1901.

Perepletnikov, A. *Materialy po obsledovaniiu khoziaistva i zemlepol'zovaniia kirgiz Semipalatinskoi oblasti.* 3 vols. St. Petersburg, 1912–1913.

Plotnikov, V. N. "Zametki na stat'iu g. Altynsarina 'Ocherk Kirgizskikh obychaev pri svatovstve i svad'be.'" *Zapiski Orenburgskogo otdela imperatorskogo russkogo geograficheskogo obshchestva* 1 (1870): 117–121.

"Po povodu pozdnei vesny." *Kirgizskaia stepnaia gazeta*, March 22, 1898.

Polnoe sobranie uchenykh puteshestvii po Rossii, izdavaemoe Imperatorskoiu Akademieiu nauk, po predlozheniiu eia prezidenta. 7 vols. St. Petersburg, 1818–1825.

Polnoe sobranie zakonov Rossiiskoi imperii. Sobranie pervoe (1649–1825). St. Petersburg, 1830. 45 vols. *Sobranie tretie (1881–1913).* St. Petersburg, 1885–1916. 33 vols.

Polozhenie ob upravlenii Orenburgskimi kirgizami. St. Petersburg, 1844.

"Prostoi sposob bor'by s dzhutom." *Kirgizskaia stepnaia gazeta,* November 23, 1897.

Qoigeldiev, M. Q., ed. *Alash qozghalïsï: qŭzhattar men materialdar zhinaghy,* vol. 2. Almaty, 2004.

Qunanbaev, Abai. *Qara söz: Poemalar/Kniga slov: Poemy.* Edited and translated by K. Serikbaeva and R. Seisenbaev. Alma-Ata, 1992.

"Raznye izvestiia." *Kirgizskaia stepnaia gazeta,* January 1, March 19, and July 18, 1893.

"Redkostnoe arkheologicheskoe otkrytie." *Kirgizskaia stepnaia gazeta,* April 29, 1901.

Ritter, K. *Zemlevedenie Azii Karla Rittera,* pt. 1: *Obshchee vvedenie i vostochnaia okraina Azii.* Translated by P. P. Semenov-Tian-Shanskii. St. Petersburg, 1856.

Romanov, Iu. I., ed. *Qaharlï 1916 zhïl/Groznyi 1916-i god.* Almaty, 1998.

Rousseau, Jean-Jacques. "Discourse on the Origin and Foundations of Inequality among Men." In *The Essential Writings of Rousseau,* 5–87. Translated by Peter Constantine. New York, 2013.

Rumiantsev, P. P. *Kirgizskii narod v proshlom i nastoiashchem.* St. Petersburg, 1910.

——. *Materialy po obsledovaniiu tuzemnogo i russkogo starozhil'cheskogo khoziaistva i zemlepol'zovaniia v Semirechenskoi oblasti, sostavlennye i razrabotannye pod rukovodstvom P. P. Rumiantseva.* 6 vols. St. Petersburg, 1911–1915.

——. "Usloviia kolonizatsii Semirech'ia." *Voprosy kolonizatsii* 9 (1911): 191–225.

Russov, S. "Puteshestvie iz Orenburga v Khivu samarskogo kuptsa Rukavkina v 1733 [*sic*: 1753] godu s priobshcheniem raznykh izvestii o Khive s otdalennykh vremen donyne." *Turkestanskii sbornik* 386:48–73.

Rychkov, N. P. *Dnevnye zapiski puteshestviia Kapitana Nikolaia Rychkova v kirgis-kaisatskoi stepe, 1771 godu.* St. Petersburg, 1772.

Rychkov, P. I. *Istoriia Orenburgskaia (1730–1750).* 1759. Reprint, Orenburg, 1896.

——. *Topografiia Orenburgskoi gubernii.* 1762. Reprint, Orenburg, 1887.

"Sblizhenie narodov." *Kirgizskaia stepnaia gazeta,* March 18, 1901.

Sbornik statisticheskikh svedenii po Ufimskoi gubernii. Ufa, 1898.

Sedel'nikov, T. I. *Bor'ba za zemliu v kirgizskoi stepi: Kirgizskii zemel'nyi vopros i kolonizatsionnaia politika pravitel'stva.* St. Petersburg, 1907.

Seidalin, Zh. "Kirgizskii vopros." *Rech',* April 3, 1906.

Seidïmbekov, A., ed. *Mŭsylmanshïlïqtïng tŭtqasï.* Almaty, 1991.

Semenov Tian-Shanskii, P. P. *Puteshestvie v Tian'-Shan' v 1856–7 gg.* Moscow, 1946.

Shangin, I. P. "Izvlechenie iz opisaniia ekspeditsii, byvshei v Kirgizskuiu step' v 1816 g." *Sibirskii vestnik,* pt. 9 (1820): 1–40.

Shayakhmetov, Mukhamet. *The Silent Steppe: The Story of a Kazak Nomad under Stalin.* Translated by Jan Butler. London, 2006.

Shcherbina, F. A. "Issledovaniia stepnykh oblastei." *Trudy Imperatorskogo vol'nogo ekonomicheskogo obshchestva,* no. 4 (1902): 321–339.

——. *Krest'ianskie biudzhety.* Voronezh, 1900.

——. "Prodovol'stvennye normy." *Russkoe bogatstvo,* no. 8 (1900): 1–19.

Shcherbina, F. A., et al. *Materialy po kirgizskomu zemlepol'zovaniiu.* 13 vols. St. Petersburg and Voronezh, 1898–1909.

Shidlovskii, S. I., ed. *Svod trudov mestnykh komitetov po 49 guberniiam Evropeiskoi Rossii,* vol. 6: *Zemel'nye zakhvaty i mezhevoe delo.* St. Petersburg, 1904.

Shkapskii, O. A. "Nekotoryia dannyia dlia osveshcheniia kirgizskogo voprosa." *Russkaia mysl',* no. 6 (1897): 44–58; and no. 7 (1897): 31–48.

———. "Pereselentsy i agrarnyi vopros v Semirechenskoi oblasti." *Voprosy kolonizatsii* 1 (1907): 19–52.

———. "Pereselentsy-samovol'tsy i agrarnyi vopros v Semirechenskoi oblasti." St. Petersburg, 1906.

"Shkola pri mecheti." *Kirgizskaia stepnaia gazeta*, March 19, 1895.

"Sibirskaia zheleznaia doroga." *Kirgizskaia stepnaia gazeta*, December 4, 1894.

Smirnov. *Otchet revizora zemleustroistva Smirnova po komandirovke letom 1899 g. v Akmolinskuiu i Semipaltinskuiu oblasti.* St. Petersburg, 1899.

Sosnovskii, I. V., ed. *Svod trudov mestnykh komitetov po 49 guberniiam Evropeiskoi Rossii*, vol. 4: *Zemlevladenie.* St. Petersburg, 1904.

"Sredneaziatskaia ekspeditsiia." *Kirgizskaia stepnaia gazeta*, December 19–26, 1899.

Stolypin, P. A., and A. V. Krivoshein. *Poezdka v Sibir' i Povolzh'e.* St. Petersburg, 1911.

Subkhanberdina, Ü., ed. *Dala ualaiatïnïng gazetï: Adam, qogham, tabighat, 1888–1902.* Almaty, 1994.

Subkhanberdina, Ü., and S. Däuitov, eds. *"Aiqap."* Almaty, 1995.

Subkhanberdina, Ü., Särsenbi Däuitov, Q. Sakhov, and A. Nïsanbaev, eds. *'Qazaq' gazetï: Alash azamattarïnïng rukhïna baghïshtaladï.* Almaty, 1998.

Suleimenov, B. S., ed. *I. Altynsarin: sobranie sochinenii.* 3 vols. Alma-Ata, 1975–1978.

T., M. "Novyi podvig dlia nauki." *Kirgizskaia stepnaia gazeta*, July 13, 1897.

———. "Osvobozhdenie rabov v kirgizskoi stepi." *Kirgizskaia stepnaia gazeta*, November 12, 1895.

Toikenov, Kh., ed. *Mïrzhaqïp Dŭlatŭlï: shïgharmalarï.* Almaty, 1996.

Tregubov, A. L. "Pereselencheskoe delo v Semipalatinskoi i Semriechenskoi oblastiakh." *Voprosy kolonizatsii* 6 (1910): 104–173.

Tronov, V. D. "Materialy po antropologii i etnologii Kirgiz." *Zapiski Imperatorskogo russkogo geograficheskogo obshchestva po otdeleniiu etnografii* 17, no. 2 (1891): 45–64.

Trudy mestnykh komitetov o nuzhdakh sel'skokhoziaistvennoi promyshlennosti. 59 vols. St. Petersburg, 1903.

Uspenskii, Al. "Deistvitel'nost', a ne mechty." *Voprosy kolonizatsii* 2 (1907): 1–28.

———. "Vliianie kolonizatsii na kirgizskoe khoziaistvo (po dannym povtornogo izsledovaniia Arakaragaiskoi volosti, Kustanaiskogo uezda, Turgaiskoi oblasti, proizvedennogo L. N. Tsabelem)." *Voprosy kolonizatsii* 2 (1907): 29–43.

"V chem vred dlia zhizni," *Kirgizskaia stepnaia gazeta*, April 9, 1895.

Vasil'ev, A. V. *Istoricheskii ocherk russkogo obrazovaniia v Turgaiskoi oblasti i sovremennoe ego sostoianie.* Orenburg, 1896.

Veletskii, S. "Poslednie sobytiia v Priiliiskom Kul'dzhinskom krae." *Voprosy kolonizatsii* 15 (1914): 158–189.

Veletskii, S. N. *Zemskaia statistika: Spravochnaia kniga po zemskoi statistike.* 2 pts. Moscow, 1899–1900.

Vel'iaminov-Zernov, V. V. *Istoricheskie izvestiia o kirgiz-kaisakakh i snosheniiakh Rossii s Sredneiu Azieiu so vremeni konchiny Abul-Khair khana (1748–1765 g.)*, vol. 1. Ufa, 1853.

Veniukov, M. I. "Ocherki Zailiiskogo kraia i Prichuiskoi strany." N.p., 1861.

Voitekhovskii, K. N. "Kirgizy Kustanaiskogo uezda, Turgaiskoi oblasti." Kazan', 1910.

"Vopros o zaselenii stepei i priuchenii kochevnikov k zemledeliiu." *Turkestanskii sbornik* 395:137–142.

Vremennoe polozhenie ob upravlenii v oblastiakh Ural'skoi, Turgaiskoi, Akmolinskoi, i Semipalatinskoi. N.p., n.d.

X. "Zemledelie i khlebnaia proizvoditel'nost' Semipalatinskoi oblasti." *Pamiatnaia knizhka Semipalatinskoi oblasti* (1898): 1–27.

Zagriazhskii, G. "Iuridicheskie obychai Kirgiz i o narodnom sude u kochevogo naseleniia Turkestanskogo kraia, po obychnomu pravu (zan)." In *Materialy dlia statistiki Turkestanskogo kraia*, no. 4, edited by N. Maev, 150–202. St. Petersburg, 1876.

Zavalishin, I. I. *Opisanie Zapadnoi Sibiri*, vol. 3: *Sibirsko-Kirgizskaia step'*. Moscow, 1867.

Zdravomyslov, Nik. "Prirodnye usloviia Atbasarskogo uezda i vidy na kolonizatsiiu iuzhnoi ego chasti." *Voprosy kolonizatsii* 7 (1910): 223–236.

Zeland, N. *Kirgizy—etnograficheskii ocherk*. Semipalatinsk, 1885.

Zhapanov, K. "Kochevye stoibishcha." *Kirgizskaia stepnaia gazeta*, August 20, 1895.

SECONDARY SOURCES

Abashin, S. N., D. Iu. Arapov, and N. E. Bekmakhanova. *Tsentral'naia Aziia v sostave Rossiiskoi imperii*. Moscow, 2008.

Adas, Michael. *Machines as the Measure of Men: Science, Technology, and Ideologies of Western Dominance*. Ithaca, 1989.

Afanas'eva, Anna. "'Osvobodit' . . . ot shaitanov i sharlatanov': Diskursy i praktiki Rossiiskoi meditsiny v Kazakhskoi stepi v XIX veke." *Ab Imperio*, no. 4 (2008): 113–150.

Amanzholova, D. A. *Kazakhskii avtonomizm i Rossiia: Istoriia dvizheniia Alash*. Moscow, 1994.

Ascher, Abraham. *P. A. Stolypin: The Search for Stability in Late Imperial Russia*. Stanford, 2002.

Atabaev, Q. *Qazaq baspasözï: Qazaqstan tarikhïnïng derek közi (1870–1918)*. Almaty, 2000.

Aust, Martin, Rikarda Vul'pius [Ricarda Vulpius], and Aleksei Miller, eds. *Imperium inter pares: Rol' transferov v istorii Rossiiskoi imperii*. Moscow, 2010.

Auezov, Mukhtar. *Put' Abaia*. Translated by Leonid Sobolev. Moscow, 1952.

Avrich, Paul. *Russian Rebels, 1600–1800*. New York, 1976.

Babadzhanov, Bakhtiyar. "Andizhanskoe vosstanie 1898 goda i 'Musul'manskii vopros' v Turkestane (vzgliady 'kolonizatorov' i 'kolonizirovannykh')." Ab Imperio, no. 2 (2009): 155–200.

——. "'How Will We Appear in the Eyes of *Inovertsy* and *Inorodtsy*?' Nikolai Ostroumov on the Image and Function of Russian Power." Translated by Alexander Morrison. *Central Asian Survey* 33, no. 2 (2014): 270–288.

Bailey, Scott C. Matsushita. "Travel, Science, and Empire: The Russian Geographical Society's Expeditions to Central Eurasia, 1845–1905." PhD diss., University of Hawaii, 2008.

Ballantyne, Tony. "Archive, Discipline, State: Power and Knowledge in South Asian Historiography." *New Zealand Journal of Asian Studies* 3, no. 1 (2001): 87–105.

Barrett, Thomas. *At the Edge of Empire: The Terek Cossacks and the North Caucasus Frontier, 1700–1860*. Boulder, 1999.

Baskhanov, M. K. *Russkie voennye vostokovedy do 1917 goda*. Moscow, 2005.

Bassin, Mark. *Imperial Visions: Nationalist Imagination and Geographical Expansion in the Russian Far East, 1840–1865*. Cambridge, 1999.

Batalden, Stephen K. *Seeking God: The Recovery of Religious Identity in Orthodox Russia, Ukraine, and Georgia*. DeKalb, 1993.

Batunskii, M. A. *Rossiia i Islam*, pt. 2: *Russkaia kul'tura v ee otnoshenii k Zapadu i Vostoku: Opyt istoriko-epistemologicheskoi rekonstruktsii*. Moscow, 2003.

Baumann, Robert F. "Universal Service Reform: Conception to Implementation, 1873–1883." In *Reforming the Tsar's Army: Military Innovation in Imperial Russia from*

Peter the Great to the Revolution, edited by David Schimmelpenninck van der Oye and Bruce W. Menning, 11–33. New York, 2004.

Bayly, C. A. *Empire and Information: Intelligence Gathering and Social Communication in India, 1780–1870*. New York, 1996.

Beisembiev, K. *Ideino-politicheskie techeniia v Kazakhstane kontsa XIX–nachala XX veka*. Alma-Ata, 1961.

——. *Iz istorii obshchestvennoi mysli Kazakhstana vtoroi poloviny XIX veka*. Alma-Ata, 1957.

Bell, David. *The First Total War: Napoleon's Europe and the Birth of Warfare as We Know It*. Boston, 2007.

Bekmakhanov, E. B. *Sobranie sochinenii*, vol. 4: *Istoriia Kazakhstana (uchebnik i uchebnye posobiia)*. 1959. Reprint, Pavlodar, 2005.

Berdinskikh, V. A. *Uezdnye istoriki: Russkaia provintsial'naia istoriografiia*. Moscow, 2003.

Berg, L. S. *Vsesoiuznoe geograficheskoe obshchestvo za 100 let*. Moscow, 1946.

Bodger, Alan. *The Kazakhs and the Pugachev Uprising in Russia, 1773–1775*. Bloomington, 1988.

Bradley, Joseph. *Voluntary Associations in Tsarist Russia: Science, Patriotism, and Civil Society*. Cambridge, MA, 2009.

Breckenridge, Carol, and Peter van der Veer, eds. *Orientalism and the Postcolonial Predicament: Perspectives on South Asia*. Philadelphia, 1993.

Brower, Daniel. *Turkestan and the Fate of the Russian Empire*. New York, 2003.

Brower, Daniel, and Edward Lazzerini, eds. *Russia's Orient: Imperial Borderlands and Peoples, 1700–1917*. Bloomington, 2001.

Brubaker, Rogers, and Frederick Cooper. "Identity." In *Colonialism in Question: Theory, Knowledge, History*, by Frederick Cooper, 59–90. Berkeley, 2005.

Burbank, Jane, and Frederick Cooper. *Empires in World History: Power and the Politics of Difference*. Princeton, 2010.

Burbank, Jane, Mark von Hagen, and Anatolyi Remnev, eds. *Russian Empire: Space, People, Power, 1700–1930*. Bloomington, 2007.

Butanaev, V. Ia., and Iu. S. Khudiakov. *Istoriia Eniseiskikh kyrgyzov*. Abakan, 2000.

Buttino, Marco. *Revoliutsiia naoborot: Sredniaia Aziia mezhdu padeniem tsarskoi imperii i obrazovaniem SSSR*. Translated by Nikolai Okhotin. Moscow, 2007.

Cameron, Sarah. "The Hungry Steppe: Soviet Kazakhstan and the Kazakh Famine, 1921–1934." PhD diss., Yale University, 2010.

Campbell, Elena. "The Muslim Question in Late Imperial Russia." In Burbank, von Hagen, and Remnev, *Russian Empire*, 320–347.

Carleton, Mark Alfred. *The Small Grains*. New York, 1920.

Carlson, Leonard A. *Indians, Bureaucrats, and Land: The Dawes Act and the Decline of Indian Farming*. Westport, 1981.

Chakrabarty, Dipesh. *Provincializing Europe: Postcolonial Thought and Historical Difference*. Princeton, 2000.

Charles, Loïc, and Paul Cheney. "The Colonial Machine Dismantled: Knowledge and Empire in the French Atlantic." *Past and Present* 219 (2013): 127–163.

Chatterjee, Partha. *The Black Hole of Empire: History of a Global Practice of Power*. Princeton, 2012.

——. *The Nation and Its Fragments: Colonial and Postcolonial Histories*. Princeton, 1993.

——. *Nationalist Thought and the Colonial World: A Derivative Discourse?* London, 1986.

Chu, Pey-Yi. "Encounters with Permafrost: The Rhetoric of Conquest and Practices of Adaptation in the Soviet Union." Unpublished article ms.

Coen, Deborah. "Imperial Climatographies from Tyrol to Turkestan." *Osiris* 26, no. 1 (2011): 45–65.

Cohn, Bernard. *Colonialism and Its Forms of Knowledge: The British in India.* Princeton, 1996.

Cooper, Frederick. *Colonialism in Question: Theory, Knowledge, History.* Berkeley, 2005.

Coquin, Francois-Xavier. *La Sibérie: peuplement et immigration paysanne au 19e siècle.* Paris, 1969.

Crews, Robert. *For Prophet and Tsar: Islam and Empire in Russia and Central Asia.* Cambridge, MA, 2006.

Darrow, David W. "The Politics of Numbers: Statistics and the Search for a Theory of Peasant Economy in Russia, 1861–1917." PhD diss., Univesity of Iowa, 1996.

——. "The Politics of Numbers: Zemstvo Land Assessment and the Conceptualization of Russia's Rural Economy." *Russian Review* 59, no. 1 (2000): 52–75.

Davis, Diana. *Resurrecting the Granary of Rome: Environmental History and French Colonial Expansion in North Africa.* Athens, 2007.

Davis, Mike. *Late Victorian Holocausts: El Niño Famines and the Making of the Third World.* New York, 2002.

Demko, George. *The Russian Colonization of Kazakhstan, 1896–1916.* Bloomington, 1969.

Dettelbach, Michael. "Humboldtian Science." In *Cultures of Natural History*, edited by Nicholas Jardine, James A. Secord, and E. C. Spary, 287–304. New York, 1996.

DeWeese, Devin. *Islamization and Native Religion in the Golden Horde: Baba Tükles and Conversion to Islam in Historical and Epic Tradition.* State College, 1994.

Dirks, Nicholas. "Colonial Histories and Native Informants: Biography of an Archive." In Breckenridge and van der Veer, *Orientalism and the Postcolonial Predicament*, 279–313.

Diusenbaev, I. T., ed. *Istoriia Kazakhskoi literatury*, vol. 2: *Dorevoliutsionnaia kazakhskaia literatura.* Alma-Ata, 1979.

Donnelly, Alton. *The Russian Conquest of Bashkiria, 1552–1740: A Case Study of Imperialism.* New Haven, 1986.

Dowler, Wayne. *Classroom and Empire: The Politics of Schooling Russia's Eastern Nationalities.* Montreal, 2001.

Downs, Laura. *Manufacturing Inequality: Gender Division in the French and British Metalworking Industries, 1914–1939.* Ithaca, 1995.

Driver, Felix. *Geography Militant: Cultures of Exploration and Empire.* Malden, 2001.

Eagleton, Terry. *Literary Theory: An Introduction.* 1983. 2nd ed. Minneapolis, 1996.

Edgar, Adrienne. *Tribal Nation: The Making of Soviet Turkmenistan.* Princeton, 2004.

Eklof, Ben. *Russian Peasant Schools: Officialdom, Village Culture, and Popular Pedagogy, 1861–1914.* Berkeley, 1986.

Engelstein, Laura. "Morality and the Wooden Spoon: Russian Doctors View Syphilis, Social Class, and Sexual Behavior, 1890–1905." *Representations* 14 (1986): 169–208.

Esmaghambetov, K. L. *Älem tanïghan tülgha: Mustafa Shoqaidïng dünietanïmï zhäne qairatkerlïk bolmïsï.* Almaty, 2008.

Etkind, Alexander. *Internal Colonization: Russia's Imperial Experience.* Cambridge, 2011.

Evtuhov, Catherine. *Portrait of a Russian Province: Economy, Society, and Civilization in Nineteenth-Century Nizhnii Novgorod.* Pittsburgh, 2011.

Fanon, Frantz. *Black Skin, White Masks.* Translated by Charles Lam Markmann. New York, 1967.

Ferguson, James, and Akhil Gupta. "Spatializing States: Towards an Ethnography of Neoliberal Governmentality." *American Ethnologist* 29, no. 4 (2002): 981–1002.

Ferret, Carole. "Des chevaux pour l'empire." *Cahiers d'Asie centrale* 17–18 (2009): 211–253.

Fischer, George. *Russian Liberalism: From Gentry to Intelligentsia.* Cambridge, MA, 1958.

Frank, Allen. *Muslim Religious Institutions in Imperial Russia: The Islamic World of Novouzensk District and the Kazakh Inner Horde, 1780–1910.* Boston, 2001.

Frierson, Cathy A. *All Russia Is Burning! A Cultural History of Fire and Arson in Late Imperial Russia.* Seattle, 2002.

——. *Peasant Icons: Representations of Rural People in Late Nineteenth-Century Russia.* New York, 1993.

Foucault, Michel. "Governmentality." In *The Foucault Effect: Studies in Governmentality,* edited by Graham Burchell, Colin Gordon, and Peter Miller, 87–104. Chicago, 1991.

——. *Security, Territory, Population: Lectures at the College de France, 1977–1978.* Edited by Michel Senellart, translated by Graham Burchell. New York, 2009.

Gabdullin, B. G. *Eticheskie vozzreniia Abaia.* Alma-Ata, 1970.

Galiev, V. Z. *Ssyl'nye revoliutsionery v Kazakhstane (vtoraia polovina XIX veka).* Alma-Ata, 1978.

Geraci, Robert. "Going Abroad or Going to Russia? Orthodox Missionaries in the Kazak Steppe, 1881–1917." In Geraci and Khodarkovsky, *Of Religion and Empire,* 274–310.

——. "Russian Orientalism at an Impasse: Tsarist Education Policy and the 1910 Conference on Islam." In Brower and Lazzerini, *Russia's Orient,* 138–161.

——. *Window on the East: National and Imperial Identities in Late Tsarist Russia.* Ithaca, 2001.

Geraci, Robert, and Michael Khodarkovsky, eds. *Of Religion and Empire: Missions, Conversion, and Tolerance in Tsarist Russia.* Ithaca, 2001.

Glushchenko, E. A. *Rossiia v Srednei Azii: Zavoevaniia i preobrazovaniia.* Moscow, 2010.

Goldman, Alvin I. "Why Social Epistemology Is *Real* Epistemology." In *Social Epistemology,* edited by Adrian Haddock, Alan Millar, and Duncan Pritchard, 1–29. New York, 2010.

Goodell, Edward. *The Noble Philosopher: Condorcet and the Enlightenment.* Buffalo, 1994.

Grachev, Igor, and Pavel Rykin. "A European's View of Asiatic History." Review of *Taming the Wild Field: Colonization and Empire on the Russian Steppe* by Willard Sunderland. Translated by Catriona Kelly. *Forum for Anthropology and Culture* 1 (2004): 395–401.

Grant, Bruce. *The Captive and the Gift: Cultural Histories of Sovereignty in Russia and the Caucasus.* Ithaca, 2009.

Hacking, Ian. *The Social Construction of What?* Cambridge, MA, 1999.

Hallez, Xavier. "Petite histoire des dictionnaires kazakh-russes (1861–2002): Parmi les alphabets arabe, latin, et cyrillique." *Cahiers d'Asie centrale* 11–12 (2004): 291–316.

Hannah, Matthew G. *Governmentality and the Mastery of Territory in Nineteenth-Century America.* New York, 2000.

Happel, Jörn. *Nomadische Lebenswelten und zarische Politik: Der Aufstand in Zentralasien 1916.* Stuttgart, 2010.

Hevia, James. *The Imperial Security State: British Colonial Knowledge and Empire-Building in Asia.* New York, 2012.

Hillis, Faith. *Children of Rus': Right-Bank Ukraine and the Invention of a Russian Nation.* Ithaca, 2013.

Holquist, Peter. "'In Accord with State Interests and the People's Wishes': The Technocratic Ethos of Imperial Russia's Resettlement Administration." *Slavic Review* 69, no. 1 (2010): 151–179.

Hosking, Geoffrey. *The Russian Constitutional Experiment: Government and Duma, 1907–1914.* Cambridge, 1973.

Iakaev, S. N. *Fedor Andreevich Shcherbina: Vekhi zhizni i tvorchestva.* Krasnodar, 2004.

Iğmen, Ali. *Speaking Soviet with an Accent: Culture and Power in Kyrgyzstan.* Pittsburgh, 2012.

Ivlev, N. P. "Pobornik prosveshcheniia: Novoe o Chokane." *Prostor* 10 (1993): 224–228.

Jersild, Austin. "From Savagery to Citizenship: Caucasian Mountaineers and Muslims in the Russian Empire." In Brower and Lazzerini, *Russia's Orient*, 101–114.

———. *Orientalism and Empire: North Caucasus Mountain Peoples and the Georgian Frontier, 1845–1917.* Montreal, 2003.

Jones, Ryan T. "Peter Simon Pallas, Siberia, and the European Republic of Letters." *Studies in the History of Biology* 3, no. 3 (2011): 55–67.

Judge, Edward H. *Plehve: Repression and Reform in Imperial Russia, 1902–1904.* Syracuse, 1983.

Kappeler, Andreas. *The Russian Empire: A Multiethnic History.* Translated by Alfred Clayton. Harlow, 2001.

Karpat, Kemal. "The Roots of Kazakh Nationalism: Ethnicity, Islam, or Land?" In *In a Collapsing Empire: Underdevelopment, Ethnic Conflicts, and Nationalisms in the Soviet Union*, edited by Marco Buttino, 313–333. Milan, 1993.

Kasymbaev, Zhanuzak. *Starshii sultan Kunanbai Oskenbaev i ego okruzhenie.* 2nd ed. Almaty, 2004.

Kendirbai, Gulnar. *Land and People: The Russian Colonization of the Kazak Steppe.* Berlin, 2002.

———. "We Are Children of Alash . . ." *Central Asian Survey* 18, no. 1 (1999): 5–37.

Khabizhanova, Gulnara, E. Zh. Valikhanov, and Andrei Krivkov. *Russkaia demokraticheskaia intelligentsiia v Kazakhstane (vtoraia polovina XIX–nachalo XX vv.).* Moscow, 2003.

Khalfin, N. A., and E. F. Rassadina. *N. V. Khanykov—vostokoved i diplomat.* Moscow, 1977.

Khalid, Adeeb. *Making Uzbekistan: Nation, Empire, and Revolution in the Early USSR.* Ithaca, 2015.

———. *The Politics of Muslim Cultural Reform: Jadidism in Central Asia.* Berkeley, 1998.

———. Review of *Russian Rule in Samarkand, 1868–1910: A Comparison with British India* by Alexander Morrison. *Slavic Review* 69, no. 1 (2010): 242–243.

———. "Russian History and the Debate over Orientalism." *Kritika: Explorations in Russian and Eurasian History* 1, no. 4 (2000): 691–699.

Khodarkovsky, Michael. *Russia's Steppe Frontier: The Making of a Colonial Empire, 1500–1800.* Bloomington, 2002.

———. *Where Two Worlds Met: The Russian State and the Kalmyk Nomads, 1600–1771.* Ithaca, 1992.

Kivelson, Valerie. *Cartographies of Tsardom: The Land and Its Meanings in Seventeenth-Century Russia.* Ithaca, 2006.

Knight, Nathaniel. "Constructing the Science of Nationality: Ethnography in Mid-19th Century Russia." PhD diss., Columbia University, 1995.

———. "Grigor'ev in Orenburg, 1851–1862: Russian Orientalism in the Service of Empire?" *Slavic Review* 59, no. 1 (2000): 74–100.

———. "Nikolai Kharuzin and the Quest for a Universal Human Science: Anthropological Evolutionism and the Russian Ethnographic Tradition, 1885–1900." *Kritika: Explorations in Russian and Eurasian History* 9, no. 1 (2008): 83–111.

Komatsu, Hisao. "The Andijan Uprising Reconsidered." In Muslim Societies: Historical and Comparative Perspectives, edited by Tsugitaka Sato, 29–61. London, 2004.

Kosach, G. G. *Gorod na styke dvukh kontinentov: Orenburgskoe tatarskoe men'shinstvo i gosudarstvo.* Moscow, 1998.

——. "Ibragim Altynsarin: Chelovek v potoke vremeni." *Vestnik Evrazii,* nos. 1–2 (1998): 110–130.

Kotsonis, Yanni. "How Peasants Became Backward: Agrarian Policy and Cooperatives in Russia, 1905–14." In *Transforming Peasants: Society, State, and the Peasantry, 1861–1930,* edited by Judith Pallot, 15–36. New York, 1998.

Kozybaev, M. K., ed. *Istoriia Kazakhstana s drevneishikh vremen do nashikh dnei.* 5 vols. Almaty, 2000.

Kreindler, Isabelle. "Ibrahim Altynsarin, Nikolai Il'minskii, and the Kazakh National Awakening." *Central Asian Survey* 2 (1983): 99–116.

Kuhn, Thomas. *The Structure of Scientific Revolutions.* Chicago, 1962. 2nd ed. Chicago, 1970.

Kushko, A., Viktor Taki, and Oleg Grom. *Bessarabiia v sostave Rossiiskoi imperii.* Moscow, 2012.

Kuxhausen, Anna. "Raising the Nation: Medicine, Morality and *Vospitanie* in Eighteenth-Century Russia." PhD diss., University of Michigan, 2006.

Lambert, David, and Alan Lester. *Colonial Lives across the British Empire: Imperial Careering in the Long Nineteenth Century.* New York, 2006.

Latour, Bruno. *Science in Action: How to Follow Scientists and Engineers through Society.* Cambridge, MA, 1987.

Lawrance, Benjamin, Emily Lynn Osborn, and Richard L. Roberts. "Introduction: African Intermediaries and the 'Bargain' of Collaboration." In *Intermediaries, Interpreters, and Clerks: African Employees in the Making of Colonial Africa,* edited by Benjamin Lawrance, Emily Lynn Osborn, and Richard L. Roberts, 3–34. Madison, 2006.

Lazzerini, Edward. "Beyond Renewal: The Jadid Response to Pressure for Change in the Modern Age." In *Muslims of Central Asia: Expressions of Identity and Change,* edited by Jo-Ann Gross, 151–166. Durham, 1992.

——. "Local Accommodation and Resistance to Colonialism in Nineteenth-Century Crimea." In Brower and Lazzerini, *Russia's Orient,* 169–187.

Levi, Scott C. *The Indian Diaspora in Central Asia and Its Trade, 1550–1900.* Boston, 2002.

Levin, Eve. "*Dvoeverie* and Popular Religion." In Batalden, *Seeking God,* 31–52.

Lewis, Martin W., and Kären E. Wigen. *The Myth of Continents: A Critique of Metageography.* Berkeley, 1997.

Lincoln, W. Bruce. *In the Vanguard of Reform: Russia's Enlightened Bureaucrats, 1825–1861.* DeKalb, 1982.

Ludden, David. "Orientalist Empiricism: Transformations of Colonial Knowledge." In Breckenridge and van der Veer, *Orientalism and the Postcolonial Predicament,* 250–278.

Lyons, Scott Richard. *X-Marks: Native Signatures of Assent.* Minneapolis, 2010.

Macey, David A. J. *Government and Peasant in Russia, 1861–1906: The Prehistory of the Stolypin Reforms.* DeKalb, 1987.

Malikov, Yuriy. *Tsars, Cossacks, and Nomads: The Formation of a Borderland Culture in Northern Kazakhstan in the 18th and 19th Centuries.* Berlin, 2011.

Maltusynov, S. N. *Agrarnyi vopros v Kazakhstane i Gosudarstvennaia Duma, 1906–1917 gg.: Sotsiokul'turnyi podkhod.* Almaty, 2006.

Manchester, Laurie. *Holy Fathers, Secular Sons: Clergy, Intelligentsia, and the Modern Self in Revolutionary Russia*. DeKalb, 2008.

Marchand, Suzanne. *German Orientalism in the Age of Empire: Religion, Race, and Scholarship*. Cambridge, 2009.

Marks, Steven. *Road to Power: The Trans-Siberian Railroad and the Colonization of Asian Russia, 1850–1917*. Ithaca, 1991.

Marshall, Alex. *The Russian General Staff and Asia, 1800–1917*. London, 2006.

Martin, Virginia. "Barïmta: Nomadic Custom, Imperial Crime." In Brower and Lazzerini, *Russia's Orient*, 249–270.

——. "Kazakh Chinggisids, Land, and Political Power in the Nineteenth Century: A Case Study of Syrymbet." *Central Asian Survey* 29, no. 1 (2010): 79–102.

——. *Law and Custom on the Steppe: The Kazakhs of the Middle Horde and Russian Colonialism in the Nineteenth Century*. Richmond, 2001.

Mespoulet, Martine. *Statistique et révolution en Russie: Un compromis impossible (1880–1930)*. Rennes, 2001.

Metcalf, Alida C. *Go-Betweens and the Colonization of Brazil*. Austin, 2005.

Michaels, Paula. *Curative Powers: Medicine and Empire in Stalin's Central Asia*. Pittsburgh, 2003.

Mignolo, Walter. *Local Histories/Global Designs: Coloniality, Subaltern Knowledges, and Border Thinking*. Princeton, 2000.

Miller, Aleksei. "Russifikatsiia: Klassifitsirovat' i poniat'." *Ab Imperio*, no. 2 (2002): 133–148.

Mogil'ner, Marina. *Homo Imperii: A History of Physical Anthropology in Russia*. Lincoln, 2013.

——. *Homo imperii: Istoriia fizicheskoi antropologii v Rossii*. Moscow, 2008.

Moon, David. *The Plough That Broke the Steppes: Agriculture and Environment on Russia's Grasslands, 1700–1914*. Oxford, 2013.

——. "The Russian Academy of Sciences Expeditions to the Steppes in the Late Eighteenth Century." *Slavonic and East European Review* 88, nos. 1–2 (2010): 204–236.

Morrison, Alexander. "'Applied Orientalism' in British India and Tsarist Turkestan." *Comparative Studies in Society and History* 51, no. 3 (2009): 619–647.

——. "Metropole, Colony, and Imperial Citizenship in the Russian Empire." *Kritika: Explorations in Russian and Eurasian History* 13, no. 2 (2012): 327–364.

——. "'Nechto eroticheskoe,' 'courir apres l'ombre'?—Logistical Imperatives and the Fall of Tashkent, 1859–1865." *Central Asian Survey* 33, no. 2 (2014): 153–169.

——. "Russia, Khoqand, and the Search for a Natural Frontier." *Ab Imperio*, no. 2 (2014): 165–192.

——. *Russian Rule in Samarkand, 1868–1910: A Comparison with British India*. Oxford, 2008.

——. "'Sowing the Seed of National Strife in This Alien Region': The Pahlen Report and *Pereselenie* in Turkestan, 1908–1910." *Acta Slavica Iaponica* 31 (2012): 1–29.

——. "Sufism, Pan-Islamism, and Information Panic: Nil Sergeevich Lykoshin and the Aftermath of the Andijan Uprising." *Past and Present* 214 (2012): 255–304.

——. "What Is 'Colonisation'? An Alternative View of *Taming the Wild Field*." Review of *Taming the Wild Field: Colonization and Empire on the Russian Steppe* by Willard Sunderland. *Forum for Anthropology and Culture* 1 (2004): 402–415.

——. "Writing the Russian Conquest of Central Asia." Unpublished article ms.

Musina, Makbal, and Boris Tikhomirov. *Chokan Valikhanov v Sankt-Peterburge*. St. Petersburg, 2009.

Nïsanbaev, A. *Abaidïng dünietanïmï men filosofiiasï*. Almaty, 1995.

Noack, Christian. "Retroactively Revolting: Kazan Tatar 'Conspiracies' during the 1905 Revolution." In *The Russian Revolution of 1905: Centenary Perspectives*, edited by Jonathan D. Smele and Anthony Heywood, 119–136. New York, 2005.

Novlianskaia, M. G. "Nauchnye raboty Orenburgskoi ekspeditsii." *Trudy Instituta istorii estestvoznaniia i tekhniki* 27 (1959): 26–43.

Obruchev, V. A. *Istoriia geologicheskogo issledovaniia Sibiri: Period vtoroi (1801–1850 gody)*. Leningrad, 1933.

Ohayon, Isabelle. *La sédentarisation des Kazakhs dans l'URSS de Staline: Collectivization et changement social (1928–1945)*. Paris, 2006.

Ohren, Dana M. "All the Tsar's Men: Minorities and Military Conscription in Imperial Russia, 1874–1905." PhD diss., Indiana University, 2006.

Olcott, Martha Brill. *The Kazakhs*. 2nd ed. Stanford, 2005.

O'Neill, Kelly A. "Between Submission and Subversion: The Incorporation of the Crimean Khanate into the Russian Empire, 1783–1853." PhD diss., Harvard University, 2006.

Ostler, Jeffrey. *The Plains Sioux and US Colonialism from Lewis and Clark to Wounded Knee*. New York, 2004.

Pagden, Anthony. *The Fall of Natural Man: The American Indian and the Origins of Comparative Ethnology*. New York, 1982.

Peterson, Maya. "Technologies of Rule: Water, Power, and the Modernization of Central Asia, 1867–1941." PhD diss., Harvard University, 2011.

Petrova, T. P. "K voprosu o sostave ekspeditsii F. A. Shcherbiny po issledovaniiu stepnykh oblastei Kazakstana." *Izvestiia Akademii nauk Kazakskoi SSR: Seriia obshchestvennykh nauk*, no. 4 (1980): 50–55.

——. "Organizatsiia statisticheskogo obsledovaniia kazakhskikh khoziaistv ekspeditsiei F. A. Shcherbiny." *Problemy istorii SSSR*, no. 9 (1979): 75–91.

Philliou, Christine. *Biography of an Empire: Governing Ottomans in an Age of Revolution*. Berkeley, 2011.

Pianciola, Niccolò. "Famine in the Steppe: The Collectivization of Agriculture and the Kazak Herdsmen, 1928–1934." Translated by Susan Finnel. *Cahiers du monde russe* 45, nos. 1–2 (2004): 137–191.

Pirumova, N. M. *Zemskaia intelligentsia i ee rol' v obshchestvennoi bor'be do nachala XX v.* Moscow, 1986.

Pitts, Jennifer. *A Turn to Empire: The Rise of Imperial Liberalism in Britain and France*. Princeton, 2005.

Porter, Theodore. *Trust in Numbers: The Pursuit of Objectivity in Science and Public Life*. Princeton, 1996.

Postnikov, A. V. *Stanovlenie rubezhei Rossii v Tsentral'noi i Srednei Azii (XVIII–XIX vv.): Rol' istoriko-geograficheskikh issledovanii i kartografirovaniia. Monografiia v dokumentakh*. Moscow, 2007.

Prakash, Gyan. *Another Reason: Science and the Imagination of India*. Princeton, 1999.

Pravilova, Ekaterina. *A Public Empire: Property and the Quest for the Common Good in Imperial Russia*. Princeton, 2014.

Prochaska, David. *Making Algeria French: Colonialism in Bône, 1870–1920*. New York, 1990.

Pyenson, Lewis. *Civilizing Mission: Exact Sciences and French Overseas Expansion, 1830–1940*. Baltimore, 1993.

Rafael, Vicente. *Contracting Colonialism: Translation and Christian Conversion in Tagalog Society under Early Spanish Rule*. Ithaca, 1988.

Raj, Kapil. *Relocating Modern Science: Circulation and the Construction of Knowledge in South Asia and Europe, 1650–1900*. New York, 2007.

Remnev, A. V. "Iazyk i alfavit v imperskoi politike v kazakhskoi stepi (vtoraia polovina XIX veka." In *Imperskie i natsional'nye modeli upravleniia: Rossiiskii i evropeiskii opyt*, edited by A. O. Chubar'ian, 202–225. Moscow, 2007.

——. "Kolonial'nost', postkolonial'nost', i 'istoricheskaia politika' v sovremennom Kazakhstane." *Ab Imperio*, no. 1 (2011): 169–205.

——. "Stepnoe general-gubernatorstvo v imperskoi geografii vlasti." In *Aziatskaia Rossiia: Liudi i struktury imperii*, edited by N. G. Suvorova, 163–222. Omsk, 2005.

Remnev, A. V., and N. G. Suvorova. "'Obrusenie' aziatskikh okrain Rossiiskoi imperii: optimizm i pessimizm russkoi kolonizatsii." *Istoricheskie zapiski* 11 (2008): 132–179.

Rich, David. *The Tsar's Colonels: Professionalism, Strategy, and Subversion in Late Imperial Russia*. Cambridge, MA, 1998.

Rieber, Alfred. "Bureaucratic Politics in Imperial Russia." *Social Science History* 2, no. 4 (1978): 399–413.

Riley, Patrick, ed. *The Cambridge Companion to Rousseau*. New York, 2001.

Robbins, Richard. *Famine in Russia, 1891–92: The Imperial Government Responds to a Crisis*. New York, 1975.

——. *The Tsar's Viceroys: Russian Provincial Governors in the Last Years of the Empire*. Ithaca, 1987.

Robinson, Ronald. "Non-European Foundations of European Imperialism: Sketch for a Theory of Collaboration." In *Studies in the Theory of Imperialism*, edited by E. R. J. Owen and Robert Sutcliffe, 117–142. London, 1972.

Rottier, Peter. "Creating the Kazak Nation: The Intelligentsia's Quest for Acceptance in the Russian Empire, 1905–1920." PhD diss., University of Wisconsin, 2005.

——. "The Kazakness of Sedentarization: Promoting Progress as Tradition in Response to the Land Problem." *Central Asian Survey* 22, no. 1 (2003): 67–81.

Sabol, Steven. "Comparing American and Russian Internal Colonization: The 'Touch of Civilisation' on the Sioux and Kazakhs." *Western Historical Quarterly* 43 (2012), 29–51.

——. *Russian Colonization and the Genesis of Kazak National Consciousness*. New York, 2003.

Sahadeo, Jeff. "Progress or Peril: Migrants and Locals in Russian Tashkent, 1906–1914." In *Peopling the Russian Periphery: Borderland Colonization in Eurasian History*, edited by Nicholas B. Breyfogle, Abby M. Schrader, and Willard Sunderland, 148–166. New York, 2007.

——. *Russian Colonial Society in Tashkent, 1865–1923*. Bloomington, 2007.

Said, Edward W. *Orientalism*. 1978. 2nd ed. New York, 2003.

Sanborn, Joshua. *Drafting the Russian Nation: Military Conscription, Total War, and Mass Politics, 1905–1925*. DeKalb, 2003.

Sarïbaev, Sh., and Ä. Nŭrmagambetov, eds. *Qazaq tïlïnïng dialektologiialïq sözdïgï*, vol. 1. Almaty, 1996.

Schimmelpenninck van der Oye, David. *Russian Orientalism: Asia in the Russian Mind from Peter the Great to the Emigration*. New Haven, 2010.

Scott, David. *Conscripts of Modernity: The Tragedy of Colonial Enlightenment*. Durham, 2004.

Scott, James. *The Art of Not Being Governed: An Anarchist History of Upland Southeast Asia*. New Haven, 2009.

——. *Seeing Like a State: How Certain Schemes to Improve the Human Condition Have Failed*. New Haven, 1998.

Semenov, L. S. *Puteshestvie Afanasiia Nikitina*. Moscow, 1980.

Shablei, Pavel. "Akhun Siradzh ad-din Saifulla al-Kyzyl″iari u kazakhov Sibirskogo vedomstva: Islamskaia biografiia v imperskom kontekste." *Ab Imperio*, no. 1 (2012): 175–208.

Shahrani, Nazif. *The Kirghiz and Wakhi of Afghanistan: Adaptation to Closed Frontiers.* Seattle, 1979.

Shoinbaev, T. Zh. *Dobrovol'noe vkhozhdenie kazakhskikh zemel' v sostav Rossii.* Alma-Ata, 1982.

Sibirskaia sovetskaia entsiklopediia—1929 god. "Bel'-agachskaia step." http://45f.ru/sse/bel-agachskaya-step-bel-agach-derevya-na-perevale/.

Sinel, Allen. *The Classroom and the Chancellery: State Educational Reform in Russia under Count Dmitry Tolstoy.* Cambridge, MA, 1973.

Slezkine, Yuri. *Arctic Mirrors: Russia and the Small Peoples of the North.* Ithaca, 1994.

——. "Naturalists versus Nations: Eighteenth-Century Russian Scholars Confront Ethnic Diversity." In Brower and Lazzerini, *Russia's Orient*, 27–57.

Slocum, John. "Who, and When, Were the *Inorodtsy*? The Evolution of the Category of 'Aliens' in Imperial Russia." *Russian Review* 57, no. 2 (1998): 173–190.

Smirnov, Iu. N. *Orenburgskaia ekspeditsiia (komissiia) i prisoedinenie Zavol'zhia k Rossii v 30–40-e gg. XVIII veka.* Samara, 1997.

Smith-Peter, Susan. "Bringing the Provinces into Focus: Subnational Spaces in the Recent Historiography of Russia." *Kritika: Explorations in Russian and Eurasian History* 12, no. 4 (2011): 835–848.

Söldenwagner, Philippa. *Spaces of Negotiation: European Settlement and Settlers in German East Africa, 1900–1914.* Munich, 2006.

Spurr, David. *The Rhetoric of Empire: Colonial Discourse in Journalism, Travel Writing, and Imperial Administration.* Durham, 1993.

Stebelsky, Ihor. "The Frontier in Central Asia." In *Studies in Russian Historical Geography*, vol. 1, edited by James H. Bater and R. A. French, 143–173. London, 1983.

Steinwedel, Charles. "How Bashkiria Became a Part of European Russia, 1762–1881." In Burbank, von Hagen, and Remnev, *Russian Empire*, 94–124.

Stoler, Ann Laura. *Along the Archival Grain: Epistemic Anxieties and Colonial Common Sense.* Princeton, 2009.

Stronski, Paul. *Tashkent: Forging a Soviet City, 1930–1966.* Pittsburgh, 2010.

Sultangalieva, Gulmira. "Kazakhskoe chinovnichestva Orenburgskogo vedomstva: Formirovanie i napravlenie deiatel'nosti (XIX)." *Acta Slavica Iaponica* 27 (2009): 77–101.

——. "The Russian Empire and the Intermediary Role of Tatars in Kazakhstan: The Politics of Cooperation and Rejection." In Uyama, *Asiatic Russia*, 52–79.

Sultangalieva, Gulmira, ed. *Kazakhskie chinovniki na sluzhbe Rossiiskoi imperii: Sbornik dokumentov i materialov.* Almaty, 2013.

Sunderland, Willard. "The 'Colonization Question': Visions of Colonization in Late Imperial Russia." *Jahrbücher für Geschichte Osteuropas* 48, no. 2 (2000): 210–232.

——. "Imperial Space: Territorial Thought and Practice in the Eighteenth Century." In Burbank, von Hagen, and Remnev, *Russian Empire*, 33–66.

——. "The Ministry of Asiatic Russia: The Colonial Office That Never Was but Might Have Been." *Slavic Review* 69, no. 1 (2010): 120–150.

——. *Taming the Wild Field: Colonization and Empire on the Russian Steppe.* Ithaca, 2004.

Sytin, A. K. "'Rossiiskaia flora' Petra Simona Pallasa." In *Estestvennaia istorii v Rossii (ocherki razvitiia estestvoznaniia v Rossii v XVIII veke)*, by E. I. Kolchinskii, A. K. Sytin, and G. I. Smagina, 106–129. St. Petersburg, 2004.

Syzdykova, E. S. *Rossiiskie voennye i Kazakhstan: Voprosy sotsial'no-politicheskoi i ekonomicheskoi istorii Kazakhstana XVIII–XIX vv. v trudakh ofitserov General'nogo shtaba Rossii*. Moscow, 2005.

Tazhibaev, T. *Prosveshchenie i shkoly Kazakhstana vo vtoroi polovine XIX veka*. Alma-Ata, 1962.

Tillett, Lowell. *The Great Friendship: Soviet Historians on the Non-Russian Nationalities*. Chapel Hill, 1969.

Tolz, Vera. "Russia and the West." In *A History of Russian Thought*, edited by W. Leatherbarrow and D. Offord, 179–216. Cambridge, 2010.

——. *Russia's Own Orient: The Politics of Identity and Oriental Studies in the Late Imperial and Early Soviet Periods*. Oxford, 2011.

Treadgold, Donald. *The Great Siberian Migration: Government and Peasant in Resettlement from Emancipation to the First World War*. Princeton, 1957.

Trumbull IV, George R. *An Empire of Facts: Colonial Power, Cultural Knowledge, and Islam in Algeria, 1870–1914*. New York, 2009.

Ural'skaia istoricheskaia entsiklopediia. "Sedel'nikov, Timofei Ivanovich." http://ural.academic.ru/1760/.

Uspenskii, Boris. "The Schism and Cultural Conflict in the Seventeenth Century." In Batalden, *Seeking God*, 106–133.

Uyama, Tomohiko. "The Changing Religious Orientation of Qazaq Intellectuals in the Tsarist Period: Shari'a, Secularism, and Ethics." In *Islam, Society and States across the Qazaq Steppe (18th–Early 20th Centuries)*, edited by Niccolò Pianciola and Paolo Sartori, 95–115. Vienna, 2013.

——. "The Geography of Civilizations: A Spatial Analysis of the Kazakh Intelligentsia's Activities, from the Mid-Nineteenth to the Early Twentieth Century." In *Regions: A Prism to View the Slavic-Eurasian World*, edited by Kimitaka Matsuzato, 70–99. Sapporo, 2000.

——. "A Particularist Empire: The Russian Policies of Christianization and Military Conscription in Central Asia." In *Empire, Islam, and Politics in Central Eurasia*, edited by Tomohiko Uyama, 23–63. Sapporo, 2007.

——. "A Strategic Alliance between Kazak Intellectuals and Russian Administrators: Imagined Communities in *Dala Walayatining Gazeti* (1888–1902)." In *The Construction and Deconstruction of National Histories in Slavic Eurasia*, edited by Hayashi Tadayuki, 237–259. Sapporo, 2003.

——. "Two Attempts at Building a Qazaq State: The Revolt of 1916 and the Alash Movement." In *Islam in Politics in Russia and Central Asia (Early Eighteenth to Late Twentieth Centuries)*, edited by Stephane Dudoignon and Hisao Komatsu, 77–98. London, 2001.

Uyama, Tomohiko, ed. *Asiatic Russia: Imperial Power in Regional and International Contexts*. New York, 2012.

Veidlinger, Jeffrey. *Jewish Public Culture in the Late Russian Empire*. Bloomington, 2009.

Venturi, Franco. *Roots of Revolution: A History of the Populist and Socialist Movements in Nineteenth-Century Russia*. Translated by Francis Haskell. New York, 1960.

Vermuelen, Han. *Before Boas: The Genesis of Ethnography and Ethnology in the German Enlightenment*. Lincoln, 2015.

Vernadskii, V. I. *Trudy po istorii nauki v Rossii*. Moscow, 1988.

Vinkovetsky, Ilya. *Russian America: An Overseas Colony of a Continental Empire, 1804–1867*. New York, 2011.

Vucinich, Alexander. *Science in Russian Culture: A History to 1860*. Stanford, 1963.

Vulpius, Ricarda. "The Russian Empire's Civilizing Mission in the Eighteenth Century: A Comparative Perspective." In Uyama, *Asiatic Russia*, 13–31.

Weber, Eugen. *Peasants into Frenchmen: The Modernization of Rural France, 1870–1914.* Stanford, 1976.

Weeks, Theodore. "Between Rome and Tsargrad: The Uniate Church in Imperial Russia." In Geraci and Khodarkovsky, *Of Religion and Empire,* 70–91.

——. *Nation and State in Late Imperial Russia: Nationalism and Russification on the Western Frontier, 1863–1914.* DeKalb, 1996.

Weller, R. Charles. *Rethinking Kazakh and Central Asian Nationhood: A Challenge to Prevailing Western Views.* Los Angeles, 2006.

Werth, Paul. *At the Margins of Orthodoxy: Mission, Governance, and Confessional Politics in Russia's Volga-Kama Region, 1827–1905.* Ithaca, 2002.

——. "Big Candles and 'Internal Conversion': The Mari Animist Reformation and Its Russian Appropriations." In Geraci and Khodarkovsky, *Of Religion and Empire,* 144–172.

——. "Changing Conceptions of Difference, Assimilation, and Faith in the Volga-Kama Region, 1740–1870." In Burbank, von Hagen, and Remnev, *Russian Empire,* 169–195.

——. *The Tsar's Foreign Faiths: Toleration and the Fate of Religious Freedom in Imperial Russia.* New York, 2014.

White, Richard. *The Roots of Dependency: Subsistence, Environment, and Social Change among the Choctaws, Pawnees, and Navajos.* Lincoln, 1983.

Winner, T. G. *The Oral Art and Literature of the Kazakhs of Russian Central Asia.* Durham, 1958.

Wortman, Richard. *Scenarios of Power: Myth and Ceremony in Russian Monarchy.* 2 vols. Princeton, 1995–2000.

Yaroshevski, Dov. "Empire and Citizenship." In Brower and Lazzerini, *Russia's Orient,* 58–79.

Zaionchkovskii, P. *The Abolition of Serfdom in Russia.* Edited and translated by Susan Wobst. Gulf Breeze, 1978.

Zhirenchin, Ä. *Abai zhäne orïstïng ŭly revoliutsiiashïl demokrattarï.* Almaty, 1957.

Index

Page numbers in *italics* refer to figures and tables.

93–95; precarious position of, 11, 190; and resettlement statistics, 155–56, 164–66; roles of, 11, 186; and Steppe Commission, 38–39; tsarist state's dependency on, 63–65. *See also* Kazak intelligentsia; local knowledge
Kazak language, 212n82; importance of, 85–86; in Kazak schools, 68–71, 75–80
Kazak Reader (Altynsarin), 77–78, 107
Kazaks: administrators, 40, 99, 218n39; elites, 46, 51, 65–66; hordes, 17, 54 (*see also* Great Horde; Middle Horde; Small Horde); sedentarization, 39–44, 54–56 (*see also* sedentarism); trade, 20, 54, 56, 197n46 (*see also* commerce); as tribal confederation, 18; use of term, 17–18, 196n21. *See also* Central Asian revolt (1916); nomads; pastoral nomadism
Kazak steppe: borders, 17, 21–22, 54; as dangerous, 94–95; geography, 11, 21–24 (*see also* climate; environment); incorporation into Russian Empire, 1–2, 5, 14–15, 18–21, 30, 122, 187–88; as political term, 17–21; population, 25, 30, 32; pre-conquest, 93–94, 101–6; Russian Empire's knowledge about, 13–30, 158–59, 185–90; settlements, 35; territorial divisions, 66. *See also* Orenburg steppe; Siberian steppe
Kaznakov, N. G., 81
Khabizhanova, Gulnara, 217n33
Khakass, 17
Khalid, Adeeb, 222n125
Khanykov, Nikolai, 22–24, 58–60, 198n57, 198n69, 199n78
Kharuzin, Aleksei Nikolaevich, 14, 170, 201n117, 236n77
Khas-Mamedov, Khalil-Bek, 232n5
Khrushchov, A. P., 58
Kirgiz: as distinct ethnic group, 72; rebellion of, 157; use of term, 17–18, 196n21, 232n1. *See also* Kazaks
"Kirgiz" Autonomous Socialist Soviet Republic, 185
Kirgizskaia stepnaia gazeta. See *KSG*
Kirillov, Ivan Kirillovich, 15
knowledge: incomplete or limited, 33, 61–62, 186 (*see also* uncertainty); positivist attitude toward, 34–35, 61; and power, 2–4, 10, 33, 62, 86–89, 155–56; tsarist knowledge of steppe, 13–30, 158–59, 185–90; use of term, 191n3. *See also* epistemology; expert knowledge; facts; local knowledge; metropolitan knowledge; scientific

knowledge; secular knowledge; statistical knowledge
knowledge production, 1–4, 6, 12, 14–16, 24, 30, 33–34
Kokchetau district, 141, 154, 161
Kolpakovskii, Gerasim Alekseevich, 96, 105, 115, 220n70
Konshin, Nikolai Iakovlevich, 98, 104, 118–19
Konstantinovich, Aleksandr Petrovich, 86–87
Kopal, 170
Köpeev, Mäshhur-Zhüsïp, 117–19
Koran, 26, 67, 109, 168
Koshchygulov, Shaimerden, 161, 218n44
Kostenko, Lev Feofanovich, 14
Kotsebue, P. E., 206n93
Kozlov, Petr Kuz'mich, 108
kraevedenie, 92, 216n3. *See also* regional studies
Kraft, Ivan Ivanovich, 98–99
Krasovskii, Nikolai Ivanovich, 31–32, 40, 49, 211n54
Krivoshein, Aleksandr Vasil'evich, 149, 161–63
Krylov, I. F., 77
Kryzhanovskii, Nikolai Andreevich, 36, 50–52, 58, 62, 72, 75–76, 85, 169, 206n106
KSG (*Kirgizskaia stepnaia gazeta*), 9, 12, 92, 94, 96, 98–118, 120–24, 155, 178, 216nn3, 10, 217n25, 218n39, 221n114, 222nn122, 124, 223nn131, 146; closure, 123; creation of, 96
Kuhn, Thomas S., 193n31
Kulomzin, A. N., 140, 224n8
Kuropatkin, Aleksei Nikolaevich, 184–85
Kutler, Nikolai Nikolaevich, 233n22
Kuznetsov, Vasilii K., 140–41, 151–53, 165, 225n18, 231n156
Kyrgyz, 17, 142, 171, 183, 190

landlessness, 133
land norms, 126–54, 160–61, 165; accuracy of, 133–39; irrationality of, 148–50; lowering of, 140–43; maximal, 144, 150; Semirech'e, 150. *See also* norm-and-surplus system; norms
land rights, 139; Kazak, 161–63; Kyrgyz, 171. *See also* property
land surpluses, 125–26, 140, 142; expropriated, 92, 100–101, 125, 128, 138–39, 143–50, 155, 160–66, 189–90, 225n12, 234n45. *See also* norm-and-surplus system; zemleustroistvo
language, 65–71, 209n28
Latour, Bruno, 3, 126, 205n85
Lavrovskii, Petr Alekseevich, 76, 87
laziness, 39, 95, 114, 119, 131
Left, political, 163
legal system, 26–27, 44–48, 56–57, 61

CPSIA information can be obtained
at www.ICGtesting.com
Printed in the USA
BVOW08*0744150217

475523BV00011B/3/P

9 781501 700798